THE GOSPEL OF SELFLESS ACTION

THE GOSPEL OF SELFLESS ACTION:

OR

THE GITA ACCORDING TO GANDHI

MAHADEV DESAI

GYAN

Published by

Gyan Publishing House
5, Ansari Road
Daryaganj, New Delhi-110002
Phone: 011-47034999, 9811692060
E-mail: books@gyanbooks.com

Distribution Network
gyanbooks.com
India, USA, Canada, UK, Australia

ISBN: 978-93-6920-778-7 (HB)

First Published, 1903

2nd Impression 2025

Printed at: Gyan Press, Delhi.

THE GOSPEL OF SELFLESS ACTION
Author: MAHADEV DESAI

SWAMY

THE GOSPEL OF SELFLESS ACTION

OR

THE GITA ACCORDING TO GANDHI

(Translation of the original in Gujarati, with an additional introduction and commentary)

BY

MAHADEV DESAI

FOREWORD

The following pages by Mahadev Desai are an ambitious project. It represents his unremitting labours during his prison life in 1933-'34. Every page is evidence of his scholarship and exhaustive study of all he could lay hands upon regarding the *Bhagavad Gita,* poetically called the *Song Celestial* by the late Sir Edwin Arnold. The immediate cause of this labour of love was my translation in Gujarati of the divine book as I understood it. In trying to give a translation of my meaning of the *Gita,* he found himself writing an original commentary on the *Gita.*

The book might have been published during his lifetime, if I could have made time to go through the manuscript. I read some portions with him, but exigencies of my work had to interrupt the reading. Then followed the imprisonments of August 1942, and his sudden death within six days of our imprisonment. All of his immediate friends decided to give his reverent study of the *Gita* to the public. He had copies typed for his English friends who were impatient to see the commentary in print. And Pyarelal, who was collaborator with Mahadev Desai for many years, went through the whole manuscript and undertook to perform the difficult task of proof reading. Hence this publication.

Frankly, I do not pretend to any scholarship. I have, therefore, contented myself with showing the genesis of Mahadev Desai's effort. In so far as the translation part of the volume is concerned, I can vouch for its accuracy. He has carried out the meaning of the original translation. I may add too that Pyarelal has interfered with the original only and in rare cases where it was considered to be essential, an interference which Mahadev Desai would, in my opinion, have gladly accepted, had he been alive.

On the train to Madras, M. K. GANDHI
20th January, 1946

CONTENTS

FOREWORD — M. K. Gandhi iii

MY SUBMISSION 3–121

I PRELIMINARY 3

II DATE, TEXT, AUTHOR ETC. 5

III THE BOOK AND THE THEME 10

IV THE FUNDAMENTALS 20–54

A. The Sankhya System 22

B. The Gita View 27–54

1. Prakriti and Gunas 27

2. The Gunas 29

3. Karma and Rebirth 33

4. The Individual, World and Reality . . 39

5. Avatara 47

6. The End and the Means 52

V INTERPRETATIVE ANALYSIS 54–101

The Delusion (Discourses 1 and 2) . . . 54

Karma Yoga (Discourses 3 and 4) 61

Jnanayoga and Karmayoga Compared (Discourse 5) 68

Dhyanayoga (Discourses 6 to 8) 72

Bhaktiyoga (Discourses 9 to 11) 80

Dhyanayoga and Bhaktiyoga (Discourse 12) . 85

The World and the Reality (Discourses 13-15) 88–92

Purusha and Prakriti and Knowledge . 88

The Gunas 90

Ashvattha and Purushottama (Discourse 15) . 92

Individual Ethics (Discourses 16 and 17) . . 93

Delusion Destroyed (Discourse 18) . . . 97

VI A FEW QUESTIONS 102–114

The Four Varnas and Swadharma . . . 102

Knowledge a Talisman ? 105

Karma and Free-will 111

VII SOME CONTROVERSIES 114

VIII CONCLUSION 116

Note on the Translation 122

ANASAKTIYOGA — THE MESSAGE OF THE GITA

— M. K. Gandhi 125
DISCOURSE I 135
DISCOURSE II 148
DISCOURSE III 172
DISCOURSE IV 194
DISCOURSE V 214
DISCOURSE VI 228
DISCOURSE VII 243
DISCOURSE VIII 253
DISCOURSE IX 266
DISCOURSE X 278
DISCOURSE XI 290
DISCOURSE XII 307
DISCOURSE XIII 315
DISCOURSE XIV 328
DISCOURSE XV 337
DISCOURSE XVI 346
DISCOURSE XVII 354
DISCOURSE XVIII 363
INDEX 387

THE GOSPEL OF SELFLESS ACTION
OR
THE GITA ACCORDING TO GANDHI

MY SUBMISSION

I. PRELIMINARY

I fear that it is an act of supererogation on my part to append a long supplementary introduction and fairly profuse notes to this translation of Gandhiji's *Anasaktiyoga,* because I know that the brief introduction by Gandhiji, written in his usual succinct and direct manner, leaves nothing to be desired so far as the central message of the *Gita* is concerned, and his brief notes are enough for the purpose. But, for several reasons I have thought it necessary to add both to his introduction and his notes. For one thing, the *Anasaktiyoga* was written mainly for the Gujarati reading public, and especially the unsophisticated and even unlettered section of that public. Secondly, he wanted the book to be made available to the poorest in the country and, therefore, as small in size and as cheap as possible.* These two ends necessarily limited the scope both of Gandhiji's introduction and notes. He studiously avoided all things that would make the little book in any way difficult for the unlettered reader, and deliberately kept out of his regard the studious or the curious who would need help or enlightenment on certain points in which the readers he had in view would not be interested. Thus, for instance, there is not one mention of even the word *Upanishad* in any one of his notes, or even in his introduction, not to speak of any points of interest to the scholar or to the student : for instance, the question of the date of the *Gita,* the text of the *Gita,* the question of the Krishna Vasudeva cult. His chief concern were his readers and the message he read in the *Gita.* Not only was his scope limited, but he disowns all claim to scholarship, and thinks that some of the subjects over which keen

---

* 57,800 copies of the Gujarati *Anasaktiyoga* (price 8 As. a copy) have been sold out up to date.

controversy has raged have no intimate bearing on the message of the *Gita*. Above all, he has, as every one knows, too keen a sense of his limitations to be deflected out of the scope he sets to himself.

But this translation of his translation of the *Gita* is meant for a different, if not also a larger public. I hope and expect that a large number of English-knowing youths in India will like to have Gandhiji's interpretation of the *Gita*. I also feel that many outside India who are interested in a study of Gandhiji's life and thought may care to go in for this book. Furthermore, I have an impression that the bulk of the readers of the book will be students. It is with the needs of this public in view that I have appended additional notes to the *shlokas* (verses) and propose, by means of this "Submission" to cover a number of points that could not be dealt with in the notes, and were outside the scope of Gandhiji's book. Let me make it clear that I lay no more claim to scholarship than does Gandhiji, but I am myself a student — as I hope to remain until my dying day — and it is out of my sympathy for the needs of people of my kind that I have presumed to introduce this additional matter. I found that in the very nature of things some explanatory notes were necessary in a translation into a foreign language of a translation in an Indian language of a great Sanskrit work of philosophy and ethics ; and as I read Gandhiji's translation over and over again I felt that certain doubts and difficulties that troubled me were likely to trouble other minds too, and that I should offer what explanation I could about them. In doing so I have steered clear of all matters of purely scholastic interest, but have referred again and again to the sources — the *Upanishads* which the Divine Cowherd is said to have turned into cows to draw the nectar-like milk of the *Gita*. I have also ventured to draw parallels from the Bible and the *Koran* and the words of great seers who drew their inspiration from those great books, in order to show how, in the deepest things of life, the Hindu and the Mussalman and the Christian, the Indian and the European, in fact all who cared and endeavoured to read the truth of things, are so spiritually akin. This I thought would help, in however small a measure, to contribute to that "free sharing among religions which no longer stand in uncontaminated isolation", to the need of which Dr Radhakrishnan, that great interpreter of Hindu life and thought, has called attention in his *East and West in Religion*. Not that I went out of my way to hunt for those parallels, but I took them just as they came in the course of my quiet reading in my prison cell.

II. DATE, TEXT, AUTHOR ETC.

Let me warn the reader against expecting in this "Submission" a discussion of certain things usually discussed in such books. I have avoided them for precisely the same reason that Gandhiji would avoid them, even if he were writing for English-knowing readers. I would like to note, however, the results of research of scholars on certain points and my view regarding the bearing of some of them on the message of the *Gita*.

1. The first is the question of the date of the *Gita*. Whilst I have no fresh contribution to make on the subject, let me briefly record the results of the researches to date. Mr Hill thinks that the theory of a Christian influence to be traced in the *Gita* is "now almost universally discredited", and that "the internal evidence points to the second century B. C. as the period when the *Gita* in its present form appeared".* This is the most conservative estimate. Dr Radhakrishnan summarizes the evidence on the point thus: "We shall not, I believe, be far wrong if we assign the *Gita* to the fifth century B. C.", "though if the references in the *Dharma Sutras* are regarded as interpolated texts, then the *Gita* may be assigned to the third or the second century B. C." § Lokamanya Tilak has cited considerable evidence — that of Pali texts and other — to prove that the *Gita* existed before, and exercised considerable influence on, the growth of Mahayana

---

* Hill, *Bhagavadgita*, p. 276, and 18.

§ Dr Radhakrishnan, *Indian Philosophy*, Vol. I. p. 524.

Buddhism, and he has no doubt that the present text of the *Gita* must be assigned to the fifth century B. C. †

2. The second is the question of the text of the *Gita*. There seems to be no doubt in the mind of the scholars that the present text of the *Gita* is a redaction of a much earlier original. The question about the scope of this earlier original must remain unsolved until something like a "Code Sinaiticus" for the *Gita* is discovered. One may, however, say that, even when this original is discovered, it will not make much difference to souls like Gandhiji, every moment of whose life is a conscious effort to live the message of the *Gita*. This does not mean that Gandhiji is indifferent to the efforts of scholars in this direction. The smallest questions of historical detail interest him intensely as I can say from personal knowledge. In the quiet of the Yeravda Central Prison I have seen him spending hours discussing a reading or text. But his attitude is that in the last analysis it is the message that abides, and he is sure that no textual discovery is going to affect by a jot the essence or universality of the message.

3. The same thing may be said about questions of the historical Krishna and the genesis and history of the Krishna Vasudeva worship, i.e. the Bhagawat Dharma. While no labour and time spent on research in this connection would be ill-spent, for Gandhiji the quest of a historical Krishna has an entirely different meaning. As one may see from his intensely deep little introduction, he has already found Him, no matter whether the scholars prove him to be an inspired cowherd or an inspired charioteer driving Arjuna to victory. Substitute for "Christ" the word "Krishna" in those beautiful words of Albert Schweitzer and you find Gandhiji's attitude described to the minutest precision: "Christ comes to us as one Unknown, without a name, just as by the lake side He came to those men who knew Him not. He speaks to us the same words, 'Follow thou Me', and sets to us those

† Appendices to the *Gita Rahasya*.

tasks which He has to fulfil for our time. He commands, and to those who obey Him, whether they be wise or simple, He will reveal Himself in the toils, the conflicts, the sufferings which they shall pass through in His fellowship, and as an ineffable mystery they shall learn in their experience who He is." He has not the slightest doubt that Krishna is in every one of us, that we would feel and act on the influence of His presence if we were purged of all passion and pride and had ceased to run after the things of the earth, that He would listen to us if only we would seek refuge in Him, that He would claim us back as though we had never been away from Him. All questions of the quest for the historical Krishna become of subsidiary importance when we bear in mind the fact that the *Gita* preaches no exclusive doctrine and that when the author of the *Gita* introduces Krishna as speaking first person, it is no personal Krishna speaking but the Divine in Arjuna and in every one of us. Krishna is represented as speaking in the name of God, *Paramatman,* Supreme *Brahman.* The *Shvetashvatara Upanishad* is an unbroken praise of the Lord whom it names Siva or Rudra, but at no moment is the truth far from the seer who composed the *Upanishad* that Siva or Rudra is

> The one God, hidden in all things,
> All-pervading, the Inner Soul of all things,
> The Overseer of deeds, in all things abiding,
> The Witness, the Sole Thinker, devoid of all qualities,
> The One Controller of the inactive many,
> Who makes the one seed manifold—
> The wise who perceive Him as standing in one's self
> They, and no others, have eternal happiness.*

It is the same thing with Krishna in the *Bhagawadgita.* He is the *Atman,* He is the *Purushottama,* He is *Brahman,*

---

* Hume, *Shve. Up.* 6. 11-12.

एको देवः सर्वभूतेषु गूढः सर्वव्यापी सर्वभूतान्तरात्मा ।
कर्माध्यक्षः सर्वभूताधिवासः साक्षी चेता केवलो निर्गुणश्च ।।११।।
एको वशी निष्क्रियाणां बहूनाम् एकं बीजं बहुधा यः करोति ।
तमात्मस्थं येऽनुपश्यन्ति धीरास्तेषां सुखं शाश्वतं नेतरेषाम् ।।१२।।

He is the God of gods, the Lord of the Universe seated in the heart of all. Mr Hill calls the *Gita* "an uncompromising eirenicon" — uncompromising because the author of the *Gita* will "not abate one jot of Krishna's claim to be Supreme, to be the All." It is a mistake, I think, to talk of anything like "Krishna's claim". It is not so much the purpose of the author to advance the claim of a particular person, however divine, as the deity, as to direct the mind and the heart and the soul of man to the only abiding Reality. The name *Vasudeva* is defined in the *Mahabharata* thus: "Because I have my abode (*vasa*) in all creation, I am Vasudeva." A person deified and described as Vasudeva was already being worshipped; no doubt the author of the *Gita* may or may not have seen him physically, but that his whole being was suffused with him is certain, and it is to that devotion that he gives name and form and reality. The characteristics of the ideal devotee — "in whom My soul delights" — quoted by Gandhiji in his introduction from the twelfth discourse, are not the characteristics of the devotee of a particular god. They are to be found — and must be found — in *any* true devotee of God, whether he calls Him Krishna or Christ or God or Allah. The 'ME' in "Abandon all duties and come to ME the only refuge" (XVIII. 66) does not and cannot mean the person called Krishna — that person no longer exists — but it means the ever-abiding Lord in every one of us. "In Him alone take thy refuge, with all thy heart. By His grace thou shalt win to the eternal heaven of supreme peace" (XVIII. 62). The emphasis is not on ME as the Lord, but on the Lord speaking through ME, and further, as we shall see in the sequel, not on the profession of His name but on doing His work and His will: "He alone comes to Me, Pandava, who does My work, who makes Me his goal, who is My devotee, who has banished all attachment, who has ill-will towards none" (XI. 55). Did St. Paul mean an exclusive Jesus when he said: "That Christ may dwell in your hearts by faith; that ye, being rooted and grounded in love, may be able to comprehend with all saints what is the breadth and length, and depth, and height; and to know the love of Christ which passeth knowledge" (Eph. 3. 17-18-19); "As ye have received Christ Jesus, so walk in Him, rooted and built up in Him" (Col. 1. 6-7)? I submit not.

4. Vyasa, the reputed author of the *Mahabharata,* is believed to be the author of the *Gita,* as it forms part of the epic, but there is no conclusive evidence to prove this, nor have we any evidence on the facts regarding the life of Vyasa.

Evidence about Krishna Vasudeva cannot be said to be scanty, as references to a "Krishna" can be traced even in the early Vedic hymns. But there is no evidence of a conclusive nature to establish his identity or to prove that the *rishi* Krishna of the Vedic hymns and the pupil Krishna the son of Devaki, and the disciple of Ghora Angirasa, of whom the *Chhandogya Upanishad* speaks; and the Krishna of the *Mahabharata* now playing the role of a charioteer and warrior, now being described as worshipping Mahadeva, now being hailed as an incarnation of the Supreme Deity even by Dhritarashtra and Bhishma and now being decried by scoffers as built of common clay; and the Krishna of the Puranas — whether all these are one and the same. There can be no doubt, however, that an extraordinary personality combining in himself the qualities of a hero and a statesman, a warrior and a philosopher, did exist at a time of which we have no record, that he grew to enormous proportions in the race-memory of the Aryans, so much so that he came to be revered as an *avatara* and later on as the Incarnation, and countless traditions and legends grew up about "the ideal man", according to the varying psychological and spiritual levels of the ages that followed.

I would thus sum up my attitude — and perhaps Gandhiji's also — on this and similar questions. An aspirant will not make himself uneasy over the absence or uncertainty of evidence regarding the author of the *Gita* or the identity of Krishna. Let the scholars not tire of effort in this direction. But for us laymen there is much comfort to be derived from the thought that the seers of old practised *anasakti* (detachment), which is the message of the *Gita,* to an extent that puzzles our sophisticated generation. The doctrine of detachment, or selflessness, or work in the spirit of sacrifice is as old as Creation, as Lord Krishna assures us in the *Gita.* It must have been practised to perfection by the seers who revealed the message to mankind. It is delivered in a concentrated form in the *Gita* and argued out in it as in no other scriptures. The author of the *Gita* felt and saw and knew and lived Krishna and left his experience as an abiding heritage for mankind.

III. THE BOOK AND THE THEME

Is not then the *Gita* anything in the nature of a historical narrative, forming as it does, part of the great war-epic? Gandhiji has challenged the description of the *Mahabharata* as a historical war-epic. In support of the challenge, I venture to enforce its argument by a few more considerations to show that the *Gita* can, in no sense of the term, be regarded as a historical dialogue. That a war named the Mahabharata War or some other took place, need not be disputed, but that the author of the epic and the *Gita* had anything like the object of a historical narrative in mind is certainly disputed.

1. Look at the intensely significant artistry of the way in which the jewel of the *Gita* is set in the field of gold of the great epic. The reputed author Vyasa is supposed to be one of the deathless ones — *Chiranjivas* — and he is said to be the progenitor of Pandu and Dhritarashtra whose sons fought on the field of Kurukshetra. It is this 'deathless one' who approaches Dhritarashtra, the blind king, before the commencement of the fight and asks him if he would care to have his eyes opened in order to see the fighting. He is said to have declined the privilege, lest his heart should subside in him to see the fearful carnage, but at a certain stage he evinces anxiety to know the happenings from day to day. Sanjaya was endowed with divine vision and without being on the battlefield narrated the happenings to the blind king. As though this much was not enough to open the eyes of the blind student trying to read history in a spiritual epic, Vyasa goes

further and reassures the king that Sanjaya's divine vision would serve him better than his natural vision, for "this Sanjaya will narrate the battle to you (in a unique way), for he shall know whatever happens, within the sight of or unknown to all, whether by day or by night, *whether actually or in the mind of any of the actors.* Weapons shall not touch Sanjaya and fatigue shall not tire him." It is Sanjaya thus endowed with supernatural vision who narrates the dialogue which is said to have taken place between Arjuna and Krishna. And how does he satisfy the old king's curiosity ? The old king, in the only question that is put into his mouth in the whole poem, asks to know "what my sons and Pandu's did, assembled, on battle intent, on the Field of Kuru". The reply is the narration of an intensely philosophical dialogue between Arjuna and Krishna through eighteen discourses, and at the end of the narration he describes not what the king's sons did or what Pandu's sons did, but that he was intensely exultant to have had the superb privilege of listening to that unique dialogue and that "where is the Master of Yoga and where is Partha, the bowman, there, I am sure, are Fortune, Victory, Prosperity and Eternal Right". Does it need any argument after this that it is not a historical dialogue that we are reading, but a profoundly meaningful poem ?

There is, therefore, no wonder that to quite a considerable class of readers the *Gita* conveys an allegorical meaning: some likening the Pandavas to the forces of light and the Kauravas to the forces of darkness, and making the human body the field of *dharma* ; some putting various meanings on the obviously meaningful names of the various characters of the epic and pressing allegory to distant lengths. To some Dhritarashtra, the blind king, is the individual ego blindly holding on to the flesh, as his name indicates, listening to the dialogue between Krishna, the In-dweller, and Arjuna, the humble and transparently pure intellect obeying His behest and fighting the forces of darkness and winning the victory. To use a phrase of Dr Carid, Dhritarashtra, to these interpreters, becomes

" at once the combatants and the conflict and the field that is torn with strife ". Some, on the other hand, would make Arjuna the individual ego torn with internal conflict and approaching Krishna, the Self for guidance.

2. Even if one assumes that the epic is a historical narrative, is it necessary that the *Gita* too must be the narration of a dialogue that took place on the field of battle ? Instances are not wanting of genuine works of history containing imaginary dialogues. Thucydides, the most conscientious historian known to antiquity, did not hesitate to introduce such imaginary dialogues between, and to invent speeches for, historical characters in order to elucidate situations, and has himself said that he had deliberately done so. As for poetical works, many poets of a transcendental vision have picked up historical or semi-historical incidents and used them for depicting imperishable visions of the soul of man struggling with grim facts of life. To take only one instance — that of that master painter of human passions, Shakespeare. We see in his dramas men and women thrown into situations as profoundly tragic as that in which we find Arjuna in the first discourse of the *Gita*. See how Lady Blanch, in *King John*, feels herself torn between different interests, and talks almost in the language of Arjuna :

> Which is the side that I must go withal ?
> I am with both : each army has a hand :
> And in their rage, I having hold of both,
> They whirl asunder and dismember me.
> Husband, I cannot pray that thou mayst win ;
> Uncle, I needs must pray that thou must lose ;
> Father, I may not wish the fortune thine ;
> Whoever wins, on that side shall I lose ;
> Assured loss before the match be played.

But Shakespeare simply describes her sad predicament and leaves her to her fate. We do not hear of her again. Macbeth he does not leave to his fate but puts in charge of the devil, who at one time as witches and at another as Lady Macbeth fans the flame of his ambition, dries up all the milk of human kindness in him, and drives him to the dire deed. Hamlet he tosses on the boisterous seas of a devastating indecision. Brutus loses his sleep, his mind suffers "the nature of an insurrection", he walks about "musing and sighing with arms across", avoids the counsel of his noble wife, lest she should cure him of the "sick offence within his mind", and finally decides to do what he thinks is for the "general good", not in the spirit of a butcher but that of a sacrificer:

> Let's kill him boldly, but not wrathfully;
> Let's carve him as a dish fit for the gods.

And throughout the drama he retains such a composed selflessness that it makes even his enemies declare him to be "the noblest Roman of them all". The author of the *Gita,* centuries before Shakespeare, made Arjuna's mind also suffer "the nature of an insurrection", but neither did he leave him to his fate nor fling him to the devil. He put him face to face with God — as Shakespeare put Brutus face to face with his self — and made God quell the insurrection and surround him with light and peace and bliss. We have not only the whole insurrection described, the delusion exposed, the doubter with his doubts fully depicted, but we have something more revealed to us — the Dispeller of doubts and the Bringer of Peace. It is this which to my mind makes the *Gita* the Bible of Humanity. The *Gita* says: When you are torn with doubt and despair and anguish, go to the Dweller in the Innermost, listen to His counsel, obey it implicitly and you will have no cause to grieve. Every mystic, burning with genuine aspiration, seeks comfort and solace from his God in matters of doubt, and Miss Underhill had referred to so many "internal conversations" between the contemplative soul of the mystic and his God. Is it any way unreasonable to imagine that the author of the *Gita* — one of the supreme mystics of the world — had himself a similar "internal conversation", and so visualized Arjuna, an aspirant, as having such "internal conversations" and left the picture as an inspiring heritage for all the spiritual aspirants of the world? It may not be unreasonable, but it is heretical, some one might perhaps say. Heretical it is, I admit, but the heresy should in no way hurt one's faith. If it is an actual discourse between Krishna and Arjuna that is narrated by the author of the *Gita,* one can think of him as nothing more than a reporter. I for one should prefer to think of him as a *Kavi* (poet-seer, a word we often find applied to God Himself) who has given us God's authentic message as was revealed to him and as was believed by him. The *Gita,* seen in this light, becomes none the less adorable for me, than it would be if some one proved to me that it was an actual dialogue between Krishna and Arjuna that was reported therein.

3. The barest examination of the contents of the *Gita* shows that the author, saturated with the teachings of the *Upanishads,* and a devotee of Krishna, as he was, wanted to leave to mankind an expression of what he had felt and seen and lived. Hopkins' charge that the *Gita* is an "ill-assorted cabinet of primitive philosophical opinions" has value only in that it proves that the poem is certainly not a historical narrative. But the charge betrays gross ignorance of philosophy and a most superficial reading of the *Gita.* Modern philosophical opinion has wellnigh accepted the *Upanishadic* philosophy or is at least coming near it. What appears to be a jumble is nothing more than a reflection of the state of things in the days when the poem was written. The Vedas with their apparently many gods and occasionally expressed monotheism were there; the *Upanishads* had raised a noble protest against the Vedic ritual which had still a hold on the people and in decrying paradise-seeking ritual had laid an excessive emphasis on the life of renunciation as the only means of salvation; the Sankhya and *Yoga* principles were there in the atmosphere not yet crystalized into definite systems; the Bhagawat cult of Krishna Vasudeva was also there. Whether Buddha and Buddhism were there it is not yet definitely established, but atheistic doctrines were certainly

prevalent. It was the unique, though very uphill, task of the author of the *Gita* to pick up scattered and heterogeneous material, to sift the true from the false, to attenuate seeming contradictions, and to present a new philosophy and new art of life. There is Sankhya, there is *Yoga*, there is *Yajna*, there is *Bhakti*, and there are the gods too, everywhere in the *Gita*, but all in their proper place and setting and some with a connotation and meaning which they did not possess before. As regards the relation of the *Upanishads* to the *Gita*, I have already referred to the well-known metaphor of the cows, the milker and the milk. If I may venture to change the metaphor, without incurring the charge of heresy, I may say that the meadows of the *Upanishads* provided for the author of the *Gita* a rich verdure which was converted into the nectar-like milk of the *Gita*. For whilst one finds the influence of the *Upanishads* throughout the *Gita*, whilst one finds words and whole verses taken from them, they are so digested and assimilated that one can scarcely think that they went into the making of the rich product.

For what is there in the *Gita*, one may ask, that is not in the *Upanishads*? What Dr Radhakrishnan calls the "fundamental ultimates" are there borrowed bodily from the *Upanishads*; the *Atman* (Self) and the *Brahman* are there in the very language of the *Upanishads*—in the seemingly mutually contradictory language of the evolving *Upanishads*, as my notes on II. 19, II. 20, II. 29, XIII. 12-17, and other verses will show; but whilst one has to trace the evolution and reconcile the contradictions in the *Upanishads* (as Prof. Ranade has ably done in his *Constructive Survey of Upanishadic Philosophy*) the author of the *Gita* has woven them in with such consummate skill that they are all in their appropriate place on the pattern for which they are used and to which they seem to belong in a most vital manner. Where he has adopted a thought from the *Upanishads* it seems as though he had simply chosen a text to produce a most inspiring sermon.

I shall take just a few examples. Take this well-known text * from that very brief *Upanishad* containing all the philosophy of the *Upanishads,* I mean the *Ishopanishad*: "Even while engaged in action here, a man may look forward to living a hundred years; for even thus and not otherwise the actions will not smear the man." As it is, it almost reads like a conundrum. But the author of the *Gita* related it to the preceding verse "renouncing that, thou must enjoy", and out of the two produced his whole philosophy of action that binds and action that does not bind but frees.

I have pointed out in detail in its proper place in my notes the way in which the author has summarized one whole section of the *Mundaka Upanishad* and clothed it with a new meaning (IV. 32-38). He had a lively sense of the essentials and had no hesitation in jettisoning the unessentials as we find in so many places in the *Gita.* For instance, he refers to the ancient eschatology, summarizes a string of verses from the *Chhandogya Upanishad* (5. 10. 1-6) in two neat *shlokas* and in a third gives us the significance of the belief (see my note on VIII. 24-26).

Take now the Sankhyan principles which we shall have occasion to study in some detail in the next section. The *Prashna Upanishad* (4.8) contains a full enumeration of them, and indeed the Sankhyan *Purusha* is already turned into the empirical self, the seer, toucher, taster, hearer, smeller, thinker, whose abode is the Supreme Imperishable *Atman* — *Paramatman* — the Universal Self. The *gunas* also are there in the germ in other *Upanishads.* But the author of the *Gita* has constructed a whole philosophy and ethics out of these scattered elements and given them a new and rich meaning.

For the *Yoga* of meditation take the sections in the *Maitri Upanishad* 6. 18-22, on which one may say the whole

---

* *Isha.* 1. 2.

तेन त्यक्तेन भुंजीथाः . . . . . ॥ १ ॥
कुर्वन्नेवेह कर्माणि जिजीविषेच्छतं समाः ।
एवं त्वयि नान्यथेतोऽस्ति न कर्म लिप्यते नरे ॥ २ ॥

of the sixth and part of the eighth discourses are based. I shall not enter into the comparison here, but the reader who will care to go to the sources in the pages of Hume will not fail to see that the *Gita* exposition of the method of meditative mysticism, shorn of the technical details described in the *Upanishad,* is a vast development on the latter, and the final part of the sixth discourse containing the covenant of the Lord to the failed aspirant is the *Gita's* most original and inspiring contribution.

The gods of the Vedas are there, and the worshippers of different gods are also referred to, but each of these worshippers, whilst fully recognized, has been given his proper desert, and the gods are brought under the numerous manifestations of the one All-pervading God who is to be worshipped and adored, through those manifestations, if one will. The tenth discourse, read in this light, is a luminous commentary on the Vedas. I do not know how far Prof. Ranade is justified in tracing the seeds of the full-grown tree of *bhakti* (devotion) to the instances of humble discipleship that we come across in the *Upanishads* : Narada who approaches Sanatkumara with a broken and contrite heart — " I have heard from those like you, sir, that he who knows the Atman passes beyond sorrow. Such a sorrowing one I am ; pray help me to pass beyond sorrow " ; or Brihadratha who in the same spirit begs his *guru* to " deliver " him from *sansara* wherein he was lying like a frog in a waterless well. Well, we must not forget that the *Gita* too is described as an *Upanishad* — though not counted as one — and the spirit of discipleship has been in India ever since the beginnings of philosophy. I would rather read in these and other instances of disciples going to their masters to learn *brahmavidya* (divine knowledge) a strong suggestion that Arjuna's is also a similar case, in a different background of course. The seeds of the tree of *bhakti* are to be looked for in the praises and prayers with which the Vedas are full — the *upasana* in which the Vedic seer " bows to God over and over again — God who is in fire and in water, who pervades the whole world, who is in the annual crops as well as in the perennial trees " ; or in those glorious *Upanishadic* prayers where the soul implores the Nourisher (*Pushan*) to uncover for the votary of Truth its face hidden in a golden veil; or where the *Upanishad* prescribes for the sacrificer that sublime form of prayer for being led from the unreal to the Real, from darkness to Light, from death to Deathlessness. The atmosphere was there ready with the Krishna Vasudeva cult for the *upasana* of the Vedas to be systematized and converted into the life-giving form of devotion to one God.

But Prof. Ranade is fully justified in seeing the description of the Universal form of the Lord (eleventh discourse) already in the germ in the *Mundaka Upanishad*: "When in the *Mundakopanishad* we find the description of the cosmic Person with fire as his head, the Sun and the Moon as his eyes, the quarters as his ears, the Vedas as his speech, air as his *prana*, the universe as his heart and the earth as his feet, we have in embryo a description of the *vishvaroopa* which later became the theme of the famous eleventh chapter of the *Bhagawadgita* on the transfigured personality of Krishna." *

But at this rate it is possible to trace almost everything in the *Gita* to the *Upanishads* likened to cows in the meditation verses preceding the *Gita*. If, without offending the susceptibilities of those who want to read in the *Gita* the actual words of the incarnate Lord, I might make a suggestion: I would say that the very idea of Krishna as charioteer and guide, philosopher and friend of Arjuna may be traced to the *Kathopanishad* which makes the *Atman* the master of the chariot of the body, the intellect the driver, the mind the reins, and the senses the horses. There are nearly a dozen places in which the *Gita* has actually borrowed from this great *Upanishad*. Why should not the master-artist use this beautiful image in his epic in order to weave out of the philosophy of the *Upanishad* the living religion of the *Bhagawadgita*?

I shall, however, not elaborate the point. Whoever would be a serious student of the *Gita* must go to these

---

* *Constructive Survey of the Upanishadic Philosophy*, p. 197.

source books — the "revered *Upanishads*" as Hume has called them, and he will find the truth of the metaphors of the cow, and the meadow I have referred to above. But let no one therefore run away with the impression that the *Gita* is a highly poetic echo of the *Upanishads*. The *Gita* performs the unique function of making what was an esoteric doctrine a living reality for the unlettered, the lowly and the lost, and presents the highest form of practical religion to enable each and all to realize his or her purpose in life. Above all, it blazons forth in an unmistakable manner the truth that life is worth living and teaches how it may be worth living. It is a unique synthesis and reconciliation of the two doctrines which were in those days held to be contradictory — *sannyasa* (renunciation of action) and *yoga* (performance of action).

Hinduism, remarks a Christian critic, has no New Testament, and hence no Gospel to offer to its adherents.* Well, the critic did not know that the venerable Dr Deussen had already given the reply to him: "To every Indian Brahmana today the *Upanishads* are what the New Testament is to the Christians"; and if I may venture to extend Dr Deussen's comparison, I may say that if the *Upanishads* are the New Testament, the *Gita* may well be said to constitute therein the Gospels. The author of the *Gita* having lived the teaching of the *Upanishads* summed it up thus: "Performing action without attachment, man shall attain the Supreme" (III. 19), or if I may paraphrase the language of this and other similar verses, according to the *Gita*, 'Sacrifice is the fulfilling of the law.'

But there is nothing exclusive about the *Gita* which should make it a gospel only for the Brahmana or the Hindu. Having all the light and colour of the Indian atmosphere, it naturally must have the greatest fascination for the Hindu, but the central teaching should not have any the less appeal for a non-Hindu as the central teaching of the Bible or the *Koran* should not have any the less appeal for a non-Christian or a non-Muslim.

---

* John Mackenzie, in *Hindu Ethics*.

In the verse I have just quoted is contained in a nutshell the teaching of the book. The *Gita* presents to its devotee a vision of the Supreme, tells him how to discover Him, how to recognize Him in His true nature and magnitude, how to enter Him and how to be one with Him — the End and the Means thereto as we might say in short. The colophon at the end of each discourse of the *Gita* is noteworthy. It has come down to us from an ancient date and though the title of each discourse given in this colophon differs in various editions, the colophon itself is the same in all editions: "Thus ends discourse (number) entitled (name) in the converse of Lord Krishna and Arjuna, on the science of Yoga as part of the knowledge of *brahman* in the *Upanishad* called the *Bhagawadgita* (Sung by the Lord)." *Upanishad* etymologically means what the pupil learns sitting at the feet of the master; it may also mean the knowledge which by taking one near the Supreme helps to cut off earthly ties. Thus, in one sense, *brahmavidya* and *upanishad* are synonymous. The *Gita* is, therefore, the science and art of *Yoga* — or shall we call it the Art of Life — for the attainment of the knowledge of *brahman*, or the Wisdom and the Art of Life? This phrase in the colophon may also be translated, "the science of *Yoga* rooted in *brahmavidya*." It goes without saying that unless the Art of Life is rooted in the Wisdom of Life it will never lead to it. There seems to be no doubt, however we may interpret it, that Wisdom, as leading to the *summum bonum*, is the goal for the attainment of which the Art of Life or *Yoga* is the means. The *Gita* is the *Upanishad* of the *Mahabharata*.

IV. THE FUNDAMENTALS

We shall now turn to a study of that Wisdom and that Art as revealed in the *Gita*. Perhaps the best way to do so is to present a brief interpretative analysis of the various discourses. But before we start with the analysis, it would not be out of place to indicate what we might call the permanent background of the *Gita*. It starts with accepting certain "unanalysable ultimates" — the Self, the Absolute, God, and the Universe and certain fundamental postulates. It presents no philosophical treatment, as it is really addressed to those who assume these ultimates, for the simple reason that the author's purpose was to expound the ordinary man's mission in life rather than to present a philosophical system. Thus, when Arjuna approaches Krishna with an appeal which recalls, 'What in me is dark, illumine,' He does so by a sudden flash light revelation of the Unborn, Ageless, Deathless, Everlasting, Indemonstrable *Atman* or Self. He uses the epithet 'Indemonstrable' indicating in a word his whole meaning. How will one demonstrate or measure Him who is the proof of all proofs and measure of all measures? As the *Kena Upanishad* puts it: "He is the very hearing of the ear, the very mind of the mind, the very voice of speech, the very breath of breath and the very vision of the eye." Or as the modern philosopher Dr Radhakrishnan puts it: "The ultimate assumption of all life is the spirit in us, the Divine in man. Life is God and the proof of it is life itself. If somewhere in ourselves we did not know with absolute certainty that God is, we could not live. Even the sun and the moon would go out if they began to doubt. Our lives are not lived within their own limits. We are not ourselves alone; we are God-men." *

About the composition of the Universe, the *Gita* takes up the theory then in vogue, as any modern thinker would start with assuming the theory of evolution. The Sankhyan cosmology was then in vogue; it was, as we have already seen, referred to in some of the *Upanishads*. Since the mention of it in the *Gita*, various *Smritis* have adopted it and it is referred to in various places in the *Mahabharata*. The system as we know it in its complete form was not then in existence; there were probably fragments of an original of which no trace can be found; there was what we might call a torso or a skeleton. At any rate the *Gita* accepted it as a skeleton, put life into it, and made use of it for its philosophy and ethics. It will be useful for our

* *An Idealist View of Life*, p. 158.

purpose to give a brief sketch of the Sankhya system in order that we may be able to see how much of it the *Gita* has adopted and how it has used the raw material. It will also familiarize us with certain terms which will occur over and over again in the *Gita*.

A. THE SANKHYA SYSTEM

Kapila, or whoever the great seer was, who brought into being the Sankhyan concepts, started not with an analysis of objective experience as Darwin did, but, perhaps as a result of elaborate experiments in the laboratory of his self, arrived at the evolutionary idea with the discovery of which Darwin concluded his researches. Darwin found the planet "cycling on" from the simple beginning of "a few forms *or one*" to "endless forms most beautiful and most wonderful", and evolving through the operation of one law — struggle for life. The Sankhya philosopher, making provision for both matter and mind, started with two eternal principles, one conscious, unconditioned, and passive, the other unconscious but active and manifesting the operation of not one law but three; or, if we may say so, a triple law evidencing not only the struggle for life, but the stage before that, namely inertia, then the struggle for life, and lastly 'the struggle for the life of others'* or sacrifice.

The Sankhya philosopher, as we have said, posits the existence of two eternal principles: *prakriti* and *purusha*. The existence of *prakriti* or primordial matter or Nature is, he says, proved by the manifested universe which is its effect. The effect really exists in the cause, which necessarily is a Causeless Cause. The evolution of the manifested universe out of this unmanifest *prakriti* arises as a result of the disturbance in the equilibrium of its three constituents which are postulated as self-evident. These constituents are called *gunas*, literally meaning threads or strands which compose the string of *prakriti*. They are

* To adopt Henry Drummond's phrase.

called *sattva, rajas* and *tamas,* the sources respectively of existence, of motion, and inertia, their functions being light, activity and restraint. They are, however, not mutually contradictory, and they exist together, in fact are never separate; they slip into one another and intermingle with one another. As soon as their equilibrium is disturbed, *prakriti* begins to evolve and whatever evolves bears an impress of these constituents, and the infinite variety of differences in the objects in the universe is due to the varying proportion of these constituents in each, and their interaction amongst themselves.

But *prakriti* cannot evolve, except under the influence of *purusha,* a principle as eternal as *prakriti* and of which the existence is posited and proved by the Sankhyan philosopher by various arguments into which we need not go. *Purusha* is the Soul that informs the body—*prakriti*; unlike the *prakriti* he is inactive, he is without *gunas,* and the subject and seer of all objects possessing the *gunas.* uncaused and unproductive. But whilst *prakriti* is one, the *purushas* are taken to be countless, for while the constitutive stuff is essentially one and the same in all, there are separate births and deaths, separate organs and varying functions in different individuals. The process of evolution of the *prakriti* may be thus tabularly shown:

(1) Prakriti (unmanifest) — (25) Purusha
becoming manifest in

|

(2) Buddhi (Intellect or Will)

|

(3) Ahamkara (Individuation)

|

Organic	Inorganic
(4) Manas (mind)	(15-19) Five Tanmatras (subtle elements)
(5-9) Five senses of Perception	(20-24) Five Mahabhootas (gross elements)
(10-14) Five organs of action	

The Sankhya system, as we find it in Ishvarachandra's *karika* has no Supreme or God, *prakriti* and *purusha* being the only two eternal principles. The presence of the inactive *purusha* is said somehow to disturb the equilibrium of the unmanifest *prakriti* which begins to evolve. The very first step in the evolution of the homogeneous *prakriti* was its determination or will (*buddhi*), however unconscious, to manifest itself; it is, therefore, regarded as its first product. The next was individuation (*ahamkar*), the product of *buddhi*, a principle whereby the *prakriti* broke up into different innumerable entities divided into two sections, organic and inorganic. Eleven elements consisting of the mind, the five senses of perception (hearing, touch, sight, taste, and smell) and the five organs of action (the hands, the feet, the tongue, and the two organs of evacuation) were evolved out of individuation, for the formation of the organic world, and five subtle elements (sound, touch, form, savour, and smell) for the formation of the inorganic world composed of the five gross elements. These three quintets really suggest one another. Each sense has a single realm — the eye, for instance, has the realm of form and no other; the ears have the realm of sound and no other, and so on — and so there could be no more than five realms (also called sense-objects) corresponding to the five senses of perception and no more than five gross elements, Ether, Wind, Fire, Water, Earth could reflect the five subtle ones.

This shows *prakriti* in its cosmic aspect. No doubt the seer who arrived at this process of evolution as evident in Nature did so from an observation of the small human physical and mental frame. This microcosm was to him the macrocosm in miniature. In the individual the senses of perception provide the material to the mind which forms percepts out of it, then individuation refers them to the self and passes them on to *buddhi* or the determining principle which forms concepts and decisions and sends them back to the mind which gets them executed by means of the five organs of action.

How *purusha* is entrapped in *prakriti* is sought to be explained somewhat in this manner. *Buddhi,* which after the evolution starts, plays an important part, almost simulating as the *purusha. Buddhi* coloured in *sattvika* character helps to release, and coloured in *tamas* and *rajas* character, helps to tighten, the bondage of *purusha.* In fact all the psychic experiences — desire, hate, likes and dislikes, pleasure, pain, — are the modifications of *buddhi* which the *purusha* takes upon himself. When affected by the *Sattva guna, buddhi* gives rise to virtue, discrimination, and dispassion, the process of release begins, the distinction of *purusha* and *prakriti* becomes apparent to the *buddhi,* and *purusha* and *prakriti* are emancipated from each other. *Samsara* or the cycle of birth and death means suffering and the only means of ending that suffering permanently is this knowledge or discrimination. The individual or the lower self ever struggles to realize its identity with the higher self and as soon as the identity is realized, arises the discriminative knowledge consisting in the realization that 'I am not' (i.e. I am not *prakriti* but *purusha*), that 'nothing is mine', and that 'the ego exists not' (i.e. I am not the doer or experiencer). This knowledge is permanent release from the "dread machinery of sin and sorrow". (The 'lower self' and the 'higher self' is, however, not the language of Sankhya).

Just as there is a process of evolution, there is a similar process of dissolution. When the human organism is dissolved, the five gross elements in it mix up with the five gross elements in Nature, but the remaining eighteen, described as forming the subtle body (called *linga-sharira*), containing the impressions (*sanskaras*) of the deeds (mental and physical) done during one birth take on a new habitation and go through the fruit of the deeds of the past birth. This migration and transmigration go on in the case of all but the freed souls, and the law of *karma* carries them through all kinds of organisms — deity, man, animal or plant, until the ultimate dissolution of the world. We shall have occasion to deal with this doctrine of *karma* and rebirth in detail later on.

This in brief is the bare skeleton of the Sankhya system. The difficulties of some of the conceptions are obvious. If the presence of *purusha* helps to start the process of evolution of *prakriti*, that *purusha* must be obviously as cosmic and as much one and unified as *prakriti* itself. How they co-operate is an eternal puzzle, and the conception that *prakriti* carries on its passing show in order to release *purusha,* who by reason of his association with *prakriti* is deluded in the belief that he is bound, is more baffling still. As Keith puts it: "Unconscious Nature cannot experience misery, the spirit in itself does not experience misery, and the union of the two which results in the apparent experience of misery by spirit which wrongly thinks that the misery which it brings to light in Nature is misery which it itself endures, thus creates the very misery which it is the object of the union to abolish....The epithets given to the 'subject' in the Sankhya are applicable to the abstract conception of the subject as opposed to all its content: there can be no multiplication of this abstract conception as the Sankhya asserts. The existence of the numerous individuals who are conscious is totally a different thing, for their number and individuality are conditioned by the possession of a different objective content in consciousness and when this is removed, there would remain nothing at all, or at the most the abstract conception of subject, which could not be a multiple of individual spirits. Had the Sankhyan conception been that of a number of souls as opposed to spirits, no logical objection could be raised to the theory of multiplicity, but the sharp distinction of spirit and nature and the assertion that there is no real connection between them deprive the spirit of any possible reality." * "There is," as Dr Radhakrishnan remarks, "throughout the Sankhya a confusion

* Keith — *The Sankhyan System.*

between the *purusha* and the *jiva. Purusha* is the perfect spirit, not to be confused with the particular human spirit. The *purusha* is certainly in me as my very core and substance ; and the *jiva*, or the individual, with all his irrational caprices and selfish aims is but a distortion of *purusha.* To say that every *jiva* is striving to realize its *purusha* means that every *jiva* is potentially divine." Again, " if anything be regarded as the presupposition of all experience, it is a universal spirit on which both the tendencies of *purusha* and *prakriti* rest, for the two, *purusha* and *prakriti,* do not stand confronting each other. In the becoming of the world, the contradiction is resolved. It shows that the two things rest on a fundamental identity. The Sankhyan insistence on *purusha,* when it is not confused with *jiva,* amounts to nothing more than the recognition of a pure and perfect presence not divided by the division of things, not affected by the stress and struggle of the cosmic manifestation, within it all, while superior to it all....This Supreme personality combines within himself the peace and the bliss, the calm and the silence of *purusha* on the one hand, and the jarring multiplicity, the strife and suffering of *prakriti* on the other. The Supreme contains within itself all lives and all bodies, and each individual is nothing more than a wave of this boundless surge, a fragment of the world-soul. Only such a view can make the Sankhya philosophy more consistent." *

B. THE GITA VIEW

1. PRAKRITI AND GUNAS

The Vedanta and the *Gita* step in to make the Sankhya system a consistent whole. The *Gita* supplies the head to the torso and makes the whole the basis of its edifice. All the 24 principles of the Sankhya system are adopted by the *Gita* in one form or other, the conception of evolution to explain the breaking up of the unmanifest into the manifest world is also accepted, the idea of *gunas* is most

* *Indian Philosophy,* Vol. II.

completely worked out, but it denies any independent existence to *prakriti* and *purusha* and cuts at the root of that dualism by making Absolute *Brahman* the prime source and cause of all that exists, an All-pervading Spirit which is the *prius* of all matter, animate and inanimate. This Absolute is thus described as having two aspects or natures — the higher and the lower, the higher consisting of the Essence that vitalizes and sustains, and the lower being the world of Nature. The higher aspect — *jiva* — is the individual self in all, and the world of Nature is nothing but the Sankhyan *prakriti* shortly summed up thus: Earth, Water, Fire, Wind and Ether (which presuppose the five subtle elements), Mind, Individuation and Intellect (which are intended to include all the ten senses of perception and organs of action), which thus make up 23, and the 24th unmanifested *prakriti* being omitted as being evidenced in its manifest form (VII. 4-5). It is this *prakriti* again which is referred to in VIII. 18 where it is simply referred to as the unmanifest from which all the manifested entities spring at the coming of the Cosmic Day, and into which they dissolve at the coming of the Cosmic Night and again come into being at the coming of the Day. But higher than this Unmanifest is the Permanent, Unchanging, Unmanifest which perishes not while all beings perish, and while the unmanifest *prakriti* changes (VIII. 19). That Permanent Unmanifest is the Imperishable or the Absolute (VIII. 20) which informs and sustains the world (XV. 17). The same *prakriti* is referred to in the thirteenth discourse. *Prakriti* is here the body, the *kshetra*, or the field, made up of the 24 principles we are now familiar with, every one of them being mentioned (XIII. 5). It is called the field, as the body and the world constitute the field of toil and turmoil from which and through which the individual has to emancipate himself and to realize his unity with the Self of all universe. It is these twain — *jiva* and *prakriti* combined — which are said to form the womb of the whole creation — moving and unmoving (VII. 6; XIII. 26; XIV. 3-4), the Absolute as God being the Father depositing the seed in this great womb of all being (XIV. 4). He is thus the origin and the ultimate end of all (VII. 6), the seed itself of all (VII. 10). The individual self is the same as the Universal Self, only seeming different in different bodies, because he identifies himself with the various adjuncts, the body, the mental and the intellectual apparatus, and experiences the objective world. It is his attachment to these adjuncts — these *gunas* that binds him to the body and drags him from birth to death and death to birth.

2. THE GUNAS

The Sankhya doctrine of *gunas* as the constituents of *prakriti* has been worked out elaborately by the *Gita* and has been adopted by all the *Smriti* works, and it has taken such a hold of the Hindu mind that the words *sattva, rajas* and *tamas* and their derivatives *sattvika, rajasa* and *tamasa* are common terms of the Hindu vocabulary in every Indian language and immediately convey their ethical connotation even to an unlettered peasant. Though the word *guna* literally means " strand " and *sattva, rajas* and *tamas* in their non-technical sense mean essence, dust or foulness, and darkness respectively, the word " strand " is hardly appropriate to convey the full ethical and non-ethical content of the word *guna*. As constitutive stuff of all that exists the three *gunas* represent the three modes or modifications or moments of being — "intelligible essence, energy, and mass " to use Dr Seal's phraseology. As mental states they are the states of purity or clarity, restlessness, and torpidity. Ethically, *sattvika* state is pure, *rajasa* is alloyed, and *tamasa* is impure. The *Gita* says *sattva* binds man to his body by conscious happiness and knowledge, *rajas* by restlessness and misery, *tamas* by heedlessness, lethargy and sleep (XIV. 5-7). Knowledge, light, happiness indicate the predominance of *sattva* ; greed, restlessness, yearning indicate the predominance of *rajas* ; dulness, heedlessness, lethargy of *tamas* (XIV. 11-13). Those characterized by *sattva* rise upward, those by *rajas* remain of the earth earthy, those by *tamas* go down to the lowest species (XIV. 18). The terms are further applied to represent modes, aspects, characters or tendencies of men and things, of activity and temperament, *sattvika* indicating the highest state of selflessness, *rajasa* that of calculating selfishness, and *tamasa* of blind passion and fury.

Make as many permutations and combinations as possible of infinitely varying degrees of these constituents and you have an explanation of the astonishing diversity that you find in the universe. He who has seen the play and interplay of these *gunas* and who can detach himself from them, he who can isolate himself from them and realize the unity at the basis of this diversity is a seer — a *tattvavid* who has known the truth of things, he is free, his action does not bind him, his action is no action. That is the metaphysical aspect of the doctrine of *gunas,* as *guna* also means subordinate, not principal, and hence shadow not substance. *Prakriti,* we are told again and again, is ever active and so long as one is imprisoned in the tabernacle of *prakriti,* he has to act whether he will or no. The *gunas* are not separate from *prakriti* ; they are often described as " born of *prakriti* ", but they are the very stuff of *prakriti,* as indeed we have them described as synonymous with *prakriti.* Man's senses, mind, intellect etc. are his *prakriti* or his *gunas.* When a man's body is fat, he says ' I am fat ' identifying himself with the body ; when his feet walk or the body sleeps, he says ' I walk ', ' I sleep ', again identifying himself with the body. In a similar way man identifies himself with the mind, the will, the intellect, and arrogates to himself the various activities of those internal organs. All these constitute the *gunas,* or the not-Self, or we might say the lower ' self ', and all activity in which man identifies himself with the instrument of the activity is thus self-ful, and all activity from which man has completely detached himself is selfless. The attachment to the fruit of action in the shape of reward or pleasure springs from this identification with the not-self or lower self. This identification is described as delusion, as ignorance, as the root of bondage and the man who has cut at the root of it, who has rid himself of it, is the seer or *tattvavid* (III. 28 ; V. 8).

The Western reader will perhaps understand the distinction between the changing *gunas* and the unchanging Self, the shadows and the substance, much better from the following memorable lines from *Julius Caesar* :

> " Between the acting of a dreadful thing
> And the first motion, all the interim is
> Like a phantasma, or a hideous dream ;
> The *Genius* and the *mortal instruments*
> Are then in council ; and the state of man,
> Like to a little kingdom, suffers then
> The nature of an insurrection."

Shakespeare, as I have said more than once, had his grip on the fundamentals of things, and in this passage he sensed the distinction between the Genius (i. e. in the language of the *Gita,* the unchanging, imperishable *atman* or Self) and the " mortal instruments " (i.e. in the language of the *Gita,* the *gunas*). And no word could be happier than the word " instruments ", which indeed all *gunas* are, in the hands of the Genius, or the Master, or the Self. The self-controlled, the self-possessed, the *tattvavid,* does have an experience of the insurrection, but he quells it by making the " instruments " — *gunas* — act according to his will.

Now this state of self-control and ultimate peace can proceed from self-realization or knowledge which is the fruit of ages of endeavour. Man is, therefore, advised to take refuge in religion and ethics. He has to work himself upwards towards *sattva* dedicating all his activity and endeavour to the Giver of all good and ultimately reach beyond the three *gunas.* This state beyond is the state of true knowledge and freedom.

There is still another aspect of *prakriti* with its *gunas* which also it may be useful to indicate in this connection. There is a part of man's nature which will assert itself and no amount of coercion will avail against it. There is another part which is amenable to culture and discipline. The

Gita distinguishes the two, but does not, excepting indirectly, indicate the scope of each. It is apparent, however, that the first is the physical and mental constitution which man brings with him at birth and which normally determines his vocation. It is with a view to man's self-development and his being able to fulfil his function as a member of the social organism that his vocation is determined according to his native aptitudes and qualities. Here, says the *Gita,* let not man wrestle with nature, but obey the law of his being, of course, casting all on Him (III. 33). But there is the other part, viz. the moral part of his nature where man may not rest content until he has thoroughly cleansed himself. 'Lust, wrath and greed form the triple gateway to hell' says the *Gita.* 'Flee from that fiery hell.' (III. 34; III. 37; XVI. 21). Shakespeare, who had the heavenly gift of knowing what man's nature is, seems to make this distinction over and over again. The royal nature and material valour of King Cimbeline's sons living in captivity as barbarous rustics from their very childhood, are described as clamouring out again and again, while Hamlet tells his mother that

> "Use almost can change the stamp of nature
> And either curb the devil, or throw him out
> With wondrous potency."

This doctrine of *gunas* as the constitutive stuff of man, at least in its ethical aspect, was not quite unknown to thinkers and philosophers in the West, though they did not visualize it in all its aspects and certainly did not work it out in any detail, except perhaps Plato. His division of the springs of human behaviour into three main sources—desire, emotion and knowledge, would seem to be a recognition of the three *gunas* in another name. And his division of men according to their powers and aptitudes and later Aristotle's modification of it, were certainly due to a recognition of the three *gunas.* Was not Bacon too faintly thinking of the triple division of man's character into *sattvika, rajasa* and *tamasa* when he distinguished "the three grades of ambition in mankind"? "The first" he said, "was the desire to extend their power...which is vulgar and degenerate. The second to extend the power of their own country which has more dignity, but not less covetousness.... (The third) if a man endeavour to establish and extend the power and domination over the universe, his ambition is nobler than the other two." In the same way Spinoza was using only another language for one *guna* passing out into another when he talked of man's "emotions or modifications" as "passages or translation from a lesser state of perfection to a greater". And look at Herbert Spencer's division of knowledge into three kinds: "Knowledge of the lowest kind is ununified knowledge; science is partially unified knowledge; philosophy is completely unified knowledge."—an almost direct paraphrase, of the *Gita* (XVIII. 20-22) describing the *sattvika, rajasa,* and *tamasa* kinds of knowledge. To come to more recent times, Dr Henry Drummond when he talked of "Self-ism" and "other-ism" as the two permanent tendencies of nature—"not painted on the canvas but woven through it",* was he not describing the *rajas* and *sattva gunas*? Lastly, is not Prof. Mackenzie describing the three *gunas* in man's moral character when he says: "There are, in fact, we may say, three selves in every man. There is in the self that is revealed in occasional impulses which we cannot quite subdue, the 'sin' that after all dwelleth in us. On the other hand, there is the permanent character—the universe in which we habitually live. And finally there is the true or rational self in which alone we feel that we can rest with satisfaction—the 'Christ' that liveth in us and in whom we hope more and more to abide." Is not this last phrase almost an echo of that memorable verse (II. 45) in which Krishna asks Arjuna to "abide ever in *sattva*"?

3. KARMA AND REBIRTH

Closely allied to the doctrine of *gunas* is the doctrine of *karma* and rebirth which the *Gita* accepts as axiomatic and which has come in for a lot of criticism from Western

* In his *Ascent of man.*

thinkers. Let us see what it means and what part it plays in the Hindu view of life. We know for a fact that, although sometimes action is but 'the movement of a muscle this way or that', its consequences are infinite and untraceable beyond a certain point. If the consequences cannot thus be followed out, the roots of what apparently appears as the cause must also be too deep and hidden to trace back. For actions are not merely "things done that take the eye and have the price".

"All instincts immature,
All purposes unsure
That weighed not as his work, yet swelled the man's amount;
Thoughts hardly to be packed
Into a narrow act,
Fancies that broke through language and escaped
All I could never be
All men ignored in me,
This I was worth to God, whose wheel the pitcher shaped."

These lines from Browning's *Rabbi Ben Ezra* seem to me to bring out the content of *karma* in a striking manner. It is He, working through His law, that takes into account "all men ignore" in men. And if He is the Accountant and the Judge, His book cannot be the narrow book of a man's lifetime but the vast one of countless lifetimes. What we are, what we think, what we do is the result of what we have been through ages gone by. Locke, when he insisted that the mind at birth is a *tabula rasa* was talking from a limited experience. Bacon before him had penetrated into the truth deeper, and in his famous *Idols* he gave the world more perhaps than he knew. 'Human mind is born,' he said, composed like 'uneven mirrors' imparting 'their properties to different objects'. Those unevennesses could not but have their roots in various pre-existences. Even primitive man knew that one reaped what one sowed, but the Indian seer found out the universality of the law and made an attempt to gauge its stupendous implications.

That which ye sow, ye reap. See yonder fields!
The sesamum was sesamum; the corn
Was corn. The silence and the Darkness knew!
So is a man's fate born,
He cometh reaper of the things he sowed.*

Even in case of the sesamum we do not know how much earth and manure and water and sunshine went into the making of it. We know just the seed. Even so we do not know how much went into the making of ourselves. We have personal experience of our action affecting our lives and those of others every moment, and we also have some idea of what a share our parents' and grand-parents' characters had in our making and what share our own characters will have in the shaping of our children's character. But children sometimes manifest qualities which none of their parents or grand-parents, however remote, were ever known to have possessed. While thus heredity explains a part, it fails to explain the whole, of our make-up, and it has certainly nothing to offer in defence of the sins of the parents or grand-parents being visited on the children. The law of *karma* here steps in, supplements heredity and makes it understandable and tolerable. When a man dies, we are told, the gross elements are dissolved, dust returneth unto dust, but the self with the subtle psychic elements remains, it seeks a new home, leaving the old which is broken up (XV. 7-8). The parents provide for this unknown guest a new home with a character of its own (VI. 41-42). The guest—whom the parents fondly called their child—appropriates the home that it has deserved. Its new home, good or ill, is the result of its stock of *punya* or *papa*—not the "things that took the eye and had the price", but all that the man was worth to God,—in the language of the *Gita,* 'man's attachment to the *gunas*' (XIII. 21). It is through this home that he proceeds to work out his destiny. The effort lasts through a lifetime, the mortal coil is shuffled off once again, and

* *Light of Asia,* Edwin Arnold.

the self with the psychic apparatus, altered, developed or deteriorated, as the case may be, goes out in search of fresh fields and pastures new.

Thus if we do not know how much went into our making, we know that every one of us had an inevitable past with which we have to count. That serves to make us humble, warns us against being fretful and against judging our fellow-men. But the law of *karma* should not be mistaken for fatality or retributive justice. It is wrong to interpret it to mean that our enjoyments are a reward of a past life of virtue and our sufferings that of a past life of vice. Our enjoyments may well be the result of an inclination to a life of pleasure that we brought with us and failed to curb; and the readiness to go through suffering with joy, for the good of humanity, in a Buddha or a Jesus or a St. Francis, may be the rich harvest of nearly perfected past life. In these instances the sufferings, we will be told, were self-invited. Well, even in instances in which they seem to be imposed by nature, we may not make the mistake to think that they are the result of a life of vice. It is puerile to think that what we call 'pleasure' is the echo of virtue, and 'pain' the echo of vice. They are nature's ways of bringing into play the forces of evolution. The godly Ramakrishna Paramahamsa suffered from a fatal cancer and the Christ-like Henry Drummond who had never had an illness in his life had an excruciating disease of the bones which proved fatal. In both cases, who could say what the suffering was the result of? But it was clear to all that in both cases the suffering came in order that the world may have examples of perfected lives from which one might learn how to endure one's ailments. In both cases the doctors were amazed at the patients' reluctance to talk about their illness. No, the law of *karma* is not one to be trifled with, it is one to which we may bow with benefit, but not dare to dissect. Let us remember that neither action nor consequence may be judged by its outward form. The exquisitively sensitive balance to weigh them is in His hands, not ours. The law teaches us not to judge but to understand, not to ignore human suffering but to rush out to alleviate it, for it makes the whole world kin.

That leads us to its counterpart, the doctrine of re-birth. They are the obverse and the reverse of the same coin. If we came with something, we also pass away with something. We know that careers of the highest value abruptly come to an end, and often enough children with extraordinary gifts and attainments are born. Neither is there an abrupt end in the one case, nor a fortuitous beginning in the other. Death is but 'a sleep and a forgetting' and the individual self with the new birth wakes up in other physical environments to continue the old unfinished race towards the goal. This, being born again and again, is not "the Indian philosopher's bugbear", as Monier Williams called it; neither is it, as he thought, an escape from the quest of Truth. The doctrine was a direct product of the Indian seer's successful quest of Truth. It was a corollary of the discovery of the immortality of the soul and the indestructibility of matter. Man being ever-born endeavours to be one with God the never-born, and while each birth is a sad reminder of the race yet to run, it is also a fresh opportunity to finish it. Each rebirth is a fresh school of discipline, a fresh prison through which to work out one's release.

Does man then pass through various wombs according to his conduct here? Do those of foul conduct "enter foul wombs, either that of a dog, or a swine, or an outcaste" as the *Chhandogya Upanishad* says? One does not know. The *Gita* simply echoes the prevailing belief of the times. It of course changes the *Upanishad* phraseology and refers to three kinds of birth — birth in spotless worlds, birth among men attached to work, and in gross species; or "going upward", "remaining midway", "going downward" (XIV. 15; XIV. 18). The reference, the ancient commentators say, is to the highest type of creation — the deities, the middle type — man, and the lowest type — animals, worms, plants. The Gita does mention 'heaven' about half a dozen times (II. 2; II. 32; II. 37; II. 43; IX. 20; IX. 21) and 'hell' four times (I. 42; I. 44; XVI. 16;

XVI. 21); but it is difficult to say whether the author meant by the terms unearthly perpetual abodes of happiness and misery, as the popular judicial notion of the *karma* theory would have it. The *Mahabharata,* of which *Gita* is but a part, thus defines *svarga* and *naraka* (heaven and hell) : "Heaven, they say, is light and hell is darkness." (*Shantiparva*). The *Tattvakaumudi* (9th century A. D.) quotes a definition of *svarga* (heaven) which has no reference to a perpetual abode, but which means 'unalloyed happiness'. Hell would thus mean 'unalloyed misery'. Dr Radhakrishnan quotes a verse from the *Vishnu Purana* (belonging to the same or perhaps an earlier date) which would mean by 'heaven' pleasant mental state and by 'hell' the reverse, and identifies one with virtue and the other with vice. It would, therefore, be doing no violence to the spirit of the *Gita,* if we said that walking with God is 'heaven', walking away from God is 'hell'. The *Gita* also refers to the two paths of soul after death — that of the gods and that of the manes (VIII. 24-25), but nearly sums them up as the paths of light and of darkness, i.e. of knowledge and ignorance. There is mention often enough of *devas* (gods) and other heavenly beings. Whilst these have reference to the traditional belief in unearthly beings, let us remember that the ancient etymologist Yaska (5th century B. C.) derives the word from that which gives, shines or illumines.

However, all these terms need not detain us, inasmuch as they belong to the surface of the *Gita* and do not touch the central theme. Perhaps these references to traditional belief only serve to bring the central picture into prominent relief. Even the theory of *karma* and rebirth is an explanation and a hypothesis and need not affect the central message which does not hang on it. Whether a man believes or not in the theory, he has to work out his salvation or self-realization through the law of self-sacrifice. It may be remembered that the human birth is regarded by the Hindu as a piece of evolutionary good fortune which should be turned to the best and noblest account, and one may conceive even an orthodox Hindu completely associating himself with the Sufi who out-Darwined Darwin several centuries ago :

> I died as mineral and became a plant,
> I died as plant and rose to animal.
> I died as animal and I was man.
> Why should I fear ? When was I less by dying ?
> Yet once more I shall die as man, to soar
> With angels blest ; but even from angelhood
> I must pass on : all except God doth perish.
> When I have sacrificed my angel soul,
> I shall become what no mind e'er conceived,
> Oh let me not exist ! For non-existence
> Proclaims in organ tones, 'To Him we shall return.' *

That would seem to bring out the *Gita* ideal to perfection, though of course the *Gita* says in no uncertain terms that those who give themselves to lust and anger and greed — the triple gateway to hell — go to perdition. Indeed the language of the sixteenth discourse is not dissimilar to the terrible text : "He that is unjust, let him be unjust still : and he that is filthy, let him be filthy still : and he that is righteous, let him be righteous still : and he that is holy, let him be holy still." † But the idea is clear and unmistakable. The self which has narrowed itself and imprisoned itself 'like unto a frog in a waterless well' has to expand itself into the ocean of the Universal Self, it has to go on age after age shedding its countless trappings and extinguish them into the Eternal Radiance of Knowledge, Light and Bliss — *Brahmanirvana.*

4. THE INDIVIDUAL, WORLD AND REALITY

That brings us again to where we began. Man, as we have seen, is born in the body and in the environment that the sum of his character-impressions (*sanskaras* or *karma*) have earned for him. The physical world, with man as apparently the principal actor in it, has its

* Quoted by Nicholson, *Mystics of Islam.*

† *Rev.* 22-11.

beginning in the Absolute. How the Absolute translated itself into the universe we do not know, we cannot know; but it is a beginningless process. At every world period, says Krishna, speaking as the Creator, I send forth the world of beings, and at the end of such a period they come back to my *prakriti*. Man — physical man — as part of the world finds himself subject to this apparently endless process, but his position in the universe is unique. He observes, thinks, reflects, finds himself captive, and struggles against the captivity. He finds himself witness of ceaseless change of the elements about him and around him. His reflection tells him that he is the subject of an objective world not only inside him — composed of his body, senses, intellect etc. —, but also of the objective world that surrounds him. While both these change and apparently perish, there is an abiding something in him which certainly does not change. And if it does not change in spite of ceaseless change, how can it perish in spite of the destruction that seizes both the outside and the inside world? The world of change and the world of mortality give him intimations of an eternality and immortality. There is a secret something in him which makes the finite, imperfect, mortal in him to hanker after the Infinite, Perfect and Immortal; and he does not take long to arrive at the truth that the Infinite and the Immortal Self that informs him informs and pervades also the universe. Bound up as he is with the world of sense, he has fleeting glimpses of this oneness with the Universal Self, but those glimpses are few and far between. Unless he can completely isolate himself from all that differentiates and separates, he cannot abide in this unity.

What differentiates is the sum of adjuncts that condition the Unconditioned. As the late Mr Kirtikar said, quoting Heraclitus, "Our senses" — internal and external both — "are liars," and further quoting the French astronomer-seer Flammarion illustrated how the senses are liars: "We see the sun rise above the horizon; it is beneath us. We touch what we think is a solid body; there is no such thing (as a solid body). We hear harmonious sounds ; but the air has only brought us silently undulations that are silent themselves. We admire the effects of light and of the colours that bring vividly before our eyes the splendid scenes of Nature ; but, in fact, there is no light, there are no colours. It is the movement of opaque ether striking on our optic nerve which gives us the impression of light and colour. We burn our foot in the fire : it is not the foot that pains us ; it is in our brain only that the feeling of being burned resides. We speak of heat and cold ; there is neither heat nor cold in the universe, only motion. Thus, our senses mislead us as to the reality of objects around us." And what is true of the outer senses is truer still of the inner senses. The more complex and subtle the inner organs the more confusing the experiences thereof.

These lights, these colours, these experiences of heat and cold are the *gunas*. *Guna,* as we have noted before, etymologically means 'subordinate', the "mortal instruments". The senses show us the 'subordinate' part of things, and hide from us the primary part, show us the unreal and hide the Real. As Fichte strikingly put it, "our seeing itself hides the object we see ; our eye itself impedes our eye." The reality at the back, the substance of which the diversity is but the shadow, is seen not with the eye of flesh, but with the eye of the spirit. "It is the disciplined and the self-controlled *yogis* who see Him seated in self, with the eye of the spirit ; those without self-control do not see Him, in spite of all endeavour." (XV. 11).

It is in this sense that the *Gita* uses the much-discussed term *maya*, the mystery which deludes or cheats one of the Reality. *Maya* is not an illusion, or a mirage, but a veil or an obstacle that hides the Real, the thick strata, physical and mental, which overlay the Divine in us, the clouds that obscure the Sun in us, the golden lid that covers the face of Truth. The *gunas* or *prakriti* within us and without us are *maya* which dazzles us and blinds us and leads us astray. The bondage, the separateness, the diversity is caused by this *maya*. The world of name and form strikes on our senses, the various ornaments of gold, for instance, appear to us as so many different ornaments, the multitudinous waves appear to us as so many waves, but we do not see the gold and the unchanging sea, we do not see the Nameless and the Formless of which we see numerous forms. The *Brahman* or the Absolute is the Real substrata behind the world of name and form, which has existence only in It and through It; the "divine life appears broken up," as Fichte said, "in a multiplicity of things as the one light in the prism is broken up into a number of colour rays." The prism is the gross medium of our fleshly senses. It is because of the prism that the one looks many, and it is because of the prism of *maya* that the free self sees itself bound. "Life like a dome of many-coloured glass stains the white radiance of eternity." If the world is but a reflection of Brahman, the individual self is but a spark of the Universal effulgence. Indeed both are one, but for the limiting conditions. We have both the embodied self which finds itself united to body after body, and the Imperishable, Eternal and the Unborn identified in the Gita (II. 13; II. 18-25; XIII. 2, 13-20; XV. 7, 11), for, as a *Mahabharata* verse says: "*Atman* associated with the *gunas* of the *prakriti* is called *Kshetrajna* (knower of the field). Released from this association *Atman* is *Param-atman,* the Supreme Self." They seem separate, but they are essentially one, otherwise no identity or union would be possible, and we know that identity is an actual fact of mystical experience in all ages and climes. All mystical endeavour lies in getting rid of the bondage of *maya*. It is such a fatally delusive thing. "Of all the deceptions with which *maya* the mighty misleads the embodied self," said the venerable Dr. Besant, "of all the obstacles and difficulties that *maya* puts in the way of Self-realization, that is worst of all hypocrisies, of all delusions, which makes a man declare, with lips impure, with life unpurified, being the slave, the tool of *maya,* identifying himself with *maya*: 'I *mayavi* shell am *Brahman*'."

We have seen how Vedanta (and the *Gita*) bridges the unbridgeable gulf set up between *prakriti* and *purusha,* spirit and matter in the Sankhya system, by making both dependent on the Supreme, by making them reflections (one inferior and the other superior) of the Supreme. Let us see how this Supreme is presented in the *Gita.* One may say that we have It presented in as many aspects as the limited, no matter how spiritual, vision of man can conceive It. While It is Unmanifest, Supreme, Exhaustless and Imperishable, It displays Itself in the garment of the ever-changing phenomena and so appears to partake of their character. It transcends all and yet It pervades and permeates all. Everything is strung on It like gems on a thread (VII. 7), and yet It is above and beyond all modifications (VII. 13, VII. 24, VIII. 22, X. 22). As immanent It seems to possess the attributes of all It fills, and as transcendent It is free from any of the attributes that man can think of or human language can devise. "It is neither Being, nor not-Being. It appears to possess the functions of the senses and yet is devoid of the senses; without all beings and yet within; not moving, yet moving; far and yet so near; undivided, yet seeming to subsist divided in all beings" (XIII. 12-16) — a description which brings together several texts of the *Isha, Katha,* and *Mundaka Upanishads.* The Supreme is really neither exclusively transcendent nor exclusively immanent. It is idle to imprison the Inconceivable in finite concepts. But that should not mean that It is an abstraction or a negation. It is altogether too big and too vast to be confined in concepts, It baffles complete or anything like adequate description. As Prof. James put it in his picturesque American way, "It is superlucent, super-splendent, super-essential, super-sublime, super-everything that can be named."

And because It is not a negation but something above positive and negative, It does not exhaust Itself whilst It sustains and pervades all. It is the exhaustless source of all. Even when It becomes manifest and conditioned, It does not cease to be absolute and unconditioned. In a mathematical simile which would have gladdened the heart of Spinoza, the *Upanishad* says: "*That* is infinite, *this* is infinite. From *that* infinite *this* infinite issues. If you take *this* infinite from *that* infinite, the remainder is still infinite." * Here clearly *this* infinite is the universe *that* Infinite is *Brahman.* That is why the *Gita* says, though the universe rests in Him, He is not in it. All the modifications of the three *gunas* are due to Him, but He is not in them, they do not condition or taint Him. Whilst all reflect Him, all cannot contain Him. "With but a particle of Myself I stand upholding this universe" (X. 42). Whilst He or Vasudeva is all, everything is not Vasudeva. Hegel, in his *Philosophy of Religion,* seems to have had the Seventh and the Tenth Discourses of the *Gita* in mind when he wrote: "If you say God is all that is here, this paper etc. you have indeed committed yourselves to the pantheism with which philosophy is reproached; that is, the whole is understood as equivalent to all individual things. It has never entered into man's mind that everything is God, that is to say that God is all things in their individual and contingent existence....When Brahma says, 'In the metal I am the brightness of its shining, among the rivers I am the Ganges, I am the life of all that lives', he thereby suppresses the individual. He does not say, 'I am the metal, the rivers, the individual things of various kinds as such, nor in the fashion of their immediate existence.' The brightness is not the metal itself, but is the universal, the substantial, elevated above any individual form....What is expressed here is no longer pantheism; the idea expressed is rather that of the essence of things." Spinoza who was accused of a similar pantheism also repudiated the charge: "I take a totally different view of God and Nature from that which the later

---

* पूर्णमदः पूर्णमिदं पूर्णात्पूर्णमुदच्यते ।
पूर्णस्य पूर्णमादाय पूर्णमेवावशिष्यते ।।

Isha (*Shantipatha*)

Christians usually entertain, for I hold that God is the immanent and not the extraneous cause of all things. I say all is God ; all lives and moves in God....It is, however, a complete mistake on the part of those who say that my purpose is to say that God and Nature, under which last term they understand a certain mass of corporal matter, are one and the same. I had no such intention." The *Gita* does not believe in an extraneous God. One phrase in that sublime rhapsody of prayer and praise — the Eleventh Discourse — sums up the thing beautifully: "Thou holdest all, and, therefore, thou art all" (XI. 40). He is all, because all cannot exist independently of Him. We do find Arjuna identifying the Sun and the Moon and the Wind and Fire with the Universal Form of Krishna, but all these are described as such because He holds all, or better still because, as the Lord said, "whatever exists having any kind of richness, beauty, might, know thou that every such thing issues from a fragment of My splendour" (X. 41). In moments of vision it is possible for even ordinary mortals to see the face of God in the ugliest and evil-looking things, whilst the reborn soul of an Eckhart "is as an eye which having gazed into the Sun thence forward sees the Sun in everything." But that is far from cosmotheism. The seer, "with an eye made quiet by the power of harmony," "sees into the life of things."

But what of the personal God who is the source of all religious emotion ? That leads us really to the two view-points from which the *Gita* has treated the question. For the philosophical attitude, God as the Absolute is enough. The philosophic mystic — *jnanayogi* and the meditative mystic — *dhyanayogi* will reflect and meditate on the Supreme, but what about the erring mortal and the contrite aspirant ? Through the *Gita* we find a clear line drawn between the transcendental and the empirical view of looking at things. The self, *sub specie aeternitatis* is free and actionless, 'seated in the citadel of the nine gates', serene and blissful; but the empirical self which struggles to be one with the Universal Self is active, has agency, identifies himself with the outward trappings and has a load of *karma* to throw off. It is to this struggler that the *Gita* is addressed. Whilst the philosophical attitude is there for him who can rise or has arisen to the heights of philosophy, the struggling soul wants something to lean upon, something to throw his cares upon. Even he shall have a vision of the Reality, says the *Gita,* and the way for him is either to dedicate all his actions to God or to offer heart-felt devotion to God. A personal God becomes a fundamental necessity in this case. Man is the image of God, and as the *Bhagawata Purana* puts it, just as the reflection in a mirror will show only those ornaments which the object reflected possesses and none else, even so man superimposes all kinds of perfections on God in order that they may be reflected in him, His image. But he always finds himself far away from the ideal and hence casts himself on His exhaustless grace. In His strength does he hope to be strong, in His purity does he hope to be pure. There is no self-delusion here, no fundamental contradiction. Contradiction there could only be, if one believed in *Brahman* as a mere metaphysical concept, or a "stream of tendency" as Mathew Arnold called it and hence said that "there was not even a low degree of probability that God is a person who thinks and loves." But *Brahman* as super-conceptual and super-everything includes a personal God. "The difference between the Supreme as spirit and the Supreme as person is one of stand-point and not of essence, between God as He is and God as He seems to be," says Dr Radhakrisnan. "When we consider the abstract and impersonal aspect of the Supreme we call it the Absolute; when we consider the Supreme as self-aware and self-blissful being, we get God. The real is beyond all conceptions of personality and impersonality. We call it the Absolute to show our sense of the inadequacy of all terms and definitions. We call it God to show that it is the basis of all that exists and the goal of all. Personality is a symbol and if we ignore its symbolic character it is likely to shut us from the truth. Even those who regard personality as the ultimate category of the universe recognize that God is vast and mysterious, mighty and ultimate."* The *Gita*, whilst it mainly addresses itself to the empirical self, the aspirant, has room for all temperaments and moods, provided they do not lose sight of the might and vastness and the absoluteness of the God that they would confine in a concept or symbol. It is those who would close their eyes to the higher aspect that the *Gita* calls deluded (VII. 25 and IX. 10), and yet in a noble pragmatism recognizes all temperaments and vouchsafes them fruit according to the purity of their conception (VII. 23 ; IX. 25). "In my Father's House are many mansions," § and there is room in them for all.

5. AVATARA

I have talked in the foregoing section of the fundamental necessity, in certain cases, for positing a personal God and have shown that such an assumption involves no violence to truth. A belief, identical in origin, is the belief in *avatara* or the Lord's descent on earth in human form. In its essence the theory of *avatara* is neither strange nor peculiar to India. Almost all religions have this conception in one shape or other, though the Hindu conception has some distinctive peculiarities. Its origin, everywhere, would seem to lie in man's realization of his own powerlessness and looking to something superhuman to intervene with its unique power and infinite mercy, in all situations which baffle man's mortal resources. The Jews believed in the Messiah or the Messenger. The Christians have their son of God, whom one of the Gospels describes as identical with God : "I and my Father are one." In the *Koran* there is indeed no idolatry or anthropolatry, and the Prophet declares over and over again that he is but "a plain warner" and "a mortal messenger"; but his equally emphatic insistence that he was revealing what was inspired in him by God — "I do but follow and declare what is inspired in me" — lead the bulk of his followers to attribute to the Prophet something very much like divinity and not far removed from an *avatara*. The Jains' conception of their Arhat and

* *An Idealistic View of Life*, p. 107.

§ *John*, 14-2.

the Buddhists' of the Buddha are also similar. But broadly one may say that, while in other cases God's spirit is said to descend into a chosen human being, the Hindus believe that God descends as man, when, Right declines and wrong prevails, in order to re-establish Right. Though the word *avatara* means descent, and generally, it is the descent of God on earth that is at the back of our minds when we talk of an *avatara,* the belief in an *avatara* would seem to have several aspects. Thus belief in an *avatara,* may be belief in God incarnating as man and identifying this incarnation with a human being of extraordinary mental and spiritual dimensions striking man's mind with amazement at the qualities which make him a saviour and deliverer. That attitude is the imaginative attitude. But the same belief rationalized becomes a belief not in God embodied as man, but either in God working out the cosmic purpose through the universal law or in man ascending to the estate of God by wholly divesting himself of all his earthliness and completely spiritualizing himself, or sacrificing himself in God. Having the spark of the divine, we are all incarnations of God; but it is not usual to consider every living being an 'incarnation' for the simple reason that almost all of us reveal the human or the mortal part of us more predominantly than the immortal and the 'incarnate' part of us. Arguing thus we might say that the ultimate reach of human endeavour is the realization that the aspirant himself, as indeed everything around him, is an incarnation of the Divine. The mere belief in the Incarnation, which, as I have said, springs from the imaginative attitude, can scarcely carry one very far, and may indeed be a delusion and a snare, unless it becomes rationalized into a belief in "a perpetual cosmic and personal process", to adopt Miss Underhill's phrase. As she has so beautifully put it, "It is an everlasting bringing forth, in the universe and also in the individual ascending soul, of the divine and perfect life, the pure character of God, of which the one historical life dramatized the essential constituents. Hence the soul, like the physical embryo, resumes in its upward progress the spiritual life-history of the race. 'The one secret, the greatest of all,' says Patmore, 'is the doctrine of the Incarnation, regarded not as an historical event which occurred two thousand years ago, but as an event which is renewed in the body of every one who is in the way to the fulfilment of his original destiny.'"

We have both these aspects of the belief in *avatara* in the *Mahabharata,* though in the *Puranas* it is the exclusively imaginative aspect that predominates. It is difficult to trace the belief in *avatara* in the *Vedas* and the *Upanishads,* though two *Vedic* texts are cited as containing the belief in the germ: "The Lord of the beings travels in the wombs. Though unborn, He is born in many ways" (*Vajasaneya Yaj. Samhita* 31.19); and "this same God is in every quarter. He was born before and is born again. He was before and will be born again." (*l.c.* 32.4) * This is the rationalist aspect of the *avatara* theory. In the *Mahabharata* we have both the imaginative and the rationalistic conceptions running, so to say, a close race. Thus whilst Krishna, the warrior and the statesman is represented as the Incarnation in many places, we have also the cosmic aspect emphasized in other places. In a striking passage in the *Drona Parva* Krishna declares: "I am four-formed, ever ready to protect the worlds. One of the forms practises penance on earth; the second keeps watch over the actions of erring humanity; the third resorting to the world of men is engaged in activity; and the fourth is plunged in the slumber of a thousand years." §

---

* प्रजापतिश्चरति गर्भे अन्तरजायमानो बहुधा विजायते। ३१-१९
एषो ह देवः प्रदिशोऽनुसर्वाः पूर्वो ह जातः स उ गर्भे अन्तः।
स एव जातः स जनिष्यमाणः प्रत्यङ् जनास्तिष्ठति सर्वतोमुखः ।। ३२-४

§ चतुर्मूर्तिरहं शश्वल्लोकत्राणार्थमुद्यतः।
आत्मानं प्रविभज्येह लोकानां हितमादधे ।।
एका मूर्तिस्तपश्चर्यां कुरुते मे भुवि स्थिता।
अपरा पश्यति जगत्कुर्वाणं साध्वसाधुनी ।।
अपरा कुरुते कर्म मानुषं लोकमाश्रिता ।।
शेते चतुर्थी त्वपरा निद्रां वर्षसहस्रिकीम् ।। द्रोण० अ० २९ श्लो० ३२-३४

I feel strongly persuaded that though in the *Gita* we have Krishna referred to as the human incarnation and addressed sometimes by Arjuna as 'the slayer of foes', it is the rationalistic conception that is presented, and it is that fact which, with other things, goes to make the *Gita* the crown and culmination of the *Mahabharata*.

Thus after declaring that for the good of mankind He is born again and again, Lord Krishna says: "He who knows the secret of this divine birth and work of Mine comes to Me" (IV. 9). By 'divine birth and work' here is not meant the activities attributed to Him as warrior and slayer of foes, or as the Divine Cowherd, but the perpetual cosmic process of the victory of Right over wrong of which to know and understand the secret and which to live is to fulfil one's destiny, to experience the process of *avatara* going through at every moment of our life. In another place Lord Krishna says in effect: "Be thou unslumbering in the performance of thy duty, even as I am unslumbering" (III. 23). In a third place (IX. 9) there is again a reference to the Lord's activities. There they are patently cosmic—the creation and the dissolution of the worlds; and in the Eleventh Discourse we have a vision not of a personal incarnation but of the Divine Energy engaged in cataclysmic dissolution. It is idle to pretend that the activities referred to in all these contexts are those described in the *Mahabharata* or in the *Bhagawata Purana*. "Thou knowest not what is the way of the spirit, nor how the bones do grow in the womb of her that is with child: even so thou knowest not the works of God that maketh all," said the Jewish prophet. The author of the *Bhagawata Purana* has woven into matchless poetry the divine play of Krishna, as he had felt and seen Him, but even he has left a warning which is true for all time: 'Not even in thought should one who is not *Ishwara* (God) attempt to do these things. Should he do it, he is sure to perish, as one who would attempt to drink poison in imitation of Shiva. For those who have 'noughted' the self there is no benefit in behaving well, nor harm in behaving ill; how then does good or ill matter to Him who is the Lord of all beings on earth and in heaven ?" * Herein is contained in a nutshell the meaning and purpose of the *avatara*, whatever one may believe or imagine to be the activities of the *avatara*. To paraphrase : "Be first an *Ishvara* — God — (who is defined as having the power of doing, undoing, and transforming anything on earth and in heaven) ; achieve His supreme detachment, and then if there is any 'self' or 'will' left in you, you are welcome to will and do whatever good or ill you may." That seems to me to be the meaning also of (III. 18) and of that difficult *shloka* (XVIII. 17) which we shall have occasion to consider later on. The utmost self-purification, through action without attachment to fruit, and without thought of self, is what the *avatara* in the *Gita* teaches to us in every *shloka* that the author has put into His mouth. 'Be thou perfect even as thy Father in Heaven is perfect. Be thou holy even as I am holy,' said Christ. 'Be thou unslumbering in the performance of the duty, even as I am : Look on all alike, even as I do, and in Me shalt thou rest,' says Lord Krishna. Complete 'noughting' of self, supreme detachment and perfection are the tests that the *avatara* in the *Gita* lays down for whomsoever we would associate with the name of *avatara*, and by that test only can the activities we attribute to an incarnation be judged. Those are the only tests whereby we can measure the extent to which we might say God has descended in our own individual life. There can be no other tests. And in laying down these tests, and in presenting the perfection that a human being has to reach in the most unmistakable terms, the *Gita* stands out as unique in our literature and the crowning glory of the *Mahabharata*. As that fine verse in the *Gita Mangalacharanam* says, 'Gita is the *bharata-pankaja* — the

---

* नैतत्समाचरेज्जातु मनसापि ह्यनीश्वरः ।
विनश्यत्याचरन्मौढयाद्यथाऽरुद्रोऽब्धिजं विषम् ।। भाग० १०-३१
कुशलाचरितेनैषामिह स्वार्थो न विद्यते ।
विपर्ययेण वाऽनर्थो निरहङ्कारिणां प्रभो ।।
किमुताखिलसत्त्वानां तिर्यङ्मर्त्यदिवौकसाम् ।
ईशितुश्चेशितव्यानां कुशलाकुशलान्वयः ।। भाग० १०-३३-४

lotus sprung out of the mud of the *Bharata* (or the *Bharata* war) and the Krishna of the *Gita* or the Incarnation is the spotless, untainted embodiment of the highest aspiration of man.'

Whether we worship a personal but inconcrete God, or a personal and concrete God, we do so in order to be like unto Him. 'It is all right to be born in a church,' Swami Vivekanand used to say, 'but not to die in it,' and the devotee Narsinha Mehta, practically unlettered, who spent the bulk of his life singing the praises of the Incarnation as he had conceived Him to be, delighting himself and intoxicating himself with the worship of that Krishna, ultimately outgrew that stage and towards the end of his days broke forth in songs of matchless vision: "How am I to worship Thee, O Lord of infinite mercy? When Thou pervadest every particle of the creation, how may I limit Thee in an image? I see Thy eternal light burning without any oil or wick. Formless it is indeed to be seen without eyes, and enjoyed with the senses of the spirit."

6. THE END AND THE MEANS

The foregoing should be sufficient to show that the theme of the *Gita* is to indicate the end of man's existence on earth and the means for the attainment of it. The end is for man to realize completely what he is, what the world about him is, and to experience that what sustains him and pervades him and what sustains and pervades the world about him is the one — the Truth or the Reality. As soon as man can completely spiritualize himself he will have a vision of this Reality as also of his oneness with It. "As soon as man abolishes himself," said Fichte, "purely, entirely, to the very root, God alone remains and is all in all; man can produce no God for himself, but he can do away with his self as the great negation and then he passes into God." That is *brahma-nirvana* in the language of the *Gita*. "He will see Me, enter into Me", "He will be one *brahman*", "He will become one with My nature", "He will attain *brahma-nirvana*" are some of the expressions used by the *Gita*. These are interpreted by various schools of commentators in various ways. Let us not be drawn into those whirlpools. Fichte's phrase, 'He passes into God' is real enough for us mortals who have ages to cover before we can have a glimpse of that state. Let us concentrate on the means, the goal will reveal itself, as it may in due season.

> 'Enough if in our hearts we know
> There's such a place as Yarrow.'

Let us remember that we have to prepare for a rebirth. We have to wear off loads of *karma* by means of action, we have to be free from the trammels of the body through the body itself. As the *Bhagawata Purana* beautifully says: "This is the understanding of those who understand, and the wisdom of the wise that, with the unreal and the mortal (body), man attains to Me the Real and Immortal." We have to sublimate the *gunas* to be *nirguna,* to cease to dance to the tune of *prakriti,* but to make her dance to the tune of Self, if dance she must. In short, every one of the 'senses of the flesh' has to be turned into a 'sense of the spirit'. Every one of them has to be intimately related to the Self which alone gives them light and life, until, in the language of a famous text, 'all the senses, the whole not-Self, become Self, even as iron when every atom of it is in contact with fire, becomes like fire.'

The *Gita* sums up this means in one word — yoga, of which the varying aspects we shall see in the course of the analysis which follows. This ancient word is pressed by the *Gita* into service to mean the entire gamut of human endeavour to storm the gates of Heaven. It is derived from the verb *yuj* (tr. and intr.) which has numerous meanings: to join, to attach, to yoke; to direct, to concentrate one's attention on; to use, to apply, to employ. In the *Yoga Sutras* it is used to mean discipline or control. It thus means the yoking of all the powers of the body and the mind and soul to God; it means the discipline of the intellect, the mind, the emotions, the will, which such a yoking presupposes; it means a poise of the soul which enables one to look at life in all its aspects and evenly. The yogin is therefore one who reflects all these attributes in his life, who, in the midst of raging storm and blinding spray, will keep his vision of the Sun undisturbed, who will look difficulties and death in the face, who "goes with the same mind to the shambles and the scaffold," and "whose mind is so serene that thunder rocks him to sleep."

If we may call this many-faceted word yoga mysticism, the yogin will be a mystic. In the terms of work, the philosophic mystic will be a *Jnanayogi,* the active mystic will be a *Karmayogi* ; in the terms of devotion, the *Jnanayogi* will be a *Dhyanayogi* (meditative mystic), and the *Karmayogi* will be a *Bhaktiyogi,* worshipper mystic. We shall have both these dichotomies, but we shall also see them coincide in the end.

V. Interpretative Analysis *

THE DELUSION

(Discourses 1 and 2)

The *Gita* opens with a vivid description of men and things on the eve of the great battle of Kurukshetra. Earlier chapters in the *Mahabharata* show how all methods of persuasion and compromise have been tried and failed. Krishna has on one hand pleaded unsuccessfully with the aggressors, the Kauravas, and they in their turn have unsuccessfully appealed to the magnanimity of the Pandavas. They admitted that they had wronged the Pandavas but argued that the latter could afford to ignore the wrong, seeing that that war was sure to involve the ruin of the whole house of Kurus, that nothing but sin would accrue out of the carnage, and that their fair name would be tarnished. This unctuous appeal coming from those who on their own admission were the aggressors failed to make any impression on the Pandavas and the challenge was accepted. The dialogue between Arjuna and Krishna does not begin before these negotiations, nor even at the close of them, but *after* the seal of approval had been set to the

* In this analysis I have taken the liberty of paraphrasing the verses, i.e. to expand them in my own language. Wherever the reader is in doubt let him go to the text and reject the paraphrase without hesitation.

declaration of war by all, including of course Arjuna, the renowned Bowman, hero of many a battle in days gone by. His charioteer is no less than Krishna himself who has come at his express invitation. The war-lords on both sides are in their chariots, even the conch-shells have been sounded and the fatal arrows are about to fly. It is at this eleventh hour that an anguish seizes the soul of Arjuna, his heart sinks within him at the sight of the venerable preceptors, sires and grandsires, sons and grandsons, gathered for fratricidal carnage. He conjures up a vision of the terrible ravages of war, physical, moral and spiritual, puts aside his bow and arrow and sits down in utter distraction. His streaming eyes fail to soften Krishna who characterizes his attitude as one of impotent feeble-heartedness and unworthy of an *Arya*. But Arjuna repeats in the manner of one raving with grief: "No good do I see coming out of slaying my own kinsmen. Nor do we know which is better for us, whether that we conquer them, or that they conquer us; standing in front of us are Dhritarashtra's men, having killed whom we should have no desire to live." He is torn as much with doubt as with despair, and in the manner of a humble disciple appeals to Krishna for light and guidance (I. 1-47; II. 1-10).

I have already referred to some of the tragic situations in Shakespeare's dramas. Though in the passage quoted from *King John,* Lady Blanch's situation is different from Arjuna whose difficulty is more moral and spiritual than hers, the inertia in both cases is the result of a stupendous obsession with the sense of 'mine' or 'one's own' and 'other's'. Arjuna's situation is more tragic in that his obsession has very much a semblance of altruism. There is no doubt in Arjuna's mind that the opponents are all "proclaimed felons". Had they been "others", i.e. not kinsmen, his mind would not for a moment have suffered "the nature of an insurrection", as did that of Brutus. Brutus' inner spirit revolted against "the acting of a dreadful thing", the like of which he had not done before. For Arjuna the deed as such was not dreadful — as a *Kshatriya* he had done it over and over again. But it was made dreadful by the thought of the victims being *his* kinsmen.

There is yet another circumstance to be noted. The phantasms before Arjuna's mind were not of his creation. As I have already pointed out, some of the earlier chapters in the Epic tell us that the old king had tried in various ways to dissuade the Pandavas from the fight — the arguments used by him being the *very same* as we find Arjuna using in the First and Second Discourses. Indeed, Arjuna repeats the very language used by the messenger of Dhritarashtra, who was no other than Sanjaya who narrates now to the blind king the dialogue between Krishna and Arjuna! That is why Krishna simply brushes the arguments aside, calling them "vain words of wisdom" (II. 11). It was after all a superficial ebullition of compassion occasioned by the dark suggestion of Dhritarashtra, and not a revulsion springing from the depths of spiritual certitude. It was all right to recount the dreadful results of fratricidal warfare, but was it not a parade of wisdom? The fighting spirit was part of his innermost being, and no one knew this better than Krishna — his counsellor, the charioteer who was not only in charge of his war-chariot but who had in his hands the reins of Arjuna's inner being. That is why we find at the end of the *Gita* Krishna summing up the whole argument in these prophetically peremptory words: "If obsessed by the sense of 'I' thou thinkest 'I will not fight', vain is thy obsession; thy very nature will compel thee." (XVIII. 59).

It is this distinction between the Self and the not-Self which Krishna first brings home to Arjuna in the very language of the *Upanishads*. The specious arguments of Dhritarashtra have affected Arjuna's mind because he has identified the not-Self with the Self, the perishing with the Imperishable, the seeming and the seen which is *not*, apart from the Eternal Unseen which ever *Is*. 'The imperishable Self that inhabits the impermanent bodies pervades the universe. Him no weapons can wound, no fire can burn, no water can wet, no wind can dry. Thou art that permanent imperishable Self and not the ever-changing, ever-perishing vestment of the Self called the body, O Arjuna. It is because one identifies the perishable with the Imperishable that the delusion of 'mine' and 'thine' is caused. For when thou sayest that thou wilt be the cause of the destruction of thy kinsmen, and of thy venerable preceptors, thou art forgetting that the Dweller in those bodies called Arjuna and Duryodhana, Bhishma and Drona is the same and imperishable, as in you and me, unaffected by heat and cold, pleasure and pain. It is thy attachment to the body and those feelings of kinship that spring from it, that makes thee lament the death and destruction of things which are doomed to perish' (II. 12-30).

The argument does not still Arjuna's doubts, but checks the ebullition, makes him throw off the "unprevailing woe" and compels him furiously to think why he has thus gone off the rails. He had in the past fought many a battle, but he had not paused to think *whom* he was killing, no sense of 'sin' had obsessed him, he 'had fought because he had felt that it was part of his duty, part of his day's work, perhaps because thought of heroism and glory or an overpowering rage had prompted him on those occasions.' Indeed Krishna puts his finger on Arjuna's weak spot when he reminds Arjuna of the duty of a Kshatriya, a duty to which he was born, the fulfilling of, and not the running away from, which led to heaven and glory, (II. 31-37). Krishna knew his Arjuna better than Arjuna knew himself. The 'old Adam' was still sleeping in Arjuna's breast, whilst he was rolling out those swelling words of wisdom, and Arjuna realizes the situation in a flash. Well might he have asked: 'If the Self is imperishable, if the Self does not kill, does not act, why should I then engage in this violent undertaking at all?' But he does not interrupt the flow of Krishna's argument. The sense of reality has been quickened in him. He might even have asked: 'Dost thou indeed want me to fight as I did of old, prompted by thought of pride and glory and heroism, and to suppress the promptings of a better and a finer self?' Even that question is stilled. For as soon as Krishna feels that Arjuna's manliness has been roused, he touches the higher key in his nature and advances a loftier argument: 'Count equal loss and gain, success and failure, and gird up thy loins to do thy duty. No sin will touch thee.' That leads up to the teaching of the Art of Life — yoga. The wisdom (Sankhya) has been expounded, now follows the Art (II. 38, 39). Sin is born of ignorance and so long as man acts from ignorance, he goes on forging fresh chains of bondage. Thou hast done so in the past; I want thee to cease to do so from now. Attachment is of the essence of ignorance; cut off attachment and thou wilt cut off ignorance. In the past thou wert wont to fight with a sense of 'I', thou wert wont to attach thyself to the fruit — glory and reward and other interest perhaps. Today the attachment arises from a different obsession, but it is attachment and ignorance none the less; cast it off. Only action is thy concern and not the fruit. Forget all thought of fruit and fight. This forgetting of the fruit, this detachment from the sense of 'I', this equanimity in success and failure is yoga. Indeed in that indifference to fruit lies the secret of success. Yoga is skill in action. Herein there is no loss of effort, no going back; even a slight performance is credited to man's account. The beaten track is the one prescribed by the *Vedic* ritual, the one which puts in men's minds hopes of various rewards. That is the way of the world, which is eternally moved by the three *gunas*. The minds of men tossed about by worldly desires have no moorings. Trust thou not such as speak to thee of heaven and similar rewards. For "when they speak great swelling words of vanity, they allure through the lusts of the flesh,...those that were clean escaped from them who live in error." * Only when one steers clear of the path of success and gain, heaven and happiness in a future life, can one hitch oneself to the star of freedom — freedom from the cycle of birth and death. Be thou not conformed to the world, for the world is nothing but tribulation. Free from the pairs of opposites, free from the care of success or failure, hitch thyself to the Self. For one who has a discriminative

* 2 Peter 2.18.

knowledge of the Self will conform to the Self and not to the world. As little use will such an one have of the *Vedic* ritual as men have of a well when surrounded by an all-spreading flood of water. This path of ritual rivets one's thoughts to merit and sin, but the path of yoga cuts clear through merit and sin alike and leads to the heaven where all ills, alike of the flesh and the spirit, are unknown. Cross thou this slough of delusion (II. 40-53).

Arjuna too had probably heard of yoga before, but he now finds it presented to him in a new light. If yoga means the forgetting of all fruit, all attachment, then it means detaching oneself from the lower self and identification with the supreme Self. One has to disjoin oneself from the impermanent to join oneself to the Permanent. But so long as the Self is encased in the impermanent tabernacle, one cannot disjoin oneself from it, except by purifying it, spiritualizing it, by making the not-Self work in tune with the Self. Yoga is thus both means and end.

Were there indeed men who had achieved this yoga? Arjuna would like to know, and Krishna now describes the state of that yogin.

The yogin whose understanding is secure from all attachment to objects of senses, is free from fear and wrath and resentment, free alike from likes and dislikes, pleasure and pain. The most important step towards the haven of security is to rein in the senses, which if not kept in control carry off even the wisest to the abyss. Physical starving of the senses works but a temporary purpose; it is only when the intellect realizes its moorings in the Highest and prevents the mind from wandering that one can feel secure. But is that not a puzzling circle indeed? It is to realize the Highest that one is asked to go through the endeavour and he is told to realize the Highest before the earthly craving and yearning can be extinct! It looks a puzzle, but is not one when one remembers that the realization is in embryo in every one, and as soon as the process of self-purification starts, the full realization to come casts, so to say, a helpful flash of light on the path (II. 54-61).

With unerring psychological insight the *Gita* indicates now that ladder of doom of which the first step is brooding on sense-objects, the second is attachment to them, the third is hankering after them, the fourth, resentment over unfulfilled hankerings, the fifth, heedlessness which all resentment brings, the sixth, self-forgetfulness, the seventh, destruction of all discernment which takes one finally down to the abyss. It is not that one should close one's eyes and stuff one's ears, but that one should close and stuff them to the wrong things and open them to the right ones. The yogin closes his eyes to the things that worldly men pursue, and keeps wide awake to the things to which the latter are blind. Wordsworth has talked of the "blessed mood" in which "the heavy and the weary weight of all this intelligible world is lightened,"

—that serene and blessed mood
In which the affections gently lead us on,
Until the breath of this corporeal frame
And even the motion of our human blood,
Almost suspended, we are laid asleep
In body, and become a living soul;
While with an eye made quiet by the power
Of harmony and the deep power of joy
We see into the life of things.

With the yogin of secure understanding it is not a transient mood however, but a perpetual state of blessedness and serenity, which is the result of an ever-wakeful discipline of the soul.

And like the ocean, day by day receiving
Floods from all lands, which never overflows;
Its boundary line not leaping and not leaving,
Fed by the rivers, but unswelled by those;
So is the perfect one!
To his soul's ocean
The world of sense pours streams of witchery
They leave him, as they find, without commotion
Taking their tribute, but remaining sea.*

* Edwin Arnold, *Song Celestial.*

Having stopped all brooding on the objects of the senses, the yogin broods on the Highest, and rises towards Him ultimately resting in Him — *brahmi sthiti.* It is not a sudden conversion, but a result of incessant brooding on the Supreme. The endeavour dissolves in the achievement and what once was a conscious endeavour becomes as natural as the process of breathing (II. 62-72).

Look at this description of a Western mystic where we find the means and the end thus mixing up: "True rest in God [*brahmi sthiti* (72)] is as unchanging as God Himself. It stills all passion, restrains the imagination, steadies the mind, controls all wandering: it endures alike in the time of tribulation and in the time of wealth, in temptation and trial, as well as when the world shines brightly on us." †

KARMAYOGA

(Discourses 3 and 4)

That takes us to the third discourse. Since realization thus changes the whole man, and makes him like unto God Himself, resting in God, why not cling on to realization? At any rate, one cannot expect to wade through slaughter to that Throne of God. The secret to wade through what was inevitable slaughter with one's limbs unstained has been already told, but Arjuna forgets the means in the dazzling vision of the end. To give up the fight and sit silent musing on the Self seemed apparently easy enough to him, but it really was not so. Krishna, as we have said, knew his Arjuna better than Arjuna knew himself. Who knows, if he physically withdrew, he might still mentally brood over the progress of the war and ultimately decide to plunge, or if he did not actually do so, his mind might be still deep dyed in blood. And mind ties the knot of *karma* tighter than the body. The body may be inactive, but if the mind continually runs after things from which the senses have been held back one deceives himself and deceives the world. Freedom from the bond of action is the *summum bonum* indeed, but inertia is not freedom. There

† Quoted by C. F. Andrews in *Christ in the Silence.*

are two attitudes of life — the attitude of *Jnanayoga* (philosophical mysticism) and that of *Karmayoga* (active mysticism), but there is no such thing as an attitude of inertia. The attitude of *jnana* where there was complete Self-realization, where action and inaction were one, is a consummation devoutly to be wished, but it is not a state to be preferred to some other state. It is a state where there is no room for preferences. So long as preferences arise and are to be thought of, there is but one course and that is *Karmayoga*. Between inertia and action, action is any day better. Inactive life is a contradiction in terms. *Prakriti,* with its *gunas,* knows no inactivity and leaves no one in peace. Therefore action is inevitable (III. 1-8).

If that is the case, does it mean that one has to be always bound down to the apron-strings of *prakriti* and consequently to the cycle of birth and death ? All work, indeed, binds, says Krishna, save that done for sacrifice. For sacrifice is the law of life, the law of all creation. God whispered into the ear of man the message of sacrifice when He created him and said to him, 'by sacrifice shall ye grow and fructify.' Indeed, as the *Vedas* put it, He sacrificed Himself in order that the world may be created. In sacrifice all creation starts, by sacrifice it is sustained, sacrifice is at once the cause and the consequence. He who does anything but for sacrifice, breaks the law, sins, eats but sin, accumulates sin. For selfishness is sin, selflessness is freedom from it. And indeed those who have shed all thought of 'self', who have ceased to dance to the varying tunes of their mind, intellect and senses derive all their delight from Self, all their solace from Self, all their satisfaction from Self. For such there is nothing obligatory to do, no law is imposed on them, for they have no 'self' to serve ; then a life of sacrifice or oneness with the world is the fulfilment of the Law. That blissful state of active inactivity or inactive activity is attainable only by incessant performance of detached action which alone leads on to the Supreme (III. 9-19). So did king Janaka of old achieve his salvation. His very life-breath must have been sacrifice and service of mankind, or else how could he placidly say when his capital was burning: "Even if Mithila turn to ashes, nothing that is mine is destroyed"? And yet no one misunderstood him. While the name of Nero is a by-word for diabolical heartlessness, Janaka's name is held in reverence until today and the words in which he uttered his detachment are still remembered. He had achieved a state when every thought on his part meant the service of mankind and he might have retired to live a life of meditative calm, but he ruled his kingdom instead. There had been others too like him. They lived and worked not for themselves but for the world —

Souls heroic and good
Helpers and friends of mankind.

God Himself is ever at work, silent and slumberless, lest the worlds should come to an end. The enlightened, too, should work away if only to set an example to the unenlightened. The secret of 'free' action is detachment, the knowledge that it is the *gunas* that act, and not the Self. But the deluded attribute to the Self what belongs to the not-Self and arrogate to themselves the responsibility and claim the reward for action. To wean these from their attachment and their error, the enlightened should set an example of detached, selfless action, rather than confuse their minds with the enunciation of a principle of renunciation of action which might well lead them astray. They would sink into inertia which would be worse than the selfful activity in which they are immersed (III. 20-29).

But even for those who have not achieved the wisdom of isolating the Self from all activity, and rendering unto not-Self the things that belong to not-Self, there is a way of freedom. Let them cast off all actions on God, working as His bondslaves, taking what He gives, expecting naught. That is a saving rule of life (III. 30-32).

Men whose faith is blasted ignore the rule, so strong sometime is the force of nature. But that does not mean that man is born the slave of his nature. There is a part in one's make-up which predisposes him to a particular kind of activity and vocation. He is born to it and may not with impunity do any violence to that part of his nature. But there is another part which is entirely under man's control, viz. his moral nature. Willing obedience, in a spirit of selflessness, to that part of one's nature which is not in his hands, and control of that part which is controllable is the law of man's being — *svadharma,* if one were to free oneself. Doing aught else was not his law, but other's law, not his work, but other's work.

But one is often drawn into things which are contrary to the law of one's being, often drawn into sin. Why ? Lust and Wrath, the twin brood of the Devil, strive to subvert the law, and they do so because they make man's senses, mind and reason their home, if man be not wakeful. They are the enemy of man, as Krishna has already taught in the second discourse. He now gives the same teaching in a different psychological setting. The senses, the mind and the intellect — they are the seat of the enemy, each subtler and more difficult to control than its predecessor. But the subtlest is He the Dweller in the innermost. Let man obey His law and reject the allurements of the rest, subduing each, one by one (III. 33-43).

This again is no puzzle, for the very faintest vision of the Sun of Self is enough to put one on the path of self-control and with increasing self-control the vision grows brighter and brighter. Let the aspirant only hold fast to the master-key — let him do all for His sake and leave the rest to Him. 'Thou enjoinest continence,' said St. Augustine, addressing his prayer to God, 'give me what thou enjoinest and enjoin what Thou wilt.'

The exposition of *Karmayoga* is continued in the fourth discourse. We were told in the third discourse that God whispered 'sacrifice into the ear of man when He created him.' We are now told that this law of sacrifice Krishna taught to Vivasvat (Sun) and he to his son and so on, which means to say that God taught it to the first human being who has passed it on from generation to generation. The very first man who put himself in relation with the universe about him, that is, realized a unity, no matter how partial, with his environment, acted according to the law, and handed it down to posterity. Is there anything strange in this? The Truth has been revealed over and over again and will go on being revealed until the end of time. We hear it said that there is nothing new under the sun. Well, there need be nothing new, for the Sun of Truth, exhaustless in his manifestations, ever presents aspects and visions new. Each seer presents the aspect appropriately to his environment, but it is an aspect of the same Truth nevertheless. Whatever the Muslims may think, was the law of surrender to Allah that their Prophet revealed anything different from the law the *Gita* or the Bible teaches? "A man is right and invincible," said Carlyle, "when he joins himself to the great deep law of the world, in spite of all profit and loss calculations. This is the soul of Islam and is properly the soul of Christianity. Islam means in its way denial of self, annihilation of self. This is yet the highest wisdom revealed to our earth." "The very thing which is now called the Christian religion existed among the ancients, and never failed from the beginning of the human race up to the coming of Christ in the flesh," said St. Augustine.* Long before Islam and Christianity the same law of surrender or love or sacrifice, whatever you may call it, was delivered by the *Gita*; but it was really delivered by God to man ever since his birth on this earth. "This law of sacrifice or selfless action or yoga I taught in ages gone before us;" says Krishna to Arjuna, "thou seemest to marvel at it: Well, I tell thee that thou wast born often before; yea, even I the Unborn and Exhaustless Lord of the worlds also had many births ere this. In this marvel not. Understand the secret of My coming and of My work and cleanse thyself in the fiery ordeal of knowledge and come to Me. The ancients knew the secret and worked in the light of it. Do thou, too, likewise. I suffer myself to be born again and again whenever I find that Right declines and Wrong prevails. The yoga I taught dwindled away with the passage of time and so I have to declare it once again. I also engage Myself in establishing the fourfold

* In *Retractions* quoted by Dr. Radhakrishnan in *East and West in Religion.*

order of the human community according to their *guna* and *karma*. But nothing that I do touches Me" (IV. 1-15).

That perhaps was, for Arjuna, a further phase of the revelation. His counsellor and charioteer was God Himself descended to the state of man in order that man may ascend to the state of God. 'The incarnation was a tear of the divine compassion,' says a Christian mystic. It was not for His sake but for man's sake that God became man. It is rarely that man has a vision of such, though it is these gods become men that sustain the earth. The author of the *Gita* had evidently the vision and so makes us see Him through His dialogue with Arjuna.

It shall be
A face like my face that receives thee; a Man like to me,
Thou shalt love and be loved for ever; a Hand like this hand
Shall throw open the gates of new life to thee,
See the Christ stand.

(Browning — *Saul*)

So Arjuna saw the Lord stand before him as Krishna in order "to throw open the gates of new life to him." He realizes more clearly than ever before that it is not Krishna his friend and kinsman and charioteer but God Himself who is unfolding to him the mystery of yoga, teaching him what he was to do.

And again the Lord harks back to the doctrine in a different language. The law of yoga and sacrifice is now presented as the law of action in inaction and inaction in action. Man must go to the root from which action or inaction springs. All that springs from lust and passion is clearly binding action of the grossest type — *vikarma* — binding one in the coil of a snake; so is action with an eye to reward, binding one perhaps with a silver chain; running away from one's duty is equally binding, the chain may be of silver or of iron; what does not bind is action or refraining from action in obedience to the Law, in obedience to Him. That man is not the agent, but He the Law-giver is the agent, that man is but the instrument in His hands, that the reward is not for him to seek but for

Him to give, is true knowledge. That Knowledge makes ashes of all action, nay of all karma, i.e. potential action. Sacrifice thus not only prevents but cures all bondage (IV. 16-23).

The *Koran* * says the same thing in not very different language: "Whosoever surrendereth his purpose to Allah while doing good, he verily hath grasped the firm handhold" (31. 22). Good deeds annul ill deeds" (11. 114).

But there are sacrifices and sacrifices. Sacrifices performed in order to enter the gates of paradise were common enough. "To what purpose is the multitude of your sacrifices to Me?...Bring no more vain oblations. Wash you, make you clean, put away the evil of your doings. Learn to do well." † These were the words of the Lord as they were heard by the Jewish prophet. St. Paul paraphrased them: "Present your bodies a living sacrifice, holy, acceptable unto God." ‡ The author of the *Gita* reveals the word of the Lord on sacrifice somewhat to this effect: "Make every act of thine a sacrifice unto the Lord; sacrifice even the thought that what is so offered is a sacrifice. All is sacrifice that takes you near the Lord. Thus the discipline of the senses, of the emotions and the will, of the vital airs, the pursuit of holy knowledge, all this is sacrifice. Whatever leads to the knowledge of the Supreme is 'knowledge-sacrifice' which is the best of sacrifices. Sacrifice taught in the books of ritual—material sacrifice—is not of much account, for it does not release, it binds. Knowledge is release, and no action is of any worth unless it fulfils itself in knowledge" (IV. 24-33).

We have seen how Lord Krishna again and again harks back to the end—knowledge—even in the midst of the discourse over the means. So here too we have the true content of knowledge presented to us. True knowledge

---

* All the extracts from the *Koran* in this Analysis and in the notes are from Mr Marmaduke Pickthall's *The Glorious Koran.*

† *Is.* 13, 16.

‡ *Heb.* 10.

is that with the eye of which one sees each and every being in the universe in one's self and then in God. True spiritual knowledge makes one rest in the vision of consubstantiality of the Self in man and God. The *Upanishad* (*Mundaka*) had taught that all sacrifices based on various kinds of ritual were "unreliable boats" * and that man should leave them and resort to the properly qualified *guru,* learn the Truth from him and make that his sheet-anchor. The *Gita* succinctly sums up that long section of the *Mundaka,* declares knowledge to be the sure boat to take even the most abandoned sinner across the ocean of sin, and describes the ways and means to find that knowledge — loving homage and service and repeated questioning and inquiry of a Master of Knowledge. But it adds that this purifying knowledge which makes ashes of all sins may be won by perfecting oneself with yoga — selfless action in faith and surrender and self-control. One need not necessarily sit down at the feet of a *guru* to learn it. Arjuna must rend his doubt with the initial knowledge of Self, and cast off the bondage of action by dedicating all action to God. "Equipped with knowledge, betake thyself to yoga and arise" (IV. 33-43).

JNANAYOGA AND KARMAYOGA COMPARED

(Discourse 5)

Again Arjuna is pictured to us as puzzled, for again we have the end and the means extolled in the same breath with perhaps an added emphasis on the purifying virtue of knowledge. 'Which of the two then may be better ? Renunciation of action or performance of action, exclusive pursuit of knowledge (Sankhya) or practice of action (yoga) ?' True knowledge is the end, sure enough. May it not be that an exclusive pursuit of knowledge may be a better way than much preoccupation with the noise and bustle of the world ? It is to remain unworldly that seekers after God retire from the world and occupy themselves completely with trying to realize the mysteries of Self and God. Why then *Karmayoga* ?

---

* प्लवा ह्येते अदृढा यज्ञरूपाः । *Mundaka* I, 2, 7.

Both, says the Lord, are good; both lead to the same goal; but *Karmayoga* is better, if only because *Jnanayoga* is well nigh impossible without *Karmayoga, sannyasa* well nigh impossible without yoga. It is quite likely that he who takes a sudden leap into philosophic mysticism may come to grief, whereas he who goes through the necessary discipline of active mysticism, doing the daily duties in a spirit of selflessness, remaining in the world and yet not of it, naturally steps into the state of the Self-absorbed mystic.

When one comes to think of it, there is but a faint line of demarcation between the perfected *Karmayogi* and *Jnanayogi.* In fact one may doubt for a moment whether a particular verse in this discourse is meant to refer to one rather than to the other. Thus, verse 7 describes the active mystic: 'The yogin who has cleansed himself, who has gained mastery over his mind and the senses, and whose Self has become one with the Universal Self and all creation, though always in action, is not smeared by it.' Why should not this apply to the philosophic mystic? His action indeed may be of a different character, but act he will. Both will go through what are usually voluntary movements of all the internal and external organs as though they were all involuntary (V. 8-9). Again the philosophic mystic will sit secure in 'the city of nine gates' (body), master of himself, resting serene, doing nothing nor getting anything done (V. 13). This all may equally apply to the active mystic whose action will be inaction as it will be dedicated to God. The difference then will be a difference of attitude or emphasis: The philosophic mystic will sit secure in the wisdom that *he* is doing nothing, that it is the *gunas* that act and not the Self; the active mystic will rejoice in the knowledge that it is God who acts, that it is God who is the agent, and his limbs but instruments worked by Him. Take verses 14 and 15. The life of the *Karmayogi* and *Jnanayogi* will reflect the truth of the verses in a seemingly different way. The Self does not act, creates no agency, takes not the sin or merit of any one upon Himself. That will be the conviction of the *Jnanayogi*. The *Karmayogi* will feel and act in the conviction that he is under the rule of a law which is God's law — the Law which "doth preserve the stars from wrong".

But whereas a merely philosophical position may well be a delusion and a snare, the religious position of a *Karmayogi* is sure to lead to the *real* philosophical position. A mere assertion of the metaphysical truth, that Self does not act, may drag one into the depths of hypocrisy and worse; but he who holds his will at the disposal of God will ultimately reach the knowledge that his will and God's will are one, that he or his Self wills and acts not at all.

When in a state of complete immersion in the Absolute, Kabir sings that all outward acts of his — seeing, eating, drinking, etc. — are all so many acts of piety and dedication, he says so because for him there was no 'other' God.* Here we have the vision of the seer described in verses 8-9. But who will say that that state of self-absorption was reached automatically? It was a result of an unbroken life of self-purification (V. 11-12).

Therein lies the essence of the discourse. The true *sannyasi* will no doubt rest in serene equipoise, free from the delusion of ignorance which the Sun of knowledge has dispelled, his body and mind and intellect rivetted on the Highest whose vision he has had. He will look with an equal eye on a learned *brahmana* and a cow, on a dog and a dog-eater, resting in unity and perfection which is *brahman* (10-19), finding peace within, bliss within, light within (24). But how is the state to be achieved? Not without *Karmayoga*, which is a condition precedent. The highest intellectual effort will not put one in that condition. Intuition in some rare cases may do it, but intuition is nothing more than a result of ages of

---

* साधो सहज समाध भली।
जहँ जहँ डोलौं सो परिकरमा, जो कछु करौं सो सेवा।
जब सोवौं तब करौं दंडवत, पूजौं और न देवा।
कहौं सो नाम, सुनौं सो सुमिरन, खावौं पिवौं सो पूजा॥

endeavour. Thus *brahma-nirvana* (absorption in *brahman*) is said to be ever in front of the yogin whose sins are extinguished, whose doubts are dispelled, who is absorbed in the good of all creation, and who can withstand the flood-tides of the passions of lust and wrath (V. 25, 22-23). The description itself presupposes an intense state of selfless, God-dedicated activity — *Karmayoga*. To take another instance. The *jnani* or the philosophic mystic looks on the savant and the fool, the dog and the dog-eater with an equal eye. How will he do so? The *Bhagawata Purana,* parts of which are like a luminous commentary on the *Gita,* lays down the conditions: "The feeling that God is in every one — the saint and the sinner, the *brahmana* and the untouchable, has to be assiduously cultivated, and then only will the feeling of disgust vanish. A step to the cultivation of that feeling is to prostrate oneself on the ground in front of even the most loathsome, regardless of one's self-consciousness, prestige and of one's own sense of shame and of physical differences. This should be done unless and until one actually sees Him in every creature." St. Francis cured himself of his feeling of disgust for the lepers by adopting practically a similar course.

That is why the Lord put the truth of the matter in one word at the very opening of the discourse: "*Sannyasa* is well-nigh impossible to achieve without yoga." But we have thus far had yoga presented to us in terms of action. We shall now have it presented in terms of devotion. Here too we have two divisions exactly corresponding to the philosophic and the active mysticism, namely, meditative and devotional — *Dhyanayoga* and *Bhaktiyoga*. In the last analysis there are only two attitudes towards Reality — the philosophic and the religious, and in the ultimate analysis even these two dissolve into one, as we shall see. But for the sake of clearness we have these dichotomies given us. The *Jnanayogi,* as we have seen, has his eye fixed on the Absolute, takes his cue from it, and turns all action into inaction; the *Karmayogi* takes his cue from a God willing to take upon Himself the burden of all the actions he casts on Him in self-surrender. In the terms of prayer the former becomes *Dhyanayogi,* the mystic contemplating and meditating on the impersonal Absolute, and the latter becomes *Bhaktiyogi,* the devotee-mystic basking in the glow and warmth of His presence and His praise and His grace. We have these two fresh aspects introduced to us towards the close of the fifth discourse — meditative mysticism in V. 27-28 and devotional in V. 29. The discourses that follow deal with these two. Roughly it may be said that *Dhyanayoga* is the subject of discourses 6 to 8, and *Bhaktiyoga* that of discourses 9 to 11, both being compared in the 12th.

Dhyanayoga

(Discourses 6 to 8)

We have again (VI. 1-4) a slightly varied phraseology for the philosophic and the active mystic. The one has scaled the heights of yoga, the other has to scale them. He who would achieve those heights and enjoy tranquillity in toil, active repose, or "an attentive and recollected inaction", to use Amiel's phrase, must remember that it can only be the result of strenuous self-endeavour. By the Self does one sink or swim, for the Self is self's friend and the Self is self's foe. It is he who has thus conquered himself and mastered the art of conforming himself to the Self, that will be able to look with an equal eye upon friend and foe, happiness and misery, respect and disrespect, a clod of earth and gold. This mention of strenuous endeavour is necessary to introduce the method of meditative mysticism — *Dhyanayoga* (VI. 5-9). Verses 10-17 define in brief the spiritual qualifications of one who elects to tread this path, and the necessary physical environments which facilitate the path of one determined to retire in the sanctum of Self. External purity and *brahmacharya,* continence of the body, thought and mind, are the *sine qua non* before one thinks of choosing this path. And yet one may not violently mortify oneself. Let him give *prakriti* its moderate yet necessary toll of food and drink, rest and sleep. This yoga is a toilsome process and hence necessarily means patience and freedom from extremes. Thus equipped he should sit secure in contemplation of the Self, secure from all the winds and storms that blow, even as the steady flame of a taper in a windless spot. In spite of this effort the mind with its inveterate habit of wandering will do so. Slowly and gradually, with tireless effort, it has to be reined in, with understanding secured by will, and chained to the Self. Then all disturbing thought shall cease. The result when attained will be something ineffable which will preclude all desire for other gains and other joys. It will be a yoga or union with Supreme Bliss, meaning an extinction of union with all that is not-Self, an annulment of union with all ills. It will be the absolute bliss of an everlasting contact with *brahman.* These rare souls will not, like the stoics, " seem to bear, rather than rejoice " ; theirs will be a rejoicing which knoweth no surfeit or satiety (VI. 18-28).

But this yoga must show itself in life. Lord Krishna gives the criterion which equates the philosophic and the religious vision. Such an one will see the Universal Self in all beings, and all beings in that Self — deriving their existence and their sustenance from that Self. And since that Self is the same as Lord Himself, he will see the Lord in all, and all in the Lord. As a commentator quoting from the *Mahabharata* says, from out of the vision of the yogin who has attained self-realization, God flashes forth before him even as the lightning flashes forth from out of a raincloud. Such an one will naturally, in the vastness of his love, embrace all beings as part and parcel of himself. He will, so to say, be unique alike in his detachment and tenderness. From such an one God will never vanish, such an one will never vanish from God. It is a tremendous assurance. God will not fail him but He gives the added assurance that He knows that he will not fail God. Of such an one Lord Krishna says that however such an one may live and move he will live and move in Him. As Plotinus put it : " He becomes established in quiet and solitary union, not at all deviating from his own essence, not revolving about himself, but becoming entirely stable, becoming as it were stability itself. Neither is he then excited by anything beautiful, for he runs above the beautiful, he passes beyond even the choir of the virtues" (VI. 29-32).

But, says Arjuna, this yoga of equality with the whole creation is no easy matter. The mind is such a forward, fickle thing that one may sooner chain the wind than rein in this mind. How then is one to rest stably in that equality or union? 'Just so;' says Lord Krishna, 'but tireless effort and dispassion can overpower even the unruly mind. Indeed those two are the essentials. Yoga should not be thought of by one who has not stilled his passion; but for one who has done it, it is not difficult of achievement by the proper method.'

'But if the aspirant fail in his effort, he will be neither here nor there. Neither will he be on the path of the Vedic ritual which he has abandoned, nor on the path of *brahman* which he has lost.'

'No effort is lost,' Lord Krishna reassures him. 'A man who has chosen the path and is on it never comes to grief, here or there. Man grows by countless lives into oneness with *brahman*. What he has done in one life is a step, however inadequate, towards the goal. After a period of discarnate existence he is reborn in a family suited to help him further forward towards the goal, even from the point where he left it in the previous existence. No, there is no cause for despair. The very fact that he has chosen this path will not let him look back with longing on the path of the Vedic ritual' (VI. 33-44).

He is, however, in for an effort carried on from life to life; about that there should be no mistake. Such a yogin is better than a mere practiser of austerities, who simply tortures the flesh; he is better than one revelling in learning; he is certainly better than one wedded to the Vedic ritual (VI. 45-46). But let it be remembered that among all yogins, 'he excels who, ever attached to Me, worships Me in faith' (IV. 47). In this last verse peers out Lord Krishna's preference for *Bhaktiyoga,* which we will find demonstrated with argument in the twelfth discourse.

The seventh discourse, part of which we have summarized in the introductory background to this analysis, deals with the nature of the world and the Reality which a meditative mystic will realize. But hardly one in a thousand strains after the perfect vision and hardly one succeeds from among those who thus strive. This vision is the vision of the Absolute in Its two aspects, the higher being the vitalizing thread in all life, the lower being the physical world. The Absolute thus pervades the animate and inanimate creation, sustaining all, holding it all even as a thread sustains the gems in a necklace, immanent through and through. All that exists, where-through runs the warp and woof of the three *gunas,* exists through the Supreme, but rather than take all that as a symbol and expression of the Divine the deluded ones fix their eyes on the form and forget the substance. The world is a delusive mystery indeed, it hides what it ought to reveal, but we have to see the Unseen through the veil of the Seen. "The whole temporal world," said Henry Drummond, "is a vast transparency through which the Eternal shines." But only the blessed ones, the good-doers — not the evil-doers — have this vision, can penetrate the veil, having made the Lord their refuge. Of these devotees there are four types; he who, as a reward of devotion, seeks relief from distress; he who seeks knowledge; he who seeks material gain, and he who seeks the Lord. This last — *the jnani* — is the best, for he has no other end to serve, no other goal to think of, no other haven to hide himself in. He is the Lord's very self. It is as a result of effort which must have continued through several births that this *jnani* thus happens to win the vision and to see that Vasudeva is all (VII. 1-19).

There are, says Lord Krishna, others who have other ends to serve and who, therefore, in pursuit of those ends, seek other gods. He does not disturb their faith, on the contrary he makes them secure in their faith and dispenses them what they seek. But limited is their fruit, for they would limit Him, the Exhaustless, the Supreme, and would not look beyond their little gods. Such is the delusive mystery of the Lord that it precludes the vision of the Unborn and the Immutable. Man is born with a heritage of likes and dislikes which draw his mind and his senses to outward objects, never allowing him to look inward. Only those whose sins have come to an end are freed from that sorry heritage and resort to Him in steadfast faith. They indeed know the whole *brahman,* including *adhyatma,* karma, *adhibhuta, adhidaiva,* and *adhiyajna.* They also have a vision of the Lord at the time of death (VII. 20-30).

What, Arjuna wonders, is this *brahman* which includes so many puzzling terms. It is nothing but the several stages in which the Absolute transforms Itself into the individual and the individual comes back into the Absolute. *Brahman* thus translates Itself into the unmanifest *prakriti* (termed here *adhyatma*), *prakriti* starts evolving (which is termed karma or action), as a result we have the perishable creation (termed *adhibhuta*), the Absolute limited in each created being is *adhidaiva,* and each gifted with and purified by the power of sacrifice (*adhiyajna*) expands again into the original *brahman.* The whole mystery, bereft of its technical garb, is really nothing more or less than the mystery of the law of sacrifice which we have learnt in the Third Discourse. The Supreme Being sacrifices Itself to be the individual and the individual has to sacrifice himself to reach the original source (VIII. 1-4).

There is a secret of shuffling off one's mortal coil with a vision of this *brahman.* One has to rivet his thoughts on Him when passing away and he goes nowhere else but to Him. This thought of Him at the hour of death is no fortuitous circumstance, but the culmination of a life-long habit. 'Whatever therefore thou doest — whether thou art fighting the outward powers of darkness or the inward ones — do it at all times with the thought of Me,' says Lord Krishna. With an exclusive devotion one must concentrate one's powers of meditation on the Supreme Being (VIII. 5-8). Here follows a description of the Supreme and the way in which the Supreme is to be meditated upon. OM is the symbol of that imperishable Absolute, OM which is at once the means and the end, as the *Katha Upanishad* text * on which the *Gita* text is based declares. This and similar other *Upanishad* texts crystallize the spiritual and psychical experience of the seers who intuitively found the symbol and used it as an open sesame for their spiritual goal. As the *Prashna Upanishad* † has it: "As a snake is relieved of its skin, even so verily he (who meditates on the Supreme with the symbol OM) is freed from sin....He beholds the Being that dwells in the body and which is higher than the highest living complex....With the syllable OM in truth as a support, the knower reaches that which is peaceful, unaging, immortal, fearless Supreme" (VIII. 9-15).

The verses that follow describe the fleeting show, in order to rivet man's mind on the Unfleeting. The worlds are ceaselessly perishing and reappearing, all bound in the unending chain of karma — even those who do good deeds (for rewards). These go to the several worlds they aspire after to reap their rewards, but even those who reach the world of Brahma must be born again, for all including Brahma himself are caught in the cycle! At the beginning of each period of a thousand *yugas* — or at the beginning of each day of Brahma — the beings come into manifest existence from the unmanifest state, and at the coming of Brahma's night — of a thousand *yugas* they return to

---

* सर्वे वेदा यत्पदमामनन्ति तपांसि सर्वाणि च यद्वदन्ति।
यदिच्छन्तो ब्रह्मचर्यं चरन्ति तत्ते पदं संग्रहेण ब्रवीम्योमित्येतत्॥
एतद्ध्येवाक्षरं ब्रह्म ह्येतदेवाक्षरं परम्।
एतद्ध्येवाक्षरं ज्ञात्वा यो यदिच्छति तस्य तत्॥
एतदालम्बनं श्रेष्ठमेतदालम्बनं परम्।
एतदालम्बनं ज्ञात्वा ब्रह्मलोके महीयते॥

Katha 1, 2, 15-17.

† यथा पादोदरस्त्वचा विनिर्मुच्यत एवं ह वै स पाप्मना विनिर्मुक्तः...स एतस्माज्जीवघनात्परात्परं पुरिशयं पुरुषमीक्षते ... तमोंकारेणैवायतनेनान्वेति विद्वान्यत्तच्छान्तमजरममृतमभयं परं चेति॥

***Prashna* 5, 5-7.**

the unmanifest state. The same multitude of beings as are dissolved come to birth again at the coming of each Brahma's day and go through their cycle of existences until the coming of Brahma's night. The unceasing process goes on, whether the beings will or no (VIII. 16-19). The same idea is repeated in IX. 7-10 where the Brahma's Day is called *kalpa,* the unmanifest is referred to as '*My prakriti*' and is said to bring forth the beings "under My control."

The description strongly reminds one of the vivid stanzas in Thomson's *City of Dreadful Night* :

> This little life is all we must endure
> The grave's most holy peace is ever sure.
> We fall asleep and never wake at all.
> We finish thus ; and all our wretched race
> Shall finish with its cycle and give place
> To other beings with their own time-doom.
> Infinite aeons ere our kind began ;
> Infinite aeons after the last man
> Has joined the mammoth in earth's tomb and womb
> All substance lives and struggles evermore
> Through countless shapes continually at war
> By countless actions interknit :
> If one is born a certain day on earth
> All times and forces tended to that birth ;
> Not all the world could change or hinder it.
> I find no hint throughout the universe
> Of good or ill, of blessing or of curse,
> I find alone necessity supreme ;
> With infinite mystery, abysmal, dark
> Unlighted ever by the faintest spark
> For us the flitting shadows of a dream.

It is a powerful description of the inexorable law of karma. Only we do not "give place to other things". We ourselves take "those countless shapes", for infinite aeons indeed the show will go on, but the peace is not to be found in the "grave's most holy peace", for we fall asleep to wake up once more. The great poet contradicts himself when he says that we live and struggle evermore "by countless actions interknit", and yet says that it is all an abysmal and a dark mystery "unlighted ever by the faintest spark". We could not be interknit by countless actions, unless there was unity at the basis of this diversity, unless the whole thing was governed not by a blind necessity, but by a law which is the expression of God. The peace is not to be sought in the peace of the grave, but in the bosom of the Lord. The *Gita* verses that follow complete the thought, lest we should run away with an impression not unlike Thomson's grim vision. For, says the Lord: 'This manifest and unmanifest is not the final word. Higher than that unmanifest is *brahman* Supreme, abiding, imperishable whilst all beings perish. It is the Supreme Being, in whom all beings are and which is in all. It is the highest haven, where having reached there is no coming back. Unwavering devotion to that Being is the only way to reach It, but it also is a way which never fails (VIII. 19-22).

A day of a thousand *yugas* must hearten one, rather than dismay, for we have to work through life after life for ages, whilst our spirit strives to be one with Universal Spirit, through instruments and vestments that dissolve and decay, leaving him ever free for a fresh struggle. And after all, is not the whole picture such as to make one not only patient but feel as humble as a grain of dust? The great physicist Planck says: "Reason tells us that both the individual man and mankind as a whole, together with the entire world which we apprehend through our senses, is no more than a tiny fragment in the vastness of Nature, whose laws are in no way affected by any human brain. On the contrary they existed long before there was any life on earth, and will continue to exist long after the last physicist has perished." *

One of those laws is the law of sacrifice, as the seers have found it. The yogin has to live that law, has to annihilate self to become one with the Universal Self. Him who does this the traditional paths — known as the paths

* Quoted in *An Idealist View of Life* by Dr. Radhakrishnan.

of the gods and the manes — will not touch. He will know the secret of the paths and live by the path of light, and living thus he will travel beyond the minor rewards promised by the *Vedas* and reach the ultimate goal (VIII. 23-28).

Bhaktiyoga

(Discourses 9-11)

We have had an idea of *Dhyanayoga* and the *Dhyanayogi*, the mystic who would devote his mind and soul to a contemplation of the impersonal Absolute. It is, as we have seen, a path of strenuous endeavour. We have now described to us the path of *bhakti* — devotion to a Personal God. *Bhaktiyoga* is described as the supreme mystery, the king of sciences, purifying and of sovereign virtue, capable of direct comprehension, and easier to practise than the path we have had described. The basis of this *Bhaktiyoga* is the knowledge of the Lord as He is, and a discriminative knowledge of Him in His manifestations. Only men of faith take to this path, scoffers go and revolve through the cycle of birth and death over and over again (IX. 1-3).

This background of knowledge is now presented to us in three discourses in various ways. Lord Krishna as the Imperishable Unmanifest becomes manifest as the world which rests in Him, but He as the Unmanifest is not in it, because He transcends it. He sustains the beings and runs through them as the string in the gems. He is their ground, not they His ground. Again He contains all, nothing can contain Him fully. All beings live and move in Him without affecting Him, as does the wind in ether without affecting it (IX. 4-6). We have a description of how the Lord creates all and is in all, and is thus all — sacrifice and the oblation, the herb and the mantra, fire and the offering; Father, Mother, Creator, Friend, the Goal and the Abode, the Source and the Dissolution, Death and Deathlessness, Giver and the Withholder, and the Acceptor of all sacrifices (IX. 16-19; IX. 24).

Again He the Unborn and Unbegun is the birth of and beginning of all, even the gods, the source of all the various modifications of the mind, the supreme *brahman*, the everlasting Being, the primal Lord. "All that and more thou art," says Arjuna. "Thy amazing and unique power is recognized by even the high and the mighty gods and the *rishis*. But oh yogin (Master of that power)! May I not know these various manifestations, so that I may be constantly reminded of Thee by them?" (X. 1-8; 12-18). That gives Lord Krishna another occasion to describe just a few of his various manifestations. He, the beginning, the middle and the end of all, is all that the eye and the mind and the imagination of man holds as the highest and the noblest and the best, in all the species of creation, real or imaginary, in all classes of existence, real or imaginary, in heaven as on earth, in the universe and in the mind of man. He is the essence of all that infinity of delights for the eye and the ear and the understanding of man that exist in Nature. He is the seed of all. Anything that is possessed of richness and the beauty and majesty arises out of a fragment of His glory. Just by a part of Him is all held (X. 12-42).

Truly

> Earth's crammed with heaven
> And every common bush afire with God.

'We are complete in Him who is the head of every principle and potency,' said St. Paul.

And yet again Arjuna would have the Master reveal Himself still more. A vision would indeed be a more real revelation than hearing. For to see is to believe. He wonders if he might not have that vision of Him. The Master grants his desire. The world in front of him is not changed; his vision is transformed and made divine, and so he begins to see things he had never before seen. The Lord was there unchanged. It is not He who is transfigured, it is Arjuna who is transfigured. With this divine vision he is made to see all eternity in a moment, 'in narrow room Nature's whole wealth', the universe in one focus, the multifarious and myriad forms concentrated in One, as one. Sanjaya, the narrator who had stood aside all this while, steps in to lend colour and charm to the divine drama. He does so because the vision seems to bewilder him no less, and he for a moment breaks the narrative and exclaims his own wonder. How is he to give an idea of the vision to the blind king ? If one could conjure up a vision of the blended splendours of a thousand suns, then perhaps something like a glimpse of that glorious vision might be given. With this he narrates in Arjuna's words the awesome majesty of that vision. For, when Arjuna's eye — even the divine eye — cannot contain the vision, his tongue breaks out in speech, and when the speech fails, the eye leaps in to rest on the vision. The Universal, Infinite, All-pervading, Almighty form alternately amazes and terrifies him. The serene and the awesome aspects both are there, the Moon that soothes is one of the eyes of the Lord, the Sun that dazzles is the other eye. The Sun that gives life and warmth is there, but the Sun that scorches and burns is also there. A myriad forms are worshipping Him, and myriad forms are being devoured in His volcanic flame. And now the great war-lords are seen rushing to their doom in that divine conflagration like so many moths in a flame.

Can the Lord be terror incarnate ? The eye would for a while let the tongue express its terror. 'Not only Terror incarnate, am I,' is the answer. 'I am the very Doom. I have incarnated Myself for this very purpose. The war-lords, the prospect of whose death dismayed and made thee break out in a lament, are already devoured by Me. Be thou but an instrument.'

The first flashlight thrown on Arjuna's mind was in the second discourse with a revelation of Imperishable Self. The second comes now. 'Not *thou,* but *I* am the Agent. If thou couldst not understand it up to now, see it with thine own eyes. Cast thou thy acts on Me and fight.'

The conviction now comes in letters of living fire and makes him break out in praise and prayer. The Birthless, the Ageless, the Being and Not-Being, the Finite and the Infinite, all the elements and what not ! All and yet more in Him. He is in front and in the rear, above and below, and everywhere. Where was one to bow to Him ? We must extol Him first, Him last, Him midst, and without end.* In breathless adoration Arjuna utters his worshipful prayer to Him who is all, for He holds all. In unpardonable blindness he had limited Him in the form of a friend and a comrade, jested with Him and even slighted Him. Would he forgive him all that, as a father forgives his son, a friend his friend, and a lover the loved one ? His thanksgiving knows no bounds, as indeed his exultation also ; but so has terror too seized him. 'Wear thou again,' he prays, 'Thy form benign, and be again as Thou wast' (XI. 1-47).

What a rich vision for the *bhakta* ! He may see the Lord as Creator and 'Parent of Good' as in discourse 9 ; he may see Him as Preserver and Sustainer of all, reflected in His various manifestations which through their borrowed glory declare the parent glory, as in discourse 10 ; and he may see Him as the Destroyer, as in discourse 11. Indeed, if he be an Arjuna, he may be permitted to behold the ecstatic vision of the universal form of the Lord. But whether he happens to be vouchsafed that vision or not, if he will but walk with eyes open, he will see Him shining

> In all things, in all natures, in the stars
> Of azure heaven, the unenduring clouds,
> In flower and tree, in every pebbly stone
> That paves the brooks, the stationary rocks,
> The moving waters, and the invisible air,

and utter in humble adoration,

> We, who from the breast
> Of the frail earth, permitted to behold
> The faint reflections only of Thy face
> Are yet exalted, and in soul adore !

Singing incessantly His glory, bound in steadfast devotion to Him, the *bhaktas* worship Him (XI. 14). They leave all and follow Him, because He is their all ; they need not

---

* "If I ascend up into heaven, Thou art there : If I make my bed in hell, Thou art there. If I take the wings of the morning and dwell in the uttermost parts of the sea, even there shall Thy hand lead me, and Thy right hand shall hold me" (*Ps*. 139. 8-10).

take any thought for their all, as He takes the burden of providing all that Himself (IX. 22). Their thoughts and their lives absorbed in Him, speaking and talking only of Him, they rest content exulting in His praise. Them the Lord blesses with the power to act rightly, as also with the vision of knowledge which dispels for all time their ignorance (X. 9-11). The Lord makes the dumb speak and the halt cross the mountain. Indeed, as we have it in another scripture, the Lord has said: "I will guide thee with Mine eye."

But the *bhakta* must fulfil certain conditions. He must not lose his hold of the Reality. Whilst he may worship a god of his choice, let him not limit God in that form, let him not forget that his god is but the symbol of the Great Lord of Beings (IX. 11; IX. 23-24), let him not by a narrow vision be vain of hope and vain of work and vain of knowledge (IX. 12). "They that worship Him must worship Him in spirit and truth." * Let him know that he who worships God will go to God and he who worships stone will go to stone (IX. 25). But once the *bhakta* has hold on the Reality and steadfast faith, God expects very little of him. In one word, let him do whatever he has to do — be it working, eating, sacrificing, going through any vow or penance — let him do it as an offering to Him, let him do it to His glory. For there is nothing, however trifling, offered in earnest devotion, that the Lord does not love to accept. Shabari, the pariah woman, who tasted her wild fruit, lest it be bitter, before she offered it to the Lord, and her devotion which compelled the Lord to eat the tasted fruit with extra zest, are as much remembered as the Lord Himself. A *bhakta* in such self-effacing devotion combines both *sannyasa* and yoga and wins to the Lord. The Lord favours none, disfavours none, but belongs to them who belong to Him. And thus the most confirmed sinner, having resolved to die to sin and live to Him may earn the epithet of a saint.

* *John* 4. 24.

For, although he may have wasted his substance in riotous living, he returns to be as one of the Father's hired servants. "He was dead and is alive again, he was lost and is found." * Therefore, he is accepted right royally even as a saint.

'Rest assured, oh Arjuna, My *bhakta* perishes not.' The highest goal reached through *bhakti* is not the monopoly of caste or creed, race or sex, rank or station. The unlettered woman, and the petty shopkeeper, and the labourer going through "the narrow avenue of daily toil for daily bread", nay even those who are hated and despised as of foul birth, may through *bhakti* storm the gates of Heaven. Only let them dedicate their worship, their sacrifice, their mind and all their attachment to Him (IX. 26-34). Vedas are of no avail, neither austerities, nor costly gifts, nor sacrifices. Only exclusive and unwavering devotion can avail to secure a knowledge of Him. "He who does My work, who makes Me his goal, who is My devotee, who has cast off all attachment and shed all ill-will comes to Me" (XI. 53-55).

To do His will, to live in Him — that is all the *bhakta* knows. St. Paul summed up *bhakti,* the *bhakti* that was his life and meat, in a word: 'For me to live is Christ.' †

Dhyanayoga and Bhaktiyoga

(Discourse 12)

Lord Krishna sums up the teaching about the two forms of devotion in reply to Arjuna's question as to which of the two was the better yogin — he who meditated on the impersonal Lord and he who worshipped Krishna as his all. Lord Krishna's preference for the worship of the Personal is based on the same reasoning as his preference for *karmayoga* to *jnanayoga* in discourse 5. The fruit of both *dhyanayoga* and *bhaktiyoga* is the same, as we saw the fruit of *karmayoga* and *jnanayoga* was also declared to be the same. Both the meditative mystic and the *bhakta* come to the Lord. But as in discourse 5, whilst the path of

* *Luke* 15. 32.

† *Phil* 1. 21.

the *dhyanayogi* is one of hard and toilsome endeavour, that of the *bhaktiyogi* is comparatively easier. The devotee of the Absolute has to rid himself to such an extent that he sees Self everywhere and absorbs himself in the welfare of all. But inasmuch as he contemplates on the Absolute, he has nothing but his own spiritual and moral resources to draw upon. Unless the process of catharsis has reached to perfection, his effort may well be endless. But the *bhakta* with an exclusive, unwavering devotion throws himself on his Lord with all his weaknesses and imperfections, and the Lord pulls him out ere long even from the lowest depths (XII. 1-7). Perhaps the contemplative devotion to the Absolute is best achieved as a result of devotion to a personal God. Otherwise there is no difference. In the Father's many mansions there is room just as much for an iconoclast and meditative mystic like Kabir, as for Tukaram who sang: 'Be Thou formless for those who want Thee to be so, but for me take Thou on a form, O Lord! I have fallen in love with Thy name'; as much for a philosophic mystic like Akha as for Narasinha Mehta who wanted no release from birth and death but craved to be born again and again, in order to be lost in the ecstatic worship of Nandakumar (Krishna); as much for a Self-absorbed mystic like Eckhart who exclaimed: 'I ask to be rid of God, i. e. that God by His grace would bring me into the essence, that essence which is above God and above distinction,' as for St. Francis of Assissi whom the sight of the crucifix sent into trances; as much for Catherine of Siena who saw Him as 'Acceptor of Sacrifices', as for Mirabai who saw naught else in the world but Giridhar Gopala (Krishna) her beloved Lord; as much for Chaitanya whom the name of Krishna was enough to melt into ecstacies as for Ramakrishna Paramahansa whom a vision of Kali, the Mother, sent into the same rapturous trances.

Names and forms and symbols do not matter, provided the hold on the Reality is unshaken. It is gross intolerance to label the worship of a personal God as "crass idolatry". There is no idolatry so gross as the slavery to the letter and slavery to the lusts of the flesh. The true devotee never loses sight of the Reality. Vasudeva Kirtikar quotes a beautiful *abhanga* of Tukaram. The poet-saint sings :

"I made an earthen image of Shiva
But the earth is not Shiva ;
My worship reaches Shiva,
The earth remains the earth it was.
I made a stone image of Vishnu
But the stone is not Vishnu ;
My worship reaches Vishnu,
The stone remains the stone it was.
I made a pewter image of Amba,
But the pewter is not Amba ;
Amba receives my worship,
Though the pewter that pewter remains.
Even so are saints worshipped,
The worship reaches the Lord,
The saint is but His servant
An instrument, a conduit pipe." *

Easy stages in the path of *bhaktiyoga* are now suggested. Concentration on work for the Lord ; if even that is impossible, renunciation of the fruit of all action. This last is so simple and so convenient that from mere mechanical performance one rises to perfected renunciation : the mere practice leads on to a knowledge of its essence, this knowledge makes one concentrate one's energies on it and thence springs the perfected renunciation of fruit which brings everlasting peace (XII. 8-12).

The last eight verses contain the quintessence of *bhakti* and is a summing up of all the four discourses 9-12. *Bhakti* is no mere emotional rapture but the very perfection of humility and service of all that lives, the extinction of all 'otherness' and ill-will, and contentment in willing surrender, freedom from all depression and elation and from all unquiet care — a life in which the *bhakta* feels at ease with the world and the world feels at

* Quoted in Kirtikar's *Studies in Vedanta*, (translation by the author).

ease with him, where his whole joy is to do His will. And verily the man who fulfils all His will, declares the Lord, 'is the *bhakta* after Mine own heart'. That is the essence of *bhakti*, the very core of *dharma*. Dearest to the Lord are they whose life is an expression of this *bhakti*, whether they are worshippers of the Personal or the contemplative devotees of the Impersonal (XII. 13-20).

THE WORLD AND THE REALITY

(Discourses 13-15)

Purusha and Prakriti and Knowledge

We have already summarized discourses 13 and 14 in the introductory portion preceding this analysis and, hence, need touch on the contents but briefly. The thirteenth discourse puts together the scattered threads of the teaching about the world and the Reality found throughout the other discourses. We have the field of man's activity and the Knower of the Field described in the first six verses, we have them described again by their commonly accepted names as *prakriti* and *purusha*, with the *Purushottama* that pervades and transcends both. Wedged in between these two sets of description is a paradoxical description of the Supreme Spirit, seated in the heart of every being as the Knower of the Field. As Unmanifest It has all the negative attributes — if one may indeed call them attributes — of the Unmanifest — above all the supreme attribute of being without an attribute; and as manifested in the world It seems to possess all the attributes of the manifested world (XIII. 12-17). A knowledge of this Reality is what has been up to now held up before Arjuna as the end and the *summum bonum*, the goal which leads to immortality, but lest there should be any illusion about it that it was something like an intellectual process, the *Gita* gives an elaborate definition of knowledge, which in the very nature of things includes the means to the end. For knowledge to which one may claim to have leaped without having used or practised the means must be a travesty, and the means employed with the conscious end of unification with the Lord presupposes knowledge. Since it means final deliverance, the definition starts with deliverance from the little ills that the reason and the mind of man is heir to. At the top of the means is freedom from pride, which is likely to survive the extinction of all other ills like passion and attachment. 'Pride is a sin of the temper,' Henry Drummond used to say, 'and is often found with the purest moral character.' It is thus a dead weight and hence the man who aspires after true knowledge must begin by "pouring contempt on all his pride." The rest of the virtues are of course there — homage to the teachers, external and internal purity, inoffensiveness, uprightness, detachment from ties that bind one to the world, inclination to solitude and a perception of the true meaning of spiritual knowledge. It includes, too, an exclusive and "unfornicating" devotion to the Lord (to use an expression of St. Augustine, which is a literal translation of the *Gita* word *avyabhicharini bhakti*) for "the soul doth commit fornications when she turns from Thee." * Perhaps the Prophet of Islam expressed it in simple beauty when he said, "And whoever hopeth for the meeting with his Lord, let him do righteous work, and *make none sharer* of the worship due unto his Lord." § (7-11).

Towards the end of the discourse is a recapitulation of the whole teaching: (i) The four methods of knowledge of the Self are mentioned — *jnanayoga* and *karmayoga* (discourses 3-5), *dhyanayoga* and *bhaktiyoga* (discourses 9-12) (XIII. 24-25) ; (ii) the creation of the world through the connection of *Purusha* and *Prakriti* (XIII. 26); (iii) a short definition of true knowledge and true vision — seeing the Supreme dwelling alike in all things, not perishing when they perish (XIII. 27-28), and seeing that it is the not-Self (*Prakriti*) that acts, not the Self, and thus sitting content and unconcerned (XIII. 29) ; (iv) all diversity is based on unity and proceeds from it; (v) the nature of

* St. Augustine, *Confessions.*

§ *Koran*, 18. 111.

the Supreme — informing every fibre of our being and untouched by it, like the ether pervading all space, untouched by it; illuminating every pore of our being as the Sun the universe; (vi) discriminate knowledge of *Purusha* and *Prakriti,* and a perception of the secret of the release of the one from the other leads to the Supreme (XIII. 34).

Often enough even in the humdrum affairs of the world we catch a glimpse of this unity in diversity. Does not the happening of an earthquake (physical certainly, moral and political often enough) stir millions to a sudden realization of unity in diversity? And yet we soon return to the narrower vision and believe that diversity is all. The ether fills all space, the sun illumines every nook and cranny of the universe. We see it and yet we do not. "We have this treasure in earthen vessels, that the excellency of the power may be of God, and not of our selves," but we cling on to earth, as though it was all and ours.

The Gunas

The constituents of *Prakriti* are, as we have already seen, exhaustively dealt with in discourse 14. We need not go over the ground already covered. One or two points not touched before may be noted here. We are bound by the *gunas,* but we have to get free from them through them, use a thorn to get rid of a thorn. The ultimate truth is the knowledge that all action, all the world is the result of the interplay of these *gunas* and that untouched and above them is He (XIV. 19). One has to transcend them to taste of immortality. The characteristics of this spiritualized yogin who has transcended the *gunas* are described. They are, as one can easily understand, practically the same as those of the yogin of secure understanding (II. 54-72), of the *dhyanayogin* (VI. 7-9; VI. 29-32), or of the *bhakta* (XII. 12-20), for the life of perfected vision always presents the same face. The *gunatita* — the spiritualized man — is neither worried when the three *gunas* are in action, nor misses them when they have ceased to act. Though in the body, he will not identify himself with any of the internal or external organs. The body, so long as it is there, will exact its toll of conscious existence, activity and sleep, the *gunatita* will pay the toll unmoved and undisturbed by them. He will thus be naturally indifferent to pleasure and pain, respect or disrespect. He will look with an equal eye on friend and foe, he will have no castles to build in the air but do what comes to his lot. The secret to reach this state is exclusive and "unfornicating" devotion to the Lord. Such an one passes beyond the *gunas* and becomes one with *Brahman* for the Lord is the image of *Brahman,* eternal law and endless bliss.

The goal is to transcend the three *gunas,* but it is not reached unless we strive to reach upward from *tamas* to *sattva.* In the seventeenth and eighteenth discourses we shall see that all *sattvika* activity is selfless activity, all *rajasa* activity is selfish, and all *tamasa* activity is ignorant and blind. Every aspirant has to reach from inertia or blindness to supreme luminous selflessness. But there is a stage beyond even that. The *Gita* simply indicates it but later commentators have explained it in detail. Thus the *Bhagavata Purana* does not rest content with defining *sattvika, rajasa* and *tamasa* knowledge, happiness, and doer, as the *Gita* has done (XVIII. 19-21; XVIII. 37-39; XVIII. 26-28), but defines the fourth variety transcending the three, viz. *nirguna* knowledge, *nirguna* happiness, and *nirguna* doer — *nirguna* variety being defined as "proceeding from the Lord". Shankaracharya, with his characteristic scientific precision, defines not the three but four *gunas,* in his *Vivekachudamani* calling the third and fourth *mishra sattva* (mixed *sattva*) and *vishuddha sattva* (pure *sattva*) respectively. The characteristics of *rajas* and *tamas* are practically the same as in the *Gita,* but those of mixed *sattva* are said to be conscious performance of virtues, conscious faith and devotion etc., whereas those of pure *sattva* are serenity, light, bliss, self-realization etc. The idea is briefly this: The three *gunas* are said to adhere together and so long as *sattva* is alloyed with *rajas* and *tamas,* no matter however minutely, *sattva* is not pure; it is pure when it has shed the alloy. The purest water in its natural state is not as pure as distilled water. Even so, as long as man is not completely spiritualized his *sattva* will have a tinge of 'self' but even that 'self' will be shed when he becomes God-man. The *gunatita* of the *Gita* is the God-man, the man for whom life in tune with the Self has become as natural as the function of breathing or circulation of blood.

Ashvattha and Purushottama

(Discourse 15)

The fifteenth discourse is a restatement in different language of the truth about the world and Reality. The world is described as the *ashvattha* tree sprung from the heaven above as its root, and, therefore, ageless and changeless in its essence, the expanse of its branches coming down and showing as the manifest world. Too often we lose sight of the Root and think of the worldly roots which are below, going up into branches which again throw down in the earth rootlets in the shape of actions which shoot up again to bear their consequences. The tree is sustained on the sap of the *gunas,* its offshoots are the sense-objects. We do not discern its beginning, basis or end. It is attachment that sustains it and through attachment man remains tied down to it. The wise hew it down with the sure axe of detachment. "Every tree that my Father hath not planted must be rooted out." Even thus can man seize hold of the Imperishable Root — the Abiding, the Imperishable Abode, whence there is no returning, which is all light, not needing a sun and moon to illumine it. Only those who have shed all self-sense, delusion and selfish desires, who are hitched on to the Supreme, and free from the pairs reach that imperishable haven (XV. 1-6).

The process of how the cycle of birth and death goes on is now described — i.e. how the tree is planted and kept alive, how a part of the Lord embodies himself as *jiva* (individual soul) and passes from birth to death and death to birth, taking the psychic apparatus of the mind and the senses of perception from every body he leaves. It is in association with this apparatus that he experiences the sense objects, stays in and departs from the body. Him, the Supreme who is untouched by the *gunas,* only the yogins who have cleansed themselves see with the eye of the spirit, not the intellectual vision, which is, after all, the eye of the flesh (XV. 7-11).

The immanence of Him seated in the heart of all is again described (XV. 12-15), and *Purushottama* is held up as the supreme object of worship, called *Purushottama* (the Highest Being) inasmuch as He transcends the two beings or aspects of the world — the perishable manifest and the comparatively imperishable manifest. Transcending both He yet informs and sustains all. He who worships Him in all His forms is the man who has known all. The knowledge is the fulfilment of man's mission on earth. The supremely mysterious doctrine of which the exposition was begun in discourse 9 really finishes here, for though the description of the path of *bhakti* was concluded in the twelfth, its basis and background are concluded with this discourse.

Individual Ethics

(Discourses 16 and 17)

We have had throughout the previous discourses constant references to a pair of characters — enlightened and unenlightened (III. 25-26 ; IV. 40-41), the disciplined and the undisciplined (V. 12 ; XV. 11), the man of faith and the man without faith (III. 31-32 ; 40-41), the good-doer and the evil-doer (VII. 15-16), and so on. The author now classifies them broadly into the good and the bad, men of God and men of the devil. In doing so the *Gita* is using the language of the *Upanishads.* George Sand has somewhere divided mankind into two classes — the healthy and the unhealthy, and Coleridge says that as there is much beast and some devil in man, there is some angel and some God in him. Though broadly we may make the divisions, there are no water-tight compartments of the kind. We sometimes run towards God, harkening to the God within us, and often enough go to the devil. The stably good are the rarest on earth, and yet if one were to ask them, they would say they were far away from God. Let no one, therefore, misunderstand these labels and misapply them. We may only say that when particular characteristics predominate us we are of God, and when the opposite ones do so we are of the devil.

Naked we came out of our mother's womb and naked we must return to the womb of Mother Earth. But this is a partial truth. As we have seen in last discourse, we do not come quite naked, we come with something — the impress of our actions, our character, our karma — and we return with something, if we do. The *Gita* says that this heritage that we bring with us is either godly or ungodly, the godly helping to deliver us from the bondage of flesh, the ungodly tightening the bondage. Fearlessness is declared to be at the top of the godly heritage of virtues, and with reason. Fear presupposes otherness, and a vision of God cures one of the otherness and hence of fear. It is thus at the root of all virtues. Then follow the cardinal virtues — truth and unoffensiveness, purity and self-restraint, and a grip of the end and the means — *jnana* and yoga, and a number of other virtues like charity, compassion, spiritedness, long-suffering, etc. The opposite of these constitute the ungodly heritage — hypocrisy, snobbery, cruelty and the like. But the *Gita* goes on to describe at length the characteristics of ungodly men. Lust and lawlessness may be said to be the law of their life, anything they do is with a view to secure those ends, for they do not accept any reign of law on earth and recognize no lawgiver. There is no godly sorrow that enlightens or enlivens their lives, they carry through life a load of ungodly sorrows which drag them down to their doom. Such people, says the Lord, He casts (or do they not cast themselves ?) unto devilish wombs, the jaws of hell, for indeed they live in hell, there being no hell on earth but the one with the triple door of lust and wrath and greed (XVI. 1-21).

It is not that the path of the godly involves no struggle. He must not forget that the virtues and vices are the manifestations of the three *gunas* which coexist.

They may have a preponderance, in their nature, of *sattva,* but *rajas* and *tamas* are there — dormant yet ready to awake if *sattva* relaxes its vigilance. Sleeplessly, therefore, has the godly soul to keep watch against those heralds of hell, and fight them "by the armour of righteousness on the right hand and the left" * or "with the whole armour of God." ‡ (XVI. 22).

The Lord now sums up the whole teaching: 'Make *shastra* thy sole guide of conduct for he who forsakes the *shastra* comes to grief' (XVI. 23-24). This *shastra* (science) is none other than the *yogashastra* taught in the *Gita,* the science of selflessness or detachment, considered in terms of devotion, worshipping the One Lord of all beings.

'But,' § asks Arjuna in the opening verse of the seventeenth discourse, 'this *shastra* that thou hast expounded may not be understood by all, may not be acceptable to all. Would it do if they shaped their conduct according to their faith or belief in the scripture? Thou hast also before mentioned people worshipping gods, ghosts, manes and other beings (IX. 25). They must be doing so according to their belief in the scripture. How wouldst thou characterize their attitude — *sattvika, rajasa,* or *tamasa*?' (XVII. 1).

Lord Krishna's reply covers the rest of the discourse. It all depends, He says, on the character of their belief in scripture, for like other qualities of the mind, this belief is of three kinds — *sattviki, rajasi* and *tamasi.* Man is made of the stuff of his belief, and his object of worship will be determined by the character of his belief. Those of *sattviki* belief will worship gods, those of *rajasi* belief will worship *yakshas* and *rakshasas,* and those of *tamasi* belief will worship the spirits of the dead and

---

* 2 *Cor.* 6. 7.

‡ *Eph.* 6. 11.

§ In interpreting XVI. 23-24 and the whole of the XVII discourse I have ventured to follow my own independent line. The reader will find my argument in the notes. In the text, of course, I have faithfully followed Gandhiji's translation.

ghosts. Even in their penance or austerities their belief is bound to be reflected. Those who practise austerities not according to the science of selflessness, but out of selfishness will do so with hypocrisy and pride, passion and desire, and torture their flesh and Me the Dweller in it. Their belief is devilish indeed (XVII. 2-6). Their belief will even be reflected in the kinds of food they eat (XVII. 8-10).

Indeed the three virtues in which the whole ethical conduct of man may be summed up — sacrifice, austerity, charity — the three purifying agents as they are called (XVIII. 5) — even these virtues can become vices if divorced from the rule of selflessness or detachment. The belief in the scriptures will help little. The scriptures lay down well enough that truth, harmlessness, continence shall be practised, that sacrifice shall be offered, that charity shall be given. But it depends on the spirit in which man practises these scriptural injunctions. The science of selflessness declares the spirit in which action should be done, if it is not to bind, but to free one. Thus the *sattvika* sacrifice will be the true sacrifice — performed without an eye to reward and as a matter of duty, the *rajasa* one will be a matter of show and hypocrisy, and the *tamasa* will be miscalled 'sacrifice'; for even the belief in the scripture will not play any part there, because no scripture lays down a sacrifice in which some giving is not involved. Austerity of the body, of the word, of the mind is indeed a sum up of purity of conduct: humility, continence, inoffensiveness; speech which gives no offence, truthful, sweet and helpful; serenity of mind, silence and purity of the inner self. Now the practice of these virtues, if *sattvika*, is a power for good. But if it were *rajasa* it would become self-serving, and if *tamasa* a monstrous engine of oppression. The same is the case about charity which if done in a *sattvika* spirit would not let the left hand know what the right hand doeth; if done in a *rajasa* spirit, would be done in expectation of return and with a flourish of trumpets; and if done in a *tamasa* spirit, would be a wasteful and demoralizing excess (XVII. 11-22).

All works of austerity, sacrifice, and charity to be of liberating power should, therefore, be done in a spirit of perfect dedication. *OM TAT SAT* has been the dedicatory formula from ancient times and the worshipper and the sacrificer offering his worship and sacrifice in the name of *OM TAT SAT*—the triple symbol of *Brahman,* would dedicate them to the Absolute—the All-pervading, the Unconditioned, the True, the Beautiful and the Good. This is no theological formula—it simply expresses the rules of selflessness and dedication. Let all work be dedicated to Him—however one may think of Him and by whatever name one may call Him. And dedicated work is good, all undedicated work, divorced from selflessness and scripture is bad, availing neither here nor hereafter (XVII. 23-28).

Delusion Destroyed

(Discourse 18)

The eighteenth discourse recapitulates the teaching of the *Gita.* We have had *tyaga* (abandonment) and *sannyasa* (renunciation) mentioned over and over again. In answer to Arjuna's question Lord Krishna explains the distinction that is ordinarily made between the two and shows that it is really a distinction without a difference when one considers the essence of both.

The ordinary belief, of course, means by *sannyasa* the renunciation of all action springing from desire, and since according to those who hold that belief there is no action but springs from desire, all action must be abandoned as tainted at its source and, therefore, binding. There are some who would make an exception in favour of the three purifying principles of sacrifice, austeriy and charity. Lord Krishna's considered opinion is that what determines the nature of all action is not its outward expression, but the spirit in which it is done, the taint attaches not to the action as such but to the selfishness and attachment at the back of it. From that point of view, says the Law, even abandonment of action may be tainted and questionable if it is selfish, since like all other things abandonment too is of three kinds — *sattvika, rajasa* and *tamasa.* Therefore, even austerity, sacrifice and charity, if they are to be the purifying agents that they are known to be, have to be pursued without desire for fruit and without attachment (as we have already seen in the seventeenth discourse). Then there are obligatory acts that one has to perform as a member of the social organism, and they may not be abandoned. To abandon them out of a deluded sense of one's being above those humdrum tasks, is blind — *tamasa* — abandonment indeed. To abandon them because they are troublesome or arduous is sheer selfishness — *rajasa* abandonment. The ideal abandonment is the abandonment of fruit and of the attachment in respect of all action that comes to one's lot. That indeed is pure *tyaga* and pure *sannyasa,* call it what one will. As for *sannyasa* — renunciation of *all* action it is a physical impossibility so long as one bears the body : it is only the fruit and attachment that can be the objects of abandonment, and those must be abandoned by all aspiring to be free from the cycle of birth and death. Those who do not abandon the desire for fruit cannot escape the reward — good, bad, or mixed in the shape of rebirth in the different species (XVIII. 1-12).

The *Gita* next describes the necessary factors in all action — the body, the agent, various instruments, various processes, and the unseen element working to bring about the completed act. These factors show an interdependence of all Nature, show how " all substance lives by countless actions interknit ". It is futile, therefore, for man to take the burden of agency on oneself. From another point of view, when there are these various factors at work — which briefly described are nothing but *gunas* — the unconditioned *Atman* cannot be the agent. The wise man who has woven this truth into his life and has thus annihilated all 'self' will not be held responsible for anything he does, yea even though he annihilated all the worlds (XVIII. 13-17).

Now follows a description of the three *gunas* as they are reflected in all the things of life to show how they determine their character, and make it pure, alloyed, or impure as the case may be. Thus these three kinds of agent, act, perception, understanding, will, happiness, are described, in order that man may ever bend his energies zestfully and without thought of success or failure (XVIII. 26) to rise from the impure to the pure, from selfishness to selflessness, from darkness to light.

> 'From the unreal lead me to the Real,
> From darkness lead me to Light,
> From death lead me to Deathlessness.' *

Let him blazon on the tablet of his mind three things: pure act or pure abandonment is the performance of what comes to one's lot, without attachment, without like or dislike, without thought of reward; pure perception is the vision of unity in all diversity; pure happiness is the straining for eternal bliss through arduous, even apparently painful endeavour (XVIII. 18-40).

These *gunas* are thus woven into every fibre of man's being; no one is free from them, not even the gods (40). The four-fold division of the social organism is also based on what gifts and what special aptitudes one can bring to bear for the service of the organism. A Brahman's function or work presupposes and must evidence the qualities of serenity, self-denial, long-suffering, spiritual knowledge; a Kshatriya's work, the qualities of valour, spiritedness, magnanimity; a Vaishya's work will be the production of wealth from land, cows and commerce; and a Shudra's work is to help the rest by bodily labour (XVIII. 41-44).

Each one doing his allotted task in the proper spirit is sure to win his salvation. Only it should be done in His name, and as an offering of service to Him. Disinterested work for Him, i. e. for all God's creatures is true worship. Under the circumstances there is no occasion for choice, for choice may involve one in interestedness. One's own duty, though uninviting, is better than that of other's which, though seemingly easier of performance, may ultimately prove a snare and a delusion. A man's birth on earth is a result of bondage to one's karma and, therefore, involves

---

* असतो मा सद् गमय, तमसो मा ज्योतिर्गमय, मृत्योर्मामृतं गमय।
Brihad. 1. 3. 28.

this inherent imperfection, all actions done by the body would be inherently imperfect in some respect or other. But the alchemy of detachment will turn all imperfection into perfection. Let man go through life in a complete spirit of detachment, and his detachment will win him the supreme perfection of non-binding action (45-49).

The author now proceeds to show how the man who has achieved this secret of converting all binding action into non-binding action ultimately rests in the final stage of knowledge. We find ultimately all the yogas coalescing here. This selfless work purifies his understanding, his whole self will have been brought under the control of his will, he will cast off likes and dislikes for objects of sense, and equipped with perfect discipline and dispassion he will be intent on meditation. He will thus cast off everything that presupposes a sense of 'I' or 'mine' and thus fit himself for being one with all Nature. Having become one with all Nature, he will be at peace with himself, will regard all creation alike, and will be suffused with the purest devotion to the Lord, will know Him in all His greatness, discover Him truly and enter Him (XVIII. 50-55). Compare these verses with this passage from the mystic Ruysbroeck and note how in his description all mysticisms coalesce: "He goes towards God by inward love, in eternal work, and he goes in God by his fruitive inclination in eternal rest. And he dwells in God, and yet he goes out towards created things in a spirit of love towards all things, in the virtues and in works of righteousness. And this is the most exalted summit of the inner life."

The whole doctrine is now summed up and Arjuna finally exhorted to awake to a sense of his duty: 'Throw thyself on Me and do every thing that comes to thee at every time, as at My instance, to My glory. Thus shalt thou by My grace attain to the supreme goal, by My grace cross over every obstacle. But if thou wilt not listen to Me, fancying that thou canst escape thy duty, rest assured, thy nature will assert itself and will compel thee. What thou wilt not do at My bidding thou shalt do at the bidding of thy nature and so perish. The Lord is seated in the heart of every being. It is open to them to listen to His bidding, and put themselves in His hands ; but if they will not, then the Lord will let them be whirled round as on a machine, and dance to the tune of their *prakriti*. In Him therefore seek refuge, His grace shall lead thee to lasting peace' (XVIII. 56-62).

"That Lord," Krishna again reassures Arjuna, "am I. I have revealed to thee, My beloved, the supreme mystery. Consider it fully and act as thou wilt. Dedicate thy thought, thy worship, thy sacrifice, thy homage to Me and I solemnly promise that thou shalt come to Me. Disturb not thyself by conflicting duties. Seek refuge in Me. I will deliver thee from sin. Sorrow not" (XVIII. 63-66).

The Lord finally warns Arjuna not to waste the doctrine on those who have no qualifications to take it in — no self-restraint, no devotion, no inclination to listen. Narration of the doctrine, conveyed in the dialogue, by worthy persons to worthy persons, will endue them with true devotion. A devout study of it will be a kind of 'knowledge sacrifice' offered to God, a devout listening will earn the listeners brighter worlds of birth (XVIII. 67-71).

'Has thy ignorant delusion now been destroyed ?' asks the Lord at the end. The final flash-light revealing Krishna's knowledge of Arjuna's true make-up has clinched the matter and Arjuna exclaims with the serenity of certitude and the conviction of religious faith that his doubts have been resolved, that he has recovered his knowledge of the true Self and that he would do His bidding (XVIII. 72-73).

With that Sanjaya's story ends, but the ecstatic vision haunts him, the accents of the divine discourse reverberate in his memory. Fain would he love to linger on the memory of it all. But rather than make the blind king sadder thereby he concludes : 'What more shall I say ? Where the Lord of yoga expounds the doctrine and where there is one most fitted to carry it out, there is bound to be eternal right and hence sure victory.'

That, one takes it, made the blind king resigned to the inevitable. Perhaps he saw that therein lay the good of all.

VI. A Few Questions

I have discussed a few points which were necessary to an understanding of the analysis that followed. I propose now to discuss a few questions that arise from the teaching and are often raised.

The Four Varnas and Svadharma

Quite an amount of ignorant criticism is levelled at the doctrine of the performance of *svadharma* (one's duty or function) taught in the *Gita* and the reason for it is the much-abused *varna* system. This is no place for making out a case for or against the so-called 'caste-system'. It is necessary here to make a few points clear and to point out the bearing of the system on the *Gita* doctrine. Much of the criticism is directed against a thing which is just a shadow of what existed ages ago. There was a system which existed in ages gone by, which served the then existing social organism magnificently, which was elastic and hence made it possible for a number of different groups of the same race and several races to live together in amity and peace. What we see today is its travesty, a fossil formed out of the incrustations of customs and practices of several centuries. Let not one judge the original from the ghost of it, and say that the author of the *Gita* sought to clothe a loathsome thing with divine sanction. The system of *varnas* we find described is certainly no rigid one. The division is no division into water-tight compartments. If the *Gita* can be said to admit a division, that division is, as we have seen, into two classes — *daiva* (divine) and *asura* (devilish) — and that too would hardly appear, on examination, to be a permanent division, inasmuch as there is an eternal war going on between the divine and the devilish in us, no matter to what class or caste we belong. It is therefore difficult for man to characterize or label brother man. If he cannot label himself correctly, much less can he label any one else. Let us note then the main features of that elastic system : (i) The division was entirely vocational, in order that each might serve the best interests of the organism. If men devoted themselves to tasks for which their character and aptitude best fitted them, they would be able to give of their best to the community. The criterion was not what one needed but what one could give to the community; (ii) The division had regard to the requirements of the *then* existing society and these were broadly divided into (a) intellectual and spiritual, (b) defence, (c) production of wealth by (1) intelligent economy and by (2) labour. Each requirement was assigned to be fulfilled by a class possessing the particular gifts necessary for its fulfilment. The evident inequality of individual attainments was recognized, but the possession of gifts added to one's responsibility rather than improved one's rank. Thus to possess naught was one of the characteristics of a Brahmana whose wealth was that of spirituality and self-denial, while the production of wealth for the community was necessary for a Vaishya, to provide body labour was the privilege of a Shudra. (iii) Purity or virtue was the monopoly of none. Salvation was through the proper selfless performance of one's task. The *Bhagawata Purana* describes * what have been rather loosely described as functions (*karmani*) in the *Gita* as the natural characteristics — (*prakritayah*) — of the various classes and then says, the ethical rule of life is the same for all, viz. inoffensiveness, truth, non-thieving, freedom from wrath and greed, desire to do good to mankind. Hence salvation was more difficult for those who had greater tasks to perform and easier for those entrusted with humbler functions. For these were not cumbered with much knowledge. Whilst it was easy, for instance, for a butcher or for a scavenger to carry on his forefather's profession with equanimity and detachment and as a sacrifice offered to God, it was quite likely for a learned Brahmana to darken counsel with much learning and even "with devotion's visage and pious action sugar o'er the devil himself." Among the Indian saints we

* वर्णानामाश्रमाणां च जन्मभूम्यनुसारिणीः ।
आसन् प्रकृतयो नृणां नीचैर्नीचोत्तमोत्तमाः ।। (११, १७, १५)
अहिंसा सत्यमस्तेयमकामक्रोधलोभता ।
भूतप्रियहितेहा च धर्मोऽयं सार्ववर्णिकः ।। (११, १७, २१)

have fewer from among the Brahmanas than from the non-Brahmanas. Among the saints of revered memory, Sena was a barber, Sajana was a butcher, Gora a potter, Raidas a cobbler, Chokhamela an untouchable, Tukarama a *kunbi,* and so on. None disclaimed his profession but worked his salvation through a detached prayerful performance of it. (iv) The functions were hereditary because heredity is a law of nature, but there were no exclusive divisions, as we know from several cases of intermixture of functions and *varnas* in the *Mahabharata.* (v) The organism is shattered to pieces today and there are no defined classes that can answer to the description of the old *varnas,* but the rule to respect the law of nature may stand even today and all societies which are to any extent well-ordered would on examination be found to be based on a vocational division of some kind.

'What then is one to do when performance of one's *dharma* is considered to be the highest morality, and *dharma* is to be determined by the shattered caste system ?' is a critic's poser. The answer is that *dharma* or one's duty or the task to which one is born is no wooden phrase. It means the task to which one is born in the particular time or place we have in view.

> New occasions teach new duties,
> Time makes ancient good uncouth ;

and whilst one's allotted task may have been fighting 2500 years ago, today it may be to carry on a bloodless war to end all wars ; whilst it may have been a duty to kill a foe then, today it may be one's duty to lay down one's life in defending a sacred principle or individual or national honour. 'One's allotted task' has its natural meaning and it should not be more difficult for any one in India to find it out than it is for any one in the West. This is how a modern author * on Ethics expresses the moral law : "Thou shalt labour within thy particular province, with all thy heart and with all thy soul and with all thy strength and with all thy mind." That is too what Carlyle meant when he

* Prof. Mackenzie, *Manual of Ethics.*

said : "Know what thou canst work at, and work at it like a Hercules." The *Gita* makes the moral law clearer than any other ethical system in the world by adding to the above. somewhat to this effect: 'Work like a Hercules indeed, but offer thy work at the feet of the Lord as your humble flower of worship, without the thought of reward. A selfish performance even of the best thing would render it worse than void.' For, according to the *Gita,* doing one's duty is not the highest morality as our critic would assert; doing one's duty in complete detachment and selflessness is the highest morality. Provided the work taken up is not morally forbidden, the sole criterion to determine its moral value is detachment, selflessness. Selflessness is the sole content of right.

'But why, then, this insistence on *svadharma* and *paradharma* ?' the critic rejoins. 'The *Gita* has no answer to give but this, viz. doing of other's duty is dangerous.' Why does the critic want a better answer ? The reason lies in the experience of the seer that when one runs after a duty which is not his he runs into a pit. Duties, like things, come to those who prayerfully wait for them, not to those who run after them. As Cardinal Newman sweetly said :

"So works the All-wise ! Our services dividing
Not as we ask :
For the world's profit, by our gifts deciding
Our *duty-task*."

Knowledge a Talisman ?

Throughout the *Upanishads,* says Hume, "metaphysical knowledge" is held up as a "magic talisman" and in distinguishing the Socratic doctrine of the identity of knowledge and virtue from the *Upanishadic* doctrine, he says that in the *Upanishads,* "the possession of metaphysical knowledge actually cancels all past sins and even permits the knower unblushingly to continue in 'what seems to be much evil' with perfect impunity, although such acts are heinous crimes and are disastrous in their effect for others who lack that kind of knowledge." Later on he saves himself from this extreme position by a number of qualifications which the *Upanishads* themselves compel him to make, but finally reverts to the charge that "moral distinctions do not obtain for the man who has metaphysical knowledge." This is not the place to examine this extraordinary statement made by such an eminent scholar and apparently a votary of the *Upanishads*. But mention of it has become necessary inasmuch as he has made the same charge against the *Gita*. The *Gita*, according to him, adopts the *Upanishadic* position as stated by him, and under the authority of the *Katha Upanishad* 1. 2. 19 (repeated in *Gita* II. 19) that "This one slays not nor is slain" *, "the divine incarnation quells the scruples of Arjuna over the murdering of his enemies."

The first thing to see is whether the *Gita* adopts the position that "metaphysical knowledge" permits the perpetration of crimes. Without examining the statement in any detail that that is the position of the *Upanishads*, just one or two things may be mentioned. The doctrine that knowledge is not only virtue but that it leads to salvation and nothing else does it, may be traced to the famous Vedic text which declares: 'What will he do with a knowledge of the texts, who has not known That?' That Vedic text to my mind emphasizes the distinction between dry learning and metaphysical knowledge which suffuses every pore of one's being, that furnace-fire that turns the whole iron into fire. This distinction was never lost sight of in the *Upanishads*. The trouble is due to the unfortunate English word 'knowledge' which has not the content of *jnana*, which far from meaning mere metaphysical knowledge means a new vision, a new life, a rebirth. The Greek word *gnosis* as used by the Gnostics has that full content and means a full unification with the Universal Self, or as Prof. Nicholson points out, a complete "realization of the fact that the appearance of 'otherness' beside Oneness is a false and deluding dream. Gnosis lays the spectre which

---

* हन्ता चेन्मन्यते हन्तुं हतश्चेन्मन्यते हतम् ।
उभौ तौ न विजानीतो नायं हन्ति न हन्यते ॥

Katha. 1-2-19

haunts unenlightened men all their lives, which rises like a wall of utter darkness between them and God." The *Upanishads* make the meaning of *jnana* clear beyond any misunderstanding. But let us content ourselves with the *Gita*. If there is anything about which all the commentators of the *Gita* are agreed — for the simple reason that there is no room for misunderstanding — it is the content and the conditions of *jnana*. Is it possible to have a more comprehensive definition of *jnana* than we have in XIII. 7-11 already noticed in detail in the foregoing analysis (Pp. 88-89)? It sums up elaborately the moral life that leads up to the vision, not temporary, but permanent of the Dweller in the innermost. It is the transformed life of the seer which is the subject of those nineteen verses in the second discourse (II. 54-72) and we have the substance of it repeated at every stage. The third discourse is concluded with the statement that the spiritual enemy of man has to be killed by taking hold of the Highest (III. 43). The fourth defines knowledge over again, not by an assurance of impunity to one who has knowledge, but by declaring the unique purifying power of knowledge (IV. 38) which is no knowledge unless it makes one see the whole creation in one's Self and in God (IV. 35). The fifth is a paean of praise of the transformed life where the whole mind and heart and soul of man are cleansed of all impurity and made a worthy dwelling for the perpetual abode of the Deity (V. 17). The sixth repeats the comprehensiveness of the transformed vision in words unforgettable (VI. 29-32). But need we go on? We should then have to summarize the whole *Gita* over again. And the conditions of real knowledge are writ large on every page of the *Gita* [II. 54-72; XII. 13-20; XIV. 22-26; XV. 5; XV. 11; XVI. (whole); XVIII. 51-55 etc.]. Not with the eye of the flesh shall one see Him, but with the eye of the spirit is the burden of every verse dealing with *jnana*. It is possible for one to wrench verses from their context, as Hume has wrenched texts from the *Upanishads*, and say that *jnana* is presented as the panacea for all ills. We can quote a string of such verses — IV. 9; IV. 14; IV. 32; V. 29; IX. 1; X. 3; XIII. 18;

XIII. 23 ; XIV. 1 ; XIV. 19 and many more — but will any one have the hardihood to maintain that *jnana* in these verses has a narrower content than the *jnana* referred to in the whole contexts we cited a little while ago ? No, not even an enemy of *Gita* can misunderstand the content of knowledge. Whoever will misunderstand the famous verse in which St. John declared : "Whosoever abideth in Him sinneth not" ? For it is apparent to the meanest understanding that he who abideth in Him cannot bear to breathe anywhere else. *Jnana* is knowledge of Him in truth, and entering Him and abiding in Him (XI. 54 ; XVIII. 55). It is no intellectual or metaphysical jugglery, but a refinement of the whole soul by taking it through the fiery furnace of self-discipline. Metaphysical knowledge is necessary, but it is the beginning and not the end. "Life is different," says Dr Radhakrishnan, "from the moment of insight. The vision of the One is the beginning of the process of conversion. The soul has seen, the mind must consent, and the heart approve. The new experience must control our whole being, the word recognized as true must become flesh." The statement that sin does not touch a man of knowledge or that knowledge turns all sin to cinders means in one case that sin dare not approach a seer, and in the other that sins, or more accurately past karma, will cease to take effect like parched seeds which do not sprout. It is in this sense that the *Maitri Upanishad* in a beautiful image says :

'As to a mountain that's enflamed
Deer and birds do not resort —
So with *Brahman* knowers, faults
Do never any shelter find.' *

Are there not then *any* verses in the *Gita* which have an antinomian odour ? There are two — perhaps three — which may be cited, viz. VI. 31, XIII. 23 and XVIII. 17. But in the first the condition mentioned would leave no room for any suspicion that by knowledge anything less than the

* यथा पर्वतमादीप्तं नाऽऽश्रयन्ति मृगद्विजाः ।
तद्वद् ब्रह्मविदो दोषा नाऽऽश्रयन्ति कदाचन ॥
Hume, *Maitri Up.* 6. 18.

transformed vision is meant. For what else can be meant by, 'he who, anchored in Unity, worships Me abiding in all things'? The second must be read in the light of the whole teaching of the *Gita*. The third, i. e. XVIII. 17 would appear to have a semblance of antinomianism and a parallel verse or two (even more extravagantly worded) may be cited from the *Upanishads*. But let us see what is antinomianism and then find out if the verse in question can bear to be labelled as antinomian. Pascal who exposed the casuistry of the Jesuits of his days in his "Letters to a Provincial" thus quoted the Jesuit Father's defence of homicide: "The Father proceeded: In so far as it is in our power we turn away from forbidden things; but when we are unable to prevent the action, we at least try to purify the intention, and so correct the vice of the means by the purity of the end. That is how our Fathers have been able to permit acts of violence which are committed in defence of honour: It is only necessary to turn away one's intention from the desire of vengeance which is criminal and to restrict it to the desire of defending one's honour which is a lawful desire." Are the positions taken in *Gita* XVIII. 17 and in this quotation from Pascal the same? There is between the two positions all the difference that there is between GOD and DOG though the letters in both the words are the same. He who has rid himself of all sense of 'I' will have no 'I' left to put up any defence for anything he does. The very anxiety to defend himself will recoil on him and make a mockery of all his claim to freedom from egotism and to pure intent. The words in the *Gita* are not put in the mouth of Arjuna, but of Lord Krishna who is giving Arjuna glimpses of perfect knowledge every now and then in varying language, and asking Arjuna to fight not for himself but for His sake and in His name. As Gandhiji has said in his note on XVIII. 17 the verse describes the condition of God or a God-man — a *gunatita*. It is God alone who can slaughter all the worlds, not man.

We come now to the second charge of Hume which is already partly answered. We shall rest content with showing that the little statement that under the authority of metaphysical teaching "the divine incarnation quells the scruples of Arjuna over the murdering of his enemies" contains three misstatements. I shall briefly attempt to show this. (1) The metaphysical truth does not quell Arjuna's doubt. If it did, the *Gita* should have been finished at verse II. 19. But it is the beginning of the argument which ends in the eighteenth discourse. The metaphysical truth is mentioned to assure him that his lament was misdirected. Nowhere in the *Gita* is Arjuna represented as having grasped knowledge — metaphysical or spiritual; he is assured, and he is convinced, that if he left all conflict of duties and followed Him, and did, not what he had reasoned out as belonging to his self, but as God bade him to do, he would incur no sin, and that sort of dedicated performance of one's duty led to true knowledge. (2) Arjuna had no scruples over fighting his enemies; any scruples that he had were over having to slaughter his kinsmen. (3) Arjuna lived in an age when war was not taboo — even we are yet far off from that golden age — and he had not the slightest suspicion that killing one's enemies in war was "murder". The first argument — the statement of the metaphysical truth — makes him pause and think. The second where the climax is reached convinces him that he has to be but an instrument. Vengeance was not his, but God's who said: 'Vengeance is Mine, I have already repaid' (XI. 33). The third and the last argument is that however much he might delude himself, his nature was sure to assert itself. That dispels all delusion and doubt. He sees clearly that Krishna knew his Arjuna better than Arjuna himself. He knew how "the elements mixed in him."

But, it may be said, any man may call himself an instrument in the hands of God and perpetrate all kinds of excesses. Such an one has yet to arise and be believed in by the world! The exhortation to fight without the feverish delusion of ignorance (III. 30), and to become an instrument in His hands (XI. 33) was addressed to Arjuna who had cleansed himself of all desire for sovereignty, enjoyment and life (I. 32). Apparently, at any rate, he had no interest left in fighting and that is why he was worthy enough to be urged to fight without the thought of reward or the sense of 'I'. The divine sermon would have been lost on a Duryodhana or a Karna or even a Bhima, who could not have fought without the thought of 'I', without the thought of success or failure, without hatred or vengeance.

It is one in millions that God thus chooses to do His will, whilst the rest go on from life to life, struggling to find out what is God's will. Arjuna was that rare one whom God had chosen to make him know His will and to do it. And after all is said and done, it is God who is represented as justifying Arjuna's conduct, not Arjuna.

Let not Christian friends run away with the thought that the teaching, however one explains it away, is bound to mislead people. There is indeed the fear of the *Gita* being used in defence of murder, but the world has luckily its rough and ready standard to judge the man who makes the claim to murder in God's name. There is indeed Hitler today who, boiling with rage and burning with hate which he does not conceal, vows vengeance against the whole Jewish race and declares: "By fighting against the Jews I am doing the Lord's work." The world does not believe that he is doing God's work, nor would it do so if a follower of the *Gita* made such a claim. Besides, the Hindu has from ancient times had handed down to him the glorious example of the seer Dadhichi who laid down his life and offered his bones to be made into a thunderbolt to fight miscreants, of king Shibi who risked his life in order that the life of a dove may be saved, of Prahlad and Sudhanva who went through untold ordeals for His sake — not one Christ but many Christs if I may permit myself to say so. However, the test, after all, is not the claim advanced by the doer of the deed, but how the world judges him.

Karma and Free-will

We have already discussed the doctrine of karma and rebirth. Whilst one critic says that the author of the *Gita* contradicts himself by asserting the doctrine of karma in one breath and the doctrine of grace in the other (IX. 27-28 ; XVIII. 56, 58, 66), another critic says that there is no freedom of will in the *Gita* and man is but an automaton — 'a being spun round on a machine' (XVIII. 59), asked to be no more than an instrument (XI. 33).

The first criticism betrays ignorance of the doctrine of karma, and may be disposed of in a paragraph. The doctrine of karma or the moral law contains and comprehends the doctrine of grace. The same law that tells us that we shall reap as we shall sow, also tells us that if we throw ourselves on God in a broken and contrite spirit our contrition will by His grace result in rebirth. Mercy and grace form but another phase of God's justice, in fact mercy is ever hidden in His justice if we can but see it. The critic's objection arises solely from the orthodox Christian's belief in grace coming from somewhere outside man. But, as Principal Caird says, "that to which we thus surrender ourselves is in reality our truer self", — God who is in the heart of man.

The criticism about the absence of free-will must be dealt with in some detail, though that too involves the orthodox Christian assumption we have just mentioned. Man's *prakriti*, the make-up with which he is born is, as we have seen, the result of the past and has to be reckoned with. There is no short-cut to the goal, it must be through the handicaps and hurdles that are a necessary condition of the race. But He who has determined the race and the conditions has also endowed man with the capacity to cope with them. A man born dumb and blind cannot obviously speak and see, but a Hellen Keller born dumb and blind can do better than speak and see — infinitely better than millions who speak and see but who really don't speak and see. 'By thyself shall thou free thyself, for Self is the friend of self and Self is self's foe' (VI. 5-6).

The material is given to us, we can use that and no other, but we have freedom in the manner of using it. Dr Radhakrishnan employs a happy simile : "Life is like a game of bridge. The cards in the game are given to us:

We do not select them. They are traced to past karma, but we are free to make any call as we think fit and lead any suit. Only we are limited by the rules of the game. We are more free when we start the game than later on, when the game has developed and our choice becomes restricted. But till the very end there is always a choice. A good player will see possibilities which a bad one does not. The more skilled a player the more alternatives does he perceive. A good hand may be cut to pieces by unskilful play and bad play need not be attributed to the frowns of fortune. Even though we may not like the way in which the cards are shuffled we like the game and we want to play." * I would just add one word: the cards seem to be given to us, though really they are chosen by us, or rather they belong to us, for the law of karma works not from outside but in us and through us.

It depends on how one defines free-will. If it is a will free of all law, man has no such will, or plenty of it to go to the devil with. The fact is that our freedom is commensurate with our freedom from all that we falsely identify with Self. Even the most unfortunate of us is endowed with a consciousness of Self, and his conduct will be free to the extent that he is conscious of that Divine in him. "To thine own Self be true, and it shall follow as the night the day thou canst not then be false to any man," said Shakespeare in his immortal language. We have to be true to our Self, and "the truth shall make us free."

God is not outside us. He is in the heart of us all and we perpetually revolve round Him. The unfortunate part is that most of us forget that we revolve round Him and feel that we revolve round some other centre, the centre of our narrow selves. The centre is within us, but we have made an orbit with a centre outside us. When we are under that delusion we fare no better than automatons, but when we live and move and have our being in Self, we can share the exultation of the Sufi who said:

* *An Idealist View of Life*, p. 279.

"I fare as one by whose majestic will
The world revolves, floods rise, rivers flow,
Stars in their courses move."

He can sing thus because his will coincides with the Divine will. When Mathew Arnold sings:

We, in some unknown Power's employ
Move on a rigorous line;
Can neither, when we will, enjoy
Nor when we will, resign;

he expresses one phase of the truth. We cannot enjoy and we cannot resign, because we want to do so when we should not. The Power knows better, and will not let us do what we should not. If we will but understand the Power we will not fret against the captivity but will sing with Newman:

So long Thy power hath blest me, sure it still
Will lead me on.

There is no freedom and no peace except in conforming our will to His will. When the *Gita* asks us to be mere instruments in His hand, it is not any outside master that we are asked to obey but the Master who is in us. We have the freedom of surrendering ourselves to the Worthiest of Masters, but we delight in pandering to unworthy ones. We pine for an unrestricted, undetermined free-will, which is but a will-o'-the-wisp, forgetting that

Our wills are ours, we know not how
Our wills are ours to make them Thine.

Seated in the heart of all He does see beings 'whirled, mounted on a machine', says the *Gita* (XVIII. 61) but we are also told: 'Go, and seek ye shelter' in Him, and by His grace not only shall you cease to be whirled, but rest in the Abode of Everlasting Peace' (XVIII. 62).

VII. Some Controversies

I fear I shall be charged with having tarried unnecessarily long over questions and controversies raised by

Western critics, and with having ignored those which have raged here. In the nature of the case, I could not ignore the former, for the readers of the book are likely to be familiar more with them than the latter. As regards these latter, it may be worth while noticing a few broad aspects here, only so far as they have a bearing on the teaching of the *Gita*. We need not go into the philosophical controversies of an earlier age which have little practical value today, but it is necessary to refer to the points at issue between Shankaracharya and Lokamanya Tilak. The Lokamanya entirely accepts the philosophical position of the great Acharya, but finds fault with him for placing an excessive emphasis on *jnana* and for having subtly but, in his opinion, unsuccessfully, argued away the necessity for action on the part of the man who has attained *jnana*. Now, though it is obvious that Shankaracharya over and over again attacks action as the root of bondage, it is Vedic ritualism that is the target of his attack and not all action as such, and he recognizes in so many words, often enough, that a *jnani's* activities, whatever they may be, will be all for the good of the world. The Lokamanya naturally impatient of the *soi-disant jnanis* of the present day, revelling in intellectual jugglery and shunning all action, unjustly attributes this philosophical lotus-eating to Shankaracharya's insistence on a man of knowledge refraining from action. The man of knowledge that Shankaracharya has in mind is the perfected man of self-realization and not the one who is the target of the Lokamanya's attack, and the activity, Shankaracharya taboos, is not *all* activity, but all self-ful activity, all activity that binds. Shankaracharya's own life of strenuous activity is an eloquent testimony to this. The two giants are thus at cross purposes and the whole controversy in the ultimate analysis would seem to be an unnecessary one. There is perhaps a difference between their conceptions of the perfected man or man-God, but it is after all a question of difference in temperaments due to the different ages in which they lived. But in spite of this difference I cannot conceive them differing as to the ultimate ideal that the *Gita* sets up before us.

Another controversy pertains to the efficacy of selfless action. The followers of Shankaracharya contend that even selfless action cannot lead to Freedom, it leads to self-purification only, and knowledge alone can lead to Freedom. The followers of the Tilak school contend, on the other hand, that selfless action leads directly to Freedom. Now this controversy is equally futile, inasmuch as one school has in mind the intermediate steps leading up to the final goal, the other thinks only of the final goal and omits the intermediate steps. An earnest aspirant will throw all the energies in the pursuit of the goal, absorbed in the means and not even thinking of the goal. And what after all is self-purification in the highest sense, but just the last step to, if not almost the same thing as, Knowledge and Freedom? The *Gita* asks us over and over again to be anchored in perfect purity. Let us see what it is. Eckhart has defined it in language which it is impossible to improve upon. 'What is purity?' he asks, and answers: 'It is that a man should have turned himself away from all creatures and have set his heart so entirely on the Pure Good that no creature is to him a comfort, that he has no desire for aught creaturely, save so far as he may apprehend therein the Pure Good which is God. And as little as the bright eye can endure aught foreign in it, so little can the pure soul bear anything in it, any stain on it, that comes between it and God.' The highest purity is thus abiding in God, oneness with God. When this is realized, it is the same thing whether you say that selfless action leads to self-purification or that selfless action leads to self-realization or Freedom.

VIII. Conclusion

I shall now conclude with a summary of the teaching of the *Gita* which stands out untouched by the dust and din of controversies. The *Gita* gives us a glimpse of Mt. Kailasa where Shiva dwells, keeps it ever before our vision even whilst we are trudging towards it, still leagues away in point of space and ages away in point of time, and declares in no uncertain terms that we have to scale the heights leading up to that highest peak where dwells the Lord of the Worlds, that we have not only to reach the peak but to realize that that really is our home whence we had fallen away and that the Lord occupying that pinnacled throne is none but the Lord in us — in a word that *Jiva* is *Shiva,* i. e. that the individual Self is the Universal Self. The *Gita* also every now and then gives us a glimpse of the souls who have scaled the heights and achieved the vision, who are "made one with Nature" — *brahmabhutah* (V. 24; XIV. 26; XVIII. 54); who like God Himself are seated 'as though indifferent, unattached to all they do' (IX. 9; XIV. 23); who work out the law of their being slumberless, even as the heavens themselves, who

> "Though so noble, share in the world's toil
> And though so tasked, keep free from dust and soil;"

who have so died to sin that "all battle of virtues" has ceased in them and who, therefore, however they live and move, live and move and have their being in Him (VI. 32). Some of these may not seem to work in our sense of the term, but their seeming inactivity will be the highest form of activity, as indeed their activity will be the purest form of repose. Their heart will throb with the heart of humanity, and their life will be lived in consonance with the great law.

> That does preserve the stars from wrong
> And the most ancient heavens through whom are fresh and strong.

Shall we presume to legislate for them? Even the *Gita* does not.

That is the ideal that we have to achieve and the *Gita* says in one word, 'if you would be one with God acquit yourselves like men.' Only by working out our destinies as men can we work up to Godhood and there is no other way. There is work that binds and work that frees. The moving finger writes and moves on inexorably, but it *can* cancel all it has written, if only one will surrender the finger to Him. As it is, the work that man is born and wedded to until his dying day is a leaden chain of bondage, but you can, says the *Gita,* transmute it into a golden ladder leading to Freedom, if only you will use the sovereign alchemy of selflessness, detachment, self-sacrifice. 'Knowledge,' says the *Gita,* 'makes ashes of all action, as the fire of the fuel.' But even as all fuel contains the fire within, all detached action contains the purifying and freedom-giving knowledge within. That is the law of dedicated activity or self-sacrifice and we must fulfil the Law, if we would reach the state that is beyond all law and legislation. "He who sacrifices himself, seeing the Self in all creation and all creation in the Self, attains *svarajya* (salvation)," says the *Manusmriti* * and that sums up the royal road of the *Gita.* That is the essential teaching of the *Gita,* and as such it has a universal appeal. All else that lends a local colour to the *Gita* is but a setting incidental to the time and place in which, and the person through whom, it took shape. All the rest of the things—karma and rebirth, and *varna* and even the belief in the Incarnation—are more or less like scaffolding to the edifice, unessentials after all. They do not touch the universal law, which has been practised in all ages and in all climes by those who, whether they believed or not in these unessentials, lived and moved in conformity with the essential law. To recount such a succession of names is, in the language of Prof. James, "to feel encouraged and washed in better air." The lives of the illustrious founders of the different faiths apart, what were the lives of those souls but lives of utter self-spending, self-effacement, self-dedication?—the lives of Job and Harishchandra; of Janaka and Marcus Aurelius, and Jalaluddin Rumi; of Plotinus and Epictetus; of St. Paul, St. Augustine and St. Ignatius; of Vidyaranya, of Shankaracharya and Eckhart; of St. Francis and St. Catherine of Siena, Sister Julian

* सर्वभूतेषु चात्मानं सर्वभूतानि चात्मनि।
समं पश्यन्नात्मयाजी स्वाराज्यमधिगच्छति।। १२-९१

and St. John of the Cross; of Chaitanya, Kabir and Tulsidas; of Jnaneshvar, Ramdas and Tukaram; of Mirabai and Andal; of Akho and Narasinha Mehta; of Spinoza and Lessing and Savonarola; of Pascal and Fenelon; of Bunyan, Wesley and Fox; of Howard and Pasteur and Madame Curie; of Father Damien and Cardinal Newman; of Lincoln, and General Gordon—not to mention the names of the living or of those of our own times.

The reader will not fail to notice that I have included in these names those of Lincoln, who directed one of the fiercest civil wars in history, and of Gordon whose hands may be said to be dripping with blood for the best part of his life, and of Pasteur much of whose work for humanity depended on his experiments involving vivisection. In doing so, I am not oblivious of Gandhiji's view that perfect renunciation or yoga is impossible without perfect observance of truth and non-violence. I have included these names because I cannot forget that if it can be said with truth of any one that he waged a war "with malice towards none, with charity for all, with firmness in the right as God gives us to see the right", it can be said of Lincoln, the whole of whose life was one of spotless self-dedication and whose every private or public individual action revealed a devotion to truth and non-violence; because in the transparent record of Gordon's life one can read the truth of his statement that he was "a chisel which cuts the wood; the carpenter directs it. If I lose the edge, He must sharpen me; if He puts me aside and takes another, it is His own good will;" because Pasteur's life was a pure flame of passionate service of humanity, even as the late M. Curie's was. "What would you say," some one might ask, "of Hitler who declares that 'by fighting against the Jews I am doing the Lord's work'?" Let us remember that he also makes no secret of the fact that he is prompted by nothing better than an implacable hatred of the Jews. Anyway, it is not for me to judge. History will judge him and many others in their proper time. That detachment is the only thing that can put life into action, is recognized by all. Even Asquith eulogizing Lloyd

George's devoted co-operation congratulated him on his "devotion, your (his) unselfishness, your (his) powers of resource, what is after all the best of all things, your (his) self-forgetfulness. These are the rare things that make the drudgery and squalor of politics, with its constant revelation of the large part played by petty and personal motives, endurable and gives to its drabness a lightening streak of nobility." But the automatic test of the purity and nobility of even that detachment is the dedication for an ideal, viz. service of God as embodied in the good of humanity. The yogin that the *Gita* regards as the ideal man is he "whose sins are wiped out, whose doubts are resolved, who has mastered himself and who is engrossed in the welfare of all beings" (V. 25).

Judged by this supreme test the names I have mentioned were, if not yogins, on the sure path of Yoga. Whilst some of them were pure mystics of devotion, some were men and women of action who were also mystics. The *Gita*'s unmistakable partiality for the man of action who is a mystic is to be seen in its repeated exhortation; "Be thou therefore a yogin" (VI. 46; VIII. 27 etc.); "Therefore at all times remember Me and fight on" (VIII. 7). "Whosoever would come after Me, let him renounce himself and take up his cross daily and follow Me," said Christ in a perfectly identical spirit. "The mystic who is also a man of action, and man of action because he is a mystic, wields a tremendous power," says Dean Inge. "He is like an invulnerable knight, fighting in magic armour." Wherever we may be placed, fight is the lot of each one of us; each one has to fight, as Arjuna was asked to do and as all these yogins fought, against the powers and principalities of darkness, within ourselves and without. The victory lies in fighting with the "magic armour" on; "Therefore, at all times remember Me and fight" (VIII. 7).

The yogins of all ages fought with the magic armour on, in a spirit of complete self-surrender, not in the interests of their narrow selves but in the interests of the Self of all mankind, and by so doing they left humanity purer, holier, nobler, stronger. They are the salt of the earth. They were called upon to play their parts on a vast stage; ours may be an infinitely narrower one, but the Master of the stage is the same. The area in which they moved was very large; ours may be very small, but the centre, round which we have to perform the divine dance, is the same. Each one of us has to sacrifice ourselves — our petty and narrow and circumscribing selves — in order to be one with the Self. We have to burn ourselves out with a heart and a will and a cheer each in his or her own sphere: our wicks may be ever so flimsy, our oil ever so poor, our flame ever so feeble, just enough to light our narrow paths, but ultimately our dim lights will blend right enough with the Universal Flame. All sacrifice, no matter how small or great, provided it is pure, reaches Him, ranks the same with Him, there is no last nor first.

NOTE ON THE TRANSLATION

I have tried to adhere as closely as possible to Gandhiji's translation of the text, but he is in no way responsible for the translation of numerous many-faceted and protean words like, for instance, *buddhi,* which in any Indian vernacular may be used in the original form in any context and yet may not be misunderstood whereas in English an equivalent word as near as possible to the sense intended in each context would be absolutely essential.

The Western reader will perhaps forgive my insistence on retaining in their original some of the strictly technical words. I have discussed them all in their several bearings in 'My Submission' and attempted to make them fairly familiar by suggesting various synonyms. These are: *Atman, Brahman, prakriti, guna, sattva, rajas, tamas,* (and their adjectives *sattvika, rajasa, tamasa*), yoga, yogin.

Then there are words like *jnana, yajna, bhakta, bhakti, tapas* which indeed have English equivalents but which mean very much more than their usual English equivalents. I have given these words in brackets along with their English equivalents, in order thereby to rivet attention of the reader on the fact that the original word is one carrying a deeper meaning. Where these words occur frequently in one context, the Sanskrit word is supplied just in the first instance.

The English vocabulary will be all the richer for these words, and as the text itself usually affords a full definition of them wherever they are treated at length, they do not put any strain on the memory of the reader.

Where, however, a protean word like yoga, for instance, is used in any sense other than the technical, I have given the appropriate English equivalent.

Krishna and Arjuna have numerous names and epithets. Some of these words are substantives whilst some are descriptive and attributive. The old commentators have not only traced even the substantival names to their supposed components, but have tried to make out that every name or epithet was chosen by the author to suit the context in which it occurs. Some of these attempted derivations are fanciful and the attempt to justify the choice in each context is often forced. It is obvious that in some cases at any rate the author had to consider the exigencies of the metre. The reader need not tax himself over the meanings of these words. For ready reference I collect here the various names (with their meanings wherever they are obvious and non-controversial) of Krishna and Arjuna :

Krishna

1. Achyuta (Unfailing)
2. Keshava
3. Govinda
4. Janardana
5. Madhusudana (Slayer of Madhu)
6. Arisudana (Slayer of foes)
7. Keshinisudana (Slayer of Keshin)
8. Madhava
9. Purushottama (Supreme Being)
10. Vasudeva (Son of Vasudeva, All-pervading)
11. Vishnu (All-pervading)
12. Hari
13. Varshneya (Descendent of Vrishni)
14. Yadava („ „ Yadu)

Arjuna

1. Kaunteya (Son of Kunti)
2. Pandava (Son of Pandu)
3. Partha (Son of Pritha or Kunti)
4. Bharata (Descendent of Bharata)
5. Gudakesha
6. Dhananjaya
7. Kurunandana (Scion of Kurus)
8. Kurushreshtha (Best of Kurus)
9. Kurusattama („)
10. Bharatarshabha (Best of Bharatas)
11. Bharatashreshtha („)
12. Bharatasattama („)
13. Parantapa (Tormentor of foes)

All these I have retained in the original, but the numerous attributive or descriptive titles I have translated. One exception I have deliberately made. In the 11th discourse I have retained even the obviously descriptive titles in the original (giving their meanings in the notes), not to break the rhythm (even in prose) of that most musical of all discourses. Mahabahu (strong-armed one), frequently used by Krishna in addressing Arjuna, and once or twice by Arjuna in addressing Krishna, I have retained in its Sanskrit form.

In some cases — I hope very few — words have been added in brackets to complete or improve the English structure of the sentences.

ANASAKTIYOGA

THE MESSAGE OF THE GITA

[It was at Kosani in Almora on 24th June, 1929, i.e. after two years' waiting, that I finished the introduction in Gujarati to my translation of the *Gita*. The whole was then published in due course. It has been translated in Hindi, Bengali and Marathi. There has been an insistent demand for an English translation. I finished the translation of the introduction at the Yeravda prison. Since my discharge it has lain with friends, and now I give it to the reader. Those, who take no interest in the Book of Life, will forgive the trespass on these columns.* To those who are interested in the poem and treat it as their guide in life, my humble attempt might prove of some help. — M. K. G.]

I

Just as, acted upon by the affection of co-workers like Swami Anand and others, I wrote *My Experiments with Truth*, so has it been regarding my rendering of the *Gita*. " We shall be able to appreciate your meaning of the message of the *Gita*, only when we are able to study a translation of the whole text by yourself, with the addition of such notes as you may deem necessary. I do not think it is just on your part to deduce *ahimsa* etc. from stray verses," thus spoke Swami Anand to me during the non-co-operation days. I felt the force of his remarks. I, therefore, told him that I would adopt his suggestion when I got the time. Shortly afterwards I was imprisoned. During my incarceration I was able to study the *Gita*

* This translation appeared in the columns of the *Young India*, 6-8-1931, from where it has been reproduced here.

more fully. I went reverently through the Gujarati translation of the Lokamanya's great work. He had kindly presented me with the Marathi original and the translations in Gujarati and Hindi, and had asked me, if I could not tackle the original, at least to go through the Gujarati translation. I had not been able to follow the advice outside the prison walls. But when I was imprisoned I read the Gujarati translation. This reading whetted my appetite for more and I glanced through several works on the *Gita*.

2. My first acquaintance with the *Gita* began in 1888-89 with the verse translation by Sir Edwin Arnold known as the *Song Celestial*. On reading it I felt a keen desire to read a Gujarati translation. And I read as many translations as I could lay hold of. But all such reading can give me no passport for presenting my own translation. Then again my knowledge of Sanskrit is limited; my knowledge of Gujarati too is in no way scholarly. How could I then dare present the public with my translation?

3. It has been my endeavour, as also that of some companions, to reduce to practice the teaching of the *Gita* as I have understood it. The *Gita* has become for us a spiritual reference book. I am aware that we ever fail to act in perfect accord with the teaching. The failure is not due to want of effort, but is in spite of it. Even through the failures we seem to see rays of hope. The accompanying rendering contains the meaning of the *Gita* message which this little band is trying to enforce in its daily conduct.

4. Again this rendering is designed for women, the commercial class, the so-called Shudras and the like, who have little or no literary equipment, who have neither the time nor the desire to read the *Gita* in the original, and yet who stand in need of its support. In spite of my Gujarati being unscholarly, I must own to having the desire to leave to the Gujaratis, through the mother tongue, whatever knowledge I may possess. I do indeed wish that, at a time when literary output of a questionable character

is pouring in upon the Gujaratis, they should have before them a rendering the majority can understand of a book that is regarded as unrivalled for its spiritual merit and so withstand the overwhelming flood of unclean literature.

5. This desire does not mean any disrespect to the other renderings. They have their own place. But I am not aware of the claim made by the translators of enforcing their meaning of the *Gita* in their own lives. At the back of my reading there is the claim of an endeavour to enforce the meaning in my own conduct for an unbroken period of forty years. For this reason I do indeed harbour the wish that all Gujarati men or women, wishing to shape their conduct according to their faith, should digest and derive strength from the translation here presented.

6. My co-workers, too, have worked at this translation. My knowledge of Sanskrit being very limited, I should not have full confidence in my literal translation. To that extent, therefore, the translation has passed before the eyes of Vinoba, Kaka Kalelkar, Mahadev Desai and Kishorlal Mashruwala.

II

7. Now about the message of the *Gita*.

8. Even in 1888-89, when I first became acquainted with the *Gita*, I felt that it was not a historical work, but that, under the guise of physical warfare, it described the duel that perpetually went on in the hearts of mankind, and that physical warfare was brought in merely to make the description of the internal duel more alluring. This preliminary intuition became more confirmed on a closer study of religion and the *Gita*. A study of the *Mahabharata* gave it added confirmation. I do not regard the *Mahabharata* as a historical work in the accepted sense. The *Adiparva* contains powerful evidence in support of my opinion. By ascribing to the chief actors superhuman or subhuman origins, the great Vyasa made short work

of the history of kings and their peoples. The persons therein described may be historical, but the author of the *Mahabharata* has used them merely to drive home his religious theme.

9. The author of the *Mahabharata* has not established the necessity of physical warfare ; on the contrary he has proved its futility. He has made the victors shed tears of sorrow and repentance, and has left them nothing but a legacy of miseries.

10. In this great work the *Gita* is the crown. Its second chapter, instead of teaching the rules of physical warfare, tells us how a perfected man is to be known. In the characteristics of the perfected man of the *Gita*, I do not see any to correspond to physical warfare. Its whole design is inconsistent with the rules of conduct governing the relations between warring parties.

11. Krishna of the *Gita* is perfection and right knowledge personified ; but the picture is imaginary. That does not mean that Krishna, the adored of his people, never lived. But perfection is imagined. The idea of a perfect incarnation is an aftergrowth.

12. In Hinduism, incarnation is ascribed to one who has performed some extraordinary service of mankind. All embodied life is in reality an incarnation of God, but it is not usual to consider every living being an incarnation. Future generations pay this homage to one who, in his own generation, has been extraordinarily religious in his conduct. I can see nothing wrong in this procedure ; it takes nothing from God's greatness, and there is no violence done to Truth. There is an Urdu saying which means, " Adam is not God but he is a spark of the Divine." And therefore he who is the most religiously behaved has most of the divine spark in him. It is in accordance with this train of thought, that Krishna enjoys, in Hinduism, the status of the most perfect incarnation.

13. This belief in incarnation is a testimony of man's lofty spiritual ambition. Man is not at peace with

himself till he has become like unto God. The endeavour to reach this state is the supreme, the only ambition worth having. And this is self-realization. This self-realization is the subject of the *Gita*, as it is of all scriptures. But its author surely did not write it to establish that doctrine. The object of the *Gita* appears to me to be that of showing the most excellent way to attain self-realization. That which is to be found, more or less clearly, spread out here and there in Hindu religious books, has been brought out in the clearest possible language in the *Gita* even at the risk of repetition.

14. *That matchless remedy is renunciation of fruits of action.*

15. This is the centre round which the *Gita* is woven. This renunciation is the central sun, round which devotion, knowledge and the rest revolve like planets. The body has been likened to a prison. There must be action where there is body. Not one embodied being is exempted from labour. And yet all religions proclaim that it is possible for man, by treating the body as the temple of God, to attain freedom. Every action is tainted, be it ever so trivial. How can the body be made the temple of God ? In other words how can one be free from action, i.e. from the taint of sin ? The *Gita* has answered the question in decisive language : " By desireless action ; by renouncing fruits of action ; by dedicating all activities to God, i.e., by surrendering oneself to Him body and soul."

16. But desirelessness or renunciation does not come for the mere talking about it. It is not attained by an intellectual feat. It is attainable only by a constant heart-churn. Right knowledge is necessary for attaining renunciation. Learned men possess a knowledge of a kind. They may recite the *Vedas* from memory, yet they may be steeped in self-indulgence. In order that knowledge may not run riot, the author of the *Gita* has insisted on devotion accompanying it and has given it the first place. Knowledge without devotion will be like a misfire. Therefore, says the *Gita*, " Have devotion, and knowledge will follow." This devotion is not mere lip worship, it is a wrestling

with death. Hence the *Gita's* assessment of the devotee's qualities is similar to that of the sage's.

17. Thus the devotion required by the *Gita* is no soft-hearted effusiveness. It certainly is not blind faith. The devotion of the *Gita* has the least to do with externals. A devotee may use, if he likes, rosaries, forehead marks, make offerings, but these things are no test of his devotion. He is the devotee who is jealous of none, who is a fount of mercy, who is without egotism, who is selfless, who treats alike cold and heat, happiness and misery, who is ever forgiving, who is always contented, whose resolutions are firm, who has dedicated mind and soul to God, who causes no dread, who is not afraid of others, who is free from exultation, sorrow and fear, who is pure, who is versed in action and yet remains unaffected by it, who renounces all fruit, good or bad, who treats friend and foe alike, who is untouched by respect or disrespect, who is not puffed up by praise, who does not go under when people speak ill of him, who loves silence and solitude, who has a disciplined reason. Such devotion is inconsistent with the existence at the same time of strong attachments.

18. We thus see that to be a real devotee is to realize oneself. Self-realization is not something apart. One rupee can purchase for us poison or nectar, but knowledge or devotion cannot buy us either salvation or bondage. These are not media of exchange. They are themselves the thing we want. In other words, if the means and the end are not identical, they are almost so. The extreme of means is salvation. Salvation of the *Gita* is perfect peace.

19. But such knowledge and devotion, to be true, have to stand the test of renunciation of fruits of action. Mere knowledge of right and wrong will not make one fit for salvation. According to common notions, a mere learned man will pass as a *pandit*. He need not perform any service. He will regard it as bondage even to lift a little *lota*. Where one test of knowledge is non-liability for

service, there is no room for such mundane work as the lifting of a *lota*.

20. Or take *bhakti*. The popular notion of *bhakti* is soft-heartedness, telling beads and the like, and disdaining to do even a loving service, lest the telling of beads etc. might be interrupted. This *bhakti*, therefore, leaves the rosary only for eating, drinking and the like, never for grinding corn or nursing patients.

21. But the *Gita* says: 'No one has attained his goal without action. Even men like Janaka attained salvation through action. If even I were lazily to cease working, the world would perish. How much more necessary then for the people at large to engage in action?'

22. While on the one hand it is beyond dispute that all action binds, on the other hand it is equally true that all living beings have to do some work, whether they will or no. Here all activity, whether mental or physical, is to be included in the term of action. Then how is one to be free from the bondage of action, even though he may be acting? The manner in which the *Gita* has solved the problem is to my knowledge unique. The *Gita* says: 'Do your allotted work but renounce its fruit — be detached and work — have no desire for reward and work.'

This is the unmistakable teaching of the *Gita*. He who gives up action falls. He who gives up only the reward rises. But renunciation of fruit in no way means indifference to the result. In regard to every action one must know the result that is expected to follow, the means thereto, and the capacity for it. He, who, being thus equipped, is without desire for the result and is yet wholly engrossed in the due fulfilment of the task before him is said to have renounced the fruits of his action.

23. Again let no one consider renunciation to mean want of fruit for the renouncer. The *Gita* reading does not warrant such a meaning. Renunciation means absence of hankering after fruit. As a matter of fact, he who renounces reaps a thousandfold. The renunciation of the *Gita* is the acid test of faith. He who is ever brooding

over result often loses nerve in the performance of his duty. He becomes impatient and then gives vent to anger and begins to do unworthy things ; he jumps from action to action never remaining faithful to any. He who broods over results is like a man given to objects of senses ; he is ever distracted, he says goodbye to all scruples, everything is right in his estimation and he therefore resorts to means fair and foul to attain his end.

24. From the bitter experiences of desire for fruit the author of the *Gita* discovered the path of renunciation of fruit and put it before the world in a most convincing manner. The common belief is that religion is always opposed to material good. " One cannot act religiously in mercantile and such other matters. There is no place for religion in such pursuits ; religion is only for attainment of salvation," we hear many worldly-wise people say. In my opinion the author of the *Gita* has dispelled this delusion. He has drawn no line of demarcation between salvation and worldly pursuits. On the contrary he has shown that religion must rule even our worldly pursuits. I have felt that the *Gita* teaches us that what cannot be followed out in day-to-day practice cannot be called religion. Thus, according to the *Gita*, all acts that are incapable of being performed without attachment are taboo. This golden rule saves mankind from many a pitfall. According to this interpretation murder, lying, dissoluteness and the like must be regarded as sinful and therefore taboo. Man's life then becomes simple, and from that simpleness springs peace.

25. Thinking along these lines, I have felt that in trying to enforce in one's life the central teaching of the *Gita*, one is bound to follow Truth and *ahimsa*. When there is no desire for fruit, there is no temptation for untruth or *himsa*. Take any instance of untruth or violence, and it will be found that at its back was the desire to attain the cherished end. But it may be freely admitted that the *Gita* was not written to establish *ahimsa*. It was an accepted and primary duty even before the *Gita* age. The *Gita* had to deliver the message

of renunciation of fruit. This is clearly brought out as early as the second chapter.

26. But if the *Gita* believed in *ahimsa* or it was included in desirelessness, why did the author take a warlike illustration ? When the *Gita* was written, although people believed in *ahimsa*, wars were not only not taboo, but nobody observed the contradiction between them and *ahimsa*.

27. In assessing the implications of renunciation of fruit, we are not required to probe the mind of the author of the *Gita* as to his limitations of *ahimsa* and the like. Because a poet puts a particular truth before the world, it does not necessarily follow that he has known or worked out all its great consequences, or that having done so, he is able always to express them fully. In this perhaps lies the greatness of the poem and the poet. A poet's meaning is limitless. Like man, the meaning of great writings suffers evolution. On examining the history of languages, we notice that the meaning of important words has changed or expanded. This is true of the *Gita*. The author has himself extended the meanings of some of the current words. We are able to discover this even on a superficial examination. It is possible that, in the age prior to that of the *Gita*, offering of animals as sacrifice was permissible. But there is not a trace of it in the sacrifice in the *Gita* sense. In the *Gita* continuous concentration on God is the king of sacrifices. The third chapter seems to show that sacrifice chiefly means body-labour for service. The third and the fourth chapters read together will give us other meanings for sacrifice, but never animal-sacrifice. Similarly has the meaning of the word *sannyasa* undergone, in the *Gita*, a transformation. The *sannyasa* of the *Gita* will not tolerate complete cessation of all activity. The *sannyasa* of the *Gita* is all work and yet no work. Thus the author of the *Gita*, by extending meanings of words, has taught us to imitate him. Let it be granted, that according to the letter of the *Gita* it is possible to say that warfare is consistent with renunciation of fruit. But after forty years' unremitting endeavour fully to enforce the

teaching of the *Gita* in my own life, I have, in all humility, felt that perfect renunciation is impossible without perfect observance of *ahimsa* in every shape and form.

28. The *Gita* is not an aphoristic work ; it is a great religious poem. The deeper you dive into it, the richer the meanings you get. It being meant for the people at large, there is pleasing repetition. With every age the important words will carry new and expanding meanings. But its central teaching will never vary. The seeker is at liberty to extract from this treasure any meaning he likes so as to enable him to enforce in his life the central teaching.

29. Nor is the *Gita* a collection of Do's and Dont's. What is lawful for one may be unlawful for another. What may be permissible at one time, or in one place, may not be so at another time, and in another place. Desire for fruit is the only universal prohibition. Desirelessness is obligatory.

30. The *Gita* has sung the praises of Knowledge, but it is beyond the mere intellect ; it is essentially addressed to the heart and capable of being understood by the heart. Therefore the *Gita* is not for those who have no faith. The author makes Krishna say :

"Do not entrust this treasure to him who is without sacrifice, without devotion, without the desire for this teaching and who denies Me. On the other hand, those who will give this precious treasure to My devotees will, by the fact of this service, assuredly reach Me. And those who, being free from malice, will with faith absorb this teaching, shall, having attained freedom, live where people of true merit go after death."

DISCOURSE I

No knowledge is to be found without seeking, no tranquillity without travail, no happiness except through tribulation. Every seeker has, at one time or another, to pass through a conflict of duties, a heart-churning.

धृतराष्ट्र उवाच ।

धर्मक्षेत्रे कुरुक्षेत्रे समवेता युयुत्सवः ।
मामकाः पांडवाश्चैव किमकुर्वत संजय ॥ १ ॥

Dhritarashtra said :

1. Tell me, O Sanjaya, what my sons and Pandu's assembled, on battle intent, did on the field of Kuru, the field of duty.

The human body is the battlefield where the eternal duel between Right and Wrong goes on. Therefore it is capable of being turned into the gateway to Freedom. It is born in sin and becomes the seed-bed of sin. Hence it is also called the field of Kuru. The Kauravas represent the forces of Evil, the Pandavas the forces of Good. Who is there that has not experienced the daily conflict within himself between the forces of Evil and the forces of Good ?

[Kurukshetra (the field of Kuru) is a vast field near modern Delhi, the ancient Hastinapura, the scene of war between the Kauravas and the Pandavas. Kuru, the ancestor of both branches of the family lived here and gave the name to the land which is supposed to have been tilled by him. *Kshetra* means both : a field and a sphere of action or a sacred spot. A text of the *Shatapatha Brahmana* shows that this field had been held sacred from earliest times and was a place where sacrifices were offered. It is also described in the Mahabharata as *tapah-kshetra* i. e. a field dedicated for the performance of austerities. About Dhritarashtra and Sanjaya, see 'My Submission,' p. 10-11.

Kauravas — sons of Kuru — would include the Pandavas — sons of Pandu, Kuru being the common ancestor of both, but generally the term 'Kauravas' is applied to Dhritarashtra's sons. Dhritarashtra had many sons, Duryodhana being the eldest. Pandu had five sons, of whom Arjuna was the most distinguished. Arjuna, however, is often addressed by Krishna as *Kurunandana* (son of Kuru), *Kurusattama* (best of Kurus), *Kurupravira* (hero among Kurus).

"The Gita," Gandhiji has said in another connection, "is not a historical discourse. A physical illustration is often needed to drive home a spiritual truth. It is the description not of war between cousins but between the two natures in us — the Good and the Evil." Also: "I regard Duryodhana and his party as the baser impulses in man, and Arjuna and his party as the higher impulses. The field of battle is our own body. An eternal battle is going on between the two camps, and the Poet-seer vividly describes it. Krishna is the Dweller within, ever whispering to a pure heart."]

संजय अुवाच ।

दृष्ट्वा तु पांडवानीकं व्यूढं दुर्योधनस्तदा ।
आचार्यमुपसंगम्य राजा वचनमब्रवीत् ।। २ ।।

Sanjaya said:

2. On seeing the Pandavas' army drawn up in battle array, King Duryodhana approached Drona, the preceptor, and addressed him thus:

[Duryodhana, the eldest son of the blind king Dhritarashtra, was king during the exile of the Pandavas, who on return asked for the restoration of their portion of the kingdom in accordance with the original agreement. Duryodhana's refusal, and the failure of efforts of all concerned towards reconciliation, forced war on the Pandavas.]

पश्यैतां पांडुपुत्राणाम् आचार्य महतीं चमूम् ।
व्यूढां द्रुपदपुत्रेण तव शिष्येण धीमता ॥ ३ ॥

3. Behold, O preceptor, this mighty army of the sons of Pandu, set in array by the son of Drupada, thy wise disciple.

[Drona, though a *Brahmana,* was the preceptor of both the Kauravas and the Pandavas. He taught them the art of warfare, especially archery. Drupada was the father of Draupadi and the father-in-law of the Pandavas. Dhrishtadyumna, his son, was the commander-in-chief of the Pandavas' hosts.]

अत्र शूरा महेष्वासा भीमार्जुनसमा युधि ।
युयुधानो विराटश्च द्रुपदश्च महारथः ॥ ४ ॥

4. Here are brave bowmen, peers of Bhima and Arjuna in fighting: Yuyudhana and Virata, and the 'Maharatha' Drupada.

[Virata was the king of the Matsyas, who gave refuge to the Pandavas during the period of their exile in disguise. 'Maharatha' is the highest military title given to one who is capable of engaging in single combat ten thousand bowmen.]

धृष्टकेतुश्चेकितानः काशिराजश्च वीर्यवान् ।
पुरुजित् कुन्तिभोजश्च शैब्यश्च नरपुंगवः ॥ ५ ॥

5. Dhrishtaketu, Chekitana, valorous Kashiraja, Purujit the Kuntibhoja, and Shaibya, chief among men;

[Dhrishtaketu was king of the Chedis. Kuntibhoja was the family name of Purujit who had adopted Kunti, the mother of the three Pandavas — Yudhishthira, Bhima and

Arjuna. Shaibya was the chief of the Shibi tribe and king of the country of the same name.]

युधामन्युश्च विक्रान्त अुत्तमौजाश्च वीर्यवान् ।
सौभद्रो द्रौपदेयाश्च सर्वे अेव महारथाः ॥ ६ ॥

6. Valiant Yudhamanyu, valorous Uttamaujas, Subhadra's son, and the sons of Draupadi — each one of them a 'Maharatha'.

[Yudhamanyu and Uttamaujas were chieftain allies of the Pandavas. Subhadra, Arjuna's second wife, had a son called Abhimanyu. Draupadi had a son by each of the five Pandavas.]

अस्माकं तु विशिष्टा ये तान् निबोध द्विजोत्तम ।
नायका मम सैन्यस्य संज्ञार्थं तान् ब्रवीमि ते ॥ ७ ॥

7. Acquaint thyself now, O best of Brahmanas, with the distinguished among us. I mention, for thy information, the names of the captains of my army.

भवान् भीष्मश्च कर्णश्च कृपश्च समितिंजयः ।
अश्वत्थामा विकर्णश्च सौमदत्तिस्तथैव च ॥ ८ ॥

8. Thy noble self, Bhishma, Karna, and Kripa, victorious in battle, Ashvatthaman, Vikarna, also Somadatta's son;

[Bhishma (lit. terrible), pledged to the terrible vow of lifelong celibacy, brought up his step-brother's sons and their sons, the Pandavas and the Kauravas. He was thus their grandsire. Karna was Kunti's son, born to her before marriage, and thus the step-brother of the three Pandavas, Yudhishthira, Bhima and Arjuna. He belonged to the opposite camp. Kripa was the brother-in-law of Drona, and Ashvatthaman was Drona's son. Vikarna was one of

Duryodhana's brothers. Somadatta was the king of the Bahikas.

All these names are mentioned to show not only that it was fratricidal war but that it was an all-India war, all parts from the north of the Narmada to the frontier of the Punjab having sent their kings and armies to fight to either side.]

अन्ये च बहवः शूरा मदर्थे त्यक्तजीविताः ।
नानाशस्त्रप्रहरणाः सर्वे युद्धविशारदाः ।। ९ ।।

9. There is many another hero, known for his skill in wielding diverse weapons, pledged to lay down his life for my sake, and all adepts in war.

अपर्याप्तं तदस्माकं बलं भीष्माभिरक्षितम् ।
पर्याप्तं त्विदमेतेषां बलं भीमाभिरक्षितम् ।। १० ।।

10. This our force, commanded by Bhishma, is all too inadequate; while theirs, commanded by Bhima, is quite adequate.

[*Aparyaptam* and *paryaptam,* translated by Gandhiji to mean 'inadequate' and 'adequate' respectively, are translated by others to mean the reverse. The reverse sense, too, is possible and perhaps more in consonance with the fact that the Kauravas' forces were vastly superior to the Pandavas'. But this interpretation gives a boastful tone to Duryodhana's utterance, which is not in keeping with the warning in the next *shloka* to every one to guard Bhishma. The point is not, however, worth a controversy, and any sense may be taken.]

अयनेषु च सर्वेषु यथाभागमवस्थिताः ।
भीष्ममेवाभिरक्षन्तु भवन्तः सर्व अेव हि ।। ११ ।।

11. Therefore, let each of you, holding your appointed places, at every entrance, guard only Bhishma.

तस्य संजनयन् हर्षं कुरुवृद्धः पितामहः ।
सिंहनादं विनद्योच्चैः शंखं दध्मौ प्रतापवान् ।। १२ ।।

12. At this, the heroic grandsire, the grand old man of the Kurus, gave a loud lion's roar and blew his conch to hearten Duryodhana.

ततः शंखाश्च भेर्यश्च पणवानकगोमुखाः ।
सहसैवाभ्यहन्यन्त स शब्दस्तुमुलोऽभवत् ।। १३ ।।

13. Thereupon, conches, drums, cymbals and trumpets were sounded all at once. Terrific was the noise.

ततः श्वेतैर्हयैर्युक्ते महति स्यन्दने स्थितौ ।
माधवः पांडवश्चैव दिव्यौ शंखौ प्रदध्मतुः ।। १४ ।।

14. Then Madhava and Pandava, standing in their great chariot yoked with white steeds, blew their divine conches.

पांचजन्यं हृषीकेशो देवदत्तं धनंजयः ।
पौण्ड्रं दध्मौ महाशंखं भीमकर्मा वृकोदरः ।। १५ ।।
अनंतविजयं राजा कुन्तीपुत्रो युधिष्ठिरः ।
नकुलः सहदेवश्च सुघोषमणिपुष्पकौ ।। १६ ।।

15. Hrishikesha blew the Panchajanya and Dhananjaya the Devadatta ; while the wolf-bellied Bhima of dread deeds sounded his great conch Paundra.

16. King Yudhishthira, Kunti's son, blew the Anantavijaya, and Nakula and Sahadeva their conches, Sughosha and Manipushpaka.

[15-16. The Pandavas are (1) Yudhishthira (2) Bhima and (3) Arjuna, all sons of Kunti, the first wife of Pandu ;

(4) Nakula and (5) Sahadeva, sons of Madri, the second wife of Pandu.]

काश्यश्च परमेष्वासः शिखंडी च महारथः ।
धृष्टद्युम्नो विराटश्च सात्यकिश्चापराजितः ।। १७ ।।

17. And Kashiraja, the great bowman, Shikhandi the 'Maharatha', Dhrishtadyumna, Virata and Satyaki, the unconquerable;

द्रुपदो द्रौपदेयाश्च सर्वशः पृथिवीपते ।
सौभद्रश्च महाबाहुः शंखान् दध्मुः पृथक् पृथक् ।।१८।।

18. Drupada, Draupadi's sons, and the strong-armed son of Subhadra, all these, O King, blew each his own conch.

स घोषो धार्तराष्ट्राणां हृदयानि व्यदारयत् ।
नभश्च पृथिवीं चैव तुमुलो व्यनुनादयन् ।। १९ ।।

19. That terrifying tumult, causing earth and heaven to resound, rent the hearts of Dhritarashtra's sons.

अथ व्यवस्थितान् दृष्ट्वा धार्तराष्ट्रान् कपिध्वजः ।
प्रवृत्ते शस्त्रसंपाते धनुरुद्यम्य पांडवः ।। २० ।।
हृषीकेशं तदा वाक्यम् अिदमाह महीपते ।
सेनयोरुभयोर्मध्ये रथं स्थापय मेऽच्युत ।। २१ ।।

20-21. Then, O King, the ape-bannered Pandava, seeing Dhritarashtra's sons arrayed and flight of arrows about to begin, took up his bow, and spoke thus to Hrishikesha: "Set my chariot between the two armies, O Achyuta!"

[Arjuna's banner bore the figure of Hanuman, the monkey-devotee, an embodiment of dedicated service, purity, and valour.]

यावदेतान् निरीक्षेऽहं योद्धुकामानवस्थितान् ।
कैर्मया सह योद्धव्यम् अस्मिन् रणसमुद्यमे ।। २२ ।।

22. That I may behold them drawn up, on battle intent, and know whom I have to engage in this fearful combat ;

योत्स्यमानानवेक्षेऽहं य अेतेऽत्र समागताः ।
धार्तराष्ट्रस्य दुर्बुद्धेः युद्धे प्रियचिकीर्षवः ।। २३ ।।

23. And that I may survey the fighters assembled here anxious to fulfil in battle perverse Duryodhana's desire.

संजय अुवाच ।

एवमुक्तो हृषीकेशो गुडाकेशेन भारत ।
सेनयोरुभयोर्मध्ये स्थापयित्वा रथोत्तमम् ।। २४ ।।
भीष्मद्रोणप्रमुखतः सर्वेषां च महीक्षिताम् ।
अुवाच पार्थ पश्यैतान् समवेतान् कुरूनिति ।। २५ ।।

Sanjaya said :

24-25. Thus addressed by Gudakesha, O King, Hrishikesha set the unique chariot between the two armies, in front of Bhishma, Drona and all the kings and said : Behold, O Partha, the Kurus assembled yonder.

[Gudakesha is Arjuna. Hrishikesha is Krishna. For the different names of Arjuna and Krishna see 'My Submission', pp. 123-24.]

तत्रापश्यत् स्थितान् पार्थः पितॄनथ पितामहान् ।
आचार्यान् मातुलान् भ्रातॄन् पुत्रान् पौत्रान् सखींस्तथा ।।२६।।
श्वशुरान् सुहृदश्चैव सेनयोरुभयोरपि ।
तान् समीक्ष्य स कौन्तेयः सर्वान् बन्धूनवस्थितान् ।।२७।।
कृपया परयाऽऽविष्टो विषीदन् अिदमब्रवीत् ।

26-28. Then did Partha see, standing there, sires, grandsires, preceptors, uncles, brothers, sons, grandsons, comrades, fathers-in-law and friends in both armies. Beholding all these kinsmen ranged before him, Kaunteya was overcome with great compassion and spake thus in anguish :

अर्जुन उवाच ।

दृष्ट्वेमं स्वजनं कृष्ण युयुत्सुं समुपस्थितम् ।। २८ ।।
सीदन्ति मम गात्राणि मुखं च परिशुष्यति ।
वेपथुश्च शरीरे मे रोमहर्षश्च जायते ।। २९ ।।

Arjuna said :

28-29. As I look upon these kinsmen, O Krishna, assembled here eager to fight, my limbs fail, my mouth is parched, a tremor shakes my frame and my hair stands on end.

गांडीवं स्रंसते हस्तात् त्वक् चैव परिदह्यते ।
न च शक्नोम्यवस्थातुं भ्रमतीव च मे मनः ।। ३० ।।

30. Gandiva slips from my hand, my skin is on fire, I cannot keep my feet, and my mind reels.

[Gandiva was the name of Arjuna's bow which was a gift to him from Indra.]

निमित्तानि च पश्यामि विपरीतानि केशव ।
न च श्रेयोऽनुपश्यामि हत्वा स्वजनमाहवे ।। ३१ ।।

31. I have unhappy forebodings, O Keshava ; and I see no good in slaying kinsmen in battle.

न कांक्षे विजयं कृष्ण न च राज्यं सुखानि च ।
किं नो राज्येन गोविंद किं भोगैर्जीवितेन वा ।। ३२ ।।

32. I seek not victory, nor sovereign power, nor earthly joys. What good are sovereign power, worldly pleasures and even life to us, O Govinda ?

येषामर्थे कांक्षितं नो राज्यं भोगाः सुखानि च ।
त इमेऽवस्थिता युद्धे प्राणांस्त्यक्त्वा धनानि च ।।३३।।

33. Those for whom we would desire sovereign power, earthly joys and delights are here arrayed in battle, having renounced life and wealth —

आचार्याः पितरः पुत्राः तथैव च पितामहाः ।
मातुलाः श्वशुराः पौत्राः श्यालाः संबंधिनस्तथा ।।३४।।

34. Preceptors, sires, grandsires, sons and even grandsons, uncles, fathers-in-law, brothers-in-law, and other kinsmen.

अेतान् न हन्तुमिच्छामि घ्नतोऽपि मधुसूदन ।
अपि त्रैलोक्यराज्यस्य हेतोः किं नु महीकृते ।। ३५ ।।

35. These I would not kill, O Madhusudana, even though they slay me, not even for kingship of the three worlds, much less for an earthly kingdom.

[The three worlds are supposed to be earth, heaven and the nether regions ; they are also said to denote the world of men, the world of semi-divine beings, and the world of divine beings.]

निहत्य धार्तराष्ट्रान् नः का प्रीतिः स्याज्जनार्दन ।
पापमेवाश्रयेदस्मान् हत्वैतानाततायिनः ।। ३६ ।।

36. What pleasure can there be in slaying these sons of Dhritarashtra, O Janardana ? Sin only can be our lot, if we slay these, usurpers though they be.

[*Atatayinah* are those who have been guilty of heinous crimes, viz: incendiaries, poisoners, assassins, robbers, usurpers of land, and ravishers. Here the Kauravas are described as *atatayinah* because they are usurpers.]

तस्मान् नार्हा वयं हन्तुं धार्तराष्ट्रान् स्वबान्धवान् ।
स्वजनं हि कथं हत्वा सुखिनः स्याम माधव ।। ३७ ।।

37. It does not therefore behove us to kill our kinsmen, these sons of Dhritarashtra. How may we be happy, O Madhava, in killing our own kins ?

यद्यप्येते न पश्यन्ति लोभोपहतचेतसः ।
कुलक्षयकृतं दोषं मित्रद्रोहे च पातकम् ।। ३८ ।।

38. Even though these, their wits warped by greed, see not the guilt that lies in destroying the family, nor the sin of treachery to comrades ;

कथं न ज्ञेयमस्माभिः पापादस्मान् निवर्तितुम् ।
कुलक्षयकृतं दोषं प्रपश्यद्भिर्जनार्दन ।। ३९ ।।

39. How can we, O Janardana, help recoiling from this sin, seeing clearly as we do the guilt that lies in such destruction ?

[It is not destruction of 'a family' or 'families' but it is the destruction of the institution of the family, as a result of fratricidal war that Arjuna deplores. "Physically, psychically, ethically, the family is the masterpiece of evolution," says Henry Drummond. "It is the generator and the repository of the forces which alone can carry out the moral and social progress of the world....Nature has produced a holy family. Not for centuries but for millenniums the family has survived. Time has not tarnished it, no later art has improved upon it ; no genius discovered any thing more lovely, nor religion any thing more divine."

To the author of the Gita the family evidently stood for all this.]

कुलक्षये प्रणश्यन्ति कुलधर्माः सनातनाः ।
धर्मे नष्टे कुलं कृत्स्नम् अधर्मोऽभिभवत्युत ।। ४० ।।

40. With the destruction of the family perish the eternal family virtues, and with the perishing of these virtues unrighteousness seizes the whole family.

अधर्माभिभवात् कृष्ण प्रदुष्यन्ति कुलस्त्रियः ।
स्त्रीषु दुष्टासु वार्ष्णेय जायते वर्णसंकरः ।। ४१ ।।

41. When unrighteousness prevails, O Krishna, the women of the family become corrupt, and their corruption, O Varshneya, causes a confusion of *varnas*.

[For *varnas*, see 'My Submission', p. 102.]

संकरो नरकायैव कुलघ्नानां कुलस्य च ।
पतन्ति पितरो ह्येषां लुप्तपिंडोदकक्रियाः ।। ४२ ।।

42. This confusion verily drags the family-slayer, as well as the family, to hell, and for want of obsequial offerings and rites their departed sires fall from blessedness.

[The author refers in this *shloka* to the *shraddha* rite which consisted in offering balls of rice and water to the manes of the deceased. The reference is to the prevailing practice. It does not mean that the author regarded it as necessary. In fact, there is no second mention of the rite in the Gita.]

दोषैरेतैः कुलघ्नानां वर्णसंकरकारकैः ।
अुत्साद्यन्ते जातिधर्माः कुलधर्माश्च शाश्वताः ।। ४३ ।।

43. By the sins of these family-slayers resulting in the confusion of *varnas*, the eternal tribal and family virtues are brought to naught.

अुत्सन्नकुलधर्माणां मनुष्याणां जनार्दन ।
नरके नियतं वासो भवतीत्यनुशुश्रुम ।। ४४ ।।

44. For we have had it handed down to us, O Janardana, that the men whose family virtues have been ruined are doomed to dwell in hell.

अहो बत महत् पापं कर्तुं व्यवसिता वयम् ।
यद् राज्यसुखलोभेन हन्तुं स्वजनमुद्यताः ॥ ४५ ॥

45. Alas! What a heinous sin we are about to commit, in that, from greed of the joy of sovereign power, we are prepared to slay our kith and kin!

यदि मामप्रतीकारम् अशस्त्रं शस्त्रपाणयः ।
धार्तराष्ट्रा रणे हन्युः तन् मे क्षेमतरं भवेत् ॥ ४६ ॥

46. Happier far would it be for me if Dhritarashtra's sons, weapons in hand, should strike me down on the battlefield, unresisting and unarmed.

संजय अुवाच ।

अेवमुक्त्वाऽर्जुनः संख्ये रथोपस्थ अुपाविशत् ।
विसृज्य सशरं चापं शोकसंविग्नमानसः ॥ ४७ ॥

Sanjaya said:

47. Thus spake Arjuna on the field of battle, and dropping his bow and arrows sank down on his seat in the chariot, overwhelmed with anguish.

अिति श्रीमद्भगवद्गीतासु अुपनिषत्सु ब्रह्मविद्यायां योगशास्त्रे श्रीकृष्णार्जुनसंवादे
अर्जुनविषादयोगो नाम प्रथमोऽध्यायः ॥ १ ॥

Thus ends the first discourse, entitled '*Arjuna Vishada Yoga*' in the converse of Lord Krishna and Arjuna, on the science of *Yoga*, as part of the knowledge of *Brahman* in the Upanishad called the Bhagawadgita.*

---

* Regarding the significance of this colophon occurring at the end of each discourse see 'My Submission', p. 20.

DISCOURSE II

By reason of delusion, man takes wrong to be right. By reason of delusion was Arjuna let to make a difference between kinsmen and non-kinsmen. To demonstrate that this is a vain distinction, Lord Krishna distinguishes between body (not-Self) and Atman (Self) and shows that whilst bodies are impermanent and several, Atman is permanent and one. Effort is within man's control, not the fruit thereof. All he has to do, therefore, is to decide his course of conduct or duty on each occasion and persevere in it, unconcerned about the result. Fulfilment of one's duty in the spirit of detachment or selflessness leads to Freedom.

संजय अुवाच ।

तं तथा कृपयाविष्टम् अश्रुपूर्णाकुलेक्षणम् ।
विषीदन्तमिदं वाक्यम् अुवाच मधुसूदनः ।। १ ।।

Sanjaya said :

1. To Arjuna, thus overcome with compassion, sorrowing, and his eyes obscured by flowing tears, Madhusudana spake these words :

श्रीभगवानुवाच ।

कुतस्त्वा कश्मलमिदं विषमे समुपस्थितम् ।
अनार्यजुष्टमस्वर्ग्यम् अकीर्तिकरमर्जुन ।। २ ।।

The Lord said :

2. How is it that at this perilous moment this delusion, unworthy of the noble, leading neither to heaven nor to glory, has overtaken thee ?

क्लैब्यं मा स्म गमः पार्थ नैतत् त्वय्युपपद्यते ।
क्षुद्रं हृदयदौर्बल्यं त्यक्त्वोत्तिष्ठ परंतप ।। ३ ।।

3. Yield not to unmanliness, O Partha; it does not become thee. Shake off this miserable faint-heartedness and arise, O Parantapa!

अर्जुन अुवाच ।
कथं भीष्ममहं संख्ये द्रोणं च मधुसूदन ।
अिषुभिः प्रतियोत्स्यामि पूजार्हावरिसूदन ।। ४ ।।

Arjuna said:

4. How shall I, with arrows, engage Bhishma and Drona in battle, O Madhusudana, they who are worthy of reverence, O Arisudana?

गुरूनहत्वा हि महानुभावान् श्रेयो भोक्तुं भैक्ष्यमपीह लोके ।
हत्वार्थकामांस्तु गुरूनिहैव भुंजीय भोगान् रुधिरप्रदिग्धान् ।।५।।

5. It were better far to live on alms in this world than to slay these venerable elders. Having slain them I should but have blood-stained enjoyments.

न चैतद् विद्मः कतरन् नो गरीयो यद्वा जयेम यदि वा नो जयेयुः ।
यानेव हत्वा न जिजीविषामस् तेऽवस्थिताः प्रमुखे धार्तराष्ट्राः ।।६।

6. Nor do we know which is better for us, that we conquer them or that they conquer us, for here stand before us Dhritarashtra's sons having killed whom we should have no desire to live.

कार्पण्यदोषोपहतस्वभावः पृच्छामि त्वां धर्मसंमूढचेताः ।
यच्छ्रेयः स्यान् निश्चितं ब्रूहि तन् मे शिष्यस्तेऽहं शाधि मां त्वां प्रपन्नम्।।७।

7. My being is paralysed by faint-heartedness; my mind discerns not duty; hence I ask thee; tell me, I pray

thee, in no uncertain language, wherein lies my good. I am thy disciple ; guide me ; I seek refuge in thee.

न हि प्रपश्यामि ममापनुद्याद् यच्छोकमुच्छोषणमिन्द्रियाणाम् ।
अवाप्य भूमावसपत्नमृद्धं राज्यं सुराणामपि चाधिपत्यम् ॥८॥

8. For I see nothing that can dispel the anguish that shrivels up my senses even if I should win on earth uncontested sovereignty over a thriving kingdom or lordship over the gods.

संजय अुवाच ।
अेवमुक्त्वा हृषीकेशम् गुडाकेशः परंतपः ।
न योत्स्य अिति गोविन्दम् अुक्त्वा तूष्णीं बभूव ह ॥ ९ ॥

Sanjaya said :

9. Thus spoke Gudakesha Parantapa to Hrishikesha Govinda, and with the words 'I will not fight' became speechless.

तमुवाच हृषीकेशः प्रहसन् अिव भारत ।
सेनयोरुभयोर्मध्ये विषीदंतमिदं वचः ॥ १० ॥

10. To him thus stricken with anguish, O Bharata ! between the two armies, Hrishikesha, as though mocking, addressed these words :

श्रीभगवानुवाच ।
अशोच्यानन्वशोचस्त्वं प्रज्ञावादांश्च भाषसे ।
गतासूनगतासूंश्च नानुशोचन्ति पंडिताः ॥ ११ ॥

The Lord said :

11. Thou mournest for them whom thou shouldst not mourn, and utterest vain words of wisdom. The wise mourn neither for the living nor for the dead.

न त्वेवाहं जातु नासं न त्वं नेमे जनाधिपाः ।
न चैव न भविष्यामः सर्वे वयमतःपरम् ।। १२ ।।

12. For never was I not, nor thou, nor these kings; nor will any of us cease to be hereafter.

देहिनोऽस्मिन् यथा देहे कौमारं यौवनं जरा ।
तथा देहांतरप्राप्तिर् धीरस्तत्र न मुह्यति ।। १३ ।।

13. As the embodied one has, in the present body, infancy, youth and age, even so does he receive another body. The wise man is not deceived therein.

मात्रास्पर्शास्तु कौन्तेय शीतोष्णसुखदुःखदाः ।
आगमापायिनोऽनित्यास् तांस्तितिक्षस्व भारत ।। १४ ।।
यं हि न व्यथयन्त्येते पुरुषं पुरुषर्षभ ।
समदुःखसुखं धीरं सोऽमृतत्वाय कल्पते ।। १५ ।।

14. O Kaunteya! contacts of the senses with their objects bring cold and heat, pleasure and pain; they come and go and are transient. Endure them, O Bharata.

15. O noblest of men, the wise man who is not disturbed by these, who is unmoved by pleasure and pain, he is fitted for immortality.

[Both 14 and 15 remind one of Keats:

"To bear all naked truths
And to envisage circumstance, all calm:
That is the top of sovereignty." (*Hyperion*)]

नासतो विद्यते भावो नाभावो विद्यते सतः ।
उभयोरपि दृष्टोऽन्तस् त्वनयोस्तत्त्वदर्शिभिः ।। १६ ।।

16. What is non-Being is never known to have been, and what is Being is never known not to have been. Of

both these the secret has been seen by the seers of the Truth.

[This emphasizes the distinction between Being which is the permanent substratum of all and the evanescent Becoming. H. P. Blavatsky said even that word 'Being' is inadequate to express what is, has been, and shall be, and she suggested the word "Be-ness" instead. All becoming, all existence (out-being) springs from what permanently is. Cf. II Cor. 4. 18: "For the things which are seen are temporal; but the things which are not seen are eternal."]

अविनाशि तु तद् विद्धि येन सर्वमिदं ततम् ।
विनाशमव्ययस्यास्य न कश्चित् कर्तुमर्हति ॥ १७ ॥

17. Know that to be imperishable whereby all this is pervaded. No one can destroy that immutable Being.

[The Sanskrit word *tatam* (ततम्) has been translated 'pervaded' by nearly all commentators; but it may certainly mean 'stretched' or 'spread out' so as to remind one, as Davis suggests, of Iss. 42. 5: "The Lord, He that created the heavens, and stretched them out; He that spread forth the earth."]

अन्तवन्त इमे देहा नित्यस्योक्ताः शरीरिणः ।
अनाशिनोऽप्रमेयस्य तस्माद् युध्यस्व भारत ॥ १८ ॥

18. These bodies of the embodied one who is eternal, imperishable and immeasurable are finite. Fight, therefore, O Bharata.

[The words 'eternal' and 'imperishable' are used to indicate both 'beyond all change', and 'beyond all destruction'. 'Immeasurable' is the word for *aprameya* of which 'indemonstrable' is just as good an equivalent, both meaning 'that which is self-evident', beyond all proof or evidence or measurement, inasmuch as the *Self* itself provides the basis of all proof and measurement. It is the prime postulate of all knowledge.]

य अेनं वेत्ति हन्तारं यश्चैनं मन्यते हतम् ।
अुभौ तौ न विजानीतो नायं हन्ति न हन्यते ।। १९ ।।
न जायते म्रियते वा कदाचिन् नायं भूत्वा भविता वा न भूयः ।
अजो नित्यः शाश्वतोऽयं पुराणो न हन्यते हन्यमाने शरीरे ।।२०।।

19. He who thinks of This (*Atman*) as slayer and he who believes This to be slain, are both ignorant. This neither slays nor is ever slain.

20. This is never born nor ever dies, nor having been will ever not be any more; unborn, eternal, everlasting, ancient, This is not slain when the body is slain.

[19-20 are an echo practically verbatim of Katha Up. 2. 19-18.] *

वेदाविनाशिनं नित्यं य अेनमजमव्ययम् ।
कथं स पुरुषः पार्थ कं घातयति हन्ति कम् ।। २१ ।।

21. He who knows This, O Partha, to be imperishable, eternal, unborn, and immutable — whom and how can that man slay or cause to be slain?

वासांसि जीर्णानि यथा विहाय नवानि गृह्णाति नरोऽपराणि ।
तथा शरीराणि विहाय जीर्णानि अन्यानि संयाति नवानि देही।।२२।।

---

* हन्ता चेन्मन्यते हन्तुं हतश्चेन्मन्यते हतम् ।
अुभौ तौ न विजानीतो नायं हन्ति न हन्यते ।।
न जायते म्रियते वा विपश्चिन्नायं कुतश्चिन्न बभूव कश्चित् ।
अजो नित्यः शाश्वतोऽयं पुराणो न हन्यते हन्यमाने शरीरे ।।
कठ. अुप. २. १९-१८

22. As a man casts off worn-out garments and takes others that are new, even so the embodied one casts off worn-out bodies and passes on to others new.

नैनं छिन्दन्ति शस्त्राणि नैनं दहति पावकः ।
न चैनं क्लेदयन्त्यापो न शोषयति मारुतः ।। २३ ।।

23. This no weapons wound, This no fire burns; This no waters wet, This no wind doth dry.

अच्छेद्योऽयमदाह्योऽयम् अक्लेद्योऽशोष्य अेव च ।
नित्यः सर्वगतः स्थाणुर् अचलोऽयं सनातनः ।। २४ ।।

24. Beyond all cutting, burning, wetting and drying is This — eternal, all-pervading, stable, immovable, everlasting.

अव्यक्तोऽयमचिन्त्योऽयम् अविकार्योऽयमुच्यते ।
तस्मादेवं विदित्वैनं नानुशोचितुमर्हसि ।। २५ ।।

25. Perceivable neither by the senses nor by the mind, This is called unchangeable; therefore knowing This as such thou shouldst not grieve.

अथ चैनं नित्यजातं नित्यं वा मन्यसे मृतम् ।
तथापि त्वं महाबाहो नैनं शोचितुमर्हसि ।। २६ ।।

26. And if thou deemest This to be always coming to birth and always dying, even then, O Mahabahu, thou shouldst not grieve.

जातस्य हि ध्रुवो मृत्युर् ध्रुवं जन्म मृतस्य च ।
तस्मादपरिहार्येऽर्थे न त्वं शोचितुमर्हसि ।। २७ ।।

27. For certain is the death of the born, and certain is the birth of the dead; therefore what is unavoidable thou shouldst not regret.

[This verse reminds of Edgar's words in *King Lear*:

"Men must endure
Their going hence, even as their coming here."]

अव्यक्तादीनि भूतानि व्यक्तमध्यानि भारत ।
अव्यक्तनिधनान्येव तत्र का परिदेवना ।। २८ ।।

28. The state of all beings before birth is unmanifest; their middle state manifest; their state after death is again unmanifest. What occasion is there for lament, O Bharata?

आश्चर्यवत् पश्यति कश्चिदेनम् आश्चर्यवद् वदति तथैव चान्यः ।
आश्चर्यवच्चैनमन्यः शृणोति श्रुत्वाऽप्येनं वेद न चैव कश्चित् ।। २९।।

29. One looks upon This as a marvel; another speaks of This as such; another hears thereof as a marvel; yet having heard of This none truly knows This.

[This is a paraphrase of Katha Up. 2. 7: *

"He whom many cannot get even to hear of; He whom many even having heard of do not know; rare is he who can describe Him; ingenious is he who has won Him; and rare he who, having been instructed by such a one, has known Him." The word 'marvel' in the Gita may apply both to 'This' (*Atman*) and to the various subjects of the verbs. Shankaracharya does not refer to the Upanishad verse but accepts both interpretations as possible.]

---

* श्रवणायापि बहुभिर्यो न लभ्यः ।
शृण्वन्तोऽपि बहवो यं न विद्युः ।।
आश्चर्यो वक्ता कुशलोऽस्य लब्धा ।
आश्चर्यो ज्ञाता कुशलानुशिष्टः ।।

कठ. उप. २. ७

देही नित्यमवध्योऽयं देहे सर्वस्य भारत ।
तस्मात् सर्वाणि भूतानि न त्वं शोचितुमर्हसि ।। ३० ।।

30. This embodied one in the body of every being is ever beyond all harm, O Bharata; thou shouldst not, therefore, grieve for any one.

Thus far Lord Krishna, by force of argument based on pure reason, has demonstrated that *Atman* is abiding while the physical body is fleeting, and has explained that if, under certain circumstances, the destruction of a physical body is deemed justifiable, it is delusion to imagine that the Kauravas should not be slain because they are kinsmen. Now he reminds Arjuna of the duty of a Kshatriya.

स्वधर्ममपि चावेक्ष्य न विकम्पितुमर्हसि ।
धर्म्याद्धि युद्धाच्छ्रेयोऽन्यत् क्षत्रियस्य न विद्यते ।। ३१ ।।

31. Again, seeing thine own duty thou shouldst not shrink from it; for there is no higher good for a Kshatriya than a righteous war.

यदृच्छया चोपपन्नं स्वर्गद्वारमपावृतम् ।
सुखिनः क्षत्रियाः पार्थ लभन्ते युद्धमीदृशम् ।। ३२ ।।

32. Such a fight, coming unsought, as a gateway to heaven thrown open, falls only to the lot of happy Kshatriyas, O Partha.

अथ चेत् त्वमिमं धर्म्यं संग्रामं न करिष्यसि ।
ततः स्वधर्मं कीर्तिं च हित्वा पापमवाप्स्यसि ।। ३३ ।।

33. But if thou wilt not fight this righteous fight, then failing in thy duty and losing thine honour thou wilt incur sin.

अकीर्तिं चापि भूतानि कथयिष्यन्ति तेऽव्ययाम् ।
संभावितस्य चाकीर्तिर् मरणादतिरिच्यते ।। ३४ ।।

34. The world will for ever recount the story of thy disgrace; and for a man of honour disgrace is worse than death.

भयाद् रणादुपरतं मंस्यन्ते त्वां महारथाः ।
येषां च त्वं बहुमतो भूत्वा यास्यसि लाघवम् ।। ३५ ।।

35. The *maharathas* will think that fear made thee retire from battle; and thou wilt fall in the esteem of those very ones who have held thee high.

[For '*maharatha*', see note on 1. 4.]

अवाच्यवादांश्च बहून् वदिष्यन्ति तवाहिताः ।
निन्दन्तस्तव सामर्थ्यं ततो दुःखतरं नु किम् ।। ३६ ।।

36. Thine enemies will deride thy prowess and speak many unspeakable words about thee. What can be more painful than that?

हतो वा प्राप्स्यसि स्वर्गं जित्वा वा भोक्ष्यसे महीम् ।
तस्मादुत्तिष्ठ कौन्तेय युद्धाय कृतनिश्चयः ।। ३७ ।।

37. Slain, thou shalt gain heaven; victorious, thou shalt inherit the earth: therefore arise, O Kaunteya, determined to fight.

Having declared the highest truth, viz. the immortality of the eternal *Atman* and the fleeting nature of the physical body (11-30), Krishna reminds Arjuna that a Kshatriya may not flinch from a fight which comes unsought (31-32). He then (33-37) shows how the highest truth and the performance of duty incidentally coincide with expediency. Next he proceeds to foreshadow the central teaching of the Gita in the following *shloka*.

सुखदुःखं समे कृत्वा लाभालाभौ जयाजयौ ।
ततो युद्धाय युज्यस्व नैवं पापमवाप्स्यसि ।। ३८ ।।

38. Hold alike pleasure and pain, gain and loss, victory and defeat, and gird up thy loins for the fight; so doing thou shalt not incur sin.

अेषा तेऽभिहिता सांख्ये बुद्धिर्योगे त्विमां शृणु ।
बुद्ध्या युक्तो यया पार्थ कर्मबन्धं प्रहास्यसि ।। ३९ ।।

39. Thus have I set before thee the attitude of Knowledge; hear now the attitude of Action; resorting to this attitude thou shalt cast off the bondage of action.

[Metaphysical truth has been clearly indicated. The knowledge of the indestructibility of *Atman* proves the futility of lamentation. But all action, so long as knowledge has not made it free, binds; it 'drags from birth to death and death to birth the soul.' How is Arjuna to be freed from the bondage of the frightful course of action that he is advised to take? The key both to free action and to knowledge that frees is now held out to Arjuna, viz. *Yoga*, the attitude of detachment or selflessness. *Yoga* is used to mean both the attitude and the action.]

नेहाभिक्रमनाशोऽस्ति प्रत्यवायो न विद्यते ।
स्वल्पमप्यस्य धर्मस्य त्रायते महतो भयात् ।। ४० ।।

40. Here no effort undertaken is lost, no disaster befalls. Even a little of this righteous course delivers one from great fear.

['Great fear' is here perhaps the fear of having to go through the cycle of birth and death.]

व्यवसायात्मिका बुद्धिर् अेकेह कुरुनन्दन ।
बहुशाखा ह्यनन्ताश्च बुद्धयोऽव्यवसायिनाम् ।। ४१ ।।

41. The attitude, in this matter, springing, as it does, from fixed resolve is but one, O Kurunandana ; but for those who have no fixed resolve the attitudes are many-branched and unending.

When the attitude ceases to be one and undivided and becomes many and divided, it ceases to be one settled will, and is broken up into various wills or desires between which man is tossed about.

यामिमां पुष्पितां वाचं प्रवदन्त्यविपश्चितः ।
वेदवादरताः पार्थ नान्यदस्तीति वादिनः ।।४२।।
कामात्मानः स्वर्गपरा जन्मकर्मफलप्रदाम् ।
क्रियाविशेषबहुलां भोगैश्वर्यगतिं प्रति ।।४३।।
भोगैश्वर्यप्रसक्तानां तयाऽपहृतचेतसाम् ।
व्यवसायात्मिका बुद्धिः समाधौ न विधीयते ।।४४।।

42-44. The ignorant, revelling in the letter of the Vedas, declare that there is naught else ; carnally-minded, holding heaven to be their goal, they utter swelling words which promise birth as the fruit of action and which dwell on the many and varied rites to be performed for the sake of pleasure and power ; intent, as they are, on pleasure and power their swelling words rob them of their wits, and they have no settled attitude which can be centred on the supreme goal.

The Vedic ritual, as opposed to the doctrine of *Yoga* laid down in the Gita, is alluded to here. The Vedic ritual lays countless ceremonies and rites with a view to attaining merit and heaven. These, divorced as they are from the essence of the Vedas and short-lived in their result, are worthless.

त्रैगुण्यविषया वेदा निस्त्रैगुण्यो भवार्जुन ।
निर्द्वन्द्वो नित्यसत्त्वस्थो निर्योगक्षेम आत्मवान् ।।४५।।

45. The Vedas have as their domain the three *gunas*; eschew them, O Arjuna. Free thyself from the pairs of opposites, abide in eternal truth, scorn to gain or guard anything, remain the master of thy soul.

[For *gunas* see 'My Submission' p. 29. The domain of the three *gunas* is the world and worldly desires. It is these *gunas* that keep the Self bound to the body (XIV. 5). "Pure religion" is "to keep himself unspotted from the world" (James 1. 27). In the world "Ye have tribulation," (John 16. 33), one must overcome the world.

Nityasattvasthah bhava (नित्यसत्त्वस्थ: भव) has been translated "abide in eternal truth", in accordance with Gandhiji's translation. That is to say, Arjuna is asked to avoid the Vedas (which direct man to seek the things of the world) and to grasp the kernel which directs him to strive towards self-realization.

But it is possible to translate the words thus: 'Be ever established in *sattva*'. This need not involve any conflict with the precept of eschewing the three *gunas,* in the same *shloka* (or in XIV. 19-27). For one who is ever established in *sattva* is as good as one who has transcended the triple bondage.]

यावानर्थ अुदपाने सर्वतः संप्लुतोदके ।
तावान् सर्वेषु वेदेषु ब्राह्मणस्य विजानतः ॥४६॥

46. To the extent that a well is of use when there is a flood of water on all sides, to the same extent are all the Vedas of use to an enlightened *Brahmana.*

['*Brahmana*' is used in its etymological sense of 'one who has realized *Brahman* or 'the man of self-realization'.

The verse has afforded the commentators a wide battleground for controversy. Some hold that the man of enlightenment has as little use for Vedic rites as one has for a well, when there is a flood of water on all sides; whilst others hold that the Vedic rites have certain uses, just as there are certain limited uses of a well in spite of a surrounding flood of water. Shankaracharya holds the latter view. Tilak clinches the matter by quoting two parallel verses, which seem to be conclusive as to what is probably the obvious meaning of the comparison in the verse in question: the first is from *Shantiparva,* 240.10: 'The enlightened do not set store by action even as those who have the river close by do not care for the well'.* The second is a Buddhist text meaning: 'Where water is everywhere available, what need is there for a well?'† Even Shankaracharya in his commentary on XVIII. 66 has used the simile in this sense: "When there is an all-spreading flood of water close by, nobody would ever think of constructing wells and tanks." The moment one accepts Vedic rites as the meaning of "Vedas" there remains little room for controversy.]

कर्मण्येवाधिकारस्ते मा फलेषु कदाचन ।
मा कर्मफलहेतुर्भूर् मा ते संगोऽस्त्वकर्मणि ॥४७॥

47. Action alone is thy province, never the fruits thereof; let not thy motive be the fruit of action, nor shouldst thou desire to avoid action.

[This need not, and certainly does not, involve the idea of "all absence of purpose", as a Christian critic would make out. The supreme purpose is before man, viz. Self-realization or Freedom, and it is with that end in view that the fruit of all action is to be abandoned. We find the same idea beautifully paraphrased and explained in Tolstoy's 'What I Believe': "The belief in a remuneration of work...rests on the assumption that we have a claim to something; but man has no rights and can have none. He is ever in debt for the welfare given him and therefore can make no demands on any one....This is a necessary condition

* न ते (ज्ञानिनः) कर्म प्रशंसन्ति। कूपं नद्यां पिबन्निव ॥
शान्तिपर्व २४०. १०

† किं कयिरा उदपानेन आपा चे सब्बदा सियुम्। पालीग्रन्थ उदान ७.९

of both service and *the true welfare of his life*." Nor yet does it mean that because a man will have no eye to fruit he will have no fruit. On the contrary, the ultimate fruit is made all the more certain by the renunciation of the desire for it. See V. 4 where the author actually refers to the fruit of *Yoga*.

The Koran has the same thought over and over again: "Whosoever surrendereth his purpose to Allah while doing good, he verily hath grasped the firm hand-hold. Unto Allah belongeth the sequel of all things." (31. 22); "My wage is the concern of Allah only" (10. 72): and "it becometh not a believing man or believing woman, when Allah has decided an affair for them, that they should claim any say in the affair." (33. 36).

Gandhiji explained the verse in another connection:

"There should be no selfish purpose behind our actions. And to be detached from the fruits of actions is not to be ignorant of them or to disregard or disown them. To be detached is never to abandon action, because the contemplated result may not follow. On the contrary, it is proof of the immovable faith in the certainty of the contemplated result following in due course." (*Young India*, 15-3-'28)]

योगस्थः कुरु कर्माणि संगं त्यक्त्वा धनंजय।
सिद्ध्यसिद्ध्योः समो भूत्वा समत्वं योग उच्यते ॥४८॥

48. Act thou, O Dhananjaya, without attachment, steadfast in *Yoga*, even-minded in success and failure. Even-mindedness is *Yoga*.

दूरेण ह्यवरं कर्म बुद्धियोगाद् धनंजय।
बुद्धौ शरणमन्विच्छ कृपणाः फलहेतवः ॥४९॥

49. For action, O Dhananjaya, is far inferior to unattached action; seek refuge in the attitude of detachment. Pitiable are those who make fruit their motive.

['Action' is here self-ful action, action with an eye to fruit. Spinoza had the same 'pitiable' people in view when he said: "Those are far astray from a true estimate of right conduct who expect for it a great reward; as if right conduct and serving God were not happiness itself and the greatest liberty."]

बुद्धियुक्तो जहातीह उभे सुकृतदुष्कृते ।
तस्माद् योगाय युज्यस्व योगः कर्मसु कौशलम् ।।५०।।

50. Here in this world a man gifted with that attitude of detachment escapes the fruit of both good and evil deeds. Gird thyself up for *Yoga*, therefore. *Yoga* is skill in action.

[Cf. with this definition of *Yoga* Epictetus' description of the 'even-minded man' as 'a man of proficiency'.]

कर्मजं बुद्धियुक्ता हि फलं त्यक्त्वा मनीषिणः ।
जन्मबन्धविनिर्मुक्ताः पदं गच्छन्त्यनामयम् ।।५१।।

51. For sages, gifted with the attitude of detachment, who renounce the fruit of action, are released from the bondage of birth and attain to the state which is free from all ills.

यदा ते मोहकलिलं बुद्धिर्व्यतितरिष्यति ।
तदा गन्तासि निर्वेदं श्रोतव्यस्य श्रुतस्य च ।।५२।।

श्रुतिविप्रतिपन्ना ते यदा स्थास्यति निश्चला ।
समाधावचला बुद्धिस् तदा योगमवाप्स्यसि ।।५३।।

52. When thy understanding will have passed through the slough of delusion, then wilt thou be indifferent alike to what thou hast heard and wilt hear.

53. When thy understanding, distracted by much hearing, will rest steadfast and unmoved in concentration, then wilt thou attain *Yoga*.

[52-53. *Shrotavya, Shruta* and *Shruti* (What has to be heard, has been heard, hearing) in these *shlokas* are said by some commentators to have reference to the Vedas. Most probably there is none ; 'what is heard' and 'hearing' have reference probably to the messages that King Dhritarashtra had repeatedly sent to Arjuna before the war began — to the effect that the slaughter of the Kurus would be a heinous sin, that the war did not become the Pandavas' noble nature, that eating the bread of beggary would be better than bloodstained enjoyments, that sovereignty gained by war would be *adharma* and would destroy all works of merit, and that even for the three worlds the Pandavas should not stain their hands in the blood of their kinsmen (*Udyoga Parva* Chs. 22-27). It is these very arguments that Arjuna has repeated (I. 32-47 and II. 3-8) and Krishna has swept them aside without even so much as mentioning them. There is just a passing reference, perhaps, to them in these *shlokas*.]

अर्जुन उवाच ।

स्थितप्रज्ञस्य का भाषा समाधिस्थस्य केशव ।
स्थितधीः किं प्रभाषेत किमासीत व्रजेत किम् ।।५४।।

Arjuna said :

54. What, O Keshava, is the mark of the man whose understanding is secure, whose mind is fixed in concentration ? How does he talk ? How sit ? How move ?

श्रीभगवानुवाच ।

प्रजहाति यदा कामान् सर्वान् पार्थ मनोगतान् ।
आत्मन्येवात्मना तुष्टः स्थितप्रज्ञस्तदोच्यते ।।५५।।

The Lord said :

55. When a man puts away, O Partha, all the cravings that arise in the mind and finds comfort for

himself only from *Atman*, then is he called the man of secure understanding.

To find comfort for oneself from *Atman* means to look to the spirit within for spiritual comfort, not to outside objects which in their very nature must give pleasure as well as pain. Spiritual comfort or bliss must be distinguished from pleasure or happiness. The pleasure I may derive from the possession of wealth, for instance, is delusive ; real spiritual comfort or bliss can be attained only if I rise superior to every temptation even though troubled by the pangs of poverty and hunger.

[Cf. 'Set your affection on things above, and not on things on the earth" (Col. 3. 2). Also "Stand with Him, and ye shall stand fast. Rest in Him, and ye shall be at rest." (St. Augustine, *Confessions*). "No creature is to him a comfort," said Eckhart, "save so far as he may apprehend therein Pure Good which is God."]

दुःखेष्वनुद्विग्नमनाः सुखेषु विगतस्पृहः ।
वीतरागभयक्रोधः स्थितधीर्मुनिरुच्यते ।।५६।।

56. Whose mind is untroubled in sorrows and longeth not for joys, who is free from passion, fear and wrath — he is called the ascetic of secure understanding.

यः सर्वत्रानभिस्नेहस् तत् तत् प्राप्य शुभाशुभम् ।
नाभिनन्दति न द्वेष्टि तस्य प्रज्ञा प्रतिष्ठिता ।।५७।।

57. Who owns attachment nowhere, who feels neither joy nor resentment whether good or bad comes his way — that man's understanding is secure.

यदा संहरते चायं कूर्मोऽङ्गानीव सर्वशः ।
अिन्द्रियाणीन्द्रियार्थेभ्यस् तस्य प्रज्ञा प्रतिष्ठिता ।।५८।।

58. And when, like the tortoise drawing in its limbs from every side, this man draws in his senses from their objects, his understanding is secure.

विषया विनिवर्तन्ते निराहारस्य देहिनः ।
रसवर्जं रसोऽप्यस्य परं दृष्ट्वा निवर्तते ।।५९।।

59. When a man starves his senses, the objects of those senses disappear from him, but not the yearning for them; the yearning too departs when he beholds the Supreme.

The *shloka* does not rule out fasting and other forms of self-restraint, but indicates their limitations. These restraints are needed for subduing the desire for sense-objects, which however is rooted out only when one has a vision of the Supreme. The higher yearning conquers all the lower yearnings.

[Cf. Plotinus: "But when we do behold Him, then we obtain the end of our wishes and rest. Then also we are no longer discordant but perform a truly divine dance about Him." Also St. John of the Cross: "I am not speaking here of the absence of things, for absence is not detachment if the desire remains — but of that detachment which consists in suppressing desire. It is this that sets the soul free, even though possession may be still retained."

For "starves his senses", Gandhiji has 'fasts'. I think there is no violence to the meaning of the verse in applying 'starvation' to all the senses, including that of hunger.

Explaining the verse Gandhiji wrote in *Young India* (22-12-'27):

"Fasting and similar discipline is one of the means to the end of self-restraint, but it is not all. And if physical fasting is not accompanied by mental fasting, it is bound to end in hypocrisy and consequent disaster."]

यततो ह्यपि कौन्तेय पुरुषस्य विपश्चितः ।
अिन्द्रियाणि प्रमाथीनि हरन्ति प्रसभं मनः ॥६०॥

60. For, in spite of the wise man's endeavour, O Kaunteya, the unruly senses distract his mind perforce.

तानि सर्वाणि संयम्य युक्त आसीत मत्परः ।
वशे हि यस्येन्द्रियाणि तस्य प्रज्ञा प्रतिष्ठिता ॥६१॥

61. Holding all these in check, the *yogi* should sit intent on Me; for he whose senses are under control is secure of understanding.

This means that without devotion and the consequent grace of God, man's endeavour is vain.

ध्यायतो विषयान् पुंसः संगस्तेषूपजायते ।
संगात् संजायते कामः कामात् क्रोधोऽभिजायते ॥६२॥

62. In a man brooding on objects of the senses, attachment to them springs up; attachment begets craving and craving begets wrath.

Craving cannot but lead to resentment, for it is unending and unsatisfied.

[Cf. The Bhagawata Purana: "Brooding on the objects of the senses the mind gets fastened to them; brooding on the Lord it is lost in Him."]

क्रोधाद् भवति संमोहः संमोहात् स्मृतिविभ्रमः ।
स्मृतिभ्रंशाद् बुद्धिनाशो बुद्धिनाशात् प्रणश्यति ॥६३॥

63. Wrath breeds stupefaction, stupefaction leads to loss of memory, loss of memory ruins the reason, and the ruin of reason spells utter destruction.

रागद्वेषवियुक्तैस्तु विषयानिन्द्रियैश्चरन् ।
आत्मवश्यैर्विधेयात्मा प्रसादमधिगच्छति ॥६४॥

64. But the disciplined soul, moving among sense-objects with the senses weaned from likes and dislikes and brought under the control of *Atman*, attains peace of mind.

प्रसादे सर्वदुःखानां हानिरस्योपजायते ।
प्रसन्नचेतसो ह्याशु बुद्धिः पर्यवतिष्ठते ॥६५॥

65. Peace of mind means the end of all ills, for the understanding of him whose mind is at peace stands secure.

नास्ति बुद्धिरयुक्तस्य न चायुक्तस्य भावना ।
न चाभावयतः शान्तिर् अशान्तस्य कुतः सुखम् ॥६६॥

66. The undisciplined man has neither understanding nor devotion ; for him who has no devotion there is no peace, and for him who has no peace whence happiness ?

['*Bhavana*' (भावना) translated 'devotion' here has been variously translated: 'Right condition' (Davies) ; 'Reflection' (Hill); 'Perseverance in the pursuit of knowledge' (Telang) ; and so on.]

अिन्द्रियाणां हि चरतां यन्मनोऽनुविधीयते ।
तदस्य हरति प्रज्ञां वायुर्नावमिवाम्भसि ॥६७॥

67. For when his mind runs after any of the roaming senses, it sweeps away his understanding, as the wind a vessel upon the waters.

[Thomas A. Kempis uses the same simile: "For, as a ship without a helm is driven to and fro by the waves, so the man who is negligent and giveth up his resolution is tempted in many ways."]

तस्माद् यस्य महाबाहो निगृहीतानि सर्वशः ।
अिन्द्रियाणीन्द्रियार्थेभ्यस् तस्य प्रज्ञा प्रतिष्ठिता ॥६८॥

68. Therefore, O Mahabahu, he, whose senses are reined in on all sides from their objects, is the man of secure understanding.

या निशा सर्वभूतानां तस्यां जागर्ति संयमी ।
यस्यां जाग्रति भूतानि सा निशा पश्यतो मुनेः ॥६९॥

69. When it is night for all other beings, the disciplined soul is awake; when all other beings are awake, it is night for the seeing ascetic.

This verse indicates the divergent paths of the disciplined ascetic and the sensual man. Whereas the ascetic is dead to the things of the world and lives in God, the sensual man is alive only to the things of the world and dead to the things of the spirit.

[Cf. This description of the gnostic or the Sufi given by Nicholson (*Mystics of Islam*) :

"At night prisoners forget their prison,
At night kings forget power,
No sorrow, no brooding over gain and loss,
No thought of this person or that person.
This is the state of the gnostic, even when he is awake;
God has said, 'Thou wouldst deem them awake while they sleep.'
He is asleep, day and night, to the affairs of the world,
Like a pen in the controlling hand of God."]

आपूर्यमाणम् अचलप्रतिष्ठम्
समुद्रमापः प्रविशन्ति यद्वत् ।
तद्वत् कामा यं प्रविशन्ति सर्वे
स शान्तिमाप्नोति न कामकामी ॥७०॥

70. He in whom all longings subside, even as the waters subside in the ocean which, though ever being filled by them, never overflows — that man finds peace; not he who cherishes longing.

विहाय कामान् यः सर्वान् पुमांश्चरति निःस्पृहः ।
निर्ममो निरहंकारः स शान्तिमधिगच्छति ॥७१॥

71. The man who sheds all longing and moves without concern, free from the sense of 'I' and 'Mine' — he attains peace.

[Cf. "Behold", says the *Theologia Germanica*, "on this sort must we cast all things from us and strip ourselves of them: we must refrain from claiming anything for our own. When we do this, we shall have the best, fullest, clearest and noblest knowledge that a man can have and also the purest and noblest desire."]

अेषा ब्राह्मी स्थितिः पार्थ नैनां प्राप्य विमुह्यति ।
स्थित्वाऽस्यामन्तकालेऽपि ब्रह्मनिर्वाणमृच्छति ॥७२॥

72. This is the state, O Partha, of the man who rests in *Brahman*; having attained to it, he is not deluded. He who abides in this state even at the hour of death passes into oneness with *Brahman*.

['He who rests in God dwells in security for ever,' said Jalaluddin Rumi, the Sufi. He who rests in God refuses to rest in anything less than God. 'What brought you to this perfection?' was the question put to one who had attained perfection, and this was his answer, says Eckhart: "My union with God. For I cannot rest in anything that was less than God." (Evelyn Underhill, *Mysticism*). *Brahma-nirvana*, translated here "oneness with *Brahman*", is explained by Gandhiji in an article in *Young India* (24-11-'27): "*Nirvana* is not utter extinction. So far as

I have been able to understand the central fact of Buddha's life, *Nirvana* is utter extinction of all that is base in us, all that is vicious in us, all that is corrupt and corruptible in us. *Nirvana* is not like the black dead peace of the grave, but the living peace, the living happiness of a soul conscious of itself and conscious of having found its own abode in the heart of the Eternal." This "abode in the heart of the Eternal" is *Brahma-nirvana*.]

इति श्रीमद्भगवद्गीतासु उपनिषत्सु ब्रह्मविद्यायां योगशास्त्रे
श्रीकृष्णार्जुनसंवादे सांख्ययोगो नाम द्वितीयोऽध्यायः ।। २।।

Thus ends the second discourse, entitled '*Sankhya Yoga*' in the converse of Lord Krishna and Arjuna, on the science of *Yoga* as part of the knowledge of *Brahman* in the Upanishad called the Bhagawadgita.

DISCOURSE III

This discourse may be said to be the key to the essence of the Gita. It makes absolutely clear the spirit and the nature of right action and shows how true knowledge must express itself in acts of selfless service.

अर्जुन उवाच ।

ज्यायसी चेत् कर्मणस्ते मता बुद्धिर्जनार्दन ।
तत् किं कर्मणि घोरे मां नियोजयसि केशव ।।१।।

Arjuna said :

1. If, O Janardana, thou holdest that the attitude of detachment is superior to action, then why, O Keshava, dost thou urge me to dreadful action ?

[See II. 49]

व्यामिश्रेणेव वाक्येन बुद्धिं मोहयसीव मे ।
तदेकं वद निश्चित्य येन श्रेयोऽहमाप्नुयाम् ।।२।।

2. Thou dost seem to confuse my understanding with perplexing speech ; tell me, therefore, in no uncertain voice, that alone whereby I may attain salvation.

Arjuna is sore perplexed, for whilst on the one hand he is rebuked for his faint-heartedness, on the other he seems to be advised to refrain from action (II. 49-50). But this, in reality, is not the case as the following *shlokas* will show.

श्रीभगवानुवाच ।

लोकेऽस्मिन् द्विविधा निष्ठा पुरा प्रोक्ता मयानघ ।
ज्ञानयोगेन सांख्यानां कर्मयोगेन योगिनाम् ।।३।।

The Lord said :

3. I have spoken, before, O sinless one, of two attitudes in this world — the *Sankhyas'*, that of *Jnana yoga* and the *Yogins'*, that of *Karma yoga*.

[' *Sankhya* ' here means follower of the path of *Sankhya* or knowledge, and ' *Yogin* ' follower of the path of *Yoga* or selfless action.]

न कर्मणामनारंभात् नैष्कर्म्यं पुरुषोऽश्नुते ।
न च संन्यसनादेव सिद्धिं समधिगच्छति ।।४।।

4. Never does man enjoy freedom from action by not undertaking action, nor does he attain that freedom by mere renunciation of action.

' Freedom from action ' is freedom from the bondage of action. This freedom is not to be gained by cessation of all activity, apart from the fact that this cessation is in the very nature of things impossible (see following *shloka*). How then may it be gained ? The following *shlokas* will explain.

[The ' bondage of action ' in Gandhiji's note is the bondage of *sansara,* the cycle of death and birth. All action will have its consequences ; the consequences in one case, as we shall see, will be the bondage of *sansara,* in the other case it will be freedom from it.]

न हि कश्चित् क्षणमपि जातु तिष्ठत्यकर्मकृत् ।
कार्यते ह्यवशः कर्म सर्वः प्रकृतिजैर्गुणैः ।।५।।

5. For none ever remains inactive even for a moment ; for all are compelled to action by the *gunas* inherent in *prakriti.*

[For *prakriti* and *gunas,* see ' My Submission ', P. 27. All creation means the disturbance of the equilibrium of the three *gunas,* and hence the existence of a created object necessarily presupposes activity of some kind.]

कर्मेन्द्रियाणि संयम्य य आस्ते मनसा स्मरन् ।
अिन्द्रियार्थान् विमूढात्मा मिथ्याचारः स अुच्यते ।।६।।

6. He who curbs the organs of action but allows the mind to dwell on the sense-objects, — such a one, wholly deluded, is called a hypocrite.

The man who curbs his tongue but mentally swears at another is a hypocrite. But that does not mean that free rein should be given to the organs of action so long as the mind cannot be brought under control. Self-imposed physical restraint is a condition precedent to mental restraint. Physical restraint should be entirely self-imposed and not super-imposed from outside, *e. g.* by fear. The hypocrite who is held up to contempt here is not the humble aspirant after self-restraint. The *shloka* has reference to the man who curbs the body because he cannot help it whilst indulging the mind, and who would indulge the body too if he possibly could. The next *shloka* puts the thing conversely.

यस्त्विन्द्रियाणि मनसा नियम्यारभतेऽर्जुन ।
कर्मेन्द्रियैः कर्मयोगम् असक्तः स विशिष्यते ।।७।।

7. But he, O Arjuna, who keeping all the senses under control of the mind, engages the organs in *Karma yoga*, without attachment — that man excels.

The mind and body should be made to accord well. Even with the mind kept in control, the body will be active in one way or another. But he whose mind is truly restrained will, for instance, close his ears to foul talk and open them only to listen to the praise of God or of good men. He will have no relish for sensual pleasures and will keep himself occupied with such activity as ennobles the soul. That is the path of action. *Karma yoga* is the *yoga* (means) which will deliver the self from the bondage of the body, and in it there is no room for self-indulgence.

नियतं कुरु कर्म त्वं कर्म ज्यायो ह्यकर्मणः ।
शरीरयात्राऽपि च ते न प्रसिद्ध्येदकर्मणः ॥८॥

8. Do thou thy allotted task; for action is superior to inaction; with inaction even life's normal course is not possible.

[I have translated the word *niyatam* 'allotted task', meaning 'task that falls to one's lot'. It seems to be a synonym for the words *svakarma,* one's own task (XVIII. 45), *svadharma,* one's duty (XVIII. 47), *svabhavaniyatam,* determined by or in accordance with one's nature (XVIII. 47), and *sahajam,* to which one is born (XVIII. 48). What falls to one's lot does not therefore mean work imposed upon one, but work which one has found out to be in accordance with one's nature, one's bent, the law of one's being.

Voltaire voiced the truth in this *shloka* in his telling way when he said: "Not to be occupied and not to exist amount to the same thing. All people are good except those who are idle." The latter half of the *shloka* reminds one of Dr Johnson's animated reply to Boswell: "Sir, action is driving on the system of life."]

यज्ञार्थात् कर्मणोऽन्यत्र लोकोऽयं कर्मबंधनः ।
तदर्थं कर्म कौन्तेय मुक्तसंगः समाचर ॥९॥

9. This world of men suffers bondage from all action save that which is done for the sake of sacrifice; to this end, O Kaunteya, perform action without attachment.

'Action for the sake of sacrifice' means acts of selfless service dedicated to God.

सहयज्ञाः प्रजाः सृष्ट्वा पुरोवाच प्रजापतिः ।
अनेन प्रसविष्यध्वम् अेष वोऽस्त्विष्टकामधुक् ॥१०॥

10. Together with sacrifice did the Lord of beings create, of old, mankind, declaring :

" By this shall ye increase ; may this be to you the giver of all your desires.

देवान् भावयतानेन ते देवा भावयन्तु वः ।
परस्परं भावयन्तः श्रेयः परमवाप्स्यथ ॥११॥

11. " With this may you cherish the gods and may the gods cherish you ; thus cherishing one another may you attain the highest good.

[9-11. Cf. Koran : " Unto each nation have we given sacred rites which they are to perform." (22. 67) and " Who is it that will lend unto Allah a goodly loan so that He may give it increased manifold ? Allah straighteneth and enlargeth." (2. 245)]

अिष्टान् भोगान् हि वो देवा दास्यन्ते यज्ञभाविताः ।
तैर्दत्तानप्रदायैभ्यो यो भुंक्ते स्तेन एव सः ॥१२॥

12. " Cherished with sacrifice, the gods will bestow on you the desired boons." He who enjoys their gifts without rendering aught unto them is verily a thief.

" Gods " in *shlokas* 11 and 12 must be taken to mean the whole creation of God. The service of all created beings is the service of the gods and the same is sacrifice.

[12. One returns nothing of one's own but what belongs to the gods or God. This sacrifice is but the repayment of our debt to Nature and God.

" *Yajna* is a word full of beauty and power. Hence with the growth of knowledge and experience and with the change of time its meaning is likely to grow and change.

'*Yajna*' literally means worship ; hence sacrifice ; hence any sacrificial act or any act of service. And in this sense every age may and should have its own particular *yajna.* For mankind lives by *yajna,* sacrifice." (*Young India*)

Also : "*Yajna* means an *act* directed to the welfare of *others,* done without receiving or desiring a return for it, whether of a temporal or a spiritual nature. *Act* must be taken in its widest sense, and includes thought and word, and *others* embraces not only humanity but all life. Therefore, it will not be a *yajna* to sacrifice lower animals even with a view to the service of humanity.................. The world cannot subsist for a single moment without '*yajna*' in this sense, and therefore the Gita, after having dealt with true wisdom in the second chapter, takes up in the third the means of attaining it, and declares in so many words, that '*yajna*' came with creation itself. This body therefore has been given us only in order that we may serve all creation with it. And therefore, says the Gita, he who eats without offering '*yajna*' eats stolen food. Every single act of one, who would lead a life of purity, should be in the nature of '*yajna*'. '*Yajna*' having come to us with our birth, we are debtors all our lives, and thus for ever bound to serve the universe. And even as a bondslave receives food, clothing and so on from the master whom he serves, so should we gratefully accept such gifts as may be assigned to us by the Lord of the universe." (*From Yeravda Mandir,* Ch. xiv)

"'Earn thy bread by the sweat of thy brow', says the Bible. Sacrifices may be of many kinds, one of them may well be bread-labour. If all laboured for their bread and no more, there would be enough food and enough leisure for all. Then there would be no cry of over-population, no disease, and no such misery as we see around us. Such labour will be the highest form of sacrifice. Men will no doubt do many other things either through their bodies or through their minds, but all this will be a labour of love for the common good. May not men earn their bread by intellectual labour? No. The needs of the body must be supplied by the body. 'Render unto Caesar that which is Caesar's' perhaps applies here well." (Gandhiji in the *Harijan*, June 29, '35)]

यज्ञशिष्टाशिनः सन्तो मुच्यन्ते सर्वकिल्बिषैः ।
भुंजते ते त्वघं पापा ये पचन्त्यात्मकारणात् ॥१३॥

13. The righteous men who eat the residue of the sacrifice are freed from all sin, but the wicked who cook for themselves eat sin.

[This seems to repeat the following Vedic text in a new setting: "He who does not nourish the guests and eats alone, eats but sin." * The similar verse from *Manusmriti* is well known: "He eats but sin who cooks but for himself; a meal of what remains after sacrifice has been offered is ordained to be the food of the good." (3. 118) ×

Cf. I. Cor. 11. 29: "For he that eateth and drinketh unworthily, eateth and drinketh damnation to himself"—'unworthily' meaning 'without remembering the Lord.']

अन्नाद् भवन्ति भूतानि पर्जन्यादन्नसंभवः ।
यज्ञाद् भवति पर्जन्यो यज्ञः कर्मसमुद्भवः ॥१४॥

14. From food springs all life, from rain is born food; from sacrifice comes rain and sacrifice is the result of action.

["Here there is propounded the theory of body-labour, called by Tolstoy bread-labour, which becomes *Yajna* or sacrifice, when performed selflessly for others. Rain comes not through intellectual feasts but through sheer bodily

---

* नार्यमणं पुष्यति नो सखायं। केवलाघो भवति केवलादी।
ऋग्वेद १०.११७.६

× अघं स केवलं भुंक्ते यः पचत्यात्मकारणात्।
यज्ञशिष्टाशनं ह्येतत् सतामन्नं विधीयते॥
मनुस्मृति ३.११८

labour. It is a well-established scientific fact that where forests are denuded of trees rains cease, where trees are planted rains are attracted and the volume of water received increases with the increase of vegetation....Who knows all the ill effects, moral and physical, of the cessation of body-labour ?" For a discourse on Bread-labour see *From Yeravda Mandir*, Ch. IX.]

कर्म ब्रह्मोद्भवं विद्धि ब्रह्माक्षरसमुद्भवम् ।
तस्मात् सर्वगतं ब्रह्म नित्यं यज्ञे प्रतिष्ठितम् ॥१५॥

15. Know that action springs from *Brahman* and *Brahman* from the Imperishable ; hence the all-pervading *Brahman* is ever firm-founded on sacrifice.

[14-15. A rather unhappy use of the word '*Brahman*' has created much unnecessary difficulty in the interpretation of *shloka* 15. '*Brahman*' in the first two mentions of it means *prakriti* and in the third and last mention it means the Imperishable, Infinite, pervading the entire creation. The idea is that sacrifice is both the cause and consequence of creation. *Shanti Parva* (267. 34) expresses the same idea : "The whole creation issues from sacrifice and sacrifice issues from creation." * Tolstoy said the same thing in simpler language, dropping out the intermediate links in the circular chain of sacrifice : "Work produces food, food produces work, that is the unending circle : the one is the consequence and cause of the other." It is the eternal process of sacrifice that makes what Browning called "this dread machinery of sin and sorrow" a well-devised plan that makes man.

"Love in turn, and be beloved,
Creative and self-sacrificing too,
And thus eventually God-like."]

अेवं प्रवर्तितं चक्रं नानुवर्तयतीह यः ।
अघायुरिन्द्रियारामो मोघं पार्थ स जीवति ॥१६॥

* अनुयज्ञं जगत् सर्वं यज्ञश्चानुजगत् सदा । शान्तिपर्व २६७–३४

16. He who does not follow the wheel thus set in motion here below, he, living in sin, sating his senses, lives, O Partha, in vain.

यस्त्वात्मरतिरेव स्याद् आत्मतृप्तश्च मानवः ।
आत्मन्येव च संतुष्टस् तस्य कार्यं न विद्यते ॥१७॥

17. But the man who revels in *Atman*, who is content in *Atman* and who is satisfied only with *Atman*, for him no action exists.

[17. This pithy *shloka* is pregnant with manifold meanings. It indicates the unfailing source of imperishable joy, and distinguishes the carnally-minded described in the preceding *shloka* from the spiritually-minded man. "It doth make a difference whence a man's joy is," said St. Augustine, and whilst the carnally-minded man, doing no sacrifice and sating his senses, lives in vain, his activity involving him in further sin and bondage, the spiritually-minded man turns his eye inward towards the perennial source of all joys — *Atman*, and in so doing wins freedom from action.

The *shloka* does not mean that for him all activity ceases, but that he is freed from all action that binds; (see IV. 23). Master of himself, having made himself one with the universe, he does not live for the self but for *Atman* or the Self which is the same as the Self of the Universe. His therefore will be the utmost freedom of action and freedom of will. Cf. the source-verses from the Upanishads: (1) Chha. Up. 7. 25. 2.*: "Verily it is *Atman* above, *Atman* below, *Atman* in the front, *Atman* in the rear, *Atman* on the right, *Atman* on the left. He who seeing this, believing this, realizing this, revels in *Atman*, sports with *Atman*, enjoys

* अथात आत्मादेश अेवात्मैवाधस्तादात्मोपरिष्टादात्मा पश्चादात्मा पुरस्तादात्मा दक्षिणत आत्मोत्तरत आत्मैवेदं सर्वमिति स वा अेष अेवं पश्यन्नेवं मन्वान अेवं विजानन्नात्मरतिरात्मक्रीड आत्ममिथुन आत्मानन्दः स स्वराड् भवति तस्य सर्वेषु लोकेषु कामचारो भवति ।

छान्दोग्य, ७.२५.२

the company of *Atman*, seeks all his joy in *Atman*, he has *Swarajya*, he has complete freedom of movement in all the three worlds." (2) *Mund.* 3.1.4.: "He who has known *Atman*, sports with *Atman*, revels in *Atman*, is ever in action and the best among all the knowers of *Brahman*." *

What his activity would be no one can say, no scripture may lay down. That the very fact of his life in the flesh will be synonymous with the good of the world is certain. Cf. *Mahaparinibbana Sutta*, 33: "Be ye as those who have the *Atman* as their light. Be ye as those who have the *Atman* as their refuge. Betake yourselves to no external refuge."]

नैव तस्य कृतेनार्थो नाकृतेनेह कश्चन ।
न चास्य सर्वभूतेषु कश्चिदर्थव्यपाश्रयः ॥१८॥

18. He has no interest whatever in anything done, nor in anything not done, nor has he need to rely on anything for personal ends.

तस्मादसक्तः सततं कार्यं कर्म समाचर ।
असक्तो ह्याचरन् कर्म परमाप्नोति पूरुषः ॥१९॥

19. Therefore, do thou ever perform without attachment the work that thou must do; for performing action without attachment man attains the Supreme.

कर्मणैव हि संसिद्धिम् आस्थिता जनकादयः ।
लोकसंग्रहमेवापि संपश्यन् कर्तुमर्हसि ॥२०॥

20. For through action alone Janaka and others achieved perfection; even with a view to the guidance of mankind thou must act.

[Janaka was the philosopher king of Mithila whose name is always cited in India as the stock instance of complete

---

* . . . . विजानन् विद्वान् . . . आत्मक्रीड आत्मरतिः क्रियावानेष ब्रह्मविदां वरिष्ठः । मुण्डक. ३.१.४

self-realization and incessant selfless activity. His sense of 'mine' was extinguished to such an extent that when he was told that his capital was on fire, he is said to have exclaimed: "If Mithila is on fire nothing that is mine is on fire." Tilak quotes a verse from Ashvaghosha's *Buddha-charita* indicating the reputation that Janaka had won: "Janaka obtained the position of *acharya* (preceptor) in *yogavidhi* (selfless action), a position never before won by anyone else."]

यद् यदाचरति श्रेष्ठः तत् तदेवेतरो जनः ।
स यत् प्रमाणं कुरुते लोकस्तदनुवर्तते ॥२१॥

21. Whatever the best man does, is also done by other men; what example he sets, the world follows.

न मे पार्थास्ति कर्तव्यं त्रिषु लोकेषु किंचन ।
नानवाप्तमवाप्तव्यं वर्त अेव च कर्मणि ॥२२॥

22. For me, O Partha, there is naught to do in the three worlds, nothing worth gaining that I have not gained; yet I am ever in action.

An objection is sometimes raised that God being impersonal is not likely to perform any physical activity, at best He may be supposed to act mentally. This is not correct. For the unceasing movement of the sun, the moon, the earth etc. signifies God in action. This is not mental but physical activity. Though God is without form and impersonal, He acts as though He had form and body. Hence though He is ever in action, He is free from action, unaffected by action. What must be borne in mind is that, just as all Nature's movements and processes are mechanical and yet guided by Divine Intelligence or Will, even so man must reduce his daily conduct to mechanical regularity and precision, but he must do so intelligently. Man's merit lies in observing divine guidance at the back of these processes and in an intelligent imitation of it rather than in emphasizing the mechanical nature thereof and reducing himself to an automaton. One has but to withdraw the self, withdraw attachment to fruit from all action, and then not only mechanical precision but security from all wear and tear will be ensured. Acting thus man remains fresh until the end of his days. His body will perish in due course, but his soul will remain evergreen without a crease or a wrinkle.

[22. For 'I am ever in action', one may even say in Biblical language, 'I live and move and have my being in action', for the verb '*varte*' has all that connotation.]

यदि ह्यहं न वर्तेयं जातु कर्मण्यतन्द्रितः ।
मम वर्त्मानुवर्तन्ते मनुष्याः पार्थ सर्वशः ॥२३॥

23. Indeed, for were I not, unslumbering, ever to remain in action, O Partha, men would follow my example in every way.

[22-23. The detached work of the Lord affords a lesson to man : Lord Krishna almost seems to say : "Take My yoke upon you and learn of Me : My yoke is easy and My burden is light." (Matt. 11. 29-30). The moment man withdraws from the attraction of his attachment, the yoke of all work becomes easy and the burden light, even as a body loses its weight if the attraction of the earth is removed.

Speaking on the birthday of Krishna, Gandhiji said : "Krishna served the people all his life, he was a real servant of the people. He could have led the hosts at Kurukshetra, but he preferred to be Arjuna's charioteer. His whole life was one unbroken Gita of *Karma*....As a child he was a cowherd and we still know him by the name of *Gopala* — cowherd....Krishna knew no sleep nor idleness. He kept a sleepless vigil over the world." (*Young India* 1-9-'27)]

उत्सीदेयुरिमे लोका न कुर्यां कर्म चेदहम् ।
संकरस्य च कर्ता स्याम् उपहन्यामिमाः प्रजाः ॥२४॥

24. If I were not to perform my task, these worlds would be ruined ; I should be the cause of chaos and of the end of all mankind.

[This *shloka* would seem to contain Lord Krishna's reply to Arjuna's fear expressed in I. 41-43. If confusion was likely to result from his doing what really is his duty, worse would result from his abstention from it, just as it would from the abstention of His task by God Himself.]

सक्ताः कर्मण्यविद्वांसो यथा कुर्वन्ति भारत ।
कुर्याद् विद्वांस्तथाऽसक्तः चिकीर्षुर्लोकसंग्रहम् ॥२५॥

25. Just as, with attachment, the unenlightened perform all actions, O Bharata, even so, but unattached, should the enlightened man act, with a desire for the welfare of humanity.

न बुद्धिभेदम् जनयेद् अज्ञानां कर्मसंगिनाम् ।
जोषयेत् सर्वकर्माणि विद्वान् युक्तः समाचरन् ॥२६॥

26. The enlightened may not confuse the mind of the unenlightened, who are attached to action ; rather must he perform all actions unattached, and thus encourage them to do likewise.

प्रकृतेः क्रियमाणानि गुणैः कर्माणि सर्वशः ।
अहंकारविमूढात्मा कर्ताऽहमिति मन्यते ॥२७॥

27. All action is entirely done by the *gunas* of *prakriti*. Man, deluded by the sense of 'I', thinks, 'I am the doer'.

तत्त्ववित् तु महाबाहो गुणकर्मविभागयोः ।
गुणा गुणेषु वर्तन्त अिति मत्वा न सज्जते ॥२८॥

28. But he, O Mahabahu, who understands the truth of the various *gunas* and their various activities, knows that it is the *gunas* that operate on the *gunas* ; he does not claim to be the doer.

As breathing, winking and similar processes are automatic and man claims no agency for them, he being conscious of the processes only when disease or similar cause arrests them, in a similar manner all his activities should be automatic, without his arrogating to himself the agency or responsibility thereof. A man of charity does not even know that he is doing charitable acts, it is his nature to do so, he cannot help it. This detachment cañ only come from tireless endeavour and God's grace.

.[27-28. For *prakriti* and *gunas* see 'My Submission' p. 27.]

प्रकृतेर्गुणसंमूढाः सज्जन्ते गुणकर्मसु ।
तानकृत्स्नविदो मन्दान् कृत्स्नविन्न विचालयेत् ॥२९॥

29. Deluded by the *gunas* of *prakriti* men become attached to the activities of the *gunas* ; he who knows the truth of things should not unhinge the slow-witted who have not the knowledge.

[26 and 29. These *shlokas* should not be taken to mean an illegitimate accommodation or compromise of truth. The enlightened man does nothing which compromises his truth, nor does he hide the truth. On the contrary, he apparently comes down to the level of the unenlightened man and prepares him for a realization of the truth. Inaction may be action for the man of knowledge, but the same would be inertia in the case of the ignorant man. Such a one has therefore to be raised from self-ful to selfless activity.

Cf. I. Cor. 8. 9 : " But take heed lest by any means this liberty of yours becomes a stumbling block to them that are weak."]

मयि सर्वाणि कर्माणि संन्यस्याध्यात्मचेतसा ।
निराशीर्निर्ममो भूत्वा युध्यस्व विगतज्वरः ॥३०॥

30. Cast all thy acts on Me, with thy mind fixed on the indwelling *Atman*, and without any thought of fruit, or sense of ' mine ' shake off thy fever and fight !

He who knows the *Atman* inhabiting the body and realizes Him to be a part of the supreme *Atman* will dedicate everything to Him, even as a faithful servant acts as a mere shadow of his master and dedicates to him all that he does. For the master is the real doer, the servant but the instrument.

[30. Cf. " Cast all your care upon Him ; for He careth for you." I Peter 5. 7.]

ये मे मतमिदं नित्यम् अनुतिष्ठन्ति मानवाः ।
श्रद्धावन्तोऽनसूयन्तो मुच्यन्ते तेऽपि कर्मभिः ॥३१॥

31. Those who always act according to the rule I have here laid down, in faith and without cavilling,— they too are released from the bondage of their actions.

ये त्वेतदभ्यसूयन्तो नानुतिष्ठन्ति मे मतम् ।
सर्वज्ञानविमूढान् तान् विद्धि नष्टानचेतसः ॥३२॥

32. But those who cavil at the rule and refuse to conform to it are fools, dead to all knowledge ; know that they are lost.

सदृशं चेष्टते स्वस्याः प्रकृतेर्ज्ञानवानपि ।
प्रकृतिं यान्ति भूतानि निग्रहः किं करिष्यति ॥३३।

33. Even a man of knowledge acts according to his nature; all creatures follow their nature; what then will constraint avail?

This does not run counter to the teaching in II. 61 and II. 68. Self-restraint is the means of salvation (VI. 35; XIII. 7). Man's energies should be bent towards achieving complete self-restraint until the end of his days. But if he does not succeed, neither will constraint help him. The *shloka* does not rule out restraint but explains that nature prevails. He who justifies himself saying, 'I cannot do this, it is not in my nature,' misreads the *shloka*. True we do not know our nature, but habit is not nature. Progress, not decline, ascent, not descent, is the nature of the soul, and therefore every threatened decline or descent ought to be resisted. The next verse makes this abundantly clear.

[33. Cf. Bacon: "Nature is often hidden, sometimes overcome, seldom extinguished. Force maketh nature more violent in the return."

Man's nature is determined by pre-natal conditions (including past actions and heredity) and post-natal conditions including physical and cultural environment. Part of this make-up is inevitable and cannot be suppressed (33), but quite a large part can be controlled (34 and 37-43). Man has to strive by self-examination to find out the inevitable part and the mendable part, or, to use Epictetus' language, 'the things in his power' and 'the things not in his power'.]

इन्द्रियस्येन्द्रियस्यार्थे रागद्वेषौ व्यवस्थितौ ।
तयोर्न वशमागच्छेत् तौ ह्यस्य परिपंथिनौ ॥३४॥

34. Each sense has its settled likes and dislikes towards its objects; man should not come under the sway of these, for they are his besetters.

Hearing, for instance, is the object of the ears which may be inclined to hear something and disinclined to hear something else. Man may not allow himself to be swayed by these likes and dislikes, but must decide for himself what is conducive to his growth, his ultimate end being to reach the state beyond happiness and misery.

श्रेयान् स्वधर्मो विगुणः परधर्मात् स्वनुष्ठितात् ।
स्वधर्मे निधनं श्रेयः परधर्मो भयावहः ॥३५॥

35. Better one's own duty, bereft of merit, than another's well-performed; better is death in the discharge of one's duty; another's duty is fraught with danger.

One man's duty may be to serve the community by working as a sweeper, another's may be to work as an accountant. An accountant's work may be more inviting, but that need not draw the sweeper away from his work. Should he allow himself to be drawn away he would himself be lost and put the community into danger. Before God the work of man will be judged by the spirit in which it is done, not by the nature of the work which makes no difference whatsoever. Whoever acts in a spirit of dedication fits himself for salvation.

[Cf. Epictetus who, though a slave, conquered his slavery by becoming the slave of God: "Remember you are an actor in a drama of such a kind as the Author pleases to make it. If short, of a short one; if long, of a long one. If it be His pleasure you should be a poor man, a cripple, a governor, or a private person, see that you act it naturally. For this is your business — to act well the part assigned to you; to choose it is another's." Also Koran: "It may happen ye hate a thing which is good for you, and it may happen that you love a thing which is bad for you. Allah knoweth, you know not." (2. 216)

Gandhiji bases his doctrine of *swadeshi* on this verse: 'Pure service of one's neighbours cannot be disservice to those who are remotely situated; rather the contrary. A man who allows himself to be lured by the distant scene and runs to the ends of the earth for service, is not only foiled in his ambition but fails also in his duty towards his neighbours. That seems to me to be the sense of the verse. Interpreted in terms of one's physical environment this gives us the law of *swadeshi*. *Swadeshi* is *Swadharma* applied to one's immediate environment." (*Young India*, June 18, 1931)]

अर्जुन अुवाच ।

अथ केन प्रयुक्तोऽयं पापं चरति पूरुषः ।
अनिच्छन्नपि वार्ष्णेय बलादिव नियोजितः ।।३६।।

Arjuna said:

36. Then what impels man to sin, O Varshneya, even against his will, as though by force compelled?

श्रीभगवानुवाच ।

काम अेष क्रोध अेष रजोगुणसमुद्भवः ।
महाशनो महापाप्मा विद्ध्येनम् अिह वैरिणम् ।।३७।।

The Lord said:

37. It is Lust, it is Wrath, born of the *guna* — *Rajas*. It is the arch-devourer, the arch-sinner. Know this to be man's enemy here.

धूमेनाव्रियते वह्निर् यथाऽऽदर्शो मलेन च ।
यथोल्बेनावृतो गर्भस् तथा तेनेदमावृतम् ।।३८।।

38. As fire is obscured by smoke, a mirror by dirt, and the embryo by the amnion, so is knowledge obscured by this.

[The amnion is the membrane which covers the embryo and which is destroyed after the birth of the child. Almost all English translators say, 'as the foetus by the womb.' *Ulba*, however, does not mean 'womb', but the amnion; and it is the amnion which obscures the foetus, not the womb; the womb protects. One destroys the amnion, and not the womb.]

आवृतं ज्ञानमेतेन ज्ञानिनो नित्यवैरिणा ।
कामरूपेण कौन्तेय दुष्पूरेणानलेन च ॥३९॥

39. Knowledge is obscured, O Kaunteya, by this eternal enemy of the wise man, in the form of Lust, the insatiable fire.

['*Kamarupa*' translated 'in the form of Lust' may also mean, 'changing shape at will', as in Hill's translation.

Cf. Dhammapada (251): "There is no fire like lust, there is no monster like hatred, there is no snare like folly, there is no torrent like greed." *]

अिन्द्रियाणि मनो बुद्धिः अस्याधिष्ठानमुच्यते ।
अेतैर्विमोहयत्येषः ज्ञानमावृत्य देहिनम् ॥४०॥

40. The senses, the mind and the reason are said to be its seat; by means of these it obscures knowledge and stupefies man.

When Lust seizes the senses, the mind is corrupted, discrimination is obscured and reason ruined. See II. 62-64.

तस्मात् त्वमिन्द्रियाण्यादौ नियम्य भरतर्षभ ।
पाप्मानं प्रजहि ह्येनं ज्ञानविज्ञाननाशनम् ॥४१॥

41. Therefore, O Bharatarshabha, bridle thou first the senses and then rid thyself of this sinner, the destroyer of knowledge and discrimination.

---

* नत्थि रागसमो अग्गि नत्थि दोससमो गहो।
नत्थि मोहसमं जालं नत्थि तण्हासमा नदी ॥ धम्मपद २५१

[*Jnana* and *Vijnana* — knowledge and discriminative knowledge — see my note on VII. 2.]

अिन्द्रियाणि पराण्याहुः अिन्द्रियेभ्यः परं मनः ।
मनसस्तु परा बुद्धिः यो बुद्धेः परतस्तु सः ॥४२॥

42. Subtle, they say, are the senses; subtler than the senses is the mind; subtler than the mind is the reason; but subtler even than the reason is He.

[Ethically man has to begin with the least subtle and therefore the most controllable, viz., the senses, and rise to a control of the whole self by the Self. Metaphysically man must start by ceasing to identify himself first with the senses, then with the mind, then with the reason, until he realizes the Self.

Here the Gita borrows the language of the *Katha Up.*, retaining the psychological categories and dropping the metaphysical ones: "Higher than the senses are their objects, higher than the objects is the mind, higher than the mind is the reason, and higher than the reason is the *mahat atman,* higher than the *mahat* is the Unmanifest, and higher than that is the Supreme than whom there is nothing higher. He is the ultimate reach, the highest goal" (*Katha Up.* 1. 3, 10-11)*. Opinion is sharply divided on the meaning of the last word in the *shloka, sah* (he). Several commentators contend that 'he' is *Kama* — Lust. The quotation from the *Katha Up.* above should make it clear that the reference is to the Supreme and not to Lust. The commentators contend that the *mahat atman* in the quotation does not mean the Supreme, but *ahankara* the ego, which is really the seat of Lust. But *sah* in the Gita *shloka* does not correspond to *mahat atman* in the

---

* अिन्द्रियेभ्यः परा ह्यर्था अर्थेभ्यश्च परं मनः ।
मनसस्तु परा बुद्धिर्बुद्धेरात्मा महान् परः ॥
महतः परमव्यक्तम् अव्यक्तात् पुरुषः परः ।
पुरुषान्न परं किंचित् सा काष्ठा सा परा गतिः ॥ कठ १.३.१०,११

Upanishad text, rather it corresponds to the Supreme at the end of the verse. Besides, the interpretation of *shlokas* 42 and 43 with *sah* as the Supreme is in consonance with the central doctrine of the Gita and the *Upanishads*. See II. 59 where yearning is said to depart "when one beholds the Supreme."]

अेवं बुद्धेः परं बुद्ध्वा संस्तभ्यात्मानमात्मना ।
जहि शत्रुं महाबाहो कामरूपं दुरासदम् ॥४३॥

43. Thus realizing Him to be subtler than the reason, and controlling the self by the Self (*Atman*), destroy, O Mahabahu, this enemy — Lust, so hard to overcome.

When man realizes Him, his mind will be under His control, not swayed by the senses. And when the mind is conquered, what power has Lust ? It is indeed a subtle enemy, but when once the senses, the mind and the reason are under the control of the subtlemost Self, Lust is extinguished.

[36-43. Chapter 7 of St. Paul's Epistle to the Romans provides a close parallel to Arjuna's question and Krishna's reply in these *shlokas*. Here is St. Paul's difficulty : "For what I would, that do I not ; but what I hate that I do." Again : "To will is present with me, but how to perform that which is good I find not" (7. 15, 18). He himself finds the answer : "Now if I do that I would not, it is no more I that do it, but the sin that dwelleth in me" (7. 20); this sin, this other law, he proceeds, finds dwelling "in my members warring against the law of the mind." What the Gita calls the senses, the mind and the reason, St. Paul calls "my members", and St. Paul's "the law of my mind" is the Gita's "control of the self by Self". St. Paul cries to be delivered from "this body of death" and ultimately finds refuge in God through Jesus — "So then with the mind I serve the law of God."

The ethical doctrine of the sufis also affords a close parallel. The sufis found moral culture "on the fact that there is in man an element of evil — the lower or appetitive soul. This evil self, the seat of passion and lust, is called *nafs,* equivalent to the flesh, and constitutes the great obstacle to the attainment of union with God." (*Mystics of Islam* by Nicholson)

इति श्रीमद्भगवद्गीतासु उपनिषत्सु ब्रह्मविद्यायां योगशास्त्रे श्रीकृष्णार्जुनसंवादे
कर्मयोगो नाम तृतीयोऽध्यायः ॥३॥

Thus ends the third discourse entitled '*Karma Yoga*' in the converse of Lord Krishna and Arjuna, on the science of *Yoga*, as part of the knowledge of *Brahman* in the Upanishad called the Bhagawadgita.

DISCOURSE IV

This discourse further explains the subject-matter of the third and describes the various kinds of sacrifice.

श्रीभगवानुवाच ।

अिमं विवस्वते योगं प्रोक्तवानहमव्ययम् ।
विवस्वान् मनवे प्राह मनुरिक्ष्वाकवेऽब्रवीत् ॥१॥
अेवं परंपराप्राप्तम् अिमं राजर्षयो विदुः ।
स कालेनेह महता योगो नष्टः परंतप ॥२॥

The Lord said :

1. I expounded this imperishable *yoga* to Vivasvat; Vivasvat communicated it to Manu, and Manu to Ikshvaku.

2. Thus handed down in succession, the royal sages learnt it; with long lapse of time it dwindled away in this world, O Parantapa.

[1-2. These summarize in a nutshell the long spiritual genealogy with regard to *Karmayoga* given in the Narayaniya section of the Mahabharata. The source is worthy of note inasmuch as it is *Karmayoga* which is there said to have been handed down from age to age, both by *Brahmana* and *Kshatriya* seers, and it is the same *yoga* that is meant here. In all the seven births of Brahma, the *yoga,* says the Mahabharata, was taught originally by Narayana to the first ancestor Brahma and then from him it was handed down to *rishis* like Vaikhanasa and Valakhilya, and then from king Daksha to Vivasvat and from Vivasvat to his son Manu and from Manu to his son Ikshvaku and so on, " for the welfare of the people ". It is wrong to suppose that this ancient doctrine was "entrusted to *Kshatriyas*," for several *Brahmarshis* are mentioned as having learnt and promulgated it.

The sense is that the doctrine is not a new one occasioned by the crisis in front of Arjuna, but the law of universal application followed from time immemorial "for the welfare of the people".]

स अेवायं मया तेऽद्य योगः प्रोक्तः पुरातनः ।
भक्तोऽसि मे सखा चेति रहस्यं ह्येतदुत्तमम् ॥३॥

3. The same ancient *yoga* have I expounded to thee today; for thou art My devotee and My friend, and this is the supreme mystery.

अर्जुन अुवाच ।
अपरं भवतो जन्म परं जन्म विवस्वतः ।
कथमेतद् विजानीयाम् त्वमादौ प्रोक्तवानिति ॥४॥

Arjuna said:

4. Later was Thy birth, my Lord, earlier that of Vivasvat. How then am I to understand that Thou didst expound it in the beginning?

श्रीभगवानुवाच ।
बहूनि मे व्यतीतानि जन्मानि तव चार्जुन ।
तान्यहं वेद सर्वाणि न त्वं वेत्थ परंतप ॥५॥

The Lord said:

5. Many births have we passed through, O Arjuna, both thou and I; I know them all, thou knowest them not, O Parantapa.

अजोऽपि सन्नव्ययात्मा भूतानामीश्वरोऽपि सन् ।
प्रकृतिं स्वामधिष्ठाय संभवाम्यात्ममायया ॥६॥

6. Though unborn and inexhaustible in My essence, though Lord of all beings, yet assuming control

over My Nature, I come into being by My mysterious power.

[Gandhiji's translation says: "because of My Nature". *Prakriti* is here Nature. God by His mysterious power — *maya* — assumes the garb of *prakriti* and looks as though He was born.]

यदा यदा हि धर्मस्य ग्लानिर्भवति भारत ।
अभ्युत्थानमधर्मस्य तदाऽऽत्मानं सृजाम्यहम् ॥७॥

7. For whenever Right declines and Wrong prevails, then O Bharata, I come to birth.

परित्राणाय साधूनां विनाशाय च दुष्कृताम् ।
धर्मसंस्थापनार्थाय संभवामि युगे युगे ॥८॥

8. To save the righteous, to destroy the wicked, and to re-establish Right I am born from age to age.

Here is comfort for the faithful and affirmation of the truth that Right ever prevails. An eternal conflict between Right and Wrong goes on. Sometimes the latter seems to get the upper hand, but it is Right which ultimately prevails. The good are never destroyed, for Right — which is Truth — cannot perish; the wicked are destroyed, because Wrong has no independent existence. Knowing this let man cease to arrogate to himself authorship and eschew untruth, violence and evil. Inscrutable Providence — the unique power of the Lord — is ever at work. This in fact is *avatara*, incarnation. Strictly speaking there can be no birth for God.

["I believe in Krishna perhaps more than the writer," said Gandhiji, in reply to a questioner who asked if Gandhiji would call Krishna Europeanized because he believed in the destruction of the wicked. "But my Krishna is the Lord of the Universe, the creator, preserver and destroyer of us all. *He* may destroy, because *He* creates." (*Young India,* 9 April, 1925). Again, "I do not regard this verse as an exhortation to physical warfare. According to the verse it is God the All-knowing who descends to the earth to punish the wicked. I may be pardoned if I refuse to regard every revolutionary as an all-knowing God or an *avatara*."]

जन्म कर्म च मे दिव्यम् एवं यो वेत्ति तत्त्वतः ।
त्यक्त्वा देहं पुनर्जन्म नैति मामेति सोऽर्जुन ॥९॥

9. He who knows the secret of this My divine birth and action is not born again, after leaving the body; he comes to Me, O Arjuna.

For, when a man is secure in the faith that Right always prevails, he never swerves therefrom, pursuing to the bitterest end and against serious odds, and as no part of the effort proceeds from his ego, but all is dedicated to Him, being ever one with Him, he is released from birth and death.

वीतरागभयक्रोधा मन्मया मामुपाश्रिताः ।
बहवो ज्ञानतपसा पूता मद्भावमागताः ॥१०॥

10. Freed from passion, fear and wrath, filled full with Me, relying on Me, and refined by the fiery ordeal of knowledge, many have become one with Me.

ये यथा मां प्रपद्यन्ते तांस्तथैव भजाम्यहम् ।
मम वर्त्मानुवर्तन्ते मनुष्याः पार्थ सर्वशः ॥११॥

11. In whatever way men resort to Me, even so do I render to them. In every way, O Partha, the path men follow is Mine.

That is, the whole world is under His ordinance. No one may break God's law with impunity. As we sow, so shall we reap. This law operates inexorably without fear or favour.

[Gandhiji's note may remind one of Rom. 2. 6 : "Who will render to every man according to his deeds" and of Gal. 6. 2 : "For whatsoever a man soweth that shall he also reap." But it would seem that it is not so much God's ordinance that is referred to here, as God's readiness to give one what one seeks *when he resorts to Him.* All depends on the faith and spirit of the seeker. Perhaps a closer parallel from the Bible would be 2 Cor. 9. 6 : "But I say, he which soweth sparingly shall reap also sparingly ; and he who soweth bountifully shall also reap bountifully." Shankaracharya puts the thing very clearly : "With whatever end or fruit in view men resort to Me, I favour them by granting it. Those who seek knowledge I give knowledge, those who seek freedom I grant freedom, and those who seek relief from distress I give relief."

The second half of the *shloka,* though the same as the second half of III. 23, slightly differs in meaning with the different context. The sense seems to be the same as in IX. 23-24 — ultimately all worshippers, no matter what god they worship, worship Me. Cf. Koran : "Unto Allah falleth prostrate whatsoever is in the heavens and the earth, willingly or unwillingly, as do their shadows in the morning and the evening hours."

Gandhiji had an interesting controversy with Lok. Tilak on the interpretation of this verse, and the latter justified 'responsive co-operation' and the Mosaic law on the strength of this verse. Gandhiji in reply said : "The Buddhist text — *akkodhena jine kodham* * — does not conflict with this. The Buddhist text lays down an eternal principle. The text from the Bhagawadgita shows how the principle of conquering hate by love, untruth by truth, can and must be applied. If it be true that God metes out the

---

* अक्कोधेन जिने कोधं असाधुं साधुना जिने।
जिने कदरियं दानेन सच्चेन अलीकवादिनं ।। धम्मपद २२३

same measure to us that we mete out to others, it follows that, if we would escape condign punishment, we may not return anger for anger but gentleness against anger. And this is the law not for the unworldly but essentially for the worldly."

With due deference to both the great spirits, I submit the controversy should not have arisen from the text, which has the same meaning as 2 Cor. 9-6 quoted above, and must be read with Gita IX. 23-24.]

कांक्षन्तः कर्मणां सिद्धिम् यजन्त इह देवताः ।
क्षिप्रं हि मानुषे लोके सिद्धिर्भवति कर्मजा ॥१२॥

12. Those who desire their actions to bear fruit worship the gods here; for in this world of men the fruit of action is quickly obtainable.

Gods, as indicated before, must not be taken to mean the heavenly beings of tradition, but whatever reflects the divine. In that sense man is also a god. Steam, electricity and the other great forces of Nature are all gods. Propitiation of these forces quickly bears fruit, as we well know, but it is short-lived. It fails to bring comfort to the soul and it certainly does not take one even a short step towards salvation.

चातुर्वर्ण्यं मया सृष्टम् गुणकर्मविभागशः ।
तस्य कर्तारमपि माम् विद्धयकर्तारमव्ययम् ॥१३॥

13. The order of the four *varnas* was created by Me according to the different *gunas* and *karma* of each; yet know that though, therefore, author thereof, being changeless I am not the author.

["The Gita does talk of *varna* being according to *guna* and *karma*, but *guna* and *karma* are inherited by birth. The law of *varna* is nothing if not by birth. But there is no superiority implied here. Brahmanism is the culmination of other *varnas* just as the head is the culmination of the body. It means capacity for superior service, not superior status. The moment superior status is arrogated, it becomes worthy to be trampled under foot." (*Young India*, 24-11-'27)]

न मां कर्माणि लिम्पन्ति न मे कर्मफले स्पृहा ।
अिति मां योऽभिजानाति कर्मभिर्न स बध्यते ॥१४॥

14. Actions do not affect Me, nor am I concerned with the fruits thereof. He who recognizes Me as such is not bound by actions.

For man has thus before him the supreme example of one who though in action is not the doer thereof. And when we are but instruments in His hands, where then is the room for arrogating responsibility for action ?

[Shankaracharya makes clear what this recognition means : "Any one who identifies himself with Me and hence realizes that he is no doer, has no desire for fruit and is freed from the bondage of action." That is to say, he must ascend to the estate of God-realization.]

अेवं ज्ञात्वा कृतं कर्म पूर्वैरपि मुमुक्षुभिः ।
कुरु कर्मैव तस्मात् त्वम् पूर्वैः पूर्वतरं कृतम् ॥१५॥

15. Knowing this did men of old, desirous of Freedom, perform action ; do thou, then, just as they did — the men of old in days gone by.

किं कर्म किमकर्मेति कवयोऽप्यत्र मोहिताः ।
तत् ते कर्म प्रवक्ष्यामि यज् ज्ञात्वा मोक्ष्यसेऽशुभात् ॥१६॥

16. 'What is action ? What inaction ?' — here even the wise are perplexed. I will then expound to thee that action knowing which thou shalt be saved from evil.

[Shrimati Sophia Wadia in her study of the Chinese spiritual classic *Tao Te Ching* quotes a passage exactly similar : "Therefore the sage relies on actionless activity."]

कर्मणो ह्यपि बोद्धव्यम् बोद्धव्यं च विकर्मणः ।
अकर्मणश्च बोद्धव्यम् गहना कर्मणो गतिः ॥१७॥

17. For it is meet to know the meaning of action, of forbidden action, as also of inaction. Impenetrable is the secret of action.

[These classes of action are here mentioned:

(1) *Karma,* i.e. action which is capable of being performed without attachment, but is not so performed and therefore binds; also including inaction or laziness which presupposes selfishness of attachment and therefore binds;

(2) *Vikarma,* forbidden action, i.e. action which by its own nature is incapable of being performed without attachment, and hence necessarily binding, e.g. murder, lying, adultery and so forth;

(3) *Akarma,* i.e. action, mental or physical, which is performed without attachment and therefore does not bind.

Shri Vinoba has made a bold departure in his interpretation of the word '*vikarma*'. It means, he says, specific action, i.e. when the mind co-operates with the body and helps to make a self-ful action selfless. Mathematically he expresses it in this formula, *karma* + *vikarma* = *akarma.*]

कर्मण्यकर्म यः पश्येद् अकर्मणि च कर्म यः ।
स बुद्धिमान् मनुष्येषु स युक्तः कृत्स्नकर्मकृत् ॥१८॥

18. Who sees inaction in action and action in inaction, he is enlightened among men, he is a *yogi*, he has done all he need do.

The 'action' of him who, though ever active, does not claim to be the doer, is inaction; and the 'inaction' of him who, though outwardly avoiding action, is always building castles in his own mind, is action. The enlightened man who has grasped the secret of action knows that no action proceeds from him, all proceeds from God and hence he selflessly remains absorbed in action. He is the true *yogi*. The man who acts self-fully misses the secret of action and cannot distinguish between Right and Wrong. The soul's natural progress is towards selflessness and purity and one might, therefore, say that the man who strays from the path of purity strays from selflessness. All actions of the selfless man are naturally pure.

यस्य सर्वे समारंभाः कामसंकल्पवर्जिताः ।
ज्ञानाग्निदग्धकर्माणम् तमाहुः पंडितं बुधाः ।।१९।।

19. He whose every undertaking is free from desire and selfish purpose, and he who has burnt all his actions in the fire of knowledge — such an one the wise call a *pandita*.

['*Pandita*' etymologically means one who has attained Self-realization. The word has now fallen from its high estate.]

त्यक्त्वा कर्मफलासंगम् नित्यतृप्तो निराश्रयः ।
कर्मण्यभिप्रवृत्तोऽपि नैव किंचित् करोति सः ।।२०।।

20. He who has renounced attachment to the fruit of action, who is ever content, and free from all dependence, — he, though immersed in action, yet acts not.

That is, his action does not bind him.

निराशीर्यतचित्तात्मा त्यक्तसर्वपरिग्रहः ।
शारीरं केवलं कर्म कुर्वन् नाप्नोति किल्बिषम् ।।२१।।

21. Expecting naught, holding his mind and body in check, putting away every possession, and going through action only in the body he incurs no stain.

The purest act, if tainted by 'self', binds. But when it is done in a spirit of dedication, it ceases to bind. When 'self' has completely subsided, it is only the body that works. For instance, in the case of a man who is asleep his body alone is working. A prisoner doing his prison task has surrendered his body to the prison authorities and only his body, therefore, works. Similarly, he who has voluntarily made himself God's prisoner, does nothing himself. His body mechanically acts, the doer is God, not he. He has reduced himself to nothingness.

यदृच्छालाभसंतुष्टो द्वन्द्वातीतो विमत्सरः ।
समः सिद्धावसिद्धौ च कृत्वाऽपि न निबध्यते ॥२२॥

22. Content with whatever chance may bring, rid of the pairs of opposites, free from ill-will, even-minded in success and failure, he is not bound though he acts.

गतसंगस्य मुक्तस्य ज्ञानावस्थितचेतसः ।
यज्ञायाचरतः कर्म समग्रं प्रविलीयते ॥२३॥

23. Of the free soul who has shed all attachment, whose mind is firmly grounded in knowledge, who acts only for sacrifice, all *karma* is extinguished.

[19-23. The *shlokas* sum up the conditions of "free" action. We have seen in III. 9 that action for sacrifice does not bind. *Shloka* 23 says that sacrifice extinguishes even *karma* i. e. action which has yet to bear fruit. Sacrifice is thus both the prevention and cure of bondage. The Gujarati mystic Narasinha Mehta likens the ignorant man to the dog who, walking under a moving cart, believes that he is pulling the cart. Pandit Satavalekar has a happy simile to illustrate the attitude of the man of knowledge. Men seated in a moving carriage move along with the carriage, but it is only the carriage that is in motion; in the same way the wise man performs his pilgrimage to the Supreme seated peacefully in the vehicle of his body, which moves while he remains still.]

ब्रह्मार्पणं ब्रह्म हविर् ब्रह्माग्नौ ब्रह्मणा हुतम् ।
ब्रह्मैव तेन गन्तव्यम् ब्रह्मकर्मसमाधिना ॥२४॥

24. The offering of sacrifice is *Brahman*; the oblation is *Brahman*; it is offered by *Brahman* in the fire that is *Brahman*; thus he whose mind is fixed on acts dedicated to *Brahman* must needs pass on to *Brahman*.

दैवमेवापरे यज्ञम् योगिनः पर्युपासते ।
ब्रह्माग्नावपरे यज्ञम् यज्ञेनैवोपजुह्वति ॥२५॥

25. Some *yogins* perform sacrifice in the form of worship of the gods, others offer sacrifice of sacrifice itself in the fire that is *Brahman*.

[24-25. The *yogi* in *shloka* 24 is one whose actions are all in tune with the Infinite. It puts one in mind of St. Augustine's phrase: 'And this is the happy life, to rejoice to Thee, of Thee, for Thee.' The *yogi* here described makes a sacrifice to Him, of Him, for Him. The second half of *shloka* 25 reproduces the language of the Vedic text: "The gods offered sacrifice of sacrifice." * Shankaracharya interprets *yajna* (sacrifice) as Self, and says: "The realization by the conditioned Self of its identity with the unconditioned Self is itself this sacrifice." But this need not mean that that alone is knowledge-sacrifice — *jnanayajna* — as Shankaracharya insists. All the processes of incessant endeavour of the self to reach and be one with the Supreme are an act of sacrifice or so many knowledge-sacrifices.

Another sense suggested by a commentator is that the sacrifice, referred to in the second half of *shloka* 25 is the

* यज्ञेन यज्ञमयजन्त देवाः । ऋ. १०. ९०. १६

sacrifice of the very consciousness that one is making a sacrifice, i. e. reducing oneself to utmost nothingness.]

श्रोत्रादीनीन्द्रियाण्यन्ये संयमाग्निषु जुह्वति ।
शब्दादीन् विषयानन्य अिन्द्रियाग्निषु जुह्वति ॥२६॥

26. Some offer as sacrifice the sense of hearing and the other senses in the fires of restraint; others sacrifice sound and the other objects of sense in the fires of the senses.

The restraint of the senses — hearing and others — is one thing; and directing them only to legitimate objects, e.g. listening to hymns in the praise of God, is another, although ultimately both amount to the same thing.

['Fires' — the plural is used to denote the different *yogic* processes of restraint — *dharana* (concentration), *dhyana* (meditation) and *samadhi* (absorption in the object of meditation) — all three constituting self-restraint — *sanyama*.]

सर्वाणीन्द्रियकर्माणि प्राणकर्माणि चापरे ।
आत्मसंयमयोगाग्नौ जुह्वति ज्ञानदीपिते ॥२७॥

27. Others again sacrifice all the activities of the senses and of the vital energy in the *yogic* fire of self-control kindled by knowledge.

That is to say, they lose themselves in the contemplation of the Supreme.

द्रव्ययज्ञास्तपोयज्ञा योगयज्ञास्तथापरे ।
स्वाध्यायज्ञानयज्ञाश्च यतयः संशितव्रताः ॥२८॥

28. Some sacrifice with material gifts; with austerities; with *yoga*; some with the acquiring and some

with the imparting of knowledge. All these are sacrifices of stern vows and serious endeavour.

अपाने जुह्वति प्राणम् प्राणेऽपानं तथापरे ।
प्राणापानगती रुद्ध्वा प्राणायामपरायणाः ॥२९॥

29. Others absorbed in the practices of the control of the vital energy sacrifice the outward in the inward and the inward in the outward, or check the flow of both the inward and the outward vital airs.

The reference here is to the three kinds of practices of the control of vital energy — *puraka, rechaka* and *kumbhaka.*

अपरे नियताहाराः प्राणान् प्राणेषु जुह्वति ।
सर्वेऽप्येते यज्ञविदो यज्ञक्षपितकल्मषाः ॥३०॥

30. Yet others, abstemious in food, sacrifice one form of vital energy in another. All these know what sacrifice is and purge themselves of all impurities by sacrifice.

[29-30. It was believed that the body functions through vital energy of which there are supposed to be five kinds, two are referred to in *shloka* 29 and all in *shloka* 30. *Puraka* practice consists in drawing the breath in and stopping all exhalation, i. e. in the language of *shloka* 29 'sacrificing the outward (called *prana*) in the inward (called *apana*)'; *rechaka* practice consists in throwing the breath outward and stopping all inhalation, i. e. in the language of *shloka* 29, 'sacrificing the inward (*apana*) in the outward (*prana*)'; *kumbhaka* practice consists in checking the flow both ways and holding it in suspense either after an exhalation or inhalation.

The different names given are according to the varying physiological functions performed by them. The energy is called *prana* when its function is breathing; it is called *apana* when it works in the colon and bladder; it is called *samana* when it is identified with the process of digestion; *vyana* when it is expressed through blood-circulation and controls all mechanical energy; *udana* when it works through the larynx.

The other three kinds of vital energy are (3) *vyana* which is said to be diffused throughout the body and which controls all mechanical activities; (4) *udana* which is supposed to escape at the time of death; (5) *samana* which is said to distribute the food essence throughout the body and thus effect digestion.]

यज्ञशिष्टामृतभुजो यान्ति ब्रह्म सनातनम् ।
नायं लोकोऽस्त्ययज्ञस्य कुतोऽन्यः कुरुसत्तम ।।३१।।

31. Those who partake of the residue of sacrifice — called *amrita* (ambrosia) — attain to everlasting *Brahman*. Even this world is not for a non-sacrificer; how then the next, O Kurusattama?

[Manusmriti * calls the residue of sacrifice *amrita* (ambrosia). Those therefore who eat without having offered any one of the sacrifices mentioned 'eat sin' in the language of *shloka* III. 13. The rule which is known to apply to the householder's obligatory *yajna* is, by the author of the Gita, made applicable to sacrifice in the widest possible sense of the term.]

अेवं बहुविधा यज्ञा वितता ब्रह्मणो मुखे ।
कर्मजान् विद्धि तान् सर्वान् अेवं ज्ञात्वा विमोक्ष्यसे ।।३२।।

32. Even so various sacrifices have been described in the Vedas; know them all to proceed from action; knowing this thou shalt be released.

Action here means mental, physical and spiritual action. No sacrifice is possible without this triple action

---

* यज्ञशेषं तथामृतम् । मनु० ३. २८५

and no salvation without sacrifice. To know this and to put the knowledge into practice is to know the secret of sacrifice. In fine, unless man uses all his physical, mental and spiritual gifts in the service of mankind, he is a thief unfit for Freedom. He who uses his intellect only and spares his body is not a full sacrificer. Unless the mind and the body and the soul are made to work in unison, they cannot be adequately used for the service of mankind. Physical, mental and spiritual purity is essential for their harmonious working. Therefore man should concentrate on developing, purifying, and turning to the best use *all* his faculties.

श्रेयान् द्रव्यमयाद् यज्ञाज् ज्ञानयज्ञः परंतप ।
सर्वं कर्माखिलं पार्थ ज्ञाने परिसमाप्यते ॥३३॥

33. Knowledge-sacrifice is better, O Parantapa, than material sacrifice, for all action which does not bind finds its consummation in Knowledge (*jnana*).

Who does not know that works of charity performed without knowledge often result in great harm? Unless every act, however noble its motive, is informed with knowledge, it lacks perfection. Hence the complete fulfilment of all action is in knowledge.

तद् विद्धि प्रणिपातेन परिप्रश्नेन सेवया ।
उपदेक्ष्यन्ति ते ज्ञानं ज्ञानिनस्तत्त्वदर्शिनः ॥३४॥

34. The masters of knowledge who have seen the Truth will impart to thee this Knowledge; learn it through humble homage and service and by repeated questioning.

The three conditions of knowledge — homage, repeated questioning and service — deserve to be carefully borne in mind in this age. Homage or obeisance means humility and service is a necessary accompaniment ; else it would be mock homage. Repeated questioning is equally essential, for without a keen spirit of inquiry there is no knowledge. All this presupposes devotion to and faith in the person approached. There can be no humility, much less service, without faith.

यज् ज्ञात्वा न पुनर्मोहम् अेवं यास्यसि पांडव ।
येन भूतान्यशेषेण द्रक्ष्यस्यात्मन्यथो मयि ।।३५।।

35. When thou hast gained this knowledge, O Pandava, thou shalt not again fall into such error ; by virtue of it thou shalt see all beings without exception in thyself and thus in Me.

The adage '*Yatha pinde tatha brahmande*' ('यथा पिंडे तथा ब्रह्मांडे' —'as with the self so with the universe') means the same thing. He who has attained Self-realization sees no difference between himself and others.

[The natural consequence of knowledge is the realization of one's unity with all creation — seeing all beings in one's self and, therefore, necessarily in God. See VI. 29-31 where the thought is expanded. This *shloka* puts in one word the test of knowledge. Cf. "He that saith he is in the light and hateth his brother is in darkness even until now. He that loveth his brother abideth in light." (1 John 2. 9-10)]

अपि चेदसि पापेभ्यः सर्वेभ्यः पापकृत्तमः ।
सर्वं ज्ञानप्लवेनैव वृजिनं संतरिष्यसि ।।३६।।

36. Even though thou be the most sinful of sinners, thou shalt cross the ocean of sin by the boat of knowledge.

यथैधांसि समिद्धोऽग्निर् भस्मसात् कुरुतेऽर्जुन ।
ज्ञानाग्निः सर्वकर्माणि भस्मसात् कुरुते तथा ।।३७।।

37. As a blazing fire turns its fuel to ashes, O Arjuna, even so the fire of Knowledge turns all actions to ashes.

न हि ज्ञानेन सदृशं पवित्रमिह विद्यते ।
तत् स्वयं योगसंसिद्धः कालेनात्मनि विन्दति ॥३८॥

38. There is nothing in this world so purifying as Knowledge. He who is perfected by *yoga* finds it in himself in the fulness of time.

[32-38. Hill has raised an interesting and even important point, about the interpretation of '*vitata brahmano mukhe*' (वितता ब्रह्मणो मुख) in *shloka* 32 translated by many, 'described in the Vedas' (as Gandhiji has done). Hill thinks that "the interpretation of *Brahman* as the Veda may be definitely rejected", and suggests that "the phrase carries on the idea in the previous *shloka* of going to *Brahman* and that all the various forms of sacrifice provided that they are performed by 'knowers of sacrifice' are represented as 'spread out at the gate of *Brahman*,'" (this being his interpretation of the phrase in question) "that each one may adopt for performance the sacrifice he prefers, and none the less enter through the door to *Brahman*." This is an interpretation which is illuminating, if not acceptable.

I think 'described in the Vedas' or 'known from the Vedas' is the only acceptable interpretation for reasons into which I must go at length to indicate the meaning of this and the following *shlokas*. This and the following *shlokas*, in my opinion, condense an important section (Sec. 2) of the *Mundaka Up*. That section begins: "The works that the sages found in the sacred hymns are manifoldly described in three Vedas" * — the last words being *tretayam bahudha santatani* (त्रतायां बहुधा संततानि)—

* ...मन्त्रेषु कर्माणि कवयो यान्यपश्यंस्तानि त्रेतायां बहुधा संततानि। तान्याचरथ नियतं सत्यकामा अेष वः पन्थाः सुकृतस्य लोके॥ ... प्रियां वाचमभिवदन्त्योऽर्चयन्त्य अेषः वः पुण्यः सुकृतो ब्रह्मलोकः॥ प्लवा ह्येते अदृढा यज्ञरूपा अष्टादशोक्तमवरं येषु कर्म। अेतच्छ्रेयो येऽभिनन्दन्ति मूढा

language very similar to the language of IV. 32. "Follow them," says the *Upanishad,* "for that is the path of merit," and then proceeds to describe the various Vedic sacrifices and closes with this important comment: "These sacrifices in which all kinds of inferior rites are spoken of may be good enough for earning merit, but *they are after all unreliable boats.* The deluded ones who commend them go again and again from old age to death." These sacrifices are deprecated in severe language and the men given to them are described as *karminah* कर्मिणः — wedded to binding action — who sink down and re-enter this world when their merits are exhausted. But as against this is the path of Knowledge followed "by those practising austerity and faith, and who therethrough go to the immortal *Atman*". "Having ascertained for himself the worlds built up by action, a man devoted to *Brahman* should be resigned, for the *Brahman* world which did not spring out of man's action cannot be won by means of action. For the sake of this knowledge let him go to none but the properly qualified *guru* in the proper manner."

I have considerably condensed the *Upanishad* section, but the argument is clear. If the reader will now read *shlokas* 32-38, he will see at once that the author of the Gita has grasped the old nettle and offered a new solution (*shloka* 38). The sacrifices based on Vedic ritual —— or the material sacrifices — are *"unreliable boats"*, in the language of the *Upanishad,* the only sure boat is the *boat of Knowledge — Jnanaplava* (*shloka* 36), in the language of the Gita which accepts the *Upanishad* argument. It not only goes to suggest the ways and means — the same as suggested by the *Upanishad* — to win that knowledge (*shloka* 34), *but also* makes the signal contribution to the solution of the difficulty by declaring that *yoga* is the key

जरामृत्युं ते पुनरेवापियन्ति ॥ . . . यत् कर्मिणो न प्रवेदयन्ति रागात् तेनातुराः क्षीणलोकाश्च्यवन्ते । . . . तपःश्रद्धे ये . . . विरजा प्रयान्ति यत्रामृतः स पुरुषो ह्यव्ययात्मा । . . . . परीक्ष्य लोकान् कर्मचितान् ब्राह्मणो निर्वेदमायान्नास्त्यकृतः कृतेन । . . तद्विज्ञानार्थं स गुरुमेवाभि- गच्छेत् समित्पाणिः श्रोत्रियं ब्रह्मनिष्ठम् । मुंडक० १. २. १-१२

to that knowledge (*shloka* 38) for one who cannot and is not fitted to renounce the world and sit at the feet of a *guru*. The Gita also supplies the corrective to the extreme *Upanishad* position by suggesting that though the material sacrifices described in the Vedas are "unreliable boats", there are knowledge-sacrifices which are far better and which may be summed up in one word *yoga* — all action without attachment to fruit and dedicated to God, and hence bound to culminate in knowledge (*shloka* 33).

Gandhiji's note on *shloka* 32, important as it is as an expression of his own view, misses the points I have urged in this note. This *Upanishad* parallel does not seem to have drawn the attention of any commentator, so far as I know.]

श्रद्धावान् लभते ज्ञानम् तत्परः संयतेन्द्रियः ।
ज्ञानं लब्ध्वा परां शान्तिम् अचिरेणाधिगच्छति ॥३९॥

39. It is the man of faith who gains knowledge — the man who is intent on it and who has mastery over his senses; having gained knowledge, he comes ere long to the supreme peace.

[These are the rock-bottom requisites for him who would have knowledge. Throughout the *Upanishads* we find austerity, faith, *brahmacharya* and truth, as the essential qualifications of a seeker after Self-realization. (*Chha. Up.* 8. 5. 3-5 ; * *Mund. Up.* 3. 1. 5 ;+ *Prashna Up.* 1. 2 † etc.)]

---

* अथ यदनाशकायनमित्याचक्षते ब्रह्मचर्यमेव तदेष ह्यात्मा न नश्यति यं ब्रह्मचर्येणानुविन्दतेऽथ यदरण्यायनमित्याचक्षते ब्रह्मचर्यमेव तत्तदरश्च ह वै ण्यश्चार्णवौ ब्रह्मलोके तृतीयस्यामितो दिवि तदैरंमदीयं सरस्तदश्वत्थः सोमसवनस्तदपराजिता पूर्ब्रह्मणः प्रभुविमितं हिरण्मयम् ॥ तद्य अेवैतावरं च ण्यं चार्णवौ ब्रह्मलोके ब्रह्मचर्येणानुविन्दन्ति तेषामेवैष ब्रह्मलोकस्तेषां सर्वेषु लोकेषु कामचारो भवति ॥ छांदोग्य ८. ५. ३–५

\+ सत्येन लभ्यस्तपसा ह्येष आत्मा। सम्यग्ज्ञानेन ब्रह्मचर्येण नित्यम् ॥
अन्तःशरीरे ज्योतिर्मयो हि शुभ्रो । यं पश्यन्ति यतयः क्षीणदोषाः ॥
मुंडक ३. १. ५

† तान्ह स ऋषिरुवाच भूय अेव तपसा ब्रह्मचर्येण श्रद्धया संवत्सरं संवत्स्यथ यथाकामं प्रश्नान् पृच्छथ यदि विज्ञास्यामः सर्वं ह वो वक्ष्याम अिति ॥ प्रश्न १.२

अज्ञश्चाश्रद्दधानश्च संशयात्मा विनश्यति ।
नायं लोकोऽस्ति न परो न सुखं संशयात्मनः ॥४०॥

40. But the man of doubt, without knowledge and without faith, is lost; for him who is given to doubt there is neither this world nor that beyond, nor happiness.

योगसंन्यस्तकर्माणम् ज्ञानसंछिन्नसंशयम् ।
आत्मवन्तं न कर्माणि निबध्नन्ति धनंजय ॥४१॥

41. He who has renounced all action by means of *yoga*, who has severed all doubt by means of knowledge —him self-possessed, no actions bind, O Dhananjaya!

तस्मादज्ञानसंभूतम् हृत्स्थं ज्ञानासिनात्मनः ।
छित्वैनं संशयं योगम् आतिष्ठोतिष्ठ भारत ॥४२॥

42. Therefore, with the sword of Self-realization sever thou this doubt, bred of ignorance, which has crept into thy heart! Betake thyself to *yoga* and arise, O Bharata!

[Cf. "Arise, and begin this very instant, and say now is the time to fight, now is the proper time to amend my life." (*Imitation of Christ*)]

अिति श्रीमद्भगवद्गीतासु अुपनिषत्सु ब्रह्मविद्यायां योगशास्त्रे श्रीकृष्णार्जुनसंवादे
ज्ञानकर्मसंन्यासयोगो नाम चतुर्थोऽध्यायः ॥४॥

Thus ends the fourth discourse, entitled '*Jnana-Karma-Sannyasa-Yoga*' in the converse of Lord Krishna and Arjuna, on the science of *Yoga*, as part of the knowledge of *Brahman* in the Upanishad called the Bhagawadgita.

DISCOURSE V

This discourse is devoted to showing that renunciation of action as such is impossible without the discipline of selfless action and that both are ultimately one.

अर्जुन अुवाच ।

संन्यासं कर्मणां कृष्ण पुनर्योगं च शंससि ।
यच्छ्रेय अेतयोरेकं तन् मे ब्रूहि सुनिश्चितम् ।।१।।

Arjuna said :

1. Thou laudest renunciation of actions, O Krishna, whilst at the same time thou laudest performance of action ; tell me for a certainty which is the better.

[The author discusses the two terms, *sannyasa* (renunciation) and *yoga* (performance) which must have been common in his time and points out how the essence of the two was very much misunderstood. The same are referred to as *sankhya* and *yoga* in *shloka* 4.]

श्रीभगवानुवाच ।

संन्यासः कर्मयोगश्च निःश्रेयसकरावुभौ ।
तयोस्तु कर्मसंन्यासात् कर्मयोगो विशिष्यते ।।२।।

The Lord said :

2. Renunciation and performance of action both lead to salvation ; but of the two, *karmayoga* (performance) is better than *sannyasa* (renunciation).

ज्ञेयः स नित्यसंन्यासी यो न द्वेष्टि न कांक्षति ।
निर्द्वंद्वो हि महाबाहो सुखं बंधात् प्रमुच्यते ।।३।।

3. Him one should know as ever renouncing who has no dislikes and likes ; for he who is free from the pairs of opposites is easily released from bondage.

That is, not renunciation of action but of attachment to the pairs determines true renunciation. A man who is always in action may be a good *sannyasi* (renouncer) and another who may be doing no work may well be a hypocrite. See III. 6.

[To use Prof. Mackenzie's phrase, he carries about himself "a continuously dominant universe" of detachment.]

सांख्ययोगौ पृथग् बाला: प्रवदन्ति न पंडिता: ।
अेकमप्यास्थित: सम्यग् अुभयोर्विन्दते फलम् ।।४।।

4. It is the ignorant who speak of *sankhya* and *yoga* as different, not so those who have knowledge. He who is rightly established even in one wins to the fruit of both.

The *yogi* engrossed in *sankhya* (knowledge) lives even in thought for the good of the world and attains the fruit of *karmayoga* by the sheer power of his thought. The *karmayogi* ever engrossed in unattached action naturally enjoys the peace of the *jnanayogi*.

यत् सांख्यै: प्राप्यते स्थानं तद् योगैरपि गम्यते ।
अेकं सांख्यं च योगं च य: पश्यति स पश्यति ।।५।।

5. The goal that the *sankhyas* attain is also reached by the *yogins*. He sees truly who sees both *sankhya* and *yoga* as one.

[For *sankhya* and *yogin* see note on III. 3.]

संन्यासस्तु महाबाहो दु:खमाप्तुमयोगत: ।
योगयुक्तो मुनिर्ब्रह्म न चिरेणाधिगच्छति ।।६।।

6. But renunciation, O Mahabahu, is hard to attain except by *yoga*; the ascetic equipped with *yoga* attains *Brahman* ere long.

[Shankaracharya says *Brahman* means here *sannyasa* (renunciation), because it is that which leads to the knowledge of the Supreme. The context would seem to justify the interpretation, the meaning being that what is difficult to attain without *yoga* is easily attained by means of *yoga*.]

योगयुक्तो विशुद्धात्मा विजितात्मा जितेन्द्रियः ।
सर्वभूतात्मभूतात्मा कुर्वन्नपि न लिप्यते ।।७।।

7. The *yogi* who has cleansed himself, has gained mastery over his mind and all his senses, who has become one with the *Atman* in all creation, although he acts he remains unaffected.

[The Gita borrows the language of *Isha Up.* 2: "Action affects not the man.*"]

नैव किंचित् करोमीति युक्तो मन्येत तत्त्ववित् ।
पश्यन् शृण्वन् स्पृशञ् जिघ्रन् अश्नन् गच्छन् स्वपन् श्वसन् ।।८।।
प्रलपन् विसृजन् गृह्णन् उन्मिषन् निमिषन्नपि ।
इंद्रियाणींद्रियार्थेषु वर्तन्त इति धारयन् ।।९।।

8. The *yogi* who has seen the Truth knows that it is not he that acts whilst seeing, hearing, touching, smelling, eating, walking, sleeping, or breathing,

9. Talking, letting go, holding fast, opening or closing the eyes — in the conviction that it is the senses that are moving in their respective spheres.

---

* न कर्म लिप्यते नरे। ईश. २.

So long as 'self' endures, this detachment cannot be achieved. A sensual man therefore may not shelter himself under the pretence that it is not he but his senses that are acting. Such a mischievous interpretation betrays a gross ignorance of the Gita and right conduct. The next *shloka* makes this clear.

[8. '*Tattvavit*' may mean 'one who has seen the Truth' or 'one who knows the principles' — the principles being the *Sankhya* principles (p. 22), all those being *gunas* or not-Self. Seeing that all the activities of the internal and external organs are all the activities of not-Self, he will not ascribe them to the Self or *Atman.* Verses 8-9 remind one of a great song of Kabir — *Sadho sahaj samadh bhali* (the natural union is the best) — where he says that for the *yogi,* every movement or position of the body is an offering to God, or an identification or union with God. Cf. the phrase 'walking with God'.]

ब्रह्मण्याधाय कर्माणि संगं त्यक्त्वा करोति यः ।
लिप्यते न स पापेन पद्मपत्रमिवांभसा ॥१०॥

10. He who dedicates his actions to *Brahman* and performs them without attachment is not smeared by sin, as the lotus-leaf by water.

[A beautiful paraphrase of *Chha. Up.** 4. 14. 3 :

"As water does not touch the lotus-leaf, even so the sinful act does not smear one who knows *Atman.*"]

कायेन मनसा बुद्ध्या केवलैरिंद्रियैरपि ।
योगिनः कर्म कुर्वन्ति संगं त्यक्त्वाऽऽत्मशुद्धये ॥११॥

11. Only with the body, mind and intellect and also with the senses, do the *yogins* perform action without attachment for the sake of self-purification.

---

* यथा पुष्करपलाश आपो न श्लिष्यन्त अेवमेवंविदि पापं कर्म न श्लिष्यत अिति। छान्दोग्य. ४. १४. ३

["Only" means "without the sense of 'I'." A day-dreamer may roam over the whole world only with the mind, an insane or intoxicated man may act only with the body, an intellectual prodigy may act only with the intellect, and a child may act only with the senses. But in each case the detachment is not a conscious act, but an accidental withdrawal of the Self from each of the agents — mind, body, intellect, and the senses. But the *yogin* withdraws the Self, with full knowledge, from the operations of each of these, and achieves the repose of the dreamer, the freedom of the insane, the absorption of the prodigy and the innocence of the child. The others act from instinct, the *yogi* from knowledge.]

युक्तः कर्मफलं त्यक्त्वा शांतिमाप्नोति नैष्ठिकीम् ।
अयुक्तः कामकारेण फले सक्तो निबध्यते ॥१२॥

12. A man of *yoga* obtains everlasting peace by abandoning the fruit of action; the man ignorant of *yoga*, selfishly attached to fruit, remains bound.

सर्वकर्माणि मनसा संन्यस्यास्ते सुखं वशी ।
नवद्वारे पुरे देही नैव कुर्वन् न कारयन् ॥१३॥

13. Renouncing with the mind all actions, the dweller in the body, who is master of himself, rests happily in his city of nine gates, neither doing nor getting anything done.

The principal gates of the body are the two eyes, the two nostrils, the two ears, the mouth, and the two organs of excretion — though really speaking the countless pores of the skin are no less gates. If the gatekeeper always remains on the alert and performs his task, letting in or out only the objects that deserve ingress or egress, then of him it can truly be said that he has no part in the ingress or egress, but that he is a passive witness. He thus does nothing nor gets anything done.

[The *Shvet. Up.* 3. 18 describes * "the embodied soul in the city of the nine gates, moving back and forth, and yet master of the whole world of the moving and unmoving."]

न कर्तृत्वं न कर्माणि लोकस्य सृजति प्रभुः ।
न कर्मफलसंयोगं स्वभावस्तु प्रवर्तते ॥१४॥

14. The Lord creates neither agency nor action for the world; neither does he connect action with its fruit. It is nature that is at work.

God is no doer. The inexorable law of *karma* prevails, and in the very fulfilment of the law — giving everyone his deserts, making everyone reap what he sows — lies God's abounding mercy and justice. In undiluted justice is mercy. Mercy which is inconsistent with justice is not mercy but its opposite. But man is not a judge knowing past, present, and future. So for him the law is reversed and mercy or forgiveness is the purest justice. Being himself ever liable to be judged, he must accord to others what he would accord to himself, viz. forgiveness. Only by cultivating the spirit of forgiveness can he reach the state of a *yogi*, whom no actions bind, the man of even-mindedness, the man skilled in action.

नादत्ते कस्यचित् पापं न चैव सुकृतं विभुः ।
अज्ञानेनावृतं ज्ञानं तेन मुह्यन्ति जंतवः ॥१५॥

15. The Lord does not take upon Himself anyone's vice or virtue; it is ignorance that veils knowledge and deludes all creatures.

---

* नवद्वारे पुरे देही हंसो लेलायते बहिः ।
वशी सर्वस्य लोकस्य स्थावरस्य चरस्य च ॥
श्वेताश्वतर ३. १८

The delusion lies in man arrogating to himself the authorship of action and the attributing to God the consequence thereof — punishment or reward as the case may be.

[14-15. These *shlokas* are an echo of the *sankhyan* doctrine that *Purusha* does not act, only *Prakriti* acts, and as Vedanta equates *Purusha* or *Atman* with the Supreme the words *prabhu* (14) and *vibhu* (15) meaning the Lord or the pervading or the presiding principle are here used. Gandhiji takes both words to mean the Supreme, while some take them to mean the individual Self. In either case, the meaning is the same. Let no one however run into the error that the Supreme of the Gita is thus like the Aristotelian God, a contemplative or abstract conception, never acting, never interesting Himself in the universe, a king that reigns but does not govern. It is the reign of the Law that is emphasized in the *shlokas,* though the ultimate source of all law is the Supreme Being pervading all, sustaining all (XV. 17). Whilst for the *sankhya* or the *jnanayogi* the Supreme, acting as the Universal Law, is enough, the *karmayogi* or *bhakta* will not be satisfied with anything less than a God willing to accept his devotion, an ever-ready friend and comforter, as we shall see in *shloka* 29 of this discourse.

With these read IX. 17-19 and XIII. 13-16.

"We are all trying to think of the Unthinkable, to describe the Indescribable, to know the Unknown. That is why our speech falters, is inadequate and contradictory. That is why the Vedas describe *Brahman* as 'not this', 'not this'. If we exist, if our parents and their parents have existed, then it is proper to believe in the Parent of the whole creation. If He is not, we are nowhere. And that is why all of us call one God differently. He is one and yet many. He is smaller than an atom and bigger than the Himalayas ; He is contained even in a drop of the ocean and yet not even the seven seas can compass Him. Reason is powerless to know Him. He is beyond the reach or grasp of reason." (Gandhiji in *Young India*, Jan. 21, 1926)]

ज्ञानेन तु तदज्ञानम् येषां नाशितमात्मनः ।
तेषामादित्यवज्ज्ञानं प्रकाशयति तत् परम् ॥१६॥

16. But to them whose ignorance is destroyed by the knowledge of *Atman*, this their knowledge, like the sun, reveals the Supreme.

तद्बुद्धयस्तदात्मानस् तन्निष्ठास्तत्परायणाः ।
गच्छंत्यपुनरावृत्तिं ज्ञाननिर्धूतकल्मषाः ॥१७॥

17. Those whose intellect is suffused with That, whose self has become one with That, who abide in That, and whose end and aim is That, wipe out their sins with knowledge, and go whence there is no return.

विद्याविनयसंपन्ने ब्राह्मणे गवि हस्तिनि ।
शुनि चैव श्वपाके च पंडिताः समदर्शिनः ॥१८॥

18. The men of Self-realization look with an equal eye on a *brahmana* possessed of learning and humility, a cow, an elephant, a dog and even a dog-eater.

That is to say, they serve every one of them alike, according to the needs of each. Treating a *brahmana* and *shwapaka* (dog-eater) alike means that the wise man will suck the poison off a snake-bitten *shwapaka* with as much eagerness and readiness as he would from a snake-bitten *brahmana*.

[Gandhiji explained this verse at great length to a meeting of Harijan workers who, Gandhiji insisted, must take the pledge of equality of status of all:

"I am not after extinguishing all differences. Who can destroy natural differences? Is there no difference between a *brahmana,* a dog and a dog-eater? There is indeed a difference between them, but the man who knows the science of life will say that there is no difference between them in status, as there is none between an elephant and an ant, a savage and a savant. A savage may be awe-struck before a savant; but the latter should not have any sense of superiority." (*Harijan*, Jan. 11, 1935)

"There is another view of the case too. We are all equal in one respect, viz. imperfection. We are all tarred with that same brush. None of us is perfect. Only the Lord is perfect. And human being is unclean by birth. Unclean we are all, if we examine our inner selves, to a greater or less extent. And yet "the inner oneness pervades all life. The forms are many, but the informing Spirit is one." (Gandhiji)

Looking with an equal eye on all is one of the attributes of the *yogi* and the *jnani,* and is mentioned over and over again in the Gita. See VI. 9, XII. 18, XIV. 25 where regarding friend and foe alike is one of the attributes of the *yogi, bhakta* and *gunatita.* The words 'equal', 'alike', 'same' in all these contexts have the same content as the word 'perfect' in the well-known verses of St. Matthew's gospel: "Love your enemies, bless them that curse you; that ye may be the children of your Father which is in Heaven; for He maketh the sun to rise on the evil and on the good; be ye therefore perfect even as your Father which is in Heaven is perfect." (5. 44, 45, 48). The last verse is a close parallel, even in language, to this *shloka.*]

इहैव तैर्जितः सर्गो येषां साम्ये स्थितं मनः ।
निर्दोषं हि समं ब्रह्म तस्माद् ब्रह्मणि ते स्थिताः ।।१९।।

19. In this very body they have conquered the round of birth and death, whose mind is anchored in sameness; for perfect *Brahman* is same to all, therefore in *Brahman* they rest.

As a man thinks, so he becomes, and therefore those whose minds are bent on being the same to all achieve that sameness and become one with *Brahman.*

[Cf. The first Epistle of John 1. 6: "He that saith he abideth in Him ought also so to walk even as He walked", which suggests the converse that he that walketh even as He walked abideth in Him: "God is love: and he that dwelleth in love dwelleth in God." (1. John 4. 16)]

न प्रहृष्येत् प्रियं प्राप्य नोद्विजेत् प्राप्य चाप्रियम् ।
स्थिरबुद्धिरसंमूढो ब्रह्मविद् ब्रह्मणि स्थितः ॥२०॥

20. He whose understanding is secure, who is undeluded, who knows *Brahman* and who rests in *Brahman*, will neither be glad to get what is pleasant, nor sad to get what is unpleasant.

बाह्यस्पर्शेष्वसक्तात्मा विन्दत्यात्मनि यत् सुखम् ।
स ब्रह्मयोगयुक्तात्मा सुखमक्षय्यमश्नुते ॥२१॥

21. He who has detached himself from contacts without, finds bliss in *Atman*; having achieved union with *Brahman* he enjoys eternal bliss.

He who has weaned himself from outward objects to the inner *Atman* is fitted for union with *Brahman* and the highest bliss. To withdraw oneself from contacts without and to bask in the sunshine of union with *Brahman* are two aspects of the same state, two sides of the same coin.

ये हि संस्पर्शजा भोगा दुःखयोनय अेव ते ।
आद्यंतवंतः कौंतेय न तेषु रमते बुधः ॥२२॥

22. For the joys derived from sense-contacts are nothing but mines of misery; they have beginning and end, O Kaunteya; the wise man does not revel therein.

[The word '*duhkhayonayah*' may be also translated 'wombs of misery'; *yoni* means 'womb' and 'mine' both. St. Augustine calls these sense-contacts "seed-plots of sorrows". For the thought cf. Col. 2. 20-22: "Touch not, taste not, handle not; which all are to perish with the using."]

शक्नोतीहैव यः सोढुं प्राक् शरीरविमोक्षणात् ।
कामक्रोधोद्भवं वेगं स युक्तः स सुखी नरः ॥२३॥

23. The man who is able even here on earth, ere he is released from the body, to hold out against the flood-tide of lust and wrath, — he is a *yogi*, he is happy.

As a corpse has no likes and dislikes, no sensibility to pleasure and pain, even so he who though alive is dead to these, he truly lives, he is truly happy.

[It is curious to note that Gandhiji's note reproduces unconsciously almost *verbatim* a *shloka* from *Yoga-vasishtha*: "If one, while alive, can be like the body, which experiences no pleasure and pain after life is extinct, he will rest in absolute bliss."]

योऽन्तःसुखोऽन्तरारामस् तथांतर्ज्योतिरेव यः ।
स योगी ब्रह्मनिर्वाणं ब्रह्मभूतोऽधिगच्छति ॥२४॥

24. He who finds happiness only within, rest only within, light only within, — that *yogi*, having become one with Nature, attains to oneness with *Brahman*.

लभन्ते ब्रह्मनिर्वाणम् ऋषयः क्षीणकल्मषाः ।
छिन्नद्वैधा यतात्मानः सर्वभूतहिते रताः ॥२५॥

25. They win oneness with *Brahman* — the seers whose sins are wiped out, whose doubts are resolved, who have mastered themselves, and who are engrossed in the welfare of all beings.

कामक्रोधवियुक्तानां यतीनां यतचेतसाम् ।
अभितो ब्रह्मनिर्वाणं वर्तते विदितात्मनाम् ।।२६।।

26. Rid of lust and wrath, masters of themselves, the ascetics who have realized *Atman* find oneness with *Brahman* everywhere around them.

स्पर्शान् कृत्वा बहिर्बाह्यान् चक्षुश्चैवांतरे भ्रुवोः ।
प्राणापानौ समौ कृत्वा नासाभ्यंतरचारिणौ ।।२७।।
यतेंद्रियमनोबुद्धिर् मुनिर्मोक्षपरायणः ।
विगतेच्छाभयक्रोधो यः सदा मुक्त अेव सः ।।२८।।

27-28. That ascetic is ever free — who, having shut out the outward sense-contacts, sits with his gaze fixed between the brows, outward and inward breathing in the nostrils made equal; his senses, mind, and reason held in check; rid of longing, fear and wrath; and intent on Freedom.

These *shlokas* refer to some of the *yogic* practices laid down in the *Yoga-sutras*. A word of caution is necessary regarding these practices. They serve for the *yogin* the same purpose as athletics and gymnastics do for the *bhogin* (who pursues worldly pleasures). His physical exercises help the latter to keep his senses of enjoyment in full vigour. The *yogic* practices help the *yogin* to keep his body in condition and his senses in subjection. Men versed in these practices are rare in these days, and few of these turn them to good account. He who has achieved the preliminary stage on the path of self-discipline, he who has a passion for Freedom, and who having rid himself of the pairs of opposites has conquered fear, would do well to go in for these practices which will surely help him. It is such a disciplined man alone who can, through these practices, render his body a holy temple of God. Purity both of the mind and body is a *sine qua non,* without which these processes are likely, in the first instance, to lead a man astray and then drive him deeper into the slough of delusion. That this has been the result in some cases many know from actual experience. That is why that prince of *yogins,* Patanjali gave the first place to *yamas* (cardinal vows) and *niyamas* (casual vows), and held as eligible for *yogic* practices only those who have gone through the preliminary discipline.

The five cardinal vows are: non-violence, truth, non-stealing, celibacy, non-possession. The five casual vows are: bodily purity, contentment, the study of the scriptures, austerity, and meditation of God.

भोक्तारं यज्ञतपसां सर्वलोकमहेश्वरम् ।
सुहृदं सर्वभूतानां ज्ञात्वा मां शांतिमृच्छति ॥२९॥

29. Knowing Me as the Acceptor of sacrifice and austerity, the great Lord of all the worlds, the Friend of all creation, the *yogi* attains to peace.

This *shloka* may appear to be in conflict with *shlokas* 14 and 15 of this discourse and similar ones in other discourses. It is not really so. Almighty God is Doer and non-Doer, Enjoyer and non-Enjoyer both. He is indescribable, beyond the power of human speech. Man somehow strives to have a glimpse of Him and in so doing invests Him with diverse and even contradictory attributes.

[27-29: The reader will perhaps do well to study the argument of this discourse in "My Submission" pp. 68-72.

We have had in the discourse a comparison of the *jnana-yogi* or the philosophic mystic and the *karmayogi* or the active mystic. The *shlokas* V. 27-29 start a new comparison now — quite a parallel dichotomy as it evidences itself in the life of the devotee. *Shlokas* 27-28 introduce to us the contemplative or meditative mystic — *dhyanayogi* — to be described in discourses VI, VII and VIII, while *shloka* 29 describes the devotional mystic, the *bhaktiyogi* who worships the Supreme in His one or many manifestations, to be described in discourses IX-XII. To him God appears or reveals Himself as the Acceptor of all sacrifices and the Friend of all creation, as indeed He did appear to St. Catherine of Siena. To her He appeared as the all-demanding Lover from Whom she heard the solemn words: "I, Fire, the Acceptor of sacrifices, ravishing away from them their darkness, give the light.' (Evelyn Underhill, *Mysticism*). Cf. with V. 29, *shlokas* IX. 18 and IX. 24.

It is interesting to note that the Bible also applies to God the epithets "Father" and "Comforter", and in the Koran He is again and again referred to as the *Wali* — the Patron and Friend: "He verily is the Absolute, the Owner of praise" (22. 64); "He is your Protecting Friend, a Blessed Patron and a Blessed Helper." (22. 78)]

इति श्रीमद्भगवद्गीतासु उपनिषत्सु ब्रह्मविद्यायां योगशास्त्रे श्रीकृष्णार्जुनसंवादे
संन्यासयोगो नाम पंचमोऽध्यायः ॥५॥

Thus ends the fifth discourse, entitled '*Sannyasa Yoga*' in the converse of Lord Krishna and Arjuna, on the science of *Yoga* as part of the knowledge of *Brahman*, in the Upanishad called the Bhagawadgita.

DISCOURSE VI

This discourse deals with some of the means for the accomplishment of Yoga or the discipline of the mind and its activities.

श्रीभगवानुवाच ।

अनाश्रितः कर्मफलं कार्यं कर्म करोति यः ।
स संन्यासी च योगी च न निरग्निर्न चाक्रियः ।।१।।

The Lord said:

1. He who performs all obligatory action, without depending on the fruit thereof, is a *sannyasin* and a *yogin* — not the man who neglects the sacrificial fire nor he who neglects action.

Fire here may be taken to mean all possible instruments of action. Fire was needed when sacrifices used to be performed with its help. Assuming that spinning were a means of universal service in this age, a man by neglecting the spinning wheel would not become a *sannyasi.*

यं संन्यासमिति प्राहुर् योगं तं विद्धि पांडव ।
न ह्यसंन्यस्तसंकल्पो योगी भवति कश्चन ।।२।।

2. What is called *sannyasa,* know thou to be *yoga,* O Pandava; for none can become a *yogin* who has not renounced selfish purpose.

[Cf. the converse in V. 6 where *sannyasa* is said to be hard to attain without *yoga.*]

आरुरुक्षोर्मुनेर्योगं कर्म कारणमुच्यते ।
योगारूढस्य तस्यैव शमः कारणमुच्यते ।।३।।

3. For the man who seeks to scale the heights of *yoga,* action is said to be the means; for the same man,

when he has scaled those heights, repose is said to be the means.

He who has purged himself of all impurities and who has achieved even-mindedness will easily achieve Self-realization. But this does not mean that he who has scaled the heights of *yoga* will disdain to work for the guidance of the world. On the contrary that work will be to him not only as the breath of his nostrils, but also as natural to him as breathing. He will do so by the sheer force of his will. See V. 4.

[This partly repeats the thought of V. 4. 'Repose' is *not* inaction. The word in Sanskrit is *shamah* as opposed to '*ashamah*' in XIV. 12 which is restlessness or 'toil without tranquillity'. 'Repose' — *shamah* — will therefore be "toil unsevered from tranquillity", to use Mathew Arnold's phrase. Perhaps the meaning of the whole *shloka* will be still better expressed by adopting Lao Tze's language: The seer who has scaled the heights of *yoga* will have acquired perfection enough "to teach without words and to be useful without action."]

यदा हि नेंद्रियार्थेषु न कर्मस्वनुषज्जते ।
सर्वसंकल्पसंन्यासी योगारूढस्तदोच्यते ।।४।।

4. When a man is not attached either to the objects of sense or to actions and sheds all selfish purpose, then he is said to have scaled the heights of *yoga*.

उद्धरेदात्मनाऽऽत्मानं नात्मानमवसादयेत् ।
आत्मैव ह्यात्मनो बंधुर् आत्मैव रिपुरात्मनः ।।५।।
बंधुरात्माऽऽत्मनस्तस्य येनात्मैवात्मना जितः ।
अनात्मनस्तु शत्रुत्वे वर्तेतात्मैव शत्रुवत् ।।६।।

5. By one's Self should one raise oneself, and not allow oneself to fall; for *Atman* (Self) alone is the friend of self, and Self alone is self's foe.

6. His Self alone is friend, who has conquered himself by his Self; but to him who has not conquered himself and is thus inimical to himself, even his Self behaves as foe.

[5-6. Cf. Dhammapada, 160: "Self is the lord of self; who else can be the lord? With self well-subdued one finds the Lord who is difficult to find." Also *Ibid,* 165: "One's sin taints oneself, one's abstinence from sin keeps oneself clean. One can be clean or unclean by oneself, none else can make one so." Also *Ibid,* 379: "The *bhikkhu* should elevate himself by himself, he should be his own neighbour; thus self-protected and self-possessed he becomes happy."; *Ibid* 380: "Self is the lord of self; Self is the goal of self." *

I have in my translation distinguished '*Atman*' the higher Self from the lower self, though it is not quite clear whether Gandhiji does so in his translation. *Atman* is really speaking, neither friend nor foe, but the lower self makes Him friend or foe, according as it strives to lift itself up to Him or drag itself down from Him. In order that the moral end of perfection may be fulfilled, the self has to look to Him as "the Goal, the Witness, the Refuge, the Friend" (IX. 18); but it often makes Him his enemy as mortal men know to their cost.

Cf. Koran: "Whoso committeth sin committeth it only against himself" (4. 111) and "Whoso goeth right it is only for his own soul that he goeth right, and whosoever erreth

---

* अत्ता ही अत्तनो नाथो को हि नाथो परो सिया।
अत्तना हि सुदन्तेन नाथं लभति दुल्लभं ॥१६०॥
अत्तना व कत्तं पापं अत्तना संकिलिस्सति।
अत्तना अकतं पापं अत्तना व विसुज्झति।
सुद्धी असुद्धी पच्चत्तं नाञ्ञो अञ्ञं विसोधये ॥१६५॥
अत्तना चोदयत्तानं पटिमासे अत्तमत्तना।
सो अत्तगुत्तो सतिमा सुख भिक्खु विहाहिसि ॥३७९॥
अत्ता हि अत्तनो नाथो अत्ता हि अत्तनो गति ॥३८०॥ धम्मपद

erreth only to its hurt." (17. 15). Also cf. 'Imitation of Christ', "There is not a more troublesome or worse enemy to the soul than thou thyself art when not well agreeing with Spirit."]

जितात्मनः प्रशांतस्य परमात्मा समाहितः ।
शीतोष्णसुखदुःखेषु तथा मानापमानयोः ॥७॥

7. Of him who has conquered himself and who rests in perfect calm the self is completely composed, in cold and heat, in pleasure and pain, in honour and dishonour.

ज्ञानविज्ञानतृप्तात्मा कूटस्थो विजितेंद्रियः ।
युक्त अित्युच्यते योगी समलोष्टाश्मकांचनः ॥८॥

8. The *yogin* who is filled with the contentment of wisdom and discriminative knowledge, who is firm as a rock, who has mastered his senses, and to whom a clod of earth, a stone and gold are the same, is possessed of *yoga*.

सुहृन्मित्रार्युदासीनमध्यस्थद्वेष्यबंधुषु ।
साधुष्वपि च पापेषु समबुद्धिर्विशिष्यते ॥९॥

9. He excels who regards alike the boon companion, the friend, the enemy, the stranger, the mediator, the alien and the ally, as also the saint and the sinner.

योगी युंजीत सततम् आत्मानं रहसि स्थितः ।
अेकाकी यतचित्तात्मा निराशीरपरिग्रहः ॥१०॥

10. Let the *yogi* constantly apply his thought to *Atman* remaining alone in a secluded place, his mind and body in control, rid of desires and possessions.

[In the whole of this context (*shlokas* 10-16) '*yogi*' often means the aspirant *yogi*, one set on *yoga*; and *yoga* means the discipline of the mind and the intellect and of the vital airs in order to concentrate the whole psychical apparatus on *Atman,* briefly to concentrate the self on the Self. For *shlokas* 10-14 cf. *Shve. Up.* 2-8-12 where the posture and the spot and other conditions are described in greater detail. But the rest of the portion is the Gita's own contribution on the subject of *yoga* practice.]

शुचौ देशे प्रतिष्ठाप्य स्थिरमासनमात्मनः ।
नात्युच्छ्रितं नातिनीचं चैलाजिनकुशोत्तरम् ।।११।।

11. Fixing for himself, in a pure spot, a firm seat, neither too high nor yet too low, covered with *kusha* grass, thereon a deerskin, and thereon a cloth ;

तत्रैकाग्रं मनः कृत्वा यतचित्तेंद्रियक्रियः ।
उपविश्यासने युंज्याद् योगमात्मविशुद्धये ।।१२।।

12. Sitting on that seat, with mind concentrated, the functions of thought and sense in control, he should set himself to the practice of *yoga* for the sake of self-purification.

समं कायशिरोग्रीवं धारयन्नचलं स्थिरः ।
संप्रेक्ष्य नासिकाग्रं स्वं दिशश्चानवलोकयन् ।।१३।।
प्रशांतात्मा विगतभीर् ब्रह्मचारिव्रते स्थितः ।
मनः संयम्य मच्चित्तो युक्त आसीत मत्परः ।।१४।।

13. Keeping himself steady, holding the trunk, the neck and the head in a straight line and motionless, fixing his eye on the tip of his nose, and looking not around.

14. Tranquil in spirit, free from fear, steadfast in the vow of *brahmacharya*, holding his mind in control, the *yogi* should sit, with all his thoughts on Me, absorbed in Me.

Brahmacharya (usually translated 'celibacy') means not only sexual continence but observance of all the cardinal vows for the attainment of *Brahman*.

युंजन्नेवं सदाऽऽत्मानं योगी नियतमानसः ।
शांतिं निर्वाणपरमां मत्संस्थामधिगच्छति ।।१५।।

15. The *yogi*, who ever thus, with mind controlled, unites himself to *Atman*, wins the peace which culminates in *Nirvana*, the peace that is in Me.

[For *Nirvana*, see my note on II. 72.]

नात्यश्नतस्तु योगोऽस्ति न चैकान्तमनश्नतः ।
न चातिस्वप्नशीलस्य जाग्रतो नैव चार्जुन ।।१६।।

16. *Yoga* is not for him who eats too much, nor for him who fasts too much, neither for him who sleeps too much, nor yet for him who is too wakeful.

युक्ताहारविहारस्य युक्तचेष्टस्य कर्मसु ।
युक्तस्वप्नावबोधस्य योगो भवति दुःखहा ।।१७।।

17. To him who is disciplined in food and recreation, in effort in all activities, and in sleep and waking, *yoga* (discipline) becomes a relief from all ills.

[Cf. I Co. 9. 25: "And every man that striveth for the mastery is temperate in all things."]

यदा विनियतं चित्तम् आत्मन्येवावतिष्ठते ।
निःस्पृहः सर्वकामेभ्यो युक्त अित्युच्यते तदा ।।१८।।

18. When one's thought, completely controlled, rests steadily only on *Atman*, when one is free from longing for all objects of desire, then one is called a *yogin*.

[All longing for 'other' things ceases, one's soul being consumed by the sole longing for union with Him. "If God gave to man all the gifts which the saints possess, and all that He has to offer, but without giving Himself, the craving spirit would remain hungry and unfulfilled." (Ruysbroeck)]

यथा दीपो निवातस्थो नेंगते सोपमा स्मृता ।
योगिनो यतचित्तस्य युंजतो योगमात्मनः ।।१९।।

19. As a taper in a windless spot flickers not, even so is a *yogin*, with his thought controlled, seeking to unite himself with *Atman*.

यत्रोपरमते चित्तं निरुद्धं योगसेवया ।
यत्र चैवात्मनाऽऽत्मानं पश्यन्नात्मनि तुष्यति ।।२०।।

20. Where thought curbed by the practice of *yoga* completely ceases, where a man sits content within himself, *Atman* having seen *Atman* ;

["To see and to have seen that Vision," says Plotinus, "is reason no longer. And perhaps we should not here speak of *sight* : for that which is seen...is not discerned by the seer, nor perceived by him as a second thing... therefore this vision is hard to tell of : for how can a man describe as other than himself that which, when he discerned it, seemed not other, but one with himself indeed ?" The Gita simply says *Atman* sees *Atman*.]

सुखमात्यंतिकं यत् तद् बुद्धिग्राह्यमतींद्रियम् ।
वेत्ति यत्र न चैवायं स्थितश्चलति तत्त्वतः ।।२१।।

21. Where he experiences that endless bliss beyond the senses which can be grasped by reason alone ; wherein established he swerves not from the Truth ;

यं लब्ध्वा चापरं लाभं मन्यते नाधिकं ततः ।
यस्मिन् स्थितो न दुःखेन गुरुणापि विचाल्यते ।।२२।।

22. Where he holds no other gain greater than that which he has gained; and where, securely seated, he is not shaken by any calamity however great;

तं विद्याद् दुःखसंयोगवियोगं योगसंज्ञितम् ।
स निश्चयेन योक्तव्यो योगोऽनिर्विण्णचेतसा ॥२३॥

23. That state should be known as *yoga* (union with the Supreme), the disunion from all union with pain. This *yoga* must one practise with firm resolve and unwearing zeal.

[23. Cf. Tauler: "His spirit is, as it were, sunk and lost in the Abyss of the Deity and loses the consciousness of all creature-distinctions....The man's spirit is so sunk in God in divine union, that he loses all sense of distinction...and there remains a secret, still union, without cloud or colour."

We have seen one phase of the synthesis between *Sankhya* and *Yoga* achieved by the Gita. Here is another phase. The very first aphorism of the *Sankhya Karika* states the inquiry in question to be about the means of complete extinction of all possible kinds of pain; and the *Yoga Bhashya* says: *Sanśara* which is full of misery must be shunned; the *Purusha* must be freed from the union with *Prakriti,* complete destruction of this union is escape and union with the Supreme is the only means of escape from *sansara* which is full of misery. The severance of the union with all misery, declares the Gita, is to be achieved by the accomplishment of the union of the *Atman* with the Supreme.

The 'unwearying zeal' may be described in the famous words of Gaudapada: 'The zeal of a man trying to empty the sea drop by drop by means of a blade of grass.' It must be unshaken by doubt and despair, in spite of the obstacles to the achievement of *yoga* which are well-known, e.g. fear of mishap, heedlessness, sleepiness, hallucination, doubt etc.]

संकल्पप्रभवान् कामान् त्यक्त्वा सर्वानशेषतः ।
मनसैवेन्द्रियग्रामं विनियम्य समंततः ।।२४।।

24. Shaking oneself completely free from longings born of selfish purpose; reining in the whole host of senses, from all sides, with the mind itself;

शनैः शनैरुपरमेद् बुद्धया धृतिगृहीतया ।
आत्मसंस्थं मनः कृत्वा न किंचिदपि चिंतयेत् ।।२५।।

25. With reason held securely by the will, he should gradually attain calm and with the mind established in *Atman* think of nothing.

यतो यतो निश्चरति मनश्चंचलमस्थिरम् ।
ततस्ततो नियम्यैतद् आत्मन्येव वशं नयेत् ।।२६।।

26. Wherever the fickle and unsteady mind wanders, thence should it be reined in and brought under the sole sway of *Atman.*

[25-26. Dr Radhakrishnan quotes from Plato's *Phaedo*: "Thought is best when the mind is gathered into herself and none of these things trouble her—neither sound, nor sight, nor pain, nor pleasure, when she has as little as possible to do with the body and has no bodily sense or feeling, but is aspiring after Being."]

प्रशांतमनसं ह्येनं योगिनं सुखमुत्तमम् ।
अुपैति शांतरजसं ब्रह्मभूतमकल्मषम् ।।२७।।

27. For, supreme bliss comes to this *yogin,* who, with mind becalmed, with passions stilled, has become one with *Brahman*, and is purged of all stain.

युंजन्नेवं सदाऽऽत्मानं योगी विगतकल्मषः ।
सुखेन ब्रह्मसंस्पर्शम् अत्यंतं सुखमश्नुते ।।२८।।

28. The *yogin,* cleansed of all stain, unites himself ever thus to *Atman,* easily enjoys the endless bliss of contact with *Brahman.*

[Cf. "Being wholly absorbed in the divinity, the soul is one with it, conjoining as it were, centre with centre." Plotinus.]

सर्वभूतस्थमात्मानं सर्वभूतानि चात्मनि ।
ईक्षते योगयुक्तात्मा सर्वत्र समदर्शनः ।।२९।।

29. The man equipped with *yoga* looks on all with an impartial eye, seeing *Atman* in all beings and all beings in *Atman.*

यो मां पश्यति सर्वत्र सर्वं च मयि पश्यति ।
तस्याहं न प्रणश्यामि स च मे न प्रणश्यति ।।३०।।

30. He who sees Me everywhere and everything in Me, never vanishes from Me nor I from him.

[29-30. These *shlokas* are an echo of the great *Isha Up.* text: "For the man to whom all beings have become *Atman* what delusion and what grief is there as he sees a unity in all creation?" * Also of *Shve. Up.*: "To the wise who have seen the Absolute seated in the *Atman* belongs everlasting bliss, to none else." ×

They represent progressive steps in *yogic* experience. The result of knowledge described in IV. 35, 'Thou shalt see all beings in thyself, and then in Me', is expanded here, but the argument is the same. One starts with seeing oneself in his near neighbour, then in his distant neighbours, then in still more distant humanity, and ends in seeing himself in all; and seeing oneself in another is to love the

---

* यस्मिन्सर्वाणि भूतान्यात्मैवाभूद्विजानतः ।
तत्र को मोहः कः शोक एकत्वमनुपश्यतः ।। ईश. ७

× तमात्मस्थं येऽनुपश्यन्ति धीराः
तेषां सुखं शाश्वतं नेतरेषाम् ।। श्वेताश्वतर ६.१२

other. That is the same thing as seeing other beings in one's Self. The next natural step is to see God in everyone and everyone in God. St. John put the same thing in his epistle in less philosophical parlance but simpler and more direct manner : "If a man say, I love God, and hateth his brother, he is a liar : for he that loveth not his brother whom he hath seen, how can he love God whom he hath not seen ?" (4. 20-21). The *yogin* who worships and loves God worships and loves everyone, for he sees God in everyone. (31)]

सर्वभूतस्थितं यो मां भजत्येकत्वमास्थितः ।
सर्वथा वर्तमानोऽपि स योगी मयि वर्तते ।।३१।।

31. The *yogin* who, anchored in unity, worships Me abiding in all beings, lives and moves in Me, no matter how he live and move.

So long as 'self' subsists, the Supreme Self is absent; when 'self' is extinguished, the Supreme Self is seen everywhere. Also see note on XIII. 23.

आत्मौपम्येन सर्वत्र समं पश्यति योऽर्जुन ।
सुखं वा यदि वा दुःखं स योगी परमो मतः ।।३२।।

32. He who, by likening himself with others, senses pleasure and pain equally for all as for himself, is deemed to be the highest *yogi*, O Arjuna.

[The *shloka* concretely puts the practical consequence of the *yogic* vision. As Shankaracharya explains : "By realizing that all creatures feel the same pleasure and pain as he feels, he harms no being." Cf. the famous Biblical text : "All things whatsoever ye would that men should do to you, do ye even so to them." (Mat. 7, 12)]

अर्जुन उवाच ।
योऽयं योगस्त्वया प्रोक्तः साम्येन मधुसूदन ।
अेतस्याहं न पश्यामि चंचलत्वात् स्थितिं स्थिराम् ।।३३।।

Arjuna said :

33. I do not see, O Madhusudana, how this *yoga*, based on the equal-mindedness that Thou hast expounded to me, can steadily endure, because of fickleness (of the mind).

चंचलं हि मनः कृष्ण प्रमाथि बलवद् दृढम् ।
तस्याहं निग्रहं मन्ये वायोरिव सुदुष्करम् ।।३४।।

34. For fickle is the mind, O Krishna, unruly, overpowering and stubborn ; to curb it is, I think, as hard as to curb the wind.

श्रीभगवानुवाच ।
असंशयं महाबाहो मनो दुर्निग्रहं चलम् ।
अभ्यासेन तु कौंतेय वैराग्येण च गृह्यते ।।३५।।

The Lord said :

35. Undoubtedly, O Mahabahu, the mind is fickle and hard to curb ; yet, O Kaunteya, it can be held in check by constant practice and dispassion.

[This repeats the language of *Yoga Sutra* 12. Constant practice is studied endeavour to steady the mind, and dispassion means the converting of the natural yearning for things of the flesh into a consuming passion for things of the Spirit.]

असंयतात्मना योगो दुष्प्राप इति मे मतिः ।
वश्यात्मना तु यतता शक्योऽवाप्तुमुपायतः ।।३६।।

36. Without self-restraint, *yoga*, I hold, is difficult to attain ; but the self-governed soul can attain it by proper means, if he strive for it.

अर्जुन उवाच ।
अयतिः श्रद्धयोपेतो योगाच्चलितमानसः ।
अप्राप्य योगसंसिद्धिं कां गतिं कृष्ण गच्छति ।।३७।।

Arjuna said :

37. If one, possessed of faith, but slack of effort, because of his mind straying from *yoga*, reach not perfection in *yoga*, what end does he come to, O Krishna ?

कच्चिन्नोभयविभ्रष्टश् छिन्नाभ्रमिव नश्यति ।
अप्रतिष्ठो महाबाहो विमूढो ब्रह्मणः पथि ।।३८।।

38. Without a foothold, and floundering in the path to *Brahman* fallen from both, is he indeed not lost, O Mahabahu, like a dissipated cloud ?

['From both' i. e. from the path of reward-seeking ritual and path of *yoga*.]

अेतन् मे संशयं कृष्ण छेत्तुमर्हस्यशेषतः ।
त्वदन्यः संशयस्यास्य छेत्ता न ह्युपपद्यते ।।३९।।

39. This my doubt, O Krishna, do thou dispel utterly ; for there is to be found none other than thou to banish this doubt.

श्रीभगवानुवाच ।
पार्थ नैवेह नामुत्र विनाशस्तस्य विद्यते ।
न हि कल्याणकृत् कश्चिद् दुर्गतिं तात गच्छति ।।४०।।

The Lord said :

40. Neither in this world, nor in the next, can there be ruin for him, O Partha ; no well-doer, oh loved one, meets with a sad end.

[Plato in "Apology" uses almost identical language : "Know of a certainty that no evil can happen to a good man, either in life or in death." Cf. also Koran : "Then whoso doth good works and is a believer, there will be no rejection of his effort. Lo! We record it for him."]

प्राप्य पुण्यकृतांल्लोकान् उषित्वा शाश्वतीः समाः ।
शुचीनां श्रीमतां गेहे योगभ्रष्टोऽभिजायते ॥४१॥

41. Fallen from *yoga,* a man attains the worlds of righteous souls, and having dwelt there for numberless years is then born in a house of pure and gentle blood.

अथवा योगिनामेव कुले भवति धीमताम् ।
अेतद्धि दुर्लभतरं लोके जन्म यदीदृशम् ॥४२॥

42. Or he may even be born into a family of *yogins,* though such birth as this is all too rare in this world.

तत्र तं बुद्धिसंयोगं लभते पौर्वदेहिकम् ।
यतते च ततो भूयः संसिद्धौ कुरुनन्दन ॥४३॥

43. There, O Kurunandana, he recovers the intellectual stage he had reached in his previous birth, and thence he stretches forward again towards perfection.

पूर्वाभ्यासेन तेनैव ह्रियते ह्यवशोपि सः ।
जिज्ञासुरपि योगस्य शब्दब्रह्मातिवर्तते ॥४४॥

44. By virtue of that previous practice he is borne on, whether he will it or not; even he with a desire to know *yoga* passes beyond the Vedic ritual.

[I.e. he would have no fascination or inclination left for the path of the Vedic ritual.]

प्रयत्नाद् यतमानस्तु योगी संशुद्धकिल्बिषः ।
अनेकजन्मसंसिद्धस् ततो याति परां गतिम् ॥४५॥

45. But the *yogi* who perseveres in his striving, cleansed of sin, perfected through many births, reaches the highest state.

तपस्विभ्योऽधिको योगी ज्ञानिभ्योऽपि मतोऽधिकः ।
कर्मिभ्यश्चाधिको योगी तस्माद् योगी भवार्जुन ॥४६॥

46. The *yogin* is deemed higher than the man of austerities; he is deemed also higher than the man of knowledge; higher is he than the man engrossed in ritual; therefore be thou a *yogin,* O Arjuna!

The man of austerities means the man practising them with an eye to fruit; the man of knowledge does not mean the *jnani* who has realized the truth, but a man of learning.

योगिनामपि सर्वेषां मद्गतेनांतरात्मना ।
श्रद्धावान् भजते यो मां स मे युक्ततमो मतः ॥४७॥

47. And among all *yogins,* he who worships Me with faith, his inmost self all rapt in Me, is deemed by Me to be the best *yogin.*

[46-47: The *yogin* eulogized here is the *yogin* who has achieved complete union with the Supreme. Though he is the contemplator of the Impersonal, the meditative mystic, and although we have the meditative mystic described in discourses VI-VIII, Lord Krishna's partiality for the devotee of the Personal is obvious in *shloka* 47 as in other *shlokas.*]

अिति श्रीमद्भगवद्गीतासु अुपनिषत्सु ब्रह्मविद्यायां योगशास्त्रे श्रीकृष्णार्जुनसंवादे ध्यानयोगो नाम षष्ठोऽध्यायः ॥६॥

Thus ends the sixth discourse entitled '*Dhyana Yoga*' in the converse of Lord Krishna and Arjuna, on the science of *Yoga,* as part of the knowledge of *Brahman* in the Upanishad called the Bhagawadgita.

DISCOURSE VII

With this discourse begins an exposition of the nature of Reality and the secret of devotion.

श्रीभगवानुवाच ।

मय्यासक्तमनाः पार्थ योगं युंजन् मदाश्रयः ।
असंशयं समग्रं मां यथा ज्ञास्यसि तच्छृणु ॥१॥

The Lord said:

1. Hear, O Partha, how, with thy mind rivetted on Me, by practising *yoga* and making Me the sole refuge, thou shalt, without doubt, know Me fully.

ज्ञानं तेऽहं सविज्ञानम् अिदं वक्ष्याम्यशेषतः ।
यज्ज्ञात्वा नेह भूयोऽन्यज् ज्ञातव्यमवशिष्यते ॥२॥

2. I will declare to thee, in its entirety, this knowledge, combined with discriminative knowledge, which when thou hast known there remains here nothing more to be known.

[The words *jnana* and *vijnana* occur about half a dozen times in the Gita. Shankaracharya has always translated them 'knowledge' and 'experience' (in the sense of Self-realization). But *jnana* itself is nothing less than Self-realization, and thus it would be tautologous to say 'knowledge and experience'. Other translators (like Tilak, for instance) have taken *vijnana* to mean knowledge of the physical world. Dr Radhakrishnan takes it to mean 'the intellectual apprehension of the details of existence', and *jnana* as 'the integral knowledge of the common foundation of existence'. I am inclined to think that the explanation of these terms is to be sought in the *sankhyan* use of them. There *jnana* is experience of the Self, and *vijnana* is discriminative knowledge of the Self as distinct from all that is not-Self. The *Sankhya Karika* says that emancipation from all misery is possible only by a discriminative knowledge of the unmanifest, the manifest, and the knower. It is this discriminative knowledge that the *Upanishad* has in view when *Brh.* 2. 4. 5 says * *Atman* has to be seen, harkened to, thought on, and understood as distinct from all that is not-Self — *vijijnasitavyah.* ×]

मनुष्याणां सहस्रेषु कश्चिद् यतति सिद्धये ।
यततामपि सिद्धानां कश्चिन् मां वेत्ति तत्त्वतः ॥३॥

3. Among thousands of men hardly one strives after perfection ; among those who strive hardly one knows Me in truth.

[Cf. Dhammapada 182 "Hard it is to be born as man ; hard it is to live as one ; hard likewise to hear the Right Law said ; and rare is the birth of the Awakened" (the attainment of the state of the Buddha).] †

भूमिरापोऽनलो वायुः खं मनो बुद्धिरेव च ।
अहंकार इतीयं मे भिन्ना प्रकृतिरष्टधा ॥४॥

4. Earth, Water, Fire, Air, Ether, Mind, Reason and Ego — thus eightfold is my *prakriti* divided.

This eightfold *prakriti* is substantially the same as the field described in XIII. 5 and the perishable Being in XV. 16.

अपरेयमितस्त्वन्यां प्रकृतिं विद्धि मे पराम् ।
जीवभूतां महाबाहो ययेदं धार्यते जगत् ॥५॥

---

* आत्मा वा अरे द्रष्टव्यः श्रोतव्यो मन्तव्यो निदिध्यासितव्यः।
बृहदारण्यक. २. ४. ५

× सोऽन्वेष्टव्यः स विजिज्ञासितव्यः। छांदो० ८. ७. १

† किच्छो मनुस्सपटिलाभो । किच्छं मच्चान जीवितं ॥
किच्छं सद्धम्मसवणं । किच्छो बुद्धानमुप्पादो ॥ धम्मपद १८२

5. This is My lower aspect ; but know thou My other aspect, the higher — which is *Jiva* (the Vital Essence) by which, O Mahabahu, this world is sustained.

अेतद्योनीनि भूतानि सर्वाणीत्युपधारय ।
अहं कृत्स्नस्य जगतः प्रभवः प्रलयस्तथा ॥६॥

6. Know that these two compose the source from which all beings spring ; I am the origin and end of the entire universe.

मत्तः परतरं नान्यत् किंचिदस्ति धनंजय ।
मयि सर्वमिदं प्रोतं सूत्रे मणिगणा अिव ॥७॥

7. There is nothing higher than I, O Dhananjaya ; all this is strung on Me as a row of gems upon a thread.

[Cf. Koran : 'He hath created the heavens and the earth with truth. High be He exalted above all.' (16. 3)]

रसोऽहमप्सु कौंतेय प्रभाऽस्मि शशिसूर्ययोः ।
प्रणवः सर्ववेदेषु शब्दः खे पौरुषं नृषु ॥८॥

8. In water I am the savour, O Kaunteya ; in the sun and the moon I am the light ; the syllable *AUM* in all the Vedas ; the sound in ether, and manliness in men.

[For *AUM* see my note on VIII. 11-13.]

पुण्यो गंधः पृथिव्यां च तेजश्चास्मि विभावसौ ।
जीवनं सर्वभूतेषु तपश्चास्मि तपस्विषु ॥९॥

9. I am the sweet fragrance in earth ; the brilliance in fire ; the life in all beings ; and the austerity in ascetics.

बीजं मां सर्वभूतानां विद्धि पार्थ सनातनम् ।
बुद्धिर्बुद्धिमतामस्मि तेजस्तेजस्विनामहम् ॥१०॥

10. Know Me, O Partha, to be the primeval seed of all beings; I am the reason of rational beings and the splendour of the splendid.

बलं बलवतामस्मि कामरागविवर्जितम् ।
धर्माविरुद्धो भूतेषु कामोऽस्मि भरतर्षभ ॥११॥

11. Of the strong, I am the strength, divorced from lust and passion; in beings I am desire undivorced from righteousness.

[I. e. *sattvika* strength, devoid of lust which is the characteristic of *rajas* and passion which is that of *tamas*. The four objects of pursuit of man are known as *dharma* (righteousness), *artha* (wealth), *kama* (desire for progeny, fame etc.), *moksha* (freedom). When *artha* and *kama* are divorced from *dharma* they lead not to *moksha* but to perdition.]

ये चैव सात्त्विका भावा राजसास्तामसाश्च ये ।
मत्त अेवेति तान् विद्धि न त्वहं तेषु ते मयि ॥१२॥

12. Know that all the manifestations of the three *gunas, sattva, rajas,* and *tamas,* proceed from none but Me; yet I am not in them; they are in Me.

God is not dependent on them, they are dependent on Him. Without Him those various manifestations would be impossible.

त्रिभिर्गुणमयैर्भावैर् अेभिः सर्वमिदं जगत् ।
मोहितं नाभिजानाति मामेभ्यः परमव्ययम् ॥१३॥

13. Befogged by these manifestations of the three *gunas,* the entire world fails to recognize Me, the imperishable, as transcending them.

[The manifestations are due to Him, as we have seen in *shl.* 12, but man stands between Him and the manifestations which befog and daze him. Deluded man (14-15) thus turns his back on Him. As St. Augustine has finely said: "For I had my back to the Light and my face to the things enlightened, whence my face, with which I discerned the things enlightened, itself was not enlightened."]

दैवी ह्येषा गुणमयी मम माया दुरत्यया ।
मामेव ये प्रपद्यन्ते मायामेतां तरन्ति ते ॥१४॥

14. For this My divine delusive mystery made up of the three *gunas* is hard to pierce; but those who make Me their sole refuge pierce the veil.

[For *maya,* delusive mystery, see 'My Submission' p. 41. The world in which we should see His reflection, which does not exist but for Him, deludes us into thinking that that is all. "Some think," says Browning, "Creation's meant to show Him forth. I say it is meant to hide Him all it can." When we pierce the veil, the world does not disappear, but it ceases to hide the Real and reveals It instead. Deluded man thinks there is no sun because he is hidden by the clouds, forgetting that but for the sun he would not behold the clouds themselves. Goethe describes *maya* in exactly the language of the Gita when he makes Faust declare:

"Mysterious even in open day
Nature retains her veil, despite our clamours;
That which she doth not willingly display
Cannot be wrenched from her with levers,
screws and hammers."

But the Gita reveals the master-key in the same *shloka.*]

न मां दुष्कृतिनो मूढाः प्रपद्यन्ते नराधमाः ।
माययाऽपहृतज्ञाना आसुरं भावमाश्रिताः ॥१५॥

15. The deluded evil-doers, lowest of men, do not

seek refuge in Me ; for, by reason of this delusive mystery, they are bereft of knowledge and given to devilish ways.

चतुर्विधा भजन्ते मां जनाः सुकृतिनोऽर्जुन ।
आर्तो जिज्ञासुरर्थार्थी ज्ञानी च भरतर्षभ ॥१६॥

16. Four types of well-doers are devoted to Me, O Arjuna ; they are, O Bharatarshabha, the afflicted, the spiritual seeker, the material seeker, and the enlightened.

तेषां ज्ञानी नित्ययुक्त अेकभक्तिर्विशिष्यते ।
प्रियो हि ज्ञानिनोऽत्यर्थम् अहं स च मम प्रियः ॥१७॥

17. Of these the enlightened, ever attached to Me in single-minded devotion, is the best ; for to the enlightened I am exceedingly dear and he is dear to Me.

अुदाराः सर्वे अेवैते ज्ञानी त्वात्मैव मे मतम् ।
आस्थितः स हि युक्तात्मा मामेवानुत्तमां गतिम् ॥१८॥

18. All these are estimable indeed, but the enlightened I hold to be My very self ; for he, the true *yogi*, is stayed on Me alone, the supreme goal.

बहूनां जन्मनामंते ज्ञानवान् मां प्रपद्यते ।
वासुदेवः सर्वमिति स महात्मा सुदुर्लभः ॥१९॥

19. At the end of many births the enlightened man finds refuge in Me ; rare indeed is this great soul to whom 'Vasudeva is all'.

कामैस्तैस्तैर्हृतज्ञानाः प्रपद्यन्तेऽन्यदेवताः ।
तं तं नियममास्थाय प्रकृत्या नियताः स्वया ॥२०॥

20. Men, bereft of knowledge by reason of various longings, seek refuge in other gods, pinning their faith on diverse rites, guided by their own nature.

यो यो यां यां तनुं भक्तः श्रद्धयार्चितुमिच्छति ।
तस्य तस्याचलां श्रद्धां तामेव विदधाम्यहम् ॥२१॥

21. Whatever form one desires to worship in faith and devotion, in that very form I make that faith of his secure.

[Cf. Koran : "Whoso desireth the reward of the world, We bestow on him thereof ; and whoso desireth the reward of the hereafter We bestow on him thereof."]

स तया श्रद्धया युक्तस्तस्याराधनमीहते ।
लभते च ततः कामान् मयैव विहितान् हि तान् ॥२२॥

22. Possessed of that faith he seeks to propitiate that one, and obtains therethrough his longings, dispensed in truth by none but Me.

अंतवत् तु फलं तेषां तद् भवत्यल्पमेधसाम् ।
देवान् देवयजो यान्ति मद्भक्ता यान्ति मामपि ॥२३॥

23. But limited is the fruit that falls to those short-sighted ones ; those who worship the gods go to the gods, those who worship Me come unto Me.

[As Ramanujacharya explains : From *Brahma* to the smallest atom, all things that go by the name of the world are perishable and thus broken reeds to rely upon ; the sole refuge on whom reliance must be placed is He. Cf. *Shatapatha Brahmana* : "He who worships these finite ones wins to the finite world ; and he who worships those infinite to the infinite world." Also 2. Co. 9. 6 : "He who soweth sparingly shall reap also sparingly, and he who soweth bountifully shall reap also bountifully."]

अव्यक्तं व्यक्तिमापन्नं मन्यन्ते मामबुद्धयः ।
परं भावमजानन्तो ममाव्ययमनुत्तमम् ॥२४॥

24. Not knowing My transcendent, imperishable, supreme character, the undiscerning think Me who am unmanifest to have become manifest.

[There is a wide difference among commentators regarding the translation of this *shloka*. This is Shankaracharya's explanation: 'Not knowing My higher nature as the Supreme Self, the ignorant think that I have just now come into manifestation having been unmanifested hitherto, though I am the ever luminous Lord." Hill thinks the reference here is solely to *prakriti* and quotes Barnett whom he follows: "Some misguided men regard the Supreme who is the substrata of the universe as essentially material, existing either in a potentially determinable *avyakta* or actually determinate *vyakta* condition; but in truth He is fundamentally absolute and immaterial."

Gandhiji's translation agrees with Tilak's and Dr Radhakrishnan's (Ind. Phil. Vol. I, p. 543), and I think there is much to say in favour of it. The reference is not to *prakriti,* but to the unmanifest aspect of God, as the discourses VI, VII, VIII dealt generally with the worship of God in His unmanifest aspect (see VIII. 20-21). The *shloka* has reference to the misguided ones who worship many gods believing them to be so many gods. The *shloka* must be read with IX. 10. It is the same monotheism that speaks out there. Discourses IX-XII deal generally with the worship of God in His manifest aspect. But whether manifest or unmanifest, He is the One Imperishable Supreme Being — transcendent *Brahman* as the Unmanifest or Impersonal; and the Lord, Sustainer, and Ruler, Father, Mother and Creator (IX. 17) as the Manifest or Personal. But there are no other gods to share the worship of the One God. Those who believe in a plurality of gods are mistaken and deluded. These have been already referred to in the preceding *shlokas.* Whilst a religion like Islam would call these not only deluded but would condemn them as unbelievers, the Gita has place for them too; only "their fruit is limited" (see preceding *shloka*), as their worship and their object is limited.]

नाहं प्रकाशः सर्वस्य योगमायासमावृतः ।
मूढोऽयं नाभिजानाति लोको मामजमव्ययम् ।।२५।।

25. Veiled by the delusive mystery created by My unique power, I am not manifest to all; this bewildered world does not recognize Me, birthless and changeless.

Having the power to create this world of sense and yet unaffected by it, He is described as having unique power.

[*Yogamaya* — the delusive mystery created by My unique power is the same as the *maya* in VII. 14. There it was described as the creation of His divine nature, here as the creation of His unique power.]

वेदाहं समतीतानि वर्तमानानि चार्जुन ।
भविष्याणि च भूतानि मां तु वेद न कश्चन ।।२६।।

26. I know, O Arjuna, all creatures past, present and to be; but no one knows Me.

[Cf. *Shve. Up.*: "He knows whatever there is to be known; Him there is no one who knows." *]

इच्छाद्वेषसमुत्थेन द्वंद्वमोहेन भारत ।
सर्वभूतानि संमोहं सर्गे यान्ति परंतप ।।२७।।

27. All creatures in this universe are bewildered, O Parantapa, by virtue of the delusion of the pairs of opposites sprung from likes and dislikes, O Bharata.

[*Sarge* (सर्गे) may mean either 'at birth', or 'in this universe'. Shankaracharya translates, 'at birth'. He has a very helpful comment which I condense: "The affections of likes and dislikes cause delusion in all beings; to one such deluded the truth even of things mundane is impossible, much more so the truth about *Atman*. All creatures are born subject to this delusion, which turns their hearts

* स वेत्ति वेद्यं न च तस्यास्ति वेत्ता । श्वेत० ३.१९

away from Me, the *Atman,* to things of the world. But the virtuous conquer the delusion."]

येषां त्वंतगतं पापं जनानां पुण्यकर्मणाम् ।
ते द्वंद्वमोहनिर्मुक्ता भजन्ते मां दृढव्रताः ॥२८॥

28. But those virtuous men whose sin has come to an end, freed from the delusion of the pairs of opposites, worship Me in steadfast faith.

जरामरणमोक्षाय मामाश्रित्य यतन्ति ये ।
ते ब्रह्म तद् विदुः कृत्स्नम् अध्यात्मं कर्म चाखिलम् ॥२९॥

29. Those who endeavour for freedom from age and death by taking refuge in Me, know in full that *Brahman, Adhyatma* and all *Karma.*

साधिभूताधिदैवं मां साधियज्ञं च ये विदुः ।
प्रंयाणकालेऽपि च मां ते विदुर्युक्तचेतसः ॥३०॥

30. Those who know Me, including *Adhibhuta, Adhidaiva, Adhiyajna,* possessed of even-mindedness, they know Me even at the time of passing away.

The terms in italics are defined in the next discourse the subject of which is indicated in 29-30. The sense is that every nook and cranny of the universe is filled with *Brahman,* that He is the sole Agent of all action, and that the man who imbued with this knowledge and faith completely surrenders himself to Him, becomes one with Him at the time of passing hence. All his desires are extinguished in his vision of Him and he wins his freedom.

ॐिति श्रीमद्भगवद्गीतासु अुपनिषत्सु ब्रह्मविद्यायां योगशास्त्रे श्रीकृष्णार्जुनसंवादे
ज्ञानविज्ञानयोगो नाम सप्तमोऽध्यायः ॥७॥

Thus ends the seventh discourse, entitled '*Jnanavijnana Yoga*' in the converse of Lord Krishna and Arjuna, on the science of *Yoga* as part of the knowledge of *Brahman* in the Upanishad called the Bhagawadgita.

DISCOURSE VIII

The nature of the Supreme is further expounded in this discourse.

अर्जुन उवाच ।

किं तद् ब्रह्म किमध्यात्मं किं कर्म पुरुषोत्तम ।

अधिभूतं च किं प्रोक्तम् अधिदैवं किमुच्यते ।।१।।

Arjuna said :

1. What is that *Brahman*? What is *Adhyatma*? What *Karma,* O Purushottama? What is called *Adhibhuta*? And what *Adhidaiva*?

अधियज्ञः कथं कोऽत्र देहेऽस्मिन् मधुसूदन ।

प्रयाणकाले च कथं ज्ञेयोऽसि नियतात्मभिः ।।२।।

2. And who here in this body is *Adhiyajna* and how? And how at the time of death art Thou to be known by the self-controlled?

श्रीभगवानुवाच ।

अक्षरं ब्रह्म परमं स्वभावोऽध्यात्ममुच्यते ।

भूतभावोद्भवकरो विसर्गः कर्मसंज्ञितः ।।३।।

The Lord said :

3. The Supreme, the Imperishable is *Brahman*; its manifestation is *Adhyatma*; the creative process whereby all beings are created is called *Karma.*

अधिभूतं क्षरो भावः पुरुषश्चाधिदैवतम् ।

अधियज्ञोऽहमेवात्र देहे देहभृतां वर ।।४।।

4. *Adhibhuta* is My perishable form; *Adhidaivata* is the individual self in that form; and O best among the embodied, *Adhiyajna* am I in this body, purified by sacrifice.

That is, from the Imperishable Unmanifest down to the perishable atom everything in the universe is the Supreme and an expression of the Supreme. Why then should mortal man arrogate to himself authorship of anything rather than do His bidding and dedicate all action to Him?

[1-4. Gandhiji has summed up in his brief note the gist of this quatrain for those who will not bother about technical terms. A deeply spiritual friend has obliged me with an interpretation which lights up the apparent abracadabras with a deal of meaning: The *shlokas* describe the whole process in which the Absolute becomes conditioned and from the conditioned state becomes Absolute again. (1) We have first the Impersonal, Unmanifest, Unconditioned Absolute; (2) It chose to reveal one of Its aspects — that aspect was primordial unmanifest *prakriti* — here called *Adhyatma*; (3) *prakriti* next became active — this disturbance in the equilibrium of its *gunas* was *karma* — work, action; (4) the next step in the process were the countless manifestations of matter, with name and form — that is *Adhibhuta*; (5) then the Absolute informed these with its Ego, i. e. became conditioned; that is *Adhidaiva*; (6) but the conditioned had the potentiality to recover its pristine unconditioned state by means of giving of itself a pure sacrifice. The culmination of this self-sacrifice comes with the dissolution of the body and the merging or identification of the conditioned in the Unconditioned.

In short, it is the cycle of sacrifice that is described. The Supreme Being sacrifices Himself in the first instance and ultimately the individual sacrifices himself to be merged in the original Essence. Cf. III. 15 which describes the same cycle of sacrifice.]

अंतकाले च मामेव स्मरन् मुक्त्वा कलेवरम् ।
यः प्रयाति स मद्भावं याति नास्त्यत्र संशयः ।।५।।

5. And he who, at the last hour remembering Me only, departs leaving the body, enters into Me; of that there is no doubt.

यं यं वाऽपि स्मरन् भावं त्यजत्यन्ते कलेवरम् ।
तं तमेवैति कौंतेय सदा तद्भावभावितः ।।६।।

6. Or whatever form a man continually contemplates, that same he remembers in the hour of death, and to that very form he goes, O Kaunteya.

तस्मात् सर्वेषु कालेषु मामनुस्मर युध्य च ।
मय्यर्पितमनोबुद्धिर् मामेवैष्यस्यसंशयम् ।।७।।

7. Therefore at all times remember Me and fight on; thy mind and reason thus on Me fixed thou shalt surely come to Me.

[This *shloka* should make it abundantly clear that all through in His exhortation to Arjuna to fight, it was not only the actual warfare in front of them that was meant, but the fight — moral and spiritual — that is man's lot on earth. Cf. Jesus's words: "Whosoever would come after me, let him renounce himself and *take up his cross daily* and follow me." It is the taking up one's cross daily, at every moment, that is meant here. See also *shl.* 14. "Life is a perpetual striving. There is always a tempest raging in us, and struggle against temptation is a perpetual duty. The Gita says this in several places." (Gandhiji in *Harijan* 8-7-'33)]

अभ्यासयोगयुक्तेन चेतसा नान्यगामिना ।
परमं पुरुषं दिव्यं याति पार्थानुचिंतयन् ।।८।।

8. With thought steadied by constant practice, and wandering nowhere, he who meditates on the Supreme Celestial Being, O Partha, goes to Him.

कविं पुराणम् अनुशासितारम्
अणोरणीयांसमनुस्मरेद् यः ।
सर्वस्य धातारमचिंत्यरूपम्
आदित्यवर्णं तमसः परस्तात् ॥९॥
प्रयाणकाले मनसाऽचलेन
भक्त्या युक्तो योगबलेन चैव ।
भ्रुवोर्मध्ये प्राणमावेश्य सम्यक्
स तं परं पुरुषमुपैति दिव्यम् ॥१०॥

9-10. Whoso, at the time of death, with unwavering mind, with devotion, and fixing the breath rightly between the brows by the power of *yoga,* meditates on the Sage, the Ancient, the Ruler, subtler than the subtlest, the Supporter of all, the Inconceivable, glorious as the sun beyond the darkness, — he goes to that Supreme Celestial Being.

यदक्षरं वेदविदो वदन्ति
विशन्ति यद् यतयो वीतरागाः ।
यदिच्छन्तो ब्रह्मचर्यं चरन्ति
तत् ते पदं संग्रहेण प्रवक्ष्ये ॥११॥

11. That which the knowers of the Vedas call the Imperishable (*or* that word which the knowers of the Vedas repeat), wherein the ascetics freed from passion enter and desiring which they practise *brahmacharya,* that Goal (*or* Word) I will declare to thee in brief.

सर्वद्वाराणि संयम्य मनो हृदि निरुध्य च ।
मूर्ध्न्याधायात्मनः प्राणम् आस्थितो योगधारणाम् ॥१२॥

12. Closing all the gates, locking up the mind in the *hridaya,* fixing his breath within the head, rapt in *yogic* meditation;

[12. It is to be noticed that the Gita, both in the sixth discourse and here, omits the highly technical side of *yogic* practices and presents them as simply as possible. This *shloka* has just a passing reference to a process which is described by Dr Radhakrishnan who quotes from *Brahma Sutra* thus: "The nerve *sushumna* passes up to the cranium. At the approach of death, the knowing soul, through the grace of the Lord, breaks up the knot of the *hridaya* (a centre of the spinal cord) and enters the path of *sushumna,* and passes out of the body piercing the skull." "Through this *sushumna,*" says *Maitri Up.,* "by joining the breath, the syllable *AUM* and the mind, one may go aloft."

The kernel of the whole thing is contained in *shloka* 13 which read with *shl.* 6 and *shl.* 14 means that one should so live that one's thoughts at the hour of death may be centred on nothing but God, the sacred symbol helping one to concentrate them on Him.]

ओमित्येकाक्षरं ब्रह्म व्याहरन् मामनुस्मरन् ।
यः प्रयाति त्यजन् देहं स याति परमां गतिम् ॥१३॥

13. Whoso departs leaving the body uttering *AUM* — *Brahman* in one syllable — repeatedly thinking on Me, he reaches the highest state.

[11-13. *Shl.* 11 repeats substantially the language of *Katha Up.* 1. 2. 15: "The Goal (or Word) which all the Vedas repeat, which all the austerities speak of, desiring which men practise *brahmacharya* — that Goal (or Word) I declare to thee in brief — it is *AUM.*" * The sacred syllable, corresponding to *Logos,* is described throughout the

* सर्वे वेदा यत्पदमामनन्ति । तपांसि सर्वाणि च यद्वदन्ति ।
यदिच्छन्तो ब्रह्मचर्यं चरन्ति । तत्ते पदं संग्रहेण ब्रवीमि ओमित्येतत् ॥
कठ. १. २. १५

Upanishads as both the goal and the means of meditation. Indeed the two words *akshara* and *pada* convey both meanings, Imperishable and Word, and Goal and Word respectively. The *Mundaka Up.*, in a most beautiful metaphor, describes the whole process of meditation as the practice of archery in which one has to direct the arrow of one's *Atman,* sharpened by devotion, from the bow of *AUM,* to *Brahman* which is the target. By undistracted contemplation, we are told, can the arrow pierce the mark and become one with it.* The *Prashna Up.* describes meditation through repetition of the sacred syllable as a spiritual charm to cleanse oneself of sins, and *Mandukya* is solely devoted to expounding the spiritual content of the mystic Word.

The triple syllable is thus invariably the means of meditation as well as the goal, and has since been interpreted to stand for all kinds of trinities. It is enough for our present purpose to note that following closely, as the reference does, the description of the different processes of the evolution and involution of *Brahman,* the syllable may be understood to stand for *prakriti,* the individual self and the Supreme. '*AUM*' is *Brahman,* '*AUM*' is this all, says the *Taittiriya Up.* § It is with this knowledge that one must use the sacred symbol for meditation, and supreme is the good fortune of him who can, at the time of death, put himself in tune with the Infinite through repeating this sacred syllable.

Cf. 'Imitation of Christ' which paraphrasing the Biblical text says: "For the one Word are all things, and all things speak this one ; and this is the Beginning which also speaketh to us."]

अनन्यचेताः सततं यो मां स्मरति नित्यशः ।
तस्याहं सुलभः पार्थ नित्ययुक्तस्य योगिनः ।।१४।।

---

* प्रणवो धनुः शरो ह्यात्मा । ब्रह्म तल्लक्ष्यमुच्यते ।।
अप्रमत्तेन वेद्धव्यं । शरवत्तन्मयो भवेत् । मुंडक० २. २-४

§ ॐ अिति ब्रह्म । ॐ अितीदं सर्वम् । तैत्तिरीय० १. ८. १

14. That *yogi* easily wins to Me, O Partha, who, ever attached to Me, constantly remembers Me with undivided mind.

मामुपेत्य पुनर्जन्म दुःखालयमशाश्वतम् ।
नाप्नुवन्ति महात्मानः संसिद्धिं परमां गताः ॥१५॥

15. Great souls, having come to Me, reach the highest perfection ; they come not again to birth, unlasting and (withal) an abode of misery.

आब्रह्मभुवनाल्लोकाः पुनरावर्तिनोऽर्जुन ।
मामुपेत्य तु कौंतेय पुनर्जन्म न विद्यते ॥१६॥

16. From the world of *Brahma* down, all the worlds are subject to return, O Arjuna ; but on coming to Me there is no rebirth.

सहस्रयुगपर्यंतम् अहर् यद् ब्रह्मणो विदुः ।
रात्रिं युगसहस्रान्तां तेऽहोरात्रविदो जनाः ॥१७॥

17. Those men indeed know what is Day and what is Night, who know that Brahma's day lasts a thousand *yugas* and that his night too is a thousand *yugas* long.

That is to say, our day and night of a dozen hours each are less than the infinitesimal fraction of a moment in that vast cycle of time. Pleasures pursued during these incalculably small moments are as illusory as a mirage. Rather than waste these brief moments, we should devote them to serving God through service of mankind. On the other hand, our time is such a small drop in the ocean of eternity that if we fail of our object here, viz. Self-realization, we need not despair. We should bide our time.

अव्यक्ताद् व्यक्तयः सर्वाः प्रभवंत्यहरागमे ।
रात्र्यागमे प्रलीयन्ते तत्रैवाव्यक्तसंज्ञके ॥१८॥

18. At the coming of Day all the manifest spring forth from the Unmanifest, and at the coming of Night they are dissolved into that same Unmanifest.

Knowing this too, man should understand that he has very little power over things. The round of birth and death is ceaseless.

[17-18. This has reference to the traditional belief regarding the duration of the universe. According to it, the two *ayanas* (solstices) are the day and night of the gods, and therefore 360 human years make one year of the gods. Now time is divided into four ages each with a different duration, *krita* age of 4,000 years, *treta* of 3,000 years, *dvapara* of 2,000 and *kali* of 1,000 years. These plus 2,000 years of the transition period between these ages make 12,000 years. These however are the years of the gods! Therefore converted into human years they would be 360×12,000=43,20,000. This is one *yuga* of the gods, and one thousand such *yugas* make the day of Brahma, i. e. 4,32,00,00,000 mortal years. This is also called a *kalpa* (see IX. 7) which is the duration of a creation.

However fanciful this may seem, let it be remembered that Dr Broom whose work containing the latest research in anthropology has been recently published, reckons that man has been the main object of evolution for perhaps 1,500 million years.]

भूतग्रामः स अेवायं भूत्वा भूत्वा प्रलीयते ।
रात्र्यागमेऽवशः पार्थ प्रभवत्यहरागमे ॥१९॥

19. This same multitude of creatures come to birth, O Partha, again and again; they are dissolved at the coming of Night, whether they will or not; and at the break of Day they are re-born.

परस्तस्मात् तु भावोऽन्योऽव्यक्तोऽव्यक्तात् सनातनः ।
यः स सर्वेषु भूतेषु नश्यत्सु न विनश्यति ॥२०॥

20. But higher than that Unmanifest is another Unmanifest Being, everlasting, which perisheth not when all creatures perish.

अव्यक्तोऽक्षर इत्युक्तस् तमाहुः परमां गतिम् ।
यं प्राप्य न निवर्तन्ते तद् धाम परमं मम ॥२१॥

21. This Unmanifest, named the Imperishable, is declared to be the highest goal. For those who reach it there is no return. That is My highest abode.

पुरुषः स परः पार्थ भक्त्या लभ्यस्त्वनन्यया ।
यस्यांतःस्थानि भूतानि येन सर्वमिदं ततम् ॥२२॥

22. This Supreme Being, O Partha, may be won by undivided devotion; in It all beings dwell, by It all is pervaded.

[22. 'Pervaded' for *tatam* (ततम्), see note on II. 17.]

यत्र काले त्वनावृत्तिम् आवृत्तिं चैव योगिनः ।
प्रयाता यान्ति तं कालं वक्ष्यामि भरतर्षभ ॥२३॥

23. Now I will tell thee, Bharatarshabha, the conditions which determine the exemption from return, as also the return, of *yogins* after they pass away hence.

अग्निर्ज्योतिरहः शुक्लः षण्मासा उत्तरायणम् ।
तत्र प्रयाता गच्छन्ति ब्रह्मविदो जनाः ॥२४॥
धूमो रात्रिस्तथा कृष्णः षण्मासा दक्षिणायनम् ।
तत्र चांद्रमसं ज्योतिर् योगी प्राप्य निवर्तते ॥२५॥

24. Fire, Light, Day, the Bright Fortnight, the six

months of the Northern Solstice—through these departing men knowing *Brahman* go to *Brahman*.

25. Smoke, Night, the Dark Fortnight, the six months of the Southern Solstice—therethrough the *yogin* attains to the lunar light and thence returns.

I do not understand the meaning of these two *shlokas*. They do not seem to me to be consistent with the teaching of the Gita. The Gita teaches that he whose heart is meek with devotion, who is devoted to unattached action and has seen the Truth must win salvation, no matter when he dies. These *shlokas* seem to run counter to this. They may perhaps be stretched to mean broadly that a man of sacrifice, a man of light, a man who has known *Brahman* finds release from birth if he retains that enlightenment at the time of death, and that on the contrary the man who has none of these attributes goes to the world of the moon—not at all lasting—and returns to birth. The moon, after all, shines with borrowed light!

[24-25. There is a wide difference of opinion regarding even the verbal interpretation of these *shlokas*, much more so regarding their significance. Thus, according to some, the word *kala* in shl. 23 means not 'time', but 'path' by which a departed soul proceeds after death, and words *gati* (गति) and *sriti* (सृति) (both meaning 'paths') used by the author with reference to the same context in *shls*. 26 and 27 would seem to support the contention. On the other hand, the story of Bhishma who waited for fifty-eight days so that he might pass away when the sun entered the northern course—that being a propitious time, would go to support the view that the *shlokas* have reference to 'time'. I have used the word 'conditions' to include both meanings.

That the verses repeat the old belief handed down from the Rig Veda and the *Upanishads* (which describe the paths in much elaborate detail, e. g. *Chh. Up*. 5. 10. 1-6) is certain.

Shankaracharya says that fire, light, smoke etc. may be so-called deities presiding over the various portions of time referred to. The paths — *Devayana* (called *uttarayana* in *shl.* 24) and *Pitriyana* (called *dakshinayana* in *shl.* 25) are referred to in *Brahma Sutras* also. There, in the words of Tilak, "the author, anxious to reconcile all the passages with the practical difficulty sure to be experienced if death during the night of gods were held to be absolutely unmeritorious from a religious point of view, has recorded his opinion that we must *not* interpret these texts as predicating an uncomfortable future life for every man dying during the *dakshinayana* or the night of the gods. As an alternative, Badarayana, therefore, adds that these passages may be taken to refer to the *yogins* who desire to attain a particular kind of heaven after death. Whatever we may think of this view, we can, in this attempt of Badarayana, clearly see a distinct consciousness of the existence of tradition, which, if it did not put an absolute ban on death during the night of the gods, did, at any rate, clearly disapprove of such occurrences from a religious point of view. If the *pitriyana* originally represented, as stated above, a period of continuous darkness, the tradition can be easily and rationally explained ; for as the *pitriyana* then meant an uninterrupted night, the funeral ceremonies of any one dying during the period were deferred till the break of the dawn at the end of *pitriyana* or the commencement of *devayana*. Even now death during night is considered inauspicious, and the funeral generally takes place after daybreak." (The *Arctic Home in the Vedas*, p. 76-77)

The *shlokas* in their origin are thus of great antiquarian interest and Tilak has used them to good effect in support of his theory of the original home of the Aryans in the Arctic regions — the regions of six months' day and six months' night. The author of the Gita, however, in describing them briefly as the "bright" path and the "dark" path, struck a new departure and tried to clothe an ancient tradition with moral import, the bright path meaning that of knowledge and the dark one meaning that of ignorance. Indeed,

Gandhiji's note suggesting the moral interpretation has considerable support from two *Upanishad* texts which refer to these two paths. Thus *Prashna Up.* 1. 9-10 : "Those who worship *with the thought that they have indeed performed sacrifices* and righteous deeds go to the lunar world. This is *pitriyana.* But they who seek *Atman* by austerity, *brahmacharya,* faith, and spiritual study, they by the northern course win the sun." * See also *Mund. Up.* 1. 2. 11 : "Those who practise austerity and faith in the forest, depart passionless through the path of the sun to where there is that Imperishable Being." § This evidently was a later development of the eschatological view and the Gita in re-naming the paths would seem to have adopted this later moral interpretation. See *shl.* 27 where Arjuna is exhorted to be a true *yogin.*]

शुक्लकृष्णे गती ह्येते जगतः शाश्वते मते ।
अेकया यात्यनावृत्तिम् अन्ययाऽऽवर्तते पुनः ।।२६।।

26. These two paths — bright and dark — are deemed to be the eternal paths of the world ; by the one a man goes to return not, by the other he returns again.

The Bright one may be taken to mean the path of knowledge and the dark one that of ignorance.

नैते सृती पार्थ जानन् योगी मुह्यति कश्चन ।
तस्मात् सर्वेषु कालेषु योगयुक्तो भवार्जुन ।।२७।।

---

* तद्ये ह वै तदिष्टापूर्ते कृतमित्युपासते ते चान्द्रमसमेव लोकमभिजयन्ते ।... अथोत्तरेण तपसा ब्रह्मचर्येण श्रद्धया विद्ययात्मानमन्विष्यादित्यमभिजयन्ते ।
प्रश्न १. ९-१०

§ तपःश्रद्धे ये ह्युपवसन्त्यरण्ये ।

. . . . . .

सूर्यद्वारेण ते विरजाः प्रयान्ति ।
यत्रामृतः स पुरुषो ह्यव्ययात्मा ।। मुण्डक १. २. ११

27. The *yogin* knowing these two paths falls not into delusion, O Partha; therefore, at all times, O Arjuna, remain steadfast in *yoga*.

"Will not fall into delusion" means that he who knows the two paths and has known the secret of even-mindedness will not take the path of ignorance.

वेदेषु यज्ञेषु तपःसु चैव
दानेषु यत् पुण्यफलं प्रदिष्टम् ।
अत्येति तत् सर्वमिदं विदित्वा
योगी परं स्थानमुपैति चाद्यम् ॥२८॥

28. Whatever fruit of good deeds is laid down as accruing from (a study of) the Vedas, from sacrifices, austerities, and acts of charity—all that the *yogin* transcends, on knowing this, and reaches the Supreme and Primal Abode.

He who has achieved even-mindedness by dint of devotion, knowledge and service not only obtains the fruit of all his good actions, but also wins salvation.

['On knowing this' means, as Shankaracharya explains, on 'rightly understanding and practising the teaching imparted by the Lord in reply to the seven questions asked by Arjuna in the beginning of the discourse.']

अिति श्रीमद्भगवद्गीतासु अुपनिषत्सु ब्रह्मविद्यायां योगशास्त्रे श्रीकृष्णार्जुनसंवादे
ब्रह्मयोगो नाम अष्टमोऽध्यायः ॥८॥

Thus ends the eighth discourse entitled *Brahma Yoga* in the converse of Lord Krishna and Arjuna, on the science of *Yoga*, as part of the knowledge of *Brahman* in the Upanishad called the Bhagawadgita.

DISCOURSE IX

This discourse reveals the glory of devotion.

श्रीभगवानुवाच ।

इदं तु ते गुह्यतमं प्रवक्ष्याम्यनसूयवे ।
ज्ञानं विज्ञानसहितं यज्ज्ञात्वा मोक्ष्यसेऽशुभात् ॥१॥

The Lord said:

1. I will now declare to thee, who art uncensorious, this mysterious knowledge, together with discriminative knowledge, knowing which thou shalt be released from ill.

[Cf. What Christ said to his disciples: "Unto you it is given to know the mysteries of the Kingdom of God." Luke, 8. 10.]

राजविद्या राजगुह्यं पवित्रमिदमुत्तमम् ।
प्रत्यक्षावगमं धर्म्यं सुसुखं कर्तुमव्ययम् ॥२॥

2. This is the king of sciences, the king of mysteries, pure and sovereign, capable of direct comprehension, the essence of *dharma,* easy to practise, changeless.

अश्रद्दधानाः पुरुषा धर्मस्यास्य परंतप ।
अप्राप्य मां निवर्तन्ते मृत्युसंसारवर्त्मनि ॥३॥

3. Men who have no faith in this doctrine, O Parantapa, far from coming to Me, return repeatedly to the path of this world of death..

मया ततमिदं सर्वं जगदव्यक्तमूर्तिना ।
मत्स्थानि सर्वभूतानि न चाहं तेष्ववस्थितः ॥४॥
न च मत्स्थानि भूतानि पश्य मे योगमैश्वरम् ।
भूतभृन् न च भूतस्थो ममात्मा भूतभावनः ॥५॥

4. By Me, unmanifest in form, this whole world is pervaded ; all beings are in Me, I am not in them.

5. And yet those beings are not in Me. That indeed is My unique power as Lord ! Sustainer of all beings, I am not in them ; My Self brings them into existence.

The sovereign power of God lies in this mystery, this miracle, that all beings are in Him and yet not in Him, He is in them and yet not in them. This is the description of God in the language of mortal man. Indeed He soothes man by revealing to him all His aspects by using all kinds of paradoxes. All beings are in Him inasmuch as all creation is His ; but as He transcends it all, as He really is not the author of it all, it may be said with equal truth that the beings are not in Him. He really is in all His true devotees, He is *not*, according to them, in those who deny Him. What is this if not a mystery, a miracle of God ?

[4-5. The worship of God in His personal aspect is presented in this and the three succeeding discourses. But the paradoxes in these two *shlokas* may be explained as applicable to both the personal and the impersonal aspects of the Lord. The Invisible and the Infinite rises above and beyond the visible. Being its expression, it is in the Invisible ; but the Invisible is not in it, It transcends it. The universe as the creation of the creator reflects Him, but cannot contain Him, as the creator is greater than the creation. Again, as everything is strung on Him as gems on a thread, He, the thread, runs through them all and sustains them ; they are not in Him as they do not sustain Him. When the Lord says, 'I am not in them', perhaps it is the isolated *Atman,* unaffected by the physical frame encasing it that is referred to. Morally, of course, as Gandhiji explains in his note, He is in the hearts of all his worshippers but not, so it seems to them, in those of scoffers. As the *Atmabodha* says : "Though *Atman* is at all times and in all things it does not shine in all things. It shines only in a clear understanding as the reflection in polished surfaces." Or as the Koran says: "My earth and My heaven contain Me not, but the heart of My faithful servant containeth Me." Cf. also St. Augustine: "Thou wholly everywhere, while nothing contains Thee wholly."]

यथाऽऽकाशस्थितो नित्यं वायुः सर्वत्रगो महान् ।
तथा सर्वाणि भूतानि मत्स्थानीत्युपधारय ।।६।।

6. As the mighty wind, moving everywhere, is ever contained in ether, even so know that all beings are contained in Me.

[Ether is the subtlest of all the five elements, the next less subtle being air or wind. If there was no motion in the atmosphere, there would seem to be no distinction between ether and air. The moving air — the mighty wind moving everywhere — is ever contained in the all-pervading ether without in any way affecting it. There is no contact between the two and no amount of commotion in the atmosphere affects the ether. Even so all beings are contained in Him without affecting Him in any way.]

सर्वभूतानि कौंतेय प्रकृतिं यान्ति मामिकाम् ।
कल्पक्षये पुनस्तानि कल्पादौ विसृजाम्यहम् ।।७।।

7. All beings, O Kaunteya, merge into my *prakriti*, at the end of a *kalpa*, and I send them forth again when a *kalpa* begins.

[For *Kalpa*, see my note on VIII. 17-18.]

प्रकृतिं स्वामवष्टभ्य विसृजामि पुनः पुनः ।
भूतग्राममिमं कृत्स्नम् अवशं प्रकृतेर्वशात् ।।८।।

8. Resorting to my *prakriti*, I send forth again and again this multitude of beings, powerless under the sway of *prakriti*.

न च मां तानि कर्माणि निबध्नन्ति धनंजय ।
उदासीनवदासीनम् असक्तं तेषु कर्मसु ॥९॥

9. But all this activity, O Dhananjaya, does not bind Me, seated as one indifferent, unattached to it.

मयाऽध्यक्षेण प्रकृतिः सूयते सचराचरम् ।
हेतुनाऽनेन कौंतेय जगद् विपरिवर्तते ॥१०॥

10. With me as Presiding Witness, *prakriti* gives bīrth to all that moves and does not move; and because of this, O Kaunteya, the wheel of the world keeps going.

[Shankaracharya: "Because I am the Witness, because I preside, this universe moves on through all stages. My *maya* composed of the three *gunas* produces the universe comprising the moving and the unmoving."]

अवजानन्ति मां मूढा मानुषीं तनुमाश्रितम् ।
परं भावमजानन्तो मम भूतमहेश्वरम् ॥११॥

11. Not knowing My transcendent nature as the sovereign Lord of all beings, fools condemn Me incarnated as man.

For they deny the existence of God and do not recognize the Director in the human body.

[See my note on VII. 24.]

मोघाशा मोघकर्माणो मोघज्ञाना विचेतसः ।
राक्षसीमासुरीं चैव प्रकृतिं मोहिनीं श्रिताः ॥१२॥

12. Vain are the hopes, actions and knowledge of those witless ones who have resorted to the delusive nature of monsters and devils.

महात्मानस्तु मां पार्थ दैवीं प्रकृतिमाश्रिताः ।
भजंत्यनन्यमनसो ज्ञात्वा भूतादिमव्ययम् ॥१३॥

13. But those great souls who resort to the divine nature, O Partha, know Me as the Imperishable Source of all beings and worship Me with an undivided mind.

सततं कीर्तयन्तो मां यतन्तश्च दृढव्रताः ।
नमस्यन्तश्च मां भक्त्या नित्ययुक्ता उपासते ॥१४॥

14. Always declaring My glory, striving in steadfast faith, they do Me devout homage; ever attached to Me, they worship Me.

ज्ञानयज्ञेन चाप्यन्ये यजन्तो मामुपासते ।
अेकत्वेन पृथक्त्वेन बहुधा विश्वतोमुखम् ॥१५॥

15. Yet others, with knowledge-sacrifice, worship Me, who am to be seen everywhere, as one, as different or as many.

[I have literally translated Gandhiji's translation, but I am not sure that it is an accurate translation. Gandhiji evidently seems to follow Shankaracharya and others. I think with Hill that there is not much warrant for this translation, for there is no alternative conjunction, and it is hardly 'knowledge-sacrifice' to fix one's mind on God's manifoldness. He explains: "We have already seen (IV. 10) how Krishna claims to be one with all beings, and at the same time free from contact with them. It is with this knowledge that these men worship him, both 'with the idea of his oneness' with all existences, and at the same time 'with the idea of his separateness' from them." This is how I understand the *shloka*: *Shl.* 14 emphasizes the personal aspect, *shl.* 15 emphasizes the impersonal aspect. The worshippers of the Impersonal see Him either as one, that is immanent or as separate, i. e. transcendent, and these have been described in discourses VI-VIII. I would therefore translate it thus: "Yet others, with knowledge-sacrifice, variously worship Me, who am to be seen everywhere, (some) as immanent, (some) as transcendent." But this too is just tentative explanation.]

अहं क्रतुरहं यज्ञः स्वधाऽहमहमौषधम् ।
मन्त्रोऽहमहमेवाज्यम् अहमग्निरहं हुतम् ॥१६॥

16. I am the sacrificial vow; I am the sacrifice; I the ancestral oblation; I the herb; I the sacred text; I the clarified butter; I the fire; I the burnt offering.

पिताऽहमस्य जगतो माता धाता पितामहः ।
वेद्यं पवित्रमोंकार ऋक् साम यजुरेव च ॥१७॥

17. Of this universe I am Father, Mother, Creator, Grandsire; I am what is to be known, the sacred syllable *AUM*; the *Rig*, the *Saman* and the *Yajus*;

[For *AUM* see my note on VIII. 13; the last three are the names of the three recognized Vedas.]

गतिर्भर्ता प्रभुः साक्षी निवासः शरणं सुहृत् ।
प्रभवः प्रलयः स्थानं निधानं बीजमव्ययम् ॥१८॥

18. I am the Goal, the Sustainer, the Lord, the Witness, the Abode, the Refuge, the Friend; the Origin, the End, the Preservation, the Treasurehouse, the Imperishable Seed.

[Cf. *Imitation of Christ* which reproduces the Biblical text with comment: "Follow Me: I am the Way, the Truth, the Life. Without the way there is no going, without the truth there is no knowing, and without the life there is no living."]

तपाम्यहमहं वर्षं निगृह्णाम्युत्सृजामि च ।
अमृतं चैव मृत्युश्च सदसच्चाहमर्जुन ॥१९॥

19. I give heat; I hold back and pour forth rain; I am deathlessness and also death, O Arjuna, Being and not-Being as well.

[The seminal text for this paradoxical description is the famous *Nasadiya Sukta* of Rig Veda beginning, 'There were then neither *Asat* (not-Being) nor *Sat* (Being).' * Since then the *Prius* of all existence has sometimes been described as *Sat,* sometimes as *Asat,* from which *Asat* and *Sat* respectively were born. Thus in *Taitt. Up.* 2. 7 we have : "In the beginning was *Asat* ; from it was born *Sat.*" ; § and in *Chh. Up.* 6. 2 we have : "In the beginning verily all was *Sat* without a second." † When the *Prius* is described as *Asat* (not-Being) it is the state before being (in the sense of coming out or becoming) that is emphasized. When it is described as *Sat* it is its aspect of reality that is emphasized, that alone being the Real, all else existing because of It. The Gita sums up both the conceptions. Again we find *Br. Up.* referring to Death as the origin of all things. Why not then Deathlessness ? They are nothing but different words for not-Being and Being. In a word, God is the sum of all relatives and combines all contraries. As the *Br. Up.* says : ‡ "*Brahman* has indeed two aspects — the concrete and the inconcrete, the mortal and the immortal, the moving and the fixed, the this and the that....It is the reality of all realities for all these are realities, and It is the Supreme Reality."]

त्रैविद्या मां सोमपाः पूतपापा
यज्ञैरिष्ट्वा स्वर्गतिं प्रार्थयन्ते ।
ते पुण्यमासाद्य सुरेन्द्रलोकम्
अश्नन्ति दिव्यान् दिवि देवभोगान् ॥२०॥

---

* नासदासीन्नो सदासीत्तदानीं । ऋग्वेद, १०.१२९

§ असद्वा इदमग्र आसीत् । ततो वै सदजायत । तैत्तिरीय, २.७

† सदेव सोम्येदमग्र आसीदेकमेवाद्वितीयम् । छांदोग्य, ६.२

‡ ब्रह्मणो रूपे द्वे वाव—मूर्तं चैवामूर्तं च,
मर्त्यं चामृतं च, स्थितं च यच्च, सच्च त्यच्च ।
(बृहद्० २. ३–१)
सत्यस्य सत्यमिति; प्राणा वै सत्यम् तेषामेष सत्यम् ॥
(बृहद्० २.३–६)

20. Followers of the three Vedas, who drink the *soma* juice and are purged of sin, worship Me with sacrifice and pray for going to heaven; they reach the holy world of the gods and enjoy in heaven the divine joys of the gods.

The reference is to the sacrificial ceremonies and rites in vogue in the days of the Gita. We cannot definitely say what they were like nor what the *soma* juice exactly was.

ते तं भुक्त्वा स्वर्गलोकं विशालं
क्षीणे पुण्ये मर्त्यलोकं विशन्ति ।
अेवं त्रयीधर्ममनुप्रपन्ना
गतागतं कामकामा लभन्ते ॥२१॥

21. They enjoy the vast world of heaven, and their merit spent, they enter the world of the mortals; thus those who, following the Vedic law, long for the fruit of their action earn but the round of birth and death.

अनन्याश्चिंतयन्तो मां ये जनाः पर्युपासते ।
तेषां नित्याभियुक्तानां योगक्षेमं वहाम्यहम् ॥२२॥

22. As for those who worship Me, thinking on Me alone and nothing else, ever attached to Me, I bear the burden of getting them what they need.

There are thus three unmistakable marks of a true *yogi* or *bhakta* — even-mindedness, skill in action, undivided devotion. These three must be completely harmonized in a *yogi*. Without devotion there is no even-mindedness, without even-mindedness no devotion, and without skill in action devotion and even-mindedness might well be a pretence.

[I have written 'getting them what they need' for 'getting them what they have not and guarding for them what they have', which is more literal. Cf. "But seek ye first the kingdom of God and His righteousness, and all these things shall be added unto you." (Mat. 6. 33). Also *Imitation of Christ*: "He will provide for thee, and be thy faithful procurator in all things, so that thou needest not to trust in men."]

येऽप्यन्यदेवता भक्ता यजन्ते श्रद्धयाऽन्विताः ।
तेऽपि मामेव कौन्तेय यजंत्यविधिपूर्वकम् ।।२३।।

23. Even those who, devoted to other gods, worship them in full faith, even they, O Kaunteya, worship none but Me, though not according to the rule.

'Not according to the rule' means not knowing Me as the Impersonal and the Absolute.

अहं हि सर्वयज्ञानां भोक्ता च प्रभुरेव च ।
न तु मामभिजानन्ति तत्त्वेनातश्च्यवन्ति ते ।।२४।।

24. For I am the Acceptor and the Director of all sacrifices; but not recognizing Me as I am, they go astray.

यान्ति देवव्रता देवान् पितॄन् यान्ति पितृव्रताः ।
भूतानि यान्ति भूतेज्या यान्ति मद्याजिनोऽपि माम् ।।२५।।

25. Those who worship the gods go to the gods; those who worship the manes go to the manes; those who worship the spirits go to the spirits; but those who worship Me come to Me.

[This is a psychological truth recognized by all mystics. Sufi Jalaluddin Rumi said: "A man comes to be the thing on which he is bent." Eckhart quotes the saying of St. Augustine that "Man *is* what he loves", and adds this comment: "If he loves a stone, he is a stone; if he loves a man, he is a man; if he loves God — I dare not say more, for if I said that he would then be God, ye might stone me." (Nicholson, *Mystics of Islam*)]

पत्रं पुष्पं फलं तोयं यो मे भक्त्या प्रयच्छति ।
तदहं भक्त्युपहृतम् अश्नामि प्रयतात्मनः ॥२६॥

26. Any offering of leaf, flower, fruit or water, made to Me in devotion, by an earnest soul, I lovingly accept.

That is to say, it is the Lord in every being whom we serve with devotion who accepts the service.

यत् करोषि यदश्नासि यज्जुहोषि ददासि यत् ।
यत् तपस्यसि कौन्तेय तत् कुरुष्व मदर्पणम् ॥२७॥

27. Whatever thou doest, whatever thou eatest, whatever thou offerest as sacrifice or gift, whatever austerity thou dost perform, O Kaunteya, dedicate all to Me.

[Cf. "Whatever therefore ye eat, or drink, or whatever ye do, do all to the glory of God." 1. Co. 10. 31; also Col. 3-17]

शुभाशुभफलैरेवं मोक्ष्यसे कर्मबंधनैः ।
संन्यासयोगयुक्तात्मा विमुक्तो मामुपैष्यसि ॥२८॥

28. So doing thou shalt be released from the bondage of action, yielding good and evil fruit; having accomplished both renunciation and performance, thou shalt be released (from birth and death) and come unto Me.

[Renunciation of fruit and performance of action, *sannyasa* and *yoga* of the fifth discourse.]

समोऽहं सर्वभूतेषु न मे द्वेष्योऽस्ति न प्रियः ।
ये भजन्ति तु मां भक्त्या मयि ते तेषु चाप्यहम् ॥२९॥

29. I am the same to all beings; with Me there is none disfavoured, none favoured; but those who worship Me with devotion are in Me and I in them.

[Cf. John 15. 4: "Abide in Me, and I am in you."]

अपि चेत् सुदुराचारो भजते मामनन्यभाक् ।
साधुरेव स मंतव्यः सम्यग्व्यवसितो हि सः ॥३०॥

30. A sinner, howsoever great, if he turns to Me with undivided devotion, must indeed be counted a saint; for he has a settled resolve.

The undivided devotion subdues both his passions and his evil deeds.

[Settled resolve "to sin no more".]

क्षिप्रं भवति धर्मात्मा शश्वच्छांतिं निगच्छति ।
कौंतेय प्रतिजानीहि न मे भक्तः प्रणश्यति ॥३१॥

31. For soon he becomes righteous and wins everlasting peace; know for a certainty, O Kaunteya, that My *bhakta* never perishes.

मां हि पार्थ व्यपाश्रित्य येऽपि स्युः पापयोनयः ।
स्त्रियो वैश्यास्तथा शूद्रास् तेऽपि यान्ति परां गतिम् ॥३२॥

32. For finding refuge in Me, even those who though are born of the womb of sin, women, *vaishyas,* and *shudras* too, reach the supreme goal.

[Cf. John 3. 5: "That whosoever believeth in Him should not perish."]

किं पुनर्ब्राह्मणाः पुण्या भक्ता राजर्षयस्तथा ।
अनित्यमसुखं लोकम् अिमं प्राप्य भजस्व माम् ॥३३॥

33. How much more then, the pure *brahmanas* and seer-kings who are My devotees? Do thou worship Me, therefore, since thou hast come to this fleeting and joyless world.

मन्मना भव मद्भक्तो मद्याजी मां नमस्कुरु ।
मामेवैष्यसि युक्त्वैवम् आत्मानं मत्परायणः ॥३४॥

34. On Me fix thy mind, to Me bring thy devotion, to Me offer thy sacrifice, to Me make thy obeisance; thus having attached thyself to Me and made Me thy end and aim, to Me indeed shalt thou come.

अिति श्रीमद्भगवद्गीतासु अुपनिषत्सु ब्रह्मविद्यायां योगशास्त्रे श्रीकृष्णार्जुनसंवादे
राजविद्याराजगुह्ययोगो नाम नवमोऽध्यायः ॥९॥

Thus ends the ninth discourse entitled '*Rajavidya-rajaguhya Yoga*'
in the converse of Lord Krishna and Arjuna, on the science
of *Yoga*, as part of the knowledge of *Brahman* in
the Upanishad called the Bhagawadgita.

DISCOURSE X

For the benefit of His devotees, the Lord gives in this discourse a glimpse of His divine manifestations.

श्रीभगवानुवाच ।

भूय अेव महाबाहो श्रृणु मे परमं वचः ।
यत् तेऽहं प्रीयमाणाय वक्ष्यामि हितकाम्यया ।।१।।

The Lord said :

1. Yet once more, O Mahabahu, hear My supreme word, which I will utter to thee, gratified one, for thy benefit.

न मे विदुः सुरगणाः प्रभवं न महर्षयः ।
अहमादिर्हि देवानां महर्षीणां च सर्वशः ।।२।।

2. Neither the gods nor the great seers know My origin ; for I am, every way, the origin of them both.

['*prabhava*' (origin) may also mean 'might'. Cf. Koran : "Those whom they cry beside Allah created naught, but are themselves created." (16. 20)]

यो मामजमनादिं च वेत्ति लोकमहेश्वरम् ।
असंमूढः स मर्त्येषु सर्वपापैः प्रमुच्यते ।।३।।

3. He who knows Me, the great Lord of the worlds, as birthless and without beginning, he among mortals, undeluded, is released from sins.

बुद्धिर्ज्ञानमसंमोहः क्षमा सत्यं दमः शमः ।
सुखं दुःखं भवोऽभावो भयं चाभयमेव च ।।४।।

अहिंसा समता तुष्टिस् तपो दानं यशोऽयशः ।
भवन्ति भावा भूतानां मत्त अेव पृथग्विधाः ॥५॥

4. Discernment, knowledge, freedom from delusion, long suffering, truth, self-restraint, inward calm, pleasure, pain, birth, death, fear and fearlessness;

5. Non-violence, even-mindedness, contentment, austerity, beneficence, good and ill fame, — all these various attributes of creatures proceed verily from Me.

महर्षयः सप्त पूर्वे चत्वारो मनवस्तथा ।
मद्भावा मानसा जाता येषां लोक अिमाः प्रजाः ॥६॥

6. The seven great seers, the ancient four, and the Manus too were born of Me and of My mind, and of them were born all the creatures in the world.

[The seven sages, according to Tilak, are Marichi, Angiras, Atri, Pulastya, Pulaha, Kratu, and Vasishtha. About who the four are, so many conjectures are made that one might almost say only the author of the Gita knew who they were! Bhide Shastri suggests they may be those mentioned in *shloka* 13. The Manus are supposed to be 14, each presiding over a *manvantara* or cosmic period, known also as *kalpa* of 4320 million years. (See VIII. 17 and IX. 7.)]

अेतां विभूतिं योगं च मम यो वेत्ति तत्त्वतः ।
सोऽविकंपेन योगेन युज्यते नात्र संशयः ॥७॥

7. He who knows in truth this My immanence and My *yoga* becomes gifted with unshakable *yoga*; of this there is no doubt.

[*Yoga* — the unique power of the Lord — contains the *yoga* of even-mindedness and selfless or detached action.

He who knows Him and abides in Him naturally walks with Him, and so is gifted with unshakable *yoga*. Cf. "But as many as received Him, to them He gave power to be sons of God." John 1. 12.

Vibhuti in singular means the Lord's power and pervasiveness or immanence ; when used in the plural, I have taken it to mean manifestations revealing that immanence.]

अहं सर्वस्य प्रभवो मत्तः सर्वं प्रवर्तते ।
अिति मत्वा भजन्ते मां बुधा भावसमन्विताः ॥८॥

8. I am the source of all, all proceeds from Me; knowing this, the wise worship Me with hearts full of devotion.

मच्चित्ता मद्‌गतप्राणा बोधयन्तः परस्परम् ।
कथयन्तश्च मां नित्यं तुष्यन्ति च रमन्ति च ॥९॥

9. With Me in their thoughts, their whole soul devoted to Me, teaching one another, with Me ever on their lips, they live in contentment and joy.

["Each repetition of God's name carries you nearer and nearer to God", said Gandhiji to a friend. "This is a concrete fact, and I may tell you that I am talking here as no theorist but as one who has experienced what he says every minute of his life, so much so that it is easier for the life to stop than for this incessant process to stop. It is a definite need of the soul." (*Harijan,* May 25, 1935)]

तेषां सततयुक्तानां भजतां प्रीतिपूर्वकम् ।
ददामि बुद्धियोगं तं येन मामुपयान्ति ते ॥१०॥

10. To these, ever in tune with Me worshipping Me with affectionate devotion, I give the power of selfless action, whereby they come to Me.

[Cf. Koran : "As for those who strive in us we surely guide them to our paths, and lo! Allah is with the good." (29. 69).]

तेषामेवानुकंपार्थम् अहमज्ञानजं तमः ।
नाशयाम्यात्मभावस्थो ज्ञानदीपेन भास्वता ॥११॥

11. Out of every compassion for them, I who dwell in their hearts, destroy the darkness, born of ignorance, with the refulgent lamp of knowledge.

अर्जुन उवाच ।
परं ब्रह्म परं धाम पवित्रं परमं भवान् ।
पुरुषं शाश्वतं दिव्यम् आदिदेवमजं विभुम् ॥१२॥

Arjuna said :

12. Lord ! Thou art the supreme *Brahman,* the supreme Abode, the supreme Purifier ! Everlasting Celestial Being, the Primal God, Unborn, All-pervading.

आहुस्त्वाम् ऋषयः सर्वे देवर्षिर्नारदस्तथा ।
असितो देवलो व्यासः स्वयं चैव ब्रवीषि मे ॥१३॥

13. Thus have all the seers — the divine seer Narada, Asita, Devala, Vyasa — declared Thee ; and Thou Thyself dost tell me so.

सर्वमेतद् ऋतं मन्ये यन् मां वदसि केशव ।
न हि ते भगवन् व्यक्तिं विदुर्देवा न दानवाः ॥१४॥

14. All that Thou tellest me is true, I know, O Keshava, verily, Lord, neither the gods nor the demons know Thy manifestation.

स्वयमेवात्मनाऽऽत्मानं वेत्थ त्वं पुरुषोत्तम ।
भूतभावन भूतेश देवदेव जगत्पते ॥१५॥

15. Thyself alone Thou knowest by Thyself, O Purushottama, O Source and Lord of all beings, God of gods, O Ruler of the universe.

वक्तुमर्हस्यशेषेण दिव्या ह्यात्मविभूतयः ।
याभिर्विभूतिभिर्लोकान् अिमांस्त्वं व्याप्य तिष्ठसि ॥१६॥

16. Indeed Thou oughtest to tell me of all Thy manifestations, without a remainder, whereby Thou dost pervade these worlds.

कथं विद्यामहं योगिन् त्वां सदा परिच्चिन्तयन् ।
केषु केषु च भावेषु चिंत्योऽसि भगवन् मया ॥१७॥

17. O *Yogin*! constantly meditating on Thee, how am I to know Thee? In what various aspects am I to think of Thee, O Lord?

['*Yogin*', one possessed of the unique power. Krishna is addressed as *Yogeshvara* also in the same sense, in the next discourse.]

विस्तरेणात्मनो योगं विभूतिं च जनार्दन ।
भूयः कथय तृप्तिर्हि श्रृण्वतो नास्ति मेऽमृतम् ॥१८॥

18. Recount to me yet again, in full detail, Thy unique power and Thy immanence, O Janardana! For my ears cannot be sated with listening to Thy life-giving words.

श्रीभगवानुवाच ।
हन्त ते कथयिष्यामि दिव्या ह्यात्मविभूतयः ।
प्राधान्यतः कुरुश्रेष्ठ नास्त्यन्तो विस्तरस्य मे ॥१९॥

The Lord said:

19. Yea, I will unfold to thee, O Kurushreshtha, My divine manifestations, — the chiefest only; for there is no limit to their extent.

अहमात्मा गुडाकेश सर्वभूताशयस्थितः ।
अहमादिश्च मध्यं च भूतानामन्त अेव च ॥२०॥

20. I am the *Atman,* O Gudakesha, seated in the heart of every being; I am the beginning, the middle and the end of all beings.

आदित्यानामहं विष्णुर् ज्योतिषां रविरंशुमान् ।
मरीचिर्मरुतामस्मि नक्षत्राणामहं शशी ॥२१॥

21. Of the *Adityas* I am Vishnu; of luminaries, the radiant Sun; of *Maruts,* I am Marichi; of constellations, the moon.

[*Adityas* are twelve presiding over the twelve months. *Maruts* are the wind-gods.]

वेदानां सामवेदोऽस्मि देवानामस्मि वासवः ।
अिन्द्रियाणां मनश्चास्मि भूतानामस्मि चेतना ॥२२॥

22. Of the Vedas I am the *Sama* Veda; of the gods Indra; of the senses I am the mind; of beings I am the consciousness.

[The Gita, singing as it does the glory of devotion, gives the place of honour to *Sama Veda* which contains chants in praise of God. (Tilak)]

रुद्राणां शंकरश्चास्मि वित्तेशो यक्षरक्षसाम् ।
वसूनां पावकश्चास्मि मेरुः शिखरिणामहम् ॥२३॥

23. Of *Rudras* I am Shankara; of *Yakshas* and *Rakshasas* Kubera; of *Vasus* I am the Fire; of mountains Meru.

[*Rudras* are the deities of destruction, numbering eleven. Kubera is the Lord of Wealth, whose treasures are supposed to be guarded by *Yakshas* and *Rakshasas. Vasus* are eight — personifications of objects like fire, wind, dawn. *Meru* is the fabled mountain of gems and gold round which the planets were supposed to revolve.]

पुरोधसां च मुख्यं मां विद्धि पार्थ बृहस्पतिम् ।
सेनानीनामहं स्कंदः सरसामस्मि सागरः ।।२४।।

24. Of priests, O Partha, know Me to be the chief Brihaspati ; of army captains I am Kartikeya ; and of waters the ocean.

[Brihaspati is the preceptor of the gods. Kartikeya is the Indian Mars.]

महर्षीणां भृगुरहं गिरामस्म्येकमक्षरम् ।
यज्ञानां जपयज्ञोऽस्मि स्थावराणां हिमालयः ।।२५।।

25. Of the great seers I am Bhrigu ; of words I am the one syllable '*AUM*'; of sacrifices I am the *Japa* sacrifice ; of things immovable, the Himalaya.

[*Japa* is repetition of God's name. In this section of the Gita dealing with devotion, the sacrifice of the repetition of God's name — briefly the sacrifice of praise — is held to be the best.]

अश्वत्थः सर्ववृक्षाणां देवर्षीणां च नारदः ।
गंधर्वाणां चित्ररथः सिद्धानां कपिलो मुनिः ।।२६।।

26. Of all trees I am Ashvattha ; of the divine seers, Narada ; of the heavenly choir I am Chitraratha ; of the perfected I am Kapila the ascetic.

[*Ashvattha* is the sacred *peepul* tree. Kapila may be the supposed founder of Sankhya philosophy.]

उच्चैःश्रवसमश्वानां विद्धि माममृतोद्भवम् ।
ऐरावतं गजेन्द्राणां नराणां च नराधिपम् ।।२७।।

27. Of horses, know Me to be Uchchaihshravas born with *Amrita* ; of mighty elephants I am Airavata ; of men, the monarch.

[Uchchaihshravas, Indra's horse, one of the fourteen objects that the ocean yielded when it was churned by the gods for *Amrita* — nectar. Airavata also was one of the fourteen objects.]

आयुधानामहं वज्रं धेनूनामस्मि कामधुक् ।
प्रजनश्चास्मि कंदर्पः सर्पाणामस्मि वासुकिः ।।२८।।

28. Of weapons, I am Vajra ; of cows, Kamadhenu ; I am Kandarpa, the god of generation ; of serpants I am Vasuki.

[Vajra is Indra's thunderbolt made of the bones of sage Dadhichi who immolated himself so that the world might be saved.

Kamadhenu, supposed to be the cow yielding all objects of desire, also one of the fourteen objects yielded by the ocean.]

अनंतश्चास्मि नागानां वरुणो यादसामहम् ।
पितृणामर्यमा चास्मि यमः संयमतामहम् ।।२९।।

29. Of cobras I am Ananta ; of water-dwellers I am Varuna ; of the manes I am Aryaman ; and of the chastisers, Yama.

[Vasuki in *shloka* 28 was used as the churning rope by the gods ; Ananta is the thousand-hooded snake on which God Vishnu is supposed to rest. Yama is not so much the God of Death, as the Ruler of the dead. Varuna who held a high place among Vedic deities came later to be the Lord of the waters.]

प्रह्लादश्चास्मि दैत्यानां कालः कलयतामहम् ।
मृगाणां च मृगेन्द्रोऽहं वैनतेयश्च पक्षिणां ।।३०।।

30. Of demons I am Prahlada ; of reckoners, the Time ; of beasts I am the lion ; and of birds, Garuda.

[Prahlada is remembered throughout India as the ideal devotee who braved his father's wrath and went through untold trials rather than give up his devotion to God. Garuda is described as the mount of God Vishnu.]

पवनः पवतामस्मि रामः शस्त्रभृतामहम् ।
झषाणां मकरश्चास्मि स्रोतसामस्मि जाह्नवी ॥३१॥

31. Of cleansing agents I am the Wind ; of wielders of weapons, Rama ; of fishes I am the crocodile ; of rivers, the Ganges.

[Rama may be either Parashurama or the celebrated Rama of the Ramayana.]

सर्गाणामादिरन्तश्च मध्यं चैवाहमर्जुन ।
अध्यात्मविद्या विद्यानां वादः प्रवदतामहम् ॥३२॥

32. Of creations I am the beginning, end and middle, O Arjuna ; of sciences, the science of spiritual knowledge ; of debaters, the right argument.

['The right argument' is the dialectic style of debates as distinguished from the merely disputatious styles.]

अक्षराणामकारोऽस्मि द्वंद्वः सामासिकस्य च ।
अहमेवाक्षयः कालो धाताऽहं विश्वतोमुखः ॥३३॥

33. Of letters, the letter A ; of compounds I am the *dvandva* ; I am the imperishable Time ; I am the creator to be seen everywhere.

[*Dvandva* is a variety of Sanskrit compounds in which both the component parts are co-ordinated as distinguished from other compounds in which either of the two parts predominates.]

मृत्युः सर्वहरश्चाहम् अुद्भवश्च भविष्यताम् ।
कीर्तिः श्रीर्वाक् च नारीणां स्मृतिर्मेधा धृतिः क्षमा ॥३४॥

34. All-seizing Death am I, as also the source of things to be ; in feminine virtues I am Kirti (glory),

Shri (beauty), Vak (speech), Smriti (memory), Medha (intelligence), Dhriti (constancy) and Kshama (forgiveness).

[The other half of the *shloka* may mean either 'among nouns of feminine gender — all the abstract nouns named being feminine' or 'among feminine virtues'.]

बृहत्साम तथा साम्नां गायत्री छंदसामहम् ।
मासानां मार्गशीर्षोऽहम् ऋतूनां कुसुमाकरः ॥३५॥

35. Of *Saman* hymns I am Brihat Saman ; of metres, Gayatri ; of months I am Margashirsha ; of seasons, the spring.

[A hymn of the Sama Veda in *brihati* metre. *Gayatri* is named not as the best Vedic metre, but as containing the quintessence of all hymns. It is the daily prayer of all the twice-born. Margashirsha in those days used to be the first month of the Hindu year.]

द्यूतं छलयतामस्मि तेजस् तेजस्विनामहम् ।
जयोऽस्मि व्यवसायोऽस्मि सत्त्वं सत्त्ववतामहम् ॥३६॥

36. Of deceivers I am the dice-play ; of the splendid the splendour ; I am victory, I am resolution, I am the goodness of the good.

The 'dice-play of deceivers' need not alarm one. For the good and evil nature of things is not the matter in question, it is the directing and immanent power of God that is being described. Let the deceivers also know that they are under God's rule and judgment and put away their pride and deceit.

[Bhide Shastri translates : "I am the gamble of the deceivers", i. e. I deceive the deceivers.]

वृष्णीनां वासुदेवोऽस्मि पांडवानां धनंजयः ।
मुनीनामप्यहं व्यासः कवीनामुशना कविः ॥३७॥

37. Of Vrishnis I am Vasudeva; of Pandavas Dhananjaya; of ascetics I am Vyasa; and of seers, Ushanas.

[Among the descendents of Vrishni or Yadava, I am the son of Vasudeva — Vasudeva being the great-great-grandson of Yadava Vrishni. Ushanas is Shukra, the preceptor of the demons, or perhaps a Vedic *rishi* of that name.]

दंडो दमयतामस्मि नीतिरस्मि जिगीषताम् ।
मौनं चैवास्मि गुह्यानां ज्ञानं ज्ञानवतामहम् ।।३८।।

38. I am the rod of those that punish; the strategy of those seeking victory; of secret things I am silence, and the knowledge of those that know.

यच्चापि सर्वभूतानां बीजं तदहमर्जुन ।
न तदस्ति विना यत् स्यान् मया भूतं चराचरम् ।।३९।।

39. Whatever is the seed of every being, O Arjuna, that am I; there is nothing, whether moving or fixed, that can be without Me.

नान्तोऽस्ति मम दिव्यानां विभूतीनां परंतप ।
अेष तूद्देशतः प्रोक्तो विभूतेर्विस्तरो मया ।।४०।।

40. There is no end to my divine manifestations; what extent of them I have told thee now is only by way of illustration.

यद् यद् विभूतिमत् सत्त्वं श्रीमदूर्जितमेव वा ।
तत् तदेवावगच्छ त्वं मम तेजोंऽशसंभवम् ।।४१।।

41. Whatever is glorious, beautiful and mighty know thou that all such has issued from a fragment of My splendour.

अथवा बहुनैतेन किं ज्ञातेन तवार्जुन ।
विष्टभ्याहमिदं कृत्स्नम् अेकांशेन स्थितो जगत् ।।४२।।

42. But why needest thou to learn this at great length, O Arjuna? With but a part of Myself I stand upholding this universe.

[39-42. I have given but the briefest explanations of the various mythological and other references in the foregoing, for the kernel of the whole discourse is contained in these *shlokas*. What Shankarananda, a commentator, says explaining *shloka* 41 sums up the burden of the discourse: "Whatever there is animate or inanimate, possessed of *richness* in creative energy, power, wealth, deeds of merit, learning, austerity, in virtues like valour, austerity, fortitude, generosity; and whatever is *mighty* by virtue of vigour, splendour, energy, force, manliness, substance, size...; and whatever is to be seen possessed of *beauty* of handsomeness or learning, intellect, wealth, fame or activity — every such thing springs from a portion or phase of My majestic power." Says Jami, the Persian Sufi:

"That each one of His eternal attributes should
become manifest accordingly in a diverse form
Therefore He created the verdant fields of time and
space and the life-giving garden of the World,
That every branch and leaf and fruit might show
forth His various perfections."

And yet all this reveals but a part. As the great Vedic text of which *shloka* 42 is an echo says:

"One fourth of Him constitutes the universe below." *

Cf. also Bhagawata: "Lustre, Beauty, Glory, Might, Humility, Renunciation, Prosperity, Fortune, Valour, Forbearance, Wisdom — whatever possesses these is a fragment of Me."]

इति श्रीमद्भगवद्गीतासु उपनिषत्सु ब्रह्मविद्यायां योगशास्त्रे श्रीकृष्णार्जुनसंवादे विभूतियोगो नाम दशमोऽध्यायः ॥१०॥

Thus ends the tenth discourse, entitled '*Vibhuti Yoga*' in the converse of Lord Krishna and Arjuna, on the science of *Yoga*, as part of the knowledge of *Brahman*, in the Upanishad called the Bhagawadgita.

---

* पादोऽस्य विश्वा भूतानि । ऋग्वेद १०.९०.३

DISCOURSE XI

*In this discourse the Lord reveals to Arjuna's vision what Arjuna has heard with his ears — the Universal Form of the Lord. This discourse is a favourite with the Bhaktas. Here there is no argument, there is pure poetry. Its solemn music * reverberates in one's ears and it is not possible to tire of reading it again and again.*

अर्जुन अुवाच ।

मदनुग्रहाय परमं गुह्यमध्यात्मसंज्ञितम् ।
यत् त्वयोक्तं वचस्तेन मोहोऽयं विगतो मम ।।१।।

Arjuna said :

1. Out of Thy grace towards me, Thou hast told me the supreme mystery revealing the knowledge of the Supreme ; it has banished my delusion.

भवाप्ययौ हि भूतानां श्रुतौ विस्तरशो मया ।
त्वत्तः कमलपत्राक्ष माहात्म्यमपि चाव्ययम् ।।२।।

2. Of the origin and destruction of beings I have heard from Thee in full detail, as also of Thy imperishable majesty, O Kamala-patraksha !

[*Kamala-patraksha,* having eyes (dark, soft, and wide) like the lotus leaf.]

अेवमेतद् यथात्थ त्वम् आत्मानं परमेश्वर ।
द्रष्टुमिच्छामि ते रूपम् अैश्वरं पुरुषोत्तम ।।३।।

---

* The music, of course, of the original ! In translation, 'the glory is gone'. For a very free rendering which brings out some at least of the haunting music of the original the reader must go to Sir Edwin Arnold's flowing stanzas.

3. Thou art indeed just as Thou hast described Thyself, Parameshvara! I do crave to behold, now, that form of Thine as Ishvara.

[*Parameshvara* (Supreme Lord) and *Ishvara* are the two words in common use throughout India for 'God'. *Ishvara* is defined as "capable of doing, undoing and transforming anything".]

मन्यसे यदि तच्छक्यं मया द्रष्टुमिति प्रभो ।
योगेश्वर ततो मे त्वं दर्शयात्मानमव्ययम् ॥४॥

4. If, Lord, Thou thinkest it possible for me to bear the sight, reveal to me, O Yogeshvara, Thy imperishable form.

[*Yogeshvara* — Lord or Master of Yoga.]

श्रीभगवानुवाच ।
पश्य मे पार्थ रूपाणि शतशोऽथ सहस्रशः ।
नानाविधानि दिव्यानि नानावर्णाकृतीनि च ॥५॥

The Lord said:

5. Behold, O Partha, my forms divine in their hundreds and thousands, infinitely diverse, infinitely various in colour and aspect.

पश्यादित्यान् वसून् रुद्रान् अश्विनौ मरुतस्तथा ।
बहून्यदृष्टपूर्वाणि पश्याश्चर्याणि भारत ॥६॥

6. Behold the Adityas, the Vasus, the Rudras, the two Ashwins, and the Maruts; behold, O Bharata, numerous marvels never revealed before.

इहैकस्थं जगत् कृत्स्नं पश्याद्य सचराचरम् ।
मम देहे गुडाकेश यच्चान्यद् द्रष्टुमिच्छसि ॥७॥

7. Behold today, O Gudakesha, in my body, the whole universe, moving and unmoving, all in one, and whatever else thou cravest to see.

न तु मां शक्यसे द्रष्टुम् अनेनैव स्वचक्षुषा ।
दिव्यं ददामि ते चक्षुः पश्य मे योगमैश्वरम् ॥८॥

8. But thou canst not see Me with these thine own eyes. I give thee the eye divine; behold My sovereign power!

[We have a glimpse of what the eye divine can be like in *Chh. Up.* 8. 12. 1-5: "This body," we are told, "is mortal. It is owned by death, though it is the ground of that deathless *Atman*....For one who is bodiless pleasure and pain have no effect. The wind is bodiless, even so clouds, lightning, thunder. Even as these when they arise from space reach the highest light and appear with their own form, even so that serene *Atman* when he rises up from this body reaches the highest light and appears with his own form." This divine vision is verily to be in "that serene and blessed mood" when "we are laid asleep in body and become a living soul." *]

संजय अुवाच ।
अेवमुक्त्वा ततो राजन् महायोगेश्वरो हरिः ।
दर्शयामास पार्थाय परमं रूपमैश्वरम् ॥९॥

Sanjaya said:

9. With these words, O King, the great Lord of Yoga, Hari, then revealed to Partha His supreme form as Ishvara.

---

* मघवन्मर्त्यं वा अिदं शरीरमात्तं मृत्युना तदस्यामृतस्याशरीरस्यात्मनोऽधिष्ठानम्। . . . अशरीरं वाव सन्तं न प्रियाप्रिये स्पृशतः ॥१॥

अशरीरो वायुरभ्रं विद्युत्स्तनयित्नुरशरीराण्येतानि तद्यथैतान्यमुष्मादाकाशात्समुत्थाय परं ज्योतिरुपसंपद्य स्वेन स्वेन रूपेणाभिनिष्पद्यन्ते ॥२॥

अेवमेवैष संप्रसादोऽस्माच्छरीरात्समुत्थाय परं ज्योतिरुपसंपद्य स्वेन रूपेणाभिनिष्पद्यते . . . ॥३॥

अथ यो वेदेदं मन्वानीति स आत्मा मनोऽस्य दैवं चक्षुः स वा अेष अेतेन दैवेन चक्षुषा मनसैतान् कामान् पश्यन् रमते ॥५॥ छान्दोग्य. ८.१२.१-५

अनेकवक्त्रनयनम् अनेकाद्भुतदर्शनम् ।
अनेकदिव्याभरणं दिव्यानेकोद्यतायुधम् ॥१०॥

10. With many mouths and many eyes, many wondrous aspects, many divine ornaments, and many brandished weapons divine.

दिव्यमाल्यांबरधरं दिव्यगंधानुलेपनम् ।
सर्वाश्चर्यमयं देवम् अनन्तं विश्वतोमुखम् ॥११॥

11. Wearing divine garlands and vestments, annointed with divine perfumes, it was the form of God, all-marvellous, infinite, seen everywhere.

दिवि सूर्यसहस्रस्य भवेद् युगपदुत्थिता ।
यदि भाः सदृशी सा स्याद् भासस्तस्य महात्मनः ॥१२॥

12. Were the splendour of a thousand suns to shoot forth all at once in the sky that might perchance resemble the splendour of that Mighty One.

तत्रैकस्थं जगत् कृत्स्नं प्रविभक्तमनेकधा ।
अपश्यद् देवदेवस्य शरीरे पाण्डवस्तदा ॥१३॥

13. Then did Pandava see the whole universe in its manifold divisions gathered as one in the body of that God of gods.

ततः स विस्मयाविष्टो हृष्टरोमा धनंजयः ।
प्रणम्य शिरसा देवं कृतांजलिरभाषत ॥१४॥

14. Then Dhananjaya, wonderstruck and thrilled in every fibre of his being, bowed low his head before the Lord, addressing Him thus with folded hands.

अर्जुन उवाच ।

पश्यामि देवांस्तव देव देहे
सर्वांस्तथा भूतविशेषसंघान् ।
ब्रह्माणमीशं कमलासनस्थम्
ऋषींश्च सर्वान् उरगांश्च दिव्यान् ॥१५॥

Arjuna said :

15. Within Thy form, O Lord, I see all the gods and the diverse multitudes of beings, the Lord Brahma, on his lotus-throne and all the seers and the serpents divine.

अनेकबाहूदरवक्त्रनेत्रम्
पश्यामि त्वां सर्वतोऽनन्तरूपम् ।
नान्तं न मध्यं न पुनस्तवादिं
पश्यामि विश्वेश्वर विश्वरूप ॥१६॥

16. With many arms and bellies, mouths and eyes, I see Thy infinite form everywhere. Neither Thy end, nor middle, nor beginning, do I see, O Lord of the Universe, Universal-formed !

किरीटिनं गदिनं चक्रिणं च
तेजोराशिं सर्वतो दीप्तिमन्तम् ।
पश्यामि त्वां दुर्निरीक्ष्यं समन्ताद्
दीप्तानलार्कद्युतिमप्रमेयम् ॥१७॥

17. With crown and mace and disc, a mass of effulgence, gleaming everywhere I see Thee, so dazzling to the sight, bright with the splendour of the fiery sun blazing from all sides, — incomprehensible.

त्वमक्षरं परमं वेदितव्यम्
त्वमस्य विश्वस्य परं निधानम् ।
त्वमव्ययः शाश्वतधर्मगोप्ता
सनातनस्त्वं पुरुषो मतो मे ॥१८॥

18. Thou art the Supreme Imperishable worthy to be known ; Thou art the final resting place of this universe ; Thou art the changeless guardian of the Eternal Dharma ; Thou art, I believe, the Everlasting Being.

अनादिमध्यान्तमनन्तवीर्यम्
अनन्तबाहुं शशिसूर्यनेत्रम् ।
पश्यामि त्वां दीप्तहुताशवक्त्रम्
स्वतेजसा विश्वमिदं तपन्तम् ॥१९॥

19. Thou hast no beginning, middle nor end; infinite is Thy might; arms innumerable; for eyes, the sun and the moon; Thy mouth a blazing fire, overpowering the universe with Thy radiance.

द्यावापृथिव्योरिदमन्तरं हि
व्याप्तं त्वयैकेन दिशश्च सर्वाः ।
दृष्ट्वाऽद्भुतं रूपमुग्रं तवेदम्
लोकत्रयं प्रव्यथितं महात्मन् ॥२०॥

20. By Thee alone are filled the spaces between heaven and earth and all the quarters; at the sight of this Thy wondrous terrible form, the three worlds are sore oppressed, O Mahatman!

[19-20. These *shlokas* substantially repeat *Mund. Up.* 2. 1. 4: "Fire is His head; His eyes the moon and the sun; the region of space, His ears." *]

अमी हि त्वां सुरसंघा विशन्ति
केचिद् भीताः प्रांजलयो गृणन्ति ।
स्वस्तीत्युक्त्वा महर्षिसिद्धसंघाः
स्तुवन्ति त्वां स्तुतिभिः पुष्कलाभिः ॥२१॥

21. Here, too, the multitudes of gods are seen to enter Thee; some awe-struck praise Thee with folded arms; the hosts of great seers and siddhas, 'All Hail' on their lips, hymn Thee with songs of praise.

* अग्निमूर्धा चक्षुषी चन्द्रसूर्यौ दिशः श्रोत्रे । मुण्डक, २.१.४

रुद्रादित्या वसवो ये च साध्या
विश्वेऽश्विनौ मरुतश्चोष्मपाश्च ।
गन्धर्वयक्षासुरसिद्धसंघा
वीक्षन्ते त्वां विस्मिताश्चैव सर्वे ॥२२॥

22. The Rudras, Adityas, Vasus, Sadhyas, all the gods, the twin Ashwins, Maruts, Manes, the hosts of Gandharvas, Yakshas, Asuras and Siddhas — all gaze on Thee in wonderment.

रूपं महत् ते बहुवक्त्रनेत्रम्
महाबाहो बहुबाहूरुपादम् ।
बहूदरं बहुदंष्ट्राकरालम्
दृष्ट्वा लोकाः प्रव्यथितास्तथाऽहम् ॥२३॥

23. At the sight of Thy mighty form, O Mahabahu, many-mouthed, with eyes, arms, thighs and feet innumerable, with many vast bellies, terrible with many jaws, the worlds feel fearfully oppressed, and so do I.

नभःस्पृशं दीप्तमनेकवर्णम्
व्यात्ताननं दीप्तविशालनेत्रम् ।
दृष्ट्वा हि त्वां प्रव्यथितान्तरात्मा
धृतिं न विन्दामि शमं च विष्णो ॥२४॥

24. For as I behold Thee touching the sky, glowing, numerous-hued with gaping mouths and wide resplendent eyes, I feel oppressed in my innermost being ; no peace nor quiet I find, O Vishnu !

दंष्ट्राकरालानि च ते मुखानि
दृष्ट्वैव कालानलसंनिभानि ।
दिशो न जाने न लभे च शर्म ।
प्रसीद देवेश जगन्निवास ॥२५॥

25. And as I see Thy mouths with fearful jaws, resembling the Fire of Doom, I lose all sense of direction, and find no relief. Be gracious, O Devesha, O Jagannivasa !

[*Devesha* — Lord of gods ; *Jagannivasa* — the Refuge or Abode of the Universe. For the sake of rhythm in this musical discourse, I have retained some of these forms of address in their original form. These occur again in *Shls.* 37 and 45.]

अमी च त्वां धृतराष्ट्रस्य पुत्राः
सर्वे सहैवावनिपालसंघैः ।
भीष्मो द्रोणः सूतपुत्रस्तथासौ
सहास्मदीयैरपि योधमुख्यैः ॥२६॥
वक्त्राणि ते त्वरमाणा विशन्ति
दंष्ट्राकरालानि भयानकानि ।
केचिद् विलग्ना दशनान्तरेषु
संदृश्यन्ते चूर्णितैरुत्तमांगैः ॥२७॥

26. All the sons of Dhritarashtra, and with them the crowd of kings, Bhishma, Drona, and that Karna too, as also our chief warriors —

27. Are hastening into the fearful jaws of Thy terrible mouths. Some indeed, caught between Thy teeth, are seen, their heads being crushed to atoms.

यथा नदीनां बहवोऽम्बुवेगाः
समुद्रमेवाभिमुखा द्रवन्ति ।
तथा तवामी नरलोकवीरा
विशन्ति वक्त्राण्यभिविज्वलन्ति ॥२८॥

28. As rivers, in their numerous torrents, run headlong to the sea, even so the heroes of the world of men rush into Thy flaming mouths.

यथा प्रदीप्तं ज्वलनं पतंगा
विशन्ति नाशाय समृद्धवेगाः ।
तथैव नाशाय विशन्ति लोकास्
तवापि वक्त्राणि समृद्धवेगाः ॥२९॥

29. As moths, fast-flying, plunge into blazing fire, straight to their doom, even so these rush headlong into Thy mouths, to their destruction.

लेलिह्यसे ग्रसमानस्समंतात्
लोकान् समग्रान् वदनैर्ज्वलद्भिः ।
तेजोभिरापूर्य जगत् समग्रं
भासस्तवोग्राः प्रतपन्ति विष्णो ॥३०॥

30. Devouring all these from all sides, Thou lappest them with Thy flaming tongues; Thy fierce rays blaze forth, filling the whole universe with their lustre.

आख्याहि मे को भवानुग्ररूपो
नमोऽस्तु ते देववर प्रसीद ।
विज्ञातुमिच्छामि भवन्तमाद्यम्
न हि प्रजानामि तव प्रवृत्तिम् ॥३१॥

31. Tell me, Lord, who Thou art so dread of form! Hail to Thee, O Devavara! Be gracious! I desire to know Thee, Primal Lord; for I comprehend not what Thou dost.

[*Devavara* — same as *Devesha* — God of gods.]

श्रीभगवानुवाच ।
कालोऽस्मि लोकक्षयकृत् प्रवृद्धो
लोकान् समाहर्तुमिह प्रवृत्तः ।
ऋतेऽपि त्वां न भविष्यन्ति सर्वे
येऽवस्थिताः प्रत्यनीकेषु योधाः ॥३२॥

The Lord said :

32. Doom am I, full-ripe, dealing death to the worlds, engaged in devouring mankind. Even without thy slaying them not one of the warriors, ranged for battle against thee, shall survive.

तस्मात् त्वमुत्तिष्ठ यशो लभस्व
जित्वा शत्रून् भुंक्ष्व राज्यं समृद्धम् ।
मयैवैते निहताः पूर्वमेव
निमित्तमात्रं भव सव्यसाचिन् ।।३३।।

33. Therefore, do thou arise, and win renown! Defeat thy foes and enjoy a thriving kingdom. By Me have these already been destroyed ; be thou no more than an instrument, O Savyasachin !

द्रोणं च भीष्मं च जयद्रथं च
कर्णं तथाऽन्यानपि योधवीरान् ।
मया हतांस्त्वं जहि मा व्यथिष्ठाः
युध्यस्व जेताऽसि रणे सपत्नान् ।।३४।।

34. Droná, Bhishma, Jayadratha and Karna, as also the other warrior chiefs — already slain by Me — slay thou ! Be not dismayed ! Fight ! Victory is thine over the foes in the field.

[These four are particularly mentioned as they were supposed to be well-nigh invulnerable, gifted as they were with unique powers and celestial weapons.]

संजय अुवाच ।
अेतच्छ्रुत्वा वचनं केशवस्य
कृतांजलिर्वेपमानः किरीटी ।
नमस्कृत्वा भूय अेवाह कृष्णम्
सगद्गदं भीतभीतः प्रणम्य ।।३५।।

Sanjaya said :

35. Hearing this word of Keshava, crown-wearer Arjuna folded his hands, and trembling made obeisance. Bowing and all hesitant, in faltering accents, he proceeded to address Krishna once more.

अर्जुन उवाच ।
स्थाने हृषीकेश तव प्रकीर्त्या
जगत् प्रहृष्यत्यनुरज्यते च ।
रक्षांसि भीतानि दिशो द्रवन्ति
सर्वे नमस्यन्ति च सिद्धसंघाः ।।३६।।

Arjuna said :

36. Right proper it is, O Hrishikesha, that Thy praise should stir the world to gladness and tender emotion ; the Rakshasas in fear fly to every quarter and all the hosts of Siddhas do reverent homage.

कस्माच्च ते न नमेरन् महात्मन्
गरीयसे ब्रह्मणोऽप्यादिकर्त्रे ।
अनन्त देवेश जगन्निवास
त्वमक्षरं सदसत् तत्परं यत् ।।३७।।

37. And why should they not bow down to Thee, O Mahatman ? Thou art the First Creator, greater even than Brahma. O Ananta, O Devesha, O Jagannivasa, Thou art the Imperishable, Being, not-Being, and That which transcends even these.

त्वमादिदेवः पुरुषः पुराणस्
त्वमस्य विश्वस्य परं निधानम् ।
वेत्तासि वेद्यं च परं च धाम
त्वया ततं विश्वमनन्तरूप ।।३८।।

38. Thou art the Primal God, the Ancient Being; Thou art the Final Resting Place of this Universe; Thou art the Knower, the 'to-be-known', the Supreme Abode; by Thee, O myriad-formed, is the Universe pervaded.

वायुर्यमोऽग्निर्वरुणः शशांकः
प्रजापतिस्त्वं प्रपितामहश्च ।
नमो नमस्तेऽस्तु सहस्रकृत्वः
पुनश्च भूयोऽपि नमो नमस्ते ॥३९॥

39. Thou art Vayu, Yama, Agni, Varuna, Shashanka, Prajapati, and Prapitamaha! All hail to Thee, a thousand times all hail! Again and yet again all hail to Thee!

[*Vayu* — Wind; *Yama* — the Ruler of the dead; *Agni* — fire; *Varuna* — Water-god; *Shashanka* — the moon; *Prajapati* — The first creator Brahma; *Prapitamaha* — the great grandfather, the Ancient. This is an echo of *Shve. Up.* 4. 2: "That surely is Fire, That is the Sun, and That verily is the Wind, and That is the Moon....That is Brahma. That is Prajapati!" *]

नमः पुरस्तादथपृष्ठतस्ते
नमोऽस्तु ते सर्वत अेव सर्व ।
अनन्तवीर्यामितविक्रमस्त्वं
सर्वं समाप्नोषि ततोऽसि सर्वः ॥४०॥

40. All hail to Thee from before and behind! All hail to Thee from every side, O All; Thy prowess is infinite, Thy might is measureless! Thou holdest all; therefore Thou art all.

[39-40. Stage by stage the vision grows upon Arjuna who now sees and exclaims the fundamental Truth that

---

* तदेवाग्निस्तदादित्यस्तद्वायुस्तदु चन्द्रमाः ।
तदैव शुक्रं तद् ब्रह्म तदापस्तत् प्रजापतिः ॥ श्वेताश्वतर. ४.२

Vasudeva or *Atman* is all. Cf. *Chh. Up.*: 7. 25: "*Atman* indeed is below; *Atman* is above; *Atman* is to the West; *Atman* is to the East; *Atman* is to the South; *Atman* is to the North; *Atman* indeed is this All." *

With *Shl.* 39 cf. Koran: "Unto Allah belong the East and West, and whithersoever ye turn, there is Allah's countenance. Lo! Allah is All-embracing, All-knowing."]

सखेति मत्वा प्रसभं यदुक्तम्
हे कृष्ण हे यादव हे सखेति ।
अजानता महिमानं तवेदं
मया प्रमादात् प्रणयेन वापि ।।४१।।

41. If ever in carelessness, thinking of Thee as comrade, I addressed Thee saying, 'O Krishna!', 'O Yadava!' not knowing Thy greatness, in negligence or in affection,

यच्चावहासार्थमसत्कृतोऽसि
विहारशय्यासनभोजनेषु ।
अेकोऽथवाऽप्यच्युत तत्समक्षम्
तत् क्षामये त्वामहमप्रमेयम् ।।४२।।

42. If ever I have been rude to Thee in jest, whilst at play, at rest-time, or at meals, whilst alone or in company, O Achyuta, forgive Thou my fault — I beg of Thee, O Incomprehensible!

पिताऽसि लोकस्य चराचरस्य
त्वमस्य पूज्यश्च गुरुर्गरीयान् ।
न त्वत्समोऽस्त्यभ्यधिकः कुतोऽन्यो
लोकत्रयेऽप्यप्रतिमप्रभावः ।।४३।।

43. Thou art Father of this world, of the moving and the un-moving; Thou art its adored, its worthiest,

---

* स अेवाधस्तात् स अुपरिष्टात् स पश्चात् स पुरस्तात् स दक्षिणतः स अुत्तरतः स अेवेदं सर्वम् । छान्दोग्य. ७.२५

Master ; there is none equal to Thee ; how then any greater than Thee ? Thy power is matchless in the three worlds.

तस्मात् प्रणम्य प्रणिधाय कायम्
प्रसादये त्वामहमीशमीड्यम् ।
पितेव पुत्रस्य सखेव सख्युः
प्रियः प्रियायार्हसि देव सोढुम् ॥४४॥

44. Therefore, I prostrate myself before Thee, and beseech Thy grace, O Lord Adorable ! As father with son, as comrade with comrade, so shouldst Thou bear, beloved Lord, with me, Thy loved one.

अदृष्टपूर्वं हृषितोऽस्मि दृष्ट्वा
भयेन च प्रव्यथितं मनो मे ।
तदेव मे दर्शय देव रूपम्
प्रसीद देवेश जगन्निवास ॥४५॥

45. I am filled with joy to see what never was seen before, and yet my heart is oppressed with fear. Show me that original form of Thine, O Lord ! Be gracious, Devesha, O Jagannivasa !

किरीटिनं गदिनं चक्रहस्तम्
इच्छामि त्वाम् द्रष्टुमहं तथैव ।
तेनैव रूपेण चतुर्भुजेन
सहस्रबाहो भव विश्वमूर्ते ॥४६॥

46. I crave to see Thee even as Thou wast, with crown, with mace, and disc in hand ; wear Thou, once more, that four-armed form, O thousand-armed Vishvamurti !

[*Vishvamurti* — Universe Incarnate, Universal Form.]

श्रीभगवानुवाच ।

मया प्रसन्नेन तवार्जुनेदं
रूपं परं दर्शितमात्मयोगात् ।
तेजोमयं विश्वमनन्तमाद्यम्
यन् मे त्वदन्येन न दृष्टपूर्वम् ।।४७।।

The Lord said:

47. It is to favour thee, O Arjuna, that I have revealed to thee, by My own unique power, this My Form Supreme, Resplendent, Universal, Infinite, Primal — which none save thee has ever seen.

न वेदयज्ञाध्ययनैर्न दानैर्
न च क्रियाभिर्न तपोभिरुग्रैः ।
अेवंरूपः शक्य अहं नृलोके
द्रष्टुं त्वदन्येन कुरुप्रवीर ।।४८।।

48. Not by the study of the Vedas, not by sacrifice, not by the study of other scriptures, not by gifts, nor yet by performance of rites or of fierce austerities can I, in such a form, be seen by any one save thee in the world of men, O Kurupravira!

["Not by the study of the Vedas, not by sacrifice, not by the study of other scriptures" — so Gandhiji; "not by the Vedas, not by sacrifice, not by study" — Tilak; "not by the Vedas, not by sacrifice, not by scripture-reading" — Hill; "not by the study of the Vedas or of the science of sacrifice" — all the commentators of Shankaracharya's school.]

मा ते व्यथा मा च विमूढभावो
दृष्ट्वा रूपं घोरमीदृङ् ममेदम् ।
व्यपेतभीः प्रीतमनाः पुनस्त्वम्
तदेव मे रूपमिदं प्रपश्य ।।४९।।

49. Be thou neither oppressed nor bewildered to look on this awful form of Mine. Banish thy fear, ease thy mind, and lo ! behold Me once again as I was.

संजय अुवाच ।

अित्यर्जुनं वासुदेवस्तथोक्त्वा

स्वकं रूपं दर्शयामास भूय: ।

आश्वासयामास च भीतमेनम्

भूत्वा पुन: सौम्यवपुर्महात्मा ॥५०॥

Sanjaya said :

50. So said Vasudeva to Arjuna, and revealed to him once more His original form. Wearing again His form benign, the Mahatma consoled him terrified.

अर्जुन अुवाच ।

दृष्ट्वेदं मानुषं रूपं तव सौम्यं जनार्दन ।

अिदानीमस्मि संवृत्त: सचेता: प्रकृतिं गत: ॥५१॥

Arjuna said :

51. Beholding again Thy benign human form I am come to myself and am once more in my normal state.

श्रीभगवानुवाच ।

सुदुर्दर्शमिदं रूपं दृष्टवानसि यन् मम ।

देवा अप्यस्य रूपस्य नित्यं दर्शनकांक्षिण: ॥५२॥

The Lord said :

52. Very hard to behold is that form of Mine which thou hast seen ; even the gods always yearn to see it.

नाहं वेदैर्न तपसा न दानेन न चेज्यया ।
शक्य अेवंविधो द्रष्टुं दृष्टवानसि मां यथा ॥५३॥

53. Not by the Vedas, not by penance, nor by gifts, nor yet by sacrifice, can any behold Me in the Form that thou hast seen.

भक्त्या त्वनन्यया शक्य अहमेवंविधोऽर्जुन ।
ज्ञातुं द्रष्टुं च तत्त्वेन प्रवेष्टुं च परंतप ॥५४॥

54. But by single-minded devotion, O Arjuna, I may in this Form be known and seen, and truly entered into, O Parantapa !

मत्कर्मकृन् मत्परमो मद्भक्तः संगवर्जितः ।
निर्वैरः सर्वभूतेषु यः स मामेति पाण्डव ॥५५॥

55. He alone comes to me, O Pandava, who does My work, who has made Me his goal, who is My devotee, who has renounced attachment, who has ill-will towards none.

[Cf. 1. Cor. 15. 58 : "Be ye steadfast, unmovable, always abounding in the work of the Lord."]

अिति श्रीमद्भगवद्गीतासु अुपनिषत्सु ब्रह्मविद्यायां योगशास्त्रे श्रीकृष्णार्जुनसंवादे
विश्वरूपदर्शनयोगो नाम अेकादशोऽध्यायः ॥११॥

Thus ends the eleventh discourse, entitled '*Vishvarupadarshana Yoga*' in the converse of Lord Krishna and Arjuna, on the science of *Yoga*, as part of the knowledge of *Brahman* in the Upanishad called the Bhagawadgita.

DISCOURSE XII

Thus we see that vision of God is possible only through single-minded devotion. Contents of devotion must follow as a matter of course. This twelfth discourse should be learnt by heart even if all the discourses are not. It is one of the shortest. The marks of a devotee should be carefully noted.

[Dis. XI-XII — "What can more forcefully turn us to God than this panoramic vision of His multitudinous manifestations, and having thus prepared us for *bhakti*, the Lord gives us the essence of *bhakti* in the 12th discourse which is so brief that any one can commit it to memory to call it to his aid in moments of trial." (Gandhiji, M. D.'s Weekly Letter, *Young India*, January 12, 1928)]

अर्जुन अुवाच ।
अेवं सततयुक्ता ये भक्तास्त्वां पर्युपासते ।
ये चाप्यक्षरमव्यक्तं तेषां के योगवित्तमाः ॥१॥

Arjuna said :

1. Of the devotees who thus worship Thee, incessantly attached, and those who worship the Imperishable Unmanifest, which are the better *yogins* ?

श्रीभगवानुवाच ।
मय्यावेश्य मनो ये मां नित्ययुक्ता अुपासते ।
श्रद्धया परयोपेतास् ते मे युक्ततमा मताः ॥२॥

The Lord said :

2. Those I regard as the best *yogins* who, riveting their minds on Me, ever attached, worship Me, with the highest faith.

ये त्वक्षरमनिर्देश्यम् अव्यक्तं पर्युपासते ।
सर्वत्रगमचिंत्यं च कूटस्थमचलं ध्रुवम् ॥३॥

3. But those who worship the Imperishable, the Indefinable, the Unmanifest, the Omnipresent, the Unthinkable, the Rock-seated, the Immovable, the Unchanging,

संनियम्येन्द्रियग्रामं सर्वत्र समबुद्धयः ।
ते प्राप्नुवन्ति मामेव सर्वभूतहिते रताः ॥४॥

4. Keeping the whole host of senses in complete control, looking on all with an impartial eye, engrossed in the welfare of all beings — these come indeed to Me.

[How complete this control of the senses has to be is indicated in the sixth discourse. Not that the worshipper of the Personal God will not be self-controlled — even he who pursues the easiest path of renunciation of all fruit has to do it with self-control (see *shl.* 11) — but he has the liberty to allow his senses full play in the worship of the Lord. It is control indeed, inasmuch as the senses would be withdrawn from the things of the flesh, but it is easier than the control of the whole host of senses contemplated in the sixth discourse.]

क्लेशोऽधिकतरस्तेषाम् अव्यक्तासक्तचेतसाम् ।
अव्यक्ता हि गतिर्दुःखं देहवद्भिरवाप्यते ॥५॥

5. Greater is the travail of those whose mind is fixed on the Unmanifest; for it is hard for embodied mortals to gain the Unmanifest — Goal.

Mortal man can only imagine the Unmanifest, the Impersonal, and as his language fails him he often negatively describes It as '*Neti*', '*Neti*' (Not That, Not That). And so even iconoclasts are at bottom no better than idol-worshippers. To worship a book, to go to a church, or to pray with one's face in a particular direction — all these are forms of worshipping the Formless in an image or idol. And yet both the idol-breaker and the idol-worshipper cannot lose sight of the fact that there is something which is beyond all form, Unthinkable, Formless, Impersonal, Changeless. The highest goal of the devotee is to become one with the object of his devotion. The *bhakta* extinguishes himself and merges into, becomes, *Bhagavan.* This state can best be reached by devoting oneself to some form, and so it is said that the short cut to the Unmanifest is really the longest and the most difficult.

ये तु सर्वाणि कर्माणि मयि संन्यस्य मत्पराः ।
अनन्येनैव योगेन मां ध्यायन्त उपासते ।।६।।

6. But those who casting all their actions on Me, making Me their all in all, worship Me with the meditation of undivided devotion,

तेषामहं समुद्धर्ता मृत्युसंसारसागरात् ।
भवामि न चिरात् पार्थ मय्यावेशितचेतसाम् ।।७।।

7. Of such, whose thoughts are centred on Me, O Partha, I become ere long the Deliverer from the ocean of this world of death.

[Strongly reminiscent of St. Paul's Epistle to the Romans: "O wretched man that I am! Who shall deliver me from the body of this death?" (7. 24). "For the law of the spirit of life in Jesus hath made me free from the law of sin and death." (8. 2)]

मय्येव मन आधत्स्व मयि बुद्धिं निवेशय ।
निवसिष्यसि मय्येव अत ऊर्ध्वं न संशयः ।।८।।

8. On Me set thy mind, on Me rest thy conviction; thus without doubt shalt thou remain only in Me hereafter.

अथ चित्तं समाधातुं न शक्नोषि मयि स्थिरम् ।
अभ्यासयोगेन ततो मामिच्छाप्तुं धनंजय ॥९॥

9. If thou canst not set thy mind steadily on Me, then by the method of constant practice seek to win Me, O Dhananjaya.

अभ्यासेऽप्यसमर्थोऽसि मत्कर्मपरमो भव ।
मदर्थमपि कर्माणि कुर्वन् सिद्धिमवाप्स्यसि ॥१०॥

10. If thou art also unequal to this method of constant practice, concentrate on service for Me ; even thus serving Me thou shalt attain perfection.

अथैतदप्यशक्तोऽसि कर्तुं मद्योगमाश्रितः ।
सर्वकर्मफलत्यागं ततः कुरु यतात्मवान् ॥११॥

11. If thou art unable even to do this, then dedicating all to Me, with mind controlled, abandon the fruit of action.

श्रेयो हि ज्ञानमभ्यासाज् ज्ञानाद् ध्यानं विशिष्यते ।
ध्यानात् कर्मफलत्यागस् त्यागाच्छान्तिरनन्तरम् ॥१२॥

12. Better is knowledge than practice, better than knowledge is concentration, better than concentration is renunciation of the fruit of all action, from which directly issues peace.

'Practice' (*abhyasa*) is the practice of the *yoga* of meditation and control of psychic processes ; 'knowledge' (*jnana*) is intellectual effort ; 'concentration' (*dhyana*) is devoted worship. If as a result of all this there is no renunciation of the fruit of action, 'practice' is no 'practice', 'knowledge' is no 'knowledge', and 'concentration' is no 'concentration'.

[This *shloka* has been a perfect puzzle to all translators and commentators. Some, like Hill, have made a heroic attempt to explain it, whilst others have not faced the difficulty at all. Space forbids a discussion of the various explanations. Most of them, including Gandhiji's, fail to satisfy me. There is one (offered by Vinoba) partially supported by Bhide Shastri, which to my mind seems the best of all yet offered. I have adopted it in my 'Interpretative Analysis' (pp. 85-86) and give it here in some detail.

'Renunciation of the fruit of all action' is, it must be remembered, suggested as the easiest method in *Shl.* 11. *Shl.* 12 explains how it is the easiest. Constant practice of the method is the first stage; the next higher stage, and the natural result of the first, is a knowledge of the secret of renunciation; the stage still higher and again the natural result of the lower is concentration, i.e. concentrated devotion to the method; which last results in perfected renunciation of the fruit of all action. This perfected renunciation means lasting peace.

Much of the difficulty is caused by the author's practice of using one and the same word in varying senses, and by the commentator's attempt to relate the 12th *shloka* to *shls.* 8-10. On the other hand, Gandhiji's explanation seems to sever it violently out of context. The natural context is the simple remedy offered in the 11th *shloka*.

The reader may consider this further explanation of this verse and the following verses given by Gandhiji in another connection:

"It seems that the path of hearing, meditating and comprehending, may be easier than the path of '*yama, niyama, pranayama* and *asana*' to which I have referred; easier than that may be concentration and worship and again easier than concentration may be renunciation of the fruits of works. The same method cannot be equally easy for every one; some may have to turn for help to all these methods. They are certainly intermixed. In any case thou wishest to be a devotee. Achieve that goal by whatever method thou canst. My part is simply to tell thee whom to count a true devotee." *From Yeravda Mandir.*]

अद्वेष्टा सर्वभूतानां मैत्रः करुण अेव च ।
निर्ममो निरहंकारः समदुःखसुखः क्षमी ।।१३।।
संतुष्टः सततं योगी यतात्मा दृढनिश्चयः ।
मय्यर्पितमनोबुद्धिर् यो मद्भक्तः स मे प्रियः ।।१४।।

13. Who has ill-will towards none, who is friendly and compassionate, who has shed all thought of 'mine' or 'I', who regards pain and pleasure alike, who is long-suffering;

14. Who is ever content, gifted with *yoga,* self-restrained, of firm conviction, who has dedicated his mind and reason to Me — that devotee (*bhakta*) of Mine is dear to Me.

यस्मान्नोद्विजते लोको लोकान्नोद्विजते च यः ।
हर्षामर्षभयोद्वेगैर् मुक्तो यः स च मे प्रियः ।।१५।।

15. Who gives no trouble to the world, to whom the world causes no trouble, who is free from exultation, resentment, fear and vexation, — that man is dear to Me.

अनपेक्षः शुचिर्दक्ष अुदासीनो गतव्यथः ।
सर्वारंभपरित्यागी यो मद्भक्तः स मे प्रियः ।।१६।।

16. Who expects naught, who is pure, resourceful, unconcerned, untroubled, who indulges in no undertakings, — that devotee of Mine is dear to Me.

यो न हृष्यति न द्वेष्टि न शोचति न कांक्षति ।
शुभाशुभपरित्यागी भक्तिमान् यः स मे प्रियः ।।१७।।

17. Who rejoices not, neither frets nor grieves, who covets not, who abandons both good and ill — that devotee of Mine is dear to Me.

समः शत्रौ च मित्रे च तथा मानापमानयोः ।
शीतोष्णसुखदुःखेषु समः संगविवर्जितः ॥१८॥
तुल्यनिन्दास्तुतिर्मौनी संतुष्टो येनकेनचित् ।
अनिकेतः स्थिरमतिर् भक्तिमान् मे प्रियो नरः ॥१९॥

18. Who is same to foe and friend, who regards alike respect and disrespect, cold and heat, pleasure and pain, who is free from attachment ;

19. Who weighs in equal scale blame and praise, who is silent, content with whatever his lot, who owns no home, who is of steady mind, — that devotee of Mine is dear to Me.

[13-19. This description of the essentials of an ideal *bhakta* would suggest many a parallel. I shall content myself to reproduce a fine passage from that true *bhakta* Fenelon who would call *bhakti* 'true simplicity': "True simplicity is free and direct and gives itself up, without reserve and with a generous self-forgetfulness to the Father of spirits....Experience alone can make us comprehend the enlargement of the heart it produces. We are then like a child in the arms of its parent ; we wish nothing more, we fear nothing, we yield ourselves up to this pure attachment....We place all our interests, pleasure, reputation in His hands, receive all the sufferings that He may inflict in this scene of humiliation as trials and tests of our love to Him. Some people who are sincere are not at ease with others and others are not at ease with them ; *but the truly simple man is at ease with others and others are at ease with him.*" The last line is so beautifully reminiscent of *shl.* 15.

19. I have already commented on the spirit of even-mindedness, the spirit of looking on all pairs and on friend and foe with an equal eye, the "being perfect, even as thy Father in Heaven is perfect." Silence is here added as one more attribute ; we find it again in XVII. 16 as one of the

elements of mental or spiritual austerity. It is not so much the refraining from speech as what that Russian mystical writer Arseniew calls, "the inward silence of the spirit, that aloofness from the clamour of the passions, that silent rapt concentration upon God, accompanied, however, by ceaseless inward spiritual prayer which is conveyed to the mystics of the Eastern Church by the words : 'I sleep but my heart keeps vigil.'"]

ये तु धर्म्यामृतमिदं यथोक्तं पर्युपासते ।
श्रद्दधाना मत्परमा भक्तास्तेऽतीव मे प्रियाः ॥२०॥

20. They who follow this essence of *dharma,* as I have told it, with faith, keeping Me as their goal, — those devotees are exceeding dear to Me.

[I have translated *dharmyamrita,* 'essence of *dharma*'. It may be translated, '*dharma* leading to immortality', or 'nectar in the form of this sacred doctrine' as Gandhiji has it in his translation. I think it is best to translate it as I have done so as to relate it with IX. 2, where it is referred to as *dharmyam* and where the exposition of the subject begins ending here.

'Why are these exceeding dear to the Lord?' is a question asked and answered by an acute commentator. *Shls.* 12-19 describe the characteristics of an ideal *bhakta* — whether a worshipper of the Personal or Impersonal —, but such an ideal *bhakta,* suggests this commentator, is rare. *Shl.* 20 has reference to the aspirants striving to approach the ideal; they, he suggests, are exceeding dear to the Lord, because they deserve His special grace, the other having already won the goal — like the grandson who is held dearer than the son!]

अिति श्रीमद्भगवद्गीतासु अुपनिषत्सु ब्रह्मविद्यायां योगशास्त्रे श्रीकृष्णार्जुनसंवादे
भक्तियोगो नाम द्वादशोऽध्यायः ॥१२॥

Thus ends the twelfth discourse entitled '*Bhakti Yoga*' in the converse of Lord Krishna and Arjuna, on the science of *Yoga*, as part of the knowledge of *Brahman* in the Upanishad called the Bhagawadgita.

DISCOURSE XIII

This discourse treats of the distinction between the body (not-Self) and Atman (the Self).

श्रीभगवानुवाच ।

अिदं शरीरं कौन्तेय क्षेत्रमित्यभिधीयते ।
अेतद् यो वेत्ति तं प्राहुः क्षेत्रज्ञ अिति तद्विदः ॥१॥

The Lord said:

1. This body, O Kaunteya, is called the Field; he who knows it is called the knower of the Field by those who know.

क्षेत्रज्ञं चापि मां विद्धि सर्वक्षेत्रेषु भारत ।
क्षेत्रक्षेत्रज्ञयोर्ज्ञानं यत् तज् ज्ञानं मतं मम ॥२॥

2. And understand Me to be, O Bharata, the knower of the Field in all the Fields; and the knowledge of the Field and the knower of the Field, I hold, is true knowledge.

तत् क्षेत्रं यच्च यादृक् च यद्विकारि यतश्च यत् ।
स च यो यत्प्रभावश्च तत् समासेन मे शृणु ॥३॥

3. What that Field is, what its nature, what its modifications, and whence is what, as also who He is, and what His power — hear this briefly from Me.

ऋषिभिर्बहुधा गीतं छन्दोभिर्विविधैः पृथक् ।
ब्रह्मसूत्रपदैश्चैव हेतुमद्भिर्विनिश्चितैः ॥४॥

4. This subject has been sung by seers distinctly and

in various ways, in different hymns as also in aphoristic texts about *Brahman* well reasoned and unequivocal.

महाभूतान्यहंकारो बुद्धिरव्यक्तमेव च ।
अिंद्रियाणि दशैकं च पंच चेंद्रियगोचराः ॥५॥

5. The great elements, Individuation, Reason, the Unmanifest, the ten senses, and the one (mind), and the five spheres of the senses ;

[For a full treatment of the subject see 'My Submission' p. 88. *Shl.* 5 details all the 24 principles of *prakriti* and *shl.* 6 details the modifications of the *mind* which is part of the body and not of the Self.]

अिच्छा द्वेषः सुखं दुःखं संघातश्चेतना धृतिः ।
अेतत् क्षेत्रं समासेन सविकारमुदाहृतम् ॥६॥

6. Desire, dislike, pleasure, pain, association, consciousness, cohesion — this, in sum, is what is called the Field with its modifications.

The great elements are Earth, Water, Fire, Air and Ether. 'Individuation' is the thought of I, or that the body is 'I'; the 'Unmanifest' is *prakriti* or *maya* ; the ten senses are the five senses of perception — smell, taste, sight, touch and hearing, and the five organs of action, viz : the hands, the feet, the tongue, and the two organs of excretion. The five spheres or objects of the senses are smell, savour, form, touch and sound. 'Association' is the property of the different organs to co-operate. *Dhriti* is not patience or constancy but cohesion, i. e. the property of all the atoms in the body to hold together ; from 'individuation' springs this cohesion. Individuation is inherent in the unmanifest *prakriti.* The undeluded man is he who can cast off this individuation or ego, and having done so the shock of an inevitable thing like death and the pairs of opposites caused by sense-contacts fail to affect him. The Field, subject to all its modifications, has to be abandoned in the end by the enlightened and the unenlightened alike.

अमानित्वमदंभित्वम् अहिंसा क्षांतिरार्जवम् ।
आचार्योपासनम् शौचं स्थैर्यमात्मविनिग्रहः ॥७॥

7. Freedom from pride and pretentiousness, non-violence, forgiveness, uprightness, service of the Master, purity, steadfastness, self-restraint;

[It is noteworthy that 'freedom from pride' is the first virtue of knowledge; for pride is a sin of the temper which it is difficult to conquer even after all the sins of the flesh have been overcome. It is so subtle that one may not perceive it until the last, and it may even masquerade as humility. "Nothing is more scandalous" said Marcus Aurelius, "than a man who is proud of his humility."]

अिन्द्रियार्थेषु वैराग्यम् अनहंकार अेव च ।
जन्ममृत्युजराव्याधिदुःखदोषानुदर्शनम् ॥८॥

8. Aversion from sense-objects, absence of conceit, realization of the painfulness and evil of birth, death, age and disease;

असक्तिरनभिष्वंगः पुत्रदारगृहादिषु ।
नित्यं च समचित्तत्वं अिष्टानिष्टोपपत्तिषु ॥९॥

9. Absence of attachment, refusal to be wrapped up in one's children, wife, home and family, even-mindedness whether good or ill befall;

['Refusal to be wrapped up in one's children, wife, home and family.' Compare this with the picturesque verse in the Bible, Luke 14. 26: "If any man come to me and hate not his father, mother, wife and children...he cannot be my disciple"; or the words in the Koran: "Lo! Among your wives and children there are enemies for you, therefore beware of them;" (64. 14) "They are only a temptation." But whatever the difference in expression the emphasis is on one and the same thing, viz. "exclusive devotion of the Lord". There can be no sharer in that devotion. As the Koran puts it: "Let not your wealth, nor your children distract you from remembrance of Allah." (63. 9)]

मयि चानन्ययोगेन भक्तिरव्यभिचारिणी ।
विविक्तदेशसेवित्वम् अरतिर्जनसंसदि ॥१०॥

10. Unwavering and all-exclusive devotion to Me, resort to secluded spots, distaste for the haunts of men;

[The reason for insistence on seclusion in this *shloka* and on silence (XII. 19) in the characteristics of a true *bhakta* is beautifully expressed in *Imitation of Christ*: "No man can safely appear in public, but he who loves seclusion. No man can safely speak, but he who loves silence."]

अध्यात्मज्ञाननित्यत्वं तत्त्वज्ञानार्थदर्शनम् ।
अेतज् ज्ञानमिति प्रोक्तम् अज्ञानं यदतोऽन्यथा ॥११॥

11. Settled conviction of the nature of the *Atman*, perception of the goal of the knowledge of Truth,—

All this is declared to be Knowledge and the reverse of it is ignorance.

[7-11. It is noteworthy how the End—Knowledge—is shown to include the means, for without the means there is no end. The following verses in the Bible provide a remarkable parallel, if in somewhat different language:

"And beside this, giving all diligence, add to your faith, virtue; add to virtue, knowledge;

"And to knowledge, temperance; add to temperance patience; and to patience godliness;

"And to godliness brotherly kindness; and to brotherly kindness charity.

"For *if these things be in you* and abound, they make you that *ye shall neither be barren nor unfruitful in the knowledge* of Lord Jesus Christ.

"But *he that lacketh these things is blind,* and cannot see far off, and has forgotten that he was purged of his old sin." (II Peter I. 5-9)]

ज्ञेयं यत् तत् प्रवक्ष्यामि यज्ज्ञात्वाऽमृतमश्नुते ।
अनादिमत् परं ब्रह्म न सत् तन्नासदुच्यते ।।१२।।

12. I will (now) expound to thee that which is to be known and knowing which one enjoys immortality; it is the supreme *Brahman* which has no beginning, which is called neither Being nor non-Being.

The Supreme can be described neither as Being nor as non-Being. It is beyond definition or description, above all attributes.

[Here we find the Gita adopting the very language of the Vedic hymn referred to in the note on IX. 19. The description in IX. 19, having reference only to the Personal aspect of God, was positive. Here the absolute *Brahman* is being described also as the Impersonal, and so the author uses the familiar method of exhausting all possible attributes as inadequate. The moment we proceed to apply to *Brahman* the language of our limited experience we limit It. It is futile to imprison the Infinite in finite categories. This *shloka* is really the key to the apparent contradictions in the *shlokas* that follow.]

सर्वतः पाणिपादं तत् सर्वतोऽक्षिशिरोमुखम् ।
सर्वतः श्रुतिमल्लोके सर्वमावृत्य तिष्ठति ।।१३।।

13. Everywhere having hands and feet, everywhere having eyes, heads, mouths, everywhere having ears, It abides embracing everything in the universe.

सर्वेन्द्रियगुणाभासं सर्वेन्द्रियविवर्जितम् ।
असक्तं सर्वभृच्चैव निर्गुणं गुणभोक्तृ च ॥१४॥

14. Seeming to possess the functions of the senses, It is devoid of all the senses ; It touches naught, upholds all ; having no *gunas*, It experiences the *gunas*.

बहिरन्तश्च भूतानाम् अचरं चरमेव च ।
सूक्ष्मत्वात् तदविज्ञेयं दूरस्थं चांतिके च तत् ॥१५॥

15. Without all beings, yet within ; immovable yet moving ; so subtle that It cannot be perceived ; so far and yet so near It is.

He who knows It is within It, close to It ; mobility and immobility, peace and restlessness, we owe to It, for It has motion and yet is motionless.

अविभक्तं च भूतेषु विभक्तमिव च स्थितम् ।
भूतभर्तृ च तज्ज्ञेयं ग्रसिष्णु प्रभविष्णु च ॥१६॥

16. Undivided, It seems to subsist divided in all beings ; this *Brahman* — That which is to be known is the Sustainer of all, yet It is their Devourer and Creator.

ज्योतिषामपि तज्जोतिस् तमसः परमुच्यते ।
ज्ञानं ज्ञेयं ज्ञानगम्यं हृदि सर्वस्य धिष्ठितम् ॥१७॥

17. Light of all lights, It is said to be beyond darkness ; It is knowledge, the object of knowledge, to be gained only by knowledge ; It is seated in the hearts of all.

[13-17. These *shlokas* bring together compactly the descriptions of the Absolute in various Upanishads and sum up Its Personal and Impersonal aspects both. The whole of *shl.* 16 and the first half of *shl.* 14 have been borrowed from *Shve. Up.* 3. 16.* Part of *Shl.* 15 repeats the language of *Isha. Up.* 5 § and *Mund. Up.* 3. 1. 7 † and parts of *Shls.* 16 and 17 repeat the language of *Br. Up.* 4. 4. 16 ‡ and *Shve.* 3. 8 ¶ and *Tait.* 2. 4. $ *Shl.* 16 with its *iva — it seems* 'to be divided into different entities though one' sums up the seemingly contradictory aspects. The *Brahman* has no functions, but It functions as it were through the functions of the senses. As *Br. Up.* says : "It meditates as It were, It moves as It were." ×

Compare the language of the mystics of all ages quoted by Miss Underhill : "That nameless something which is great enough to be God, small enough to be me" (Suso); "If thou conceivest a small minute circle, as small as a grain of mustard seed, yet the Heart of God is wholly and perfectly therein ; and thou art born in God, then there is in thyself the whole Heart of God undivided" (Boehme) ; "God

* सर्वतः पाणिपादं तत्सर्वतोऽक्षिशिरोमुखम् ।
सर्वतः श्रुतिमल्लोके सर्वमावृत्य तिष्ठति ।। श्वेताश्वतर ३.१६

§ तदेजति तन्नैजति तद्दूरे तद्वन्तिके ।
तदन्तरस्य सर्वस्य तदु सर्वस्यास्य बाह्यतः ।। अीश ५

† बृहच्च तद्दिव्यमचिन्त्यरूपं
सूक्ष्माच्च तत्सूक्ष्मतरं विभाति ।
दूरात्सुदूरे तदिहान्तिके च
पश्यत्स्विहैव निहितं गुहायाम् ।। मुण्डक ३.१.७

‡ यस्मादर्वाक्संवत्सरोऽहोभिः परिवर्तते ।
तद्देवा ज्योतिषां ज्योतिरायुर्होपासतेऽमृतम् ।। बृहदारण्यक ४.४.१६

¶ वेदाहमेतं पुरुषं महान्तम्
आदित्यवर्णं तमसः परस्तात् ।
तमेव विदित्वातिमृत्युमेति
नान्यः पन्था विद्यतेऽयनाय ।। श्वेताश्वतर ३.८

$ यतो वाचो निवर्तन्ते ।
. . . .
महः पुच्छं प्रतिष्ठा ।। तैत्तिरीय २.४

× ध्यायतीव लेलायतीव । बृहदारण्यक ४.३.७

is nearer to me than I am to myself; He is just as near to wood and stone, but they don't know it" (Eckhart). Or in the language of the modern English hymn

> Closer is He than breathing;
> Nearer than hands and feet.]

अिति क्षेत्रं तथा ज्ञानं ज्ञेयं चोक्तं समासतः ।
मद्भक्त अेतद् विज्ञाय मद्भावायोपपद्यते ॥१८॥

18. Thus have I expounded in brief the Field, Knowledge and That which is to be known; My devotee, when he knows this, is worthy to become one with Me.

प्रकृतिं पुरुषं चैव विद्धयनादी अुभावपि ।
विकारांश्च गुणांश्चैव विद्धि प्रकृतिसंभवान् ॥१९॥

19. Know that *Prakriti* and *Purusha* are both without beginning; know that all the modifications and *gunas* are born of *Prakriti*.

[For *Prakriti* and *Purusha,* see 'My Submission', pp. 22-29. We have seen in the 7th discourse that these are the two aspects of the Lord, the lower and the higher, and as the Lord is beginningless, so are His aspects.]

कार्यकारणकर्तृत्वे हेतुः प्रकृतिरुच्यते ।
पुरुषः सुखदुःखानां भोक्तृत्वे हेतुरुच्यते ॥२०॥

20. *Prakriti* is described as the cause in the creation of effects from causes; *Purusha* is described as the cause of the experiencing of pleasure and pain.

[In the tree of *Prakriti* (p. 23), the ten organs of perception and action, mind, and the five gross elements are the effects and not the causes of others; reason, individuation and the five subtle elements which are both causes and effects are spoken of as effects. *Prakriti* generates them all.

पुरुषः प्रकृतिस्थो हि भुंक्ते प्रकृतिजान् गुणान् ।
कारणं गुणसंगोऽस्य सदसद्योनिजन्मसु ।।२१।।

21. For the *Purusha,* residing in *Prakriti,* experiences the *gunas* born of *Prakriti* ; attachment to these *gunas* is the cause of his birth in good or evil wombs.

Prakriti in common parlance is *Maya. Purusha* is the *Jiva. Jiva* acting in accordance with his nature experiences the fruit of actions arising out of the three *gunas.*

उपद्रष्टाऽनुमन्ता च भर्ता भोक्ता महेश्वरः ।
परमात्मेति चाप्युक्तो देहेऽस्मिन् पुरुषः परः ।।२२।।

22. What is called in this body the Witness, the Assentor, the Sustainer, the Experiencer, the Great Lord and also the Supreme *Atman,* is the Supreme Being.

[The *Jiva* or the individual Self who receives all sorts of names because of his being limited in this body is no other than He — the Supreme Being.]

य अेवं वेत्ति पुरुषं प्रकृतिं च गुणैः सह ।
सर्वथा वर्तमानोऽपि न स भूयोऽभिजायते ।।२३।।

23. He who thus knows *Purusha* and *Prakriti* with its *gunas,* is not born again, no matter how he live and move.

Read in the light of discourses II, IX and XII this *shloka* may not be taken to support any kind of libertinism. It shows the virtue of self-surrender and selfless devotion. All actions bind the self, but if all are dedicated to the Lord they do not bind, rather they release him. He who has thus extinguished the 'self' or the thought of 'I' and who acts as ever in the great Witness' eye, will never sin nor err. The self-sense is at the root of all error or sin.

Where the 'I' has been extinguished, there is no sin. This *shloka* shows how to steer clear of all sin.

[23. The subject of Gandhiji's note has been dealt with in detail in 'My Submission'.]

ध्यानेनात्मनि पश्यन्ति केचिदात्मानमात्मना ।
अन्ये सांख्येन योगेन कर्मयोगेन चापरे ।।२४।।

24. Some through meditation behold the *Atman* by themselves in their own self; others by *Sankhya Yoga*, and others by *Karma Yoga*.

अन्ये त्वेवमजानन्तः श्रुत्वाऽन्येभ्य उपासते ।
तेऽपि चातितरन्त्येव मृत्युं श्रुतिपरायणाः ।।२५।।

25. Yet others, not knowing (Him) thus, worship (Him) having heard from others; they too pass beyond death, because of devoted adherence to what they have heard.

यावत् संजायते किंचित् सत्त्वं स्थावरजंगमम् ।
क्षेत्रक्षेत्रज्ञसंयोगात् तद् विद्धि भरतर्षभ ।।२६।।

26. Wherever something is born, animate or inanimate, know, thou Bharatarshabha, that it issues from the union of the Field and the Knower of the Field.

[This union, says Shankaracharya, is illusory like the union of a rope and a mother-of-pearl respectively with a snake and silver when they are mistaken one for the other owing to the absence of discriminative knowledge. But is it? To him who knows, perhaps, it is no more than this illusory union, but to those who don't know? "Man," says Pascal, "is to himself the most wonderful object in nature; for he cannot conceive what the body is, still less what the mind is, and least of all how a body should be united to a mind. This is the consummation of his difficulties, and yet it is his very being."]

समं सर्वेषु भूतेषु तिष्ठन्तं परमेश्वरम् ।
विनश्यत्स्वविनश्यंतं यः पश्यति स पश्यति ॥२७॥

27. Who sees abiding in all beings the same *Parameshvara*, imperishable in the perishable, he sees indeed.

समं पश्यन् हि सर्वत्र समवस्थितमीश्वरम् ।
न हिनस्त्यात्मनाऽऽत्मानम् ततो याति परां गतिम् ॥२८॥

28. When he sees the same *Ishvara* abiding everywhere alike, he does not hurt himself by himself and hence he attains the highest goal.

He who sees the same God everywhere merges in Him and sees naught else ; he thus does not yield to passion, does not become his own foe and thus attains Freedom.

प्रकृत्यैव च कर्माणि क्रियमाणानि सर्वशः ।
यः पश्यति तथाऽऽत्मानम् अकर्तारं स पश्यति ॥२९॥

29. Who sees that it is *Prakriti* that performs all actions and thus (knows) that *Atman* performs them not, he sees indeed.

Just as, in the case of a man who is asleep, his "Self" is not the agent of sleep, but *Prakriti*, even so the enlightened man will detach his "Self" from all activities. To the pure everything is pure. *Prakriti* is not unchaste, it is when arrogant man takes her as wife that of these twain passion is born.

यदा भूतपृथग्भावम् अेकस्थमनुपश्यति ।
तत अेव च विस्तारं ब्रह्म संपद्यते तदा ॥३०॥

30. When he sees the diversity of beings as founded in unity and the whole expanse issuing therefrom, then he attains to *Brahman*.

To realize that everything rests in *Brahman* is to attain to the state of *Brahman*. Then *Jiva* becomes *Shiva*.

[The root of this thought lies in the famous *Br. Up.* text: "There is on earth no diversity. He goes from death to death who perceives here nothing but diversity. As a unity only is It to be perceived—this Indemonstrable, Enduring Being." (4. 4. 19-20)* It is this thought that captured the imagination of Schopenhauer who declared that the Hindu seer who can experience his own identity "with regard to everything with which he comes in contact...is certain of all virtue and blessedness and is on the direct road to salvation."]

अनादित्वान्निर्गुणत्वात् परमात्माऽयमव्ययः ।
शरीरस्थोऽपि कौन्तेय न करोति न लिप्यते ॥३१॥

31. This Imperishable Supreme *Atman*, O Kaunteya, though residing in the body, acts not and is not stained, for He has no beginning and no *gunas*.

यथा सर्वगतं सौक्ष्म्याद् आकाशं नोपलिप्यते ।
सर्वत्रावस्थितो देहे तथाऽऽत्मा नोपलिप्यते ॥३२॥

32. As the all-pervading ether, by reason of its subtlety, is not soiled even so *Atman* pervading every part of the body is not soiled.

यथा प्रकाशयत्येकः कृत्स्नं लोकमिमं रविः ।
क्षेत्रं क्षेत्री तथा कृत्स्नं प्रकाशयति भारत ॥३३॥

---

* मनसैवानुद्रष्टव्यं नेह नानास्ति किंचन ।
मृत्योः स मृत्युमाप्नोति य अिह नानेव पश्यति ॥
अेकधैवानुद्रष्टव्यमेतदप्रमेयं ध्रुवम् ।
. . . . . ॥ बृहदारण्यक ४ ४.१९-२०

33. As the one Sun illumines the whole universe, even so the Master of the Field illumines the whole field, O Bharata !

क्षेत्रक्षेत्रज्ञयोरेवम् अन्तरं ज्ञानचक्षुषा ।
भूतप्रकृतिमोक्षं च ये विदुर्यान्ति ते परम् ।।३४।।

34. Those who, with the eyes of knowledge, thus perceive the distinction between the Field and the Knower of the Field, and (the secret) of the release of beings from *Prakriti*, they attain to the Supreme.

अिति श्रीमद्भगवद्गीतासु अुपनिषत्सु ब्रह्मविद्यायां योगशास्त्रे श्रीकृष्णार्जुनसंवादे
क्षेत्रक्षेत्रज्ञविभागयोगो नाम त्रयोदशोऽध्यायः ।।१३।।

Thus ends the thirteenth discourse, entitled '*Kshetra-kshetrajna-vibhaga Yoga*' in the converse of Lord Krishna and Arjuna, on the science of *Yoga* as part of the knowledge of *Brahman* in the Upanishad called the Bhagawadgita.

DISCOURSE XIV

The description of Prakriti naturally leads on to that of its constituents, the Gunas, which form the subject of this discourse. And that, in turn, leads on to a description of the marks of him who has passed beyond the three Gunas. These are practically the same as those of the man of secure understanding (II. 54-72) as also those of the ideal Bhakta (XII. 12-20).

[The reader may read with profit the following interpretative summary of the fourteenth discourse given by Gandhiji in another connection :

"Discourse 14 and the threefold division of the qualities of nature remind me of Henry Drummond's book I read about 30 years ago — *The Natural Law in the Spiritual World*. The laws are numerous, but they have been broadly classified under three heads. The 14th discourse describes the laws to which man is subject and the 15th describes *Purushottama* — the Perfect Man. The 'ascent of man' is what we have to learn from these chapters. There is no man who is governed exclusively by one of the three *gunas* — *sattva, rajas* or *tamas*. We have each of us to rise to a state in which we are governed predominantly by the *sattva* principle, until at last we rise beyond the three and are 'Perfect Man'. I can think of an illustration from the physical world. Take water, which in its solid state remains on the earth ; it cannot ascend until it is rarefied into steam. But once it is rarefied into steam it rises up in the sky where at last it is transformed into clouds which drop down in the form of rain and fructify and bless the earth. We are all like water, we have to strive so to rarefy ourselves that all the ego in us perishes and we merge in the infinite to the eternal good of all." (M. D.'s Weekly Letter, *Young India*, January 12, 1928)]

श्रीभगवानुवाच ।

परं भूयः प्रवक्ष्यामि ज्ञानानां ज्ञानमुत्तमम् ।
यज्ज्ञात्वा मुनयः सर्वे परां सिद्धिमितो गताः ॥१॥

The Lord said :

1. Yet again will I expound the highest and the best of all knowledge, knowing which all the sages passed hence to the highest perfection.

अिदं ज्ञानमुपाश्रित्य मम साधर्म्यमागताः ।
सर्गेऽपि नोपजायन्ते प्रलये न व्यथन्ति च ॥२॥

2. By having recourse to this knowledge they became one with Me. They need not come to birth even at a creation, nor do they suffer at a dissolution.

मम योनिर्महद् ब्रह्म तस्मिन् गर्भं दधाम्यहम् ।
संभवः सर्वभूतानां ततो भवति भारत ॥३॥

3. The great *prakriti* is for me the womb in which I deposit the germ ; from it all beings come to birth, O Bharata.

सर्वयोनिषु कौन्तेय मूर्तयः संभवन्ति याः ।
तासां ब्रह्म महद्योनिर् अहं बीजप्रदः पिता ॥४॥

4. Whatever forms take birth in the various species, the great *prakriti* is their Mother and I the seed-giving Father.

[Mother, lit. 'Womb']

सत्त्वं रजस्तम अिति गुणाः प्रकृतिसंभवाः ।
निबध्नन्ति महाबाहो देहे देहिनमव्ययम् ॥५॥

5. *Sattva, rajas* and *tamas* are the *gunas* sprung from *prakriti* ; it is they, O Mahabahu, that keep the imperishable Dweller bound to the body.

तत्र सत्त्वं निर्मलत्वात् प्रकाशकमनामयम् ।
सुखसंगेन बध्नाति ज्ञानसंगेन चानघ ॥६॥

6. Of these *sattva,* being stainless, is light-giving and healing; it binds with the bond of happiness and the bond of knowledge, O sinless one.

रजो रागात्मकं विद्धि तृष्णासंगसमुद्भवम् ।
तन् निबध्नाति कौन्तेय कर्मसंगेन देहिनम् ॥७॥

7. *Rajas,* know thou, is of the nature of passion, the source of thirst and attachment; it keeps man bound with the bond of action.

तमस्त्वज्ञानजं विद्धि मोहनं सर्वदेहिनाम् ।
प्रमादालस्यनिद्राभिस् तन् निबध्नाति भारत ॥८॥

8. *Tamas,* know thou, born of ignorance, is mortal man's delusion; it keeps him bound with heedlessness, sloth and slumber, O Bharata.

सत्त्वं सुखे संजयति रजः कर्मणि भारत ।
ज्ञानमावृत्य तु तमः प्रमादे संजयत्युत ॥९॥

9. *Sattva* attaches man to happiness, *rajas* to action, and *tamas,* shrouding knowledge, attaches him to heedlessness.

रजस्तमश्चाभिभूय सत्त्वं वति भारत ।
रजः सत्त्वं तमश्चैव तमः सत्त्वं रजस्तथा ॥१०॥

10. *Sattva* prevails, O Bharata, having overcome *rajas* and *tamas*; *rajas,* when it has overpowered *sattva* and *tamas*; likewise *tamas* reigns when *sattva* and *rajas* are crushed.

सर्वद्वारेषु देहेऽस्मिन् प्रकाश अुपजायते ।
ज्ञानं यदा तदा विद्याद् विवृद्धं सत्त्वमित्युत ॥११॥

11. When the light — knowledge — shines forth from all the gates of this body, then it may be known that the *sattva* thrives.

लोभः प्रवृत्तिरारंभः कर्मणामशमः स्पृहा ।
रजस्येतानि जायन्ते विवृद्धे भरतर्षभ ॥१२॥

12. Greed, activity, assumption of undertakings, restlessness, craving — these are in evidence when *rajas* flourishes, O Bharatarshabha.

अप्रकाशोऽप्रवृत्तिश्च प्रमादो मोह अेव च ।
तमस्येतानि जायन्ते विवृद्धे कुरुनंदन ॥१३॥

13. Ignorance, dullness, heedlessness, and delusion — these are in evidence when *tamas* reigns, O Kurunandana.

यदा सत्त्वे प्रवृद्धे तु प्रलयं याति देहभृत् ।
तदोत्तमविदां लोकान् अमलान् प्रतिपद्यते ॥१४॥

14. If the embodied one meets his end whilst *sattva* prevails, then he attains to the spotless worlds of the knowers of the Highest.

[14. 'Spotless worlds of the knowers of the Highest'. It is difficult to say what exactly this means. The knowers of the Highest cannot be men of self-realization or *jnanis* for there is no birth for them, whereas here rebirth is indicated. Shankaracharya says, 'Highest means *mahat* and the other principles' — an explanation which demands a further explanation! Tilak says: 'the worlds of the gods'. Bhide Shastri: '*Satyaloka, Vaikuntha, Kailasa,* etc.' Vinoba strikes an entirely new departure, whether warranted by the text it is difficult to say: 'He is born in spotless worlds in the company of *jnanis.*' The explanation may perhaps be sought in the word *karmasangishu* (कर्मसंगिषु) in the next *shloka.* If *rajasa* people are born among *men attached to karma,* then *sattvika* people are born among men attached to *jnana,* i.e. men pursuing the path of *jnana.* It is, I feel, some such reasoning which has led Vinoba to interpret the *shloka* as he has done, and I accept it for want of a better.]

रजसि प्रलयं गत्वा कर्मसंगिषु जायते ।
तथा प्रलीनस्तमसि मूढयोनिषु जायते ॥१५॥

15. If he dies during the reign within him of *rajas,* he is born among men attached to action ; and if he dies in *tamas,* he is born in species not endowed with reason.

कर्मणः सुकृतस्याहुः सात्त्विकं निर्मलं फलम् ।
रजसस्तु फलं दुःखम् अज्ञानं तमसः फलम् ॥१६॥

16. The fruit of *sattvika* action is said to be stainless merit ; that of *rajas* is pain and that of *tamas* ignorance.

[The usual text is : '*Karmanah sukritasyahus sattvikam nirmalam phalam.*' कर्मणः सुकृतस्याहुः सात्त्विकं निर्मलं फलम् । It is obviously a kind of spoonerism. It should read : '*Karmanah sattvikasyahus sukritam nirmalam phalam.*' कर्मणः सात्त्विकस्याहुः सुकृतं निर्मलं फलम् ।]

सत्त्वात् संजायते ज्ञानं रजसो लोभ अेव च ।
प्रमादमोहौ तमसो भवतोऽज्ञानमेव च ॥१७॥

17. Of *sattva* knowledge is born, of *rajas,* greed ; of *tamas* heedlessness, delusion and ignorance.

ऊर्ध्वं गच्छन्ति सत्त्वस्था मध्ये तिष्ठन्ति राजसाः ।
जघन्यगुणवृत्तिस्था अधो गच्छन्ति तामसाः ॥१८॥

18. Those abiding in *sattva* rise upwards, those in *rajas* stay midway, those in *tamas* sink downwards.

नान्यं गुणेभ्यः कर्तारं यदा द्रष्टाऽनुपश्यति ।
गुणेभ्यश्च परं वेत्ति मद्भावं सोऽधिगच्छति ॥१९॥

19. When the seer perceives no agent other than the *gunas,* and knows Him who is above the *gunas,* he attains to My being.

As soon as a man realizes that he is not the doer, but the *gunas* are the agent, the 'self' vanishes, and he goes through all his actions spontaneously, just to sustain the body. And as the body is meant to subserve the highest end, all his actions will even reveal detachment and dispassion. Such a seer can easily have a glimpse of the One who is *above* the *gunas* and offer his devotion to Him.

गुणानेतानतीत्य त्रीन् देही देहसमुद्भवान् ।
जन्ममृत्युजरादुःखैर् विमुक्तोऽमृतमश्नुते ॥२०॥

20. When the embodied one transcends these three *gunas* which are born of his contact with the body, he is released from the pain of birth, death and age and attains deathlessness.

['Which are born of his contact with the body' is Gandhiji's translation of *dehasamudbhavan* (देहसमुद्भवान्). Hill explains the compound in a similar way: "Which exist in relation to the self because it is embodied." Many commentators follow Shankaracharya who explains: 'Which are the seed out of which the body is evolved.' I would like to interpret the compound thus: "which are the source of man's identifying his self with the body."]

अर्जुन अुवाच ।

कैर्लिङ्गैस्त्रीन् गुणानेतान् अतीतो भवति प्रभो ।
किमाचारः कथं चैतान् त्रीन् गुणानतिवर्तते ॥२१॥

Arjuna said:

21. What, O Lord, are the marks of him who has transcended the three *gunas*? How does he conduct himself? How does he transcend the three *gunas*?

श्रीभगवानुवाच ।

प्रकाशं च प्रवृत्तिं च मोहमेव च पांडव ।
न द्वेष्टि संप्रवृत्तानि न निवृत्तानि कांक्षति ॥२२॥

The Lord said:

22. He, O Pandava, who does not disdain light, activity, and delusion when they come into being, nor desires them when they vanish;

अुदासीनवदासीनो गुणैर्यो न विचाल्यते ।
गुणा वर्तन्त अित्येव योऽवतिष्ठति नेङ्गते ॥२३॥

23. He, who seated as one indifferent, is not shaken by the *gunas,* and stays still and moves not, knowing it is *gunas* playing their parts;

समदुःखसुखः स्वस्थः समलोष्टाश्मकांचनः ।
तुल्यप्रियाप्रियो धीरस् तुल्यनिंदाऽऽत्मसंस्तुतिः ॥२४॥

24. He who holds pleasure and pain alike, who is sedate, who regards as same earth, stone and gold, who is wise and weighs in equal scale things pleasant and unpleasant, who is even-minded in praise and blame;

मानापमानयोस्तुल्यस् तुल्यो मित्रारिपक्षयोः ।
सर्वारंभपरित्यागी गुणातीतः स उच्यते ॥२५॥

25. Who holds alike respect and disrespect, who is the same to friend and foe, who indulges in no undertakings — That man is called *gunatita.*

Shls. 22-25 must be read and considered together. Light, activity and delusion, as we have seen in the foregoing *shlokas,* are the products or indications of *sattva, rajas* and *tamas* respectively. The inner meaning of these verses is that he who has transcended the *gunas* will be unaffected by them. A stone does not desire light, nor does it disdain activity or inertness ; it is still, without having the will to be so. If someone puts it into motion, it does not fret ; if again, it is allowed to lie still, it does not feel that inertness or delusion has seized it. The difference between a stone and a *gunatita* is that the latter has full consciousness and with full knowledge he shakes himself free from the bonds that bind an ordinary mortal. He has, as a result of his knowledge, achieved the repose of a stone. Like the stone he is witness, but not the doer, of the activities of the *gunas* or *prakriti.* Of such *jnani* one may say that he is sitting still, unshaken in the knowledge that it is the *gunas* playing their parts. We who are every moment of our lives acting as though *we* were the doers can only imagine the state, we can hardly experience it. But we can hitch our waggon to that star and work our way closer and closer towards it by gradually withdrawing the self from our actions. A *gunatita* has experience of his own condition but he cannot describe it, for he who can describe it ceases to be one. The moment he proceeds to do so, 'self' peeps in. The peace and light and bustle and inertness of our common experience are illusory. The Gita itself has made it clear in so many words that the *sattvika* state is the one nearest that of a *gunatita.* Therefore every one should strive to develop more and more *sattva* in himself, believing that some day he will reach the goal of the state of *gunatita.*

मां च योऽव्यभिचारेण भक्तियोगेन सेवते ।
स गुणान् समतीत्यैतान् ब्रह्मभूयाय कल्पते ॥२६॥

26. He who serves Me with an unwavering and exclusive *bhaktiyoga* transcends these *gunas* and is worthy to become one with *Brahman*.

ब्रह्मणो हि प्रतिष्ठाऽहम् अमृतस्याव्ययस्य च ।
शाश्वतस्य च धर्मस्य सुखस्यैकांतिकस्य च ॥२७॥

27. For I am the very image of *Brahman,* changeless and deathless, as also of everlasting *dharma* and perfect bliss.

[The *gunatita* is not devoid of all *gunas,* but beyond all *gunas,* not full of *sattva,* which every aspirant will try to be, but pure unadulterated *sattva* itself without a particle of *rajas* or *tamas.* That Perfection is He, who is SAT-CHIT-ANANDA : being the very image of *Brahman.* He is *Sat* — the Truth or the Reality ; He is *Chit* inasmuch as He contains in Himself everlasting *Dharma* — the eternal law of cosmic evolution ; He is *Ananda* because the abode of perfect bliss.]

अिति श्रीमद्‌भगवद्‌गीतासु अुपनिषत्सु ब्रह्मविद्यायां योगशास्त्रे श्रीकृष्णार्जुनसंवादे
गुणत्रयविभागयोगो नाम चतुर्दशोऽध्यायः ॥ १४॥

Thus ends the fourteenth discourse, entitled '*Gunatrayavibhaga Yoga*' in the converse of Lord Krishna and Arjuna, on the science of *Yoga,* as part of the knowledge of *Brahman,* in the Upanishad called the Bhagawadgita.

DISCOURSE XV

This discourse deals with the Supreme Form of the Lord, transcending Kshara (perishable) and Akshara (imperishable).

श्रीभगवानुवाच ।

ऊर्ध्वमूलमधःशाखम् अश्वत्थं प्राहुरव्ययम् ।
छंदांसि यस्य पर्णानि यस्तं वेद स वेदवित् ।।१।।

The Lord said :

1. With its root above and branches below, the *ashvattha* tree, they say, is imperishable ; it has Vedic hymns for its leaves ; he who knows it knows the Vedas.

Shvah means tomorrow, and *ashvattha* (*na shvopi sthata*) means that which will not last even until tomorrow, i. e. the world of sense which is every moment in a state of flux. But even though it is perpetually changing, as its root is *Brahman* or the Supreme, it is imperishable. It has for its protection and support the leaves of the Vedic hymns, i..e *dharma.* He who knows the world of sense as such and who knows *dharma* is the real *jnani,* that man has really known the Vedas.

अधश्चोर्ध्वं प्रसृतास्तस्य शाखा
गुणप्रवृद्धा विषयप्रवालाः ।
अधश्च मूलान्यनुसंततानि
कर्मानुबंधीनि मनुष्यलोके ।।२।।

2. Above and below its branches spread, blossoming because of the *gunas,* having for their shoots the sense-objects ; deep down in the world of men are ramified its roots, in the shape of the consequences of action.

This is the description of the tree of the world of sense as the unenlightened see it. They fail to discover its Root above in *Brahman* and so they are always attached to the objects of sense. They water the tree with the three *gunas* and remain bound to *Karman* in the world of men.

[1-2. The *ashvattha* tree with the Root above and branches below is described in the *Katha Up.* as "the eternal, immortal *Brahman*", whereas here it is the tree ever perishable, but eternal in its changefulness. The *ashvattha* is the *Ficus Religiosa* or the *peepal* tree, as Tilak has conclusively shown. Its Root or Primeval Seed is *Brahman* — described poetically as "above", and its multi-branched expanse is below manifest to our eyes. But in *shl.* 2 the roots are said to be below inasmuch as ordinary mortals forget the Root and always think of the worldly roots. The branches are said to spread up and down, for the actions which are the result of past actions throw down rootlets which issue again in actions — representing the ceaseless cycle of birth and death, death and birth. Hill is mistaken in thinking that the *peepal* does not "drop down aerial roots to take fresh roots in the earth." They *do* when they grow to an old age.

Prof. Ranade (*Constructive Survey of Upanishadic Philosophy*) compares the *ashvattha* with the Tree Igdrasil in Scandinavian mythology, described in Carlyle's picturesque language in his "Heroes": "Its boughs with their buddings and disleafings — events, things suffered, things done, catastrophes — stretch through all lands and times. Is not every leaf of it a biography, every fibre there an act or word? Its boughs are histories of nations. The rustle of it is the noise of human existence, onwards from of old. It grows there, the breath of human passion rustling through it....It is Igdrasil, the Tree of Existence. It is the past, the present and the future; what was done, what is doing, what will be done; the infinite conjugation of the verb *to do.*" Prof. Ranade notices one important point of contrast, viz. that the Tree Igdrasil has "its roots deep down in the kingdom of Hela or Death." I think he seems to forget *shl.* 2 where the roots — and not the Root as in *shl.* 1 — are said to be "ramified down below". The comparison would thus seem to be closer and more instructive than the learned professor thinks. The conjugation of the verb *to do* is the eternal bondage of *Karma* or ever recurring death, if man will not open his eyes to the imperishable Root up above which is deathlessness as Gandhiji has shown in his note on XV. 2. See also XII. 7 where *sansara* is described as death itself.]

न रूपमस्येह तथोपलभ्यते
नान्तो न चादिर्न च संप्रतिष्ठा ।
अश्वत्थमेनं सुविरूढमूलम्
असंगशस्त्रेण दृढेन छित्त्वा ॥३॥
ततः पदं तत् परिमार्गितव्यम्
यस्मिन् गता न निवर्तन्ति भूयः ।
तमेव चाद्यं पुरुषं प्रपद्ये
यतः प्रवृत्तिः प्रसृता पुराणी ॥४॥

3. Its form as such is not here perceived, neither is its end, nor beginning, nor basis. Let man first hew down this deep-rooted *Ashvattha* with the sure weapon of detachment;

4. Let him pray to win to that haven from which there is no return and seek to find refuge in the Primal Being from whom has emanated this ancient world of action.

'Detachment' in *shl.* 3 here means dispassion, aversion to the objects of the senses. Unless man is determined to cut himself off from the temptations of the world of sense he will go deeper into its mire every day. These verses show that one dare not play with the objects of the senses with impunity.

निर्मानमोहा जितसंगदोषा
अध्यात्मनित्या विनिवृत्तकामाः ।
द्वंद्वैर्विमुक्ताः सुखदुःखसंज्ञैर्
गच्छन्त्यमूढाः पदमव्ययं तत् ॥५॥

5. To that imperishable haven those enlightened souls go — who are without pride and delusion, who have triumphed over the taints of attachment, who are ever in tune with the Supreme, whose passions have died, who are exempt from the pairs of opposites, such as pleasure and pain.

न तद् भासयते सूर्यो न शशांको न पावकः ।
यद् गत्वा न निवर्तन्ते तद् धाम परमं मम ॥६॥

6. Neither the sun, nor the moon, nor fire illumine it ; men who arrive there return not — that is My supreme abode.

[The same thought occurs over and over again in the *Upanishads* : " There the sun shines not, nor the moon, nor the stars, nor the lightning, much less this common fire ! All shines because He shines, all shines after Him, with His light. *Katha Up.* 2. 5. 15, *Mund. Up.* 2. 2. 10, *Shve.* 6. 14.*]

ममैवांशो जीवलोके जीवभूतः सनातनः ।
मनःषष्ठानीन्द्रियाणि प्रकृतिस्थानि कर्षति ॥७॥

7. A part indeed of Myself which has been the eternal *Jiva* in this world of life, attracts the mind and the five senses from their place in *prakriti*.

---

* न तत्र सूर्यो भाति न चन्द्रतारकं नेमा विद्युतो भान्ति कुतोऽयमग्निः ।
तमेव भान्तमनुभाति सर्वं तस्य भासा सर्वमिदं विभाति ॥
कठ २.५.१५, मुण्डक २.२.१०, श्वेताश्वतर ६.१४

[Shankaracharya says: "An integral portion of the Supreme is the individual soul manifesting himself in every one, just like the reflection of the sun in water or a part of the ether limited in a jar. The water and the jar removed; the sun is the same sun and the ether the same ether."]

शरीरं यदवाप्नोति यच्चाप्युत्क्रामतीश्वरः ।
गृहीत्वैतानि संयाति वायुर्गंधानिवाशयात् ।।८।।

8. When the Master (of the body) acquires a body and discards it he carries these with him wherever he goes, even as the wind carries scents from flower beds.

श्रोत्रं चक्षुः स्पर्शनं च रसनं घ्राणमेव च ।
अधिष्ठाय मनश्चायं विषयानुपसेवते ।।९।।

9. Having settled himself in the senses — ear, eye, touch, taste, and smell — as well as the mind, through them he frequents their objects.

These objects are the natural objects of the senses. The frequenting or enjoyment of these would be tainted if there were the sense of 'I' about it; otherwise it is pure, even as a child's enjoyment of these objects is innocent.

उत्क्रामन्तं स्थितं वाऽपि भुंजानं वा गुणान्वितम् ।
विमूढा नानुपश्यन्ति पश्यन्ति ज्ञानचक्षुषः ।।१०।।

10. The deluded perceive Him not as He leaves or settles in (a body) or enjoys (sense objects) in association with the *gunas*; it is those endowed with the eye of knowledge who alone see Him.

[I.e. perceive Him as He truly is, as one having nothing to do with the many processes mentioned here.]

यतन्तो योगिनश्चैनं पश्यंत्यात्मन्यवस्थितम् ।
यतन्तोऽप्यकृतात्मानो नैनं पश्यन्त्यचेतसः ।।११।।

11. *Yogins* who strive see Him seated in themselves; the witless ones who have not cleansed themselves see Him not, even though they strive.

This does not conflict with the covenant that God has made even with the sinner in discourse 9. *Akritatman* (अकृतात्मन्) (who has not cleansed himself) means one who has no devotion in him, who has not made up his mind to purify himself. The most confirmed sinner, if he has humility enough to seek refuge in surrender to God, purifies himself and succeeds in finding Him. Those who do not care to observe the cardinal and the casual vows and expect to find God through bare intellectual exercise are witless, Godless; they will not find Him.

यदादित्यगतं तेजो जगद् भासयतेऽखिलम् ।
यच्चंद्रमसि यच्चाग्नौ तत् तेजो विद्धि मामकम् ।।१२।।

12. The light in the sun which illumines the whole universe and which is in the moon and in fire — that light, know thou, is Mine;

गामाविश्य च भूतानि धारयाम्यहमोजसा ।
पुष्णामि चौषधीः सर्वाः सोमो भूत्वा रसात्मकः ।।१३।।

13. It is I, who penetrating the earth uphold all beings with my strength, and becoming the moon — the essence of all sap — nourish all the herbs;

अहं वैश्वानरो भूत्वा प्राणिनां देहमाश्रितः ।
प्राणापानसमायुक्तः पचाम्यन्नं चतुर्विधम् ।।१४।।

14. It is I who becoming the Vaishvanara Fire and entering the bodies of all that breathe, assimilate the four kinds of food with the help of the outward and the inward breaths.

[Four kinds: masticated, sucked, licked and drunk.]

[12-14. All the elements derive their virtue or power from Him, all the properties that we associate with matter really derive from Him, because He pervades all. In the Upanishad parable, the fire could not burn a straw, nor could the wind carry it off, and Indra had to recognize that it was verily the power of *Brahman* of which the power in all other things — the mighty elements themselves — was the reflection. (*Kena Up.* 3-4)]

सर्वस्य चाहं हृदि संनिविष्टो
मत्तः स्मृतिर्ज्ञानमपोहनं च ।
वेदैश्च सर्वैरहमेव वेद्यो
वेदांतकृद् वेदविदेव चाहम् ।।१५।।

15. And I am seated in the hearts of all, from Me proceed memory, knowledge and the dispelling of doubt; it is I who am to be known in all the Vedas, I, the author of Vedanta and the knower of the Vedas.

[Vedanta (lit. end of the Vedas) may mean the doctrine set out at the end of the Vedas, i.e. in *Upanishads* or "the essence of the Vedas", as *Muktikopanishad* * says: 'Vedanta is well-grounded in the Veda even as oil in the sesamum seed.']

द्वाविमौ पुरुषौ लोके क्षरश्चाक्षर अेव च ।
क्षरः सर्वाणि भूतानि कूटस्थोऽक्षर अुच्यते ।।१६।।

16. There are two Beings in the world: *kshara* (perishable) and *akshara* (imperishable). *Kshara* embraces all creatures and their permanent basis is *akshara.*

[One is apt to take *kshara* and *akshara* in this *shloka* as corresponding to *kshetra* and *kshetrajna* in XIII. 1 or *para prakriti* and *apara prakriti* in VII. 5, as indeed Hill has done following Ramanuja.

* तिलेषु तैलवद् वेदे वेदान्तः सुप्रतिष्ठितः। मुक्तिक. १. ९

But there are two or three serious difficulties: (1) The Lord has again and again declared His identity with *kshetrajna*—the knower of the field (XIII. 2, XIII. 22); (2) Lord Krishna is here speaking not of the two aspects of the Supreme as in VII. 5—lower nature and higher nature—, but of the two aspects of the world (*loke dvau imau purushau*) (लोके द्वौ अिमौ पुरुषौ) *akshara* being the unmanifested *prakriti* which is the permanent basis of all the manifest creation. It is *akshara*—imperishable or eternal as compared to the everchanging things of the world which are described as *kshara*—perishable. (3) This is exactly how Sankhya describes these two aspects; the Gita accepts the language of description, but declares that the real Imperishable and Unmanifest beyond what is commonly understood to be unmanifest and imperishable is the *Purushottama*—the Supreme Being (17). It is this Supreme Being that pervades and informs and supports the worlds. Compare with this *shloka* VIII. 20 which expresses the same idea. (4) Hill quotes in his support *Shve. Up.* 1. 10, but the *Shve. Up.* speaks throughout that section of *prakriti, atman,* and *paramatman.* It does not refer to the aspects of the world. Here, i.e. in *shl.* 17, there is something transcending the world or the worlds—both as *atman* and *paramatman* that is being spoken of. See *Mund. Up.* 2. 1. 2 quoted in the next note, which seems to be conclusive on this point.]

अुत्तमः पुरुषस्त्वन्यः परमात्मेत्युदाहृतः ।
यो लोकत्रयमाविश्य बिभर्त्यव्यय अीश्वरः ॥१७॥

17. The Supreme Being is surely another—called *Paramatman* who as the Imperishable *Ishvara* pervades and supports the three worlds.

यस्मात् क्षरमतीतोऽहम् अक्षरादपि चोत्तमः ।
अतोऽस्मि लोके वेदे च प्रथितः पुरुषोत्तमः ॥१८॥

18. Because I transcend the *kshara* and am also higher than the *akshara,* I am known in the world and in the Vedas as *Purushottama* (the Highest Being).

[' In the Vedas ' i.e. in the *Upanishads* particularly, though the '*Purusha*' of the famous Vedic hymn is '*Purushottama*'. In *Mund. Up.* 2. 1-2 we have the Supreme Being described as higher than " the imperishable from which diverse beings are produced ". " Divine and inconcrete is the *Purusha*, unborn, breathless, mindless, spotless, higher than the high imperishable." * Also *Shve. Up.* 1. 7-12 which describes the Supreme Being.]

यो मामेवमसंमूढो जानाति पुरुषोत्तमम् ।
स सर्वविद् भजति मां सर्वभावेन भारत ॥१९॥

19. He who, undeluded, knows Me as *Purushottama*, knows all, he worships Me with all his heart, O Bharata.

अिति गुह्यतमं शास्त्रम् अिदमुक्तं मयानघ ।
अेतद् बुद्ध्वा बुद्धिमान् स्यात् कृतकृत्यश्च भारत ॥२०॥

20. Thus I have revealed to thee, sinless one, this most mysterious *shastra*; he who understands this, O Bharata, is a man of understanding, he has fulfilled his life's mission.

अिति श्रीमद्भगवद्गीतासु अुपनिषत्सु ब्रह्मविद्यायां योगशास्त्रे श्रीकृष्णार्जुनसंवादे
पुरुषोत्तमयोगो नाम पंचदशोऽध्यायः ॥१५॥

Thus ends the fifteenth discourse, entitled '*Purushottama Yoga*' in the converse of Lord Krishna and Arjuna, on the science of *Yoga*, as part of the knowledge of *Brahman* in the Upanishad called the Bhagawadgita.

---

* तथाक्षराद्विविधाः सोम्य भावाः प्रजायन्ते तत्र चैवापियन्ति ॥१॥
दिव्यो ह्यमूर्तः पुरुषः स बाह्याभ्यन्तरो ह्यजः ।
अप्राणो ह्यमनाः शुभ्रो ह्यक्षरात्परतः परः ॥२॥ मुण्डक. २. १–२

DISCOURSE XVI

This discourse treats of the divine and the devilish heritage.

श्रीभगवानुवाच ।

अभयं सत्त्वसंशुद्धिर् ज्ञानयोगव्यवस्थितिः ।
दानं दमश्च यज्ञश्च स्वाध्यायस्तप आर्जवम् ।।१।।

The Lord said:

1. Fearlessness, purity of heart, steadfastness in *jnana* and *yoga*—knowledge and action, beneficence, self-restraint, sacrifice, spiritual study, austerity, and uprightness;

अहिंसा सत्यमक्रोधस् त्यागः शान्तिरपैशुनम् ।
दया भूतेष्वलोलुप्त्वं मार्दवं ह्रीरचापलम् ।।२।।

2. Non-violence, truth, slowness to wrath, the spirit of dedication, serenity, aversion to slander, tenderness to all that lives, freedom from greed, gentleness, modesty, freedom from levity;

तेजः क्षमा धृतिः शौचम् अद्रोहो नातिमानिता ।
भवन्ति संपदं दैवीम् अभिजातस्य भारत ।।३।।

3. Spiritedness, forgiveness, fortitude, purity, freedom from ill-will and arrogance—these are to be found in one born with the divine heritage, O Bharata.

दंभो दर्पोऽभिमानश्च क्रोधः पारुष्यमेव च ।
अज्ञानं चाभिजातस्य पार्थ संपदमासुरीम् ।।४।।

4. Pretentiousness, arrogance, self-conceit, wrath, coarseness, ignorance — these are to be found in one born with the devilish heritage.

दैवी संपद् विमोक्षाय निबंधायासुरी मता ।
मा शुचः संपदं दैवीम् अभिजातोऽसि पांडव ॥५॥

5. The divine heritage makes for Freedom, the devilish for bondage. Grieve not, O Partha ; thou art born with a divine heritage.

[1-5. : 'Walk in the spirit,' says St. Paul, 'and ye shall not fulfil the lust of the flesh.' The last verses of Gal. 4 are worth comparing with practically the whole of this discourse :

"Now the works of the flesh are manifest, which are these : adultery, fornication, uncleanliness, lasciviousness. ...I tell you that they which do such things shall not inherit the Kingdom of God. But the fruit of the spirit is love, joy, peace, long-suffering, goodness, faith, meekness, temperance. ...If we live in the spirit, let us also walk in the spirit. Let us not be desirous of vain glory, provoking one another, envying one another." (Ga. 4. 16-26)

It is perhaps better to describe the virtues as "the fruit of the spirit" than as "a divine heritage" and the vices as "the works of the flesh" rather than as "a devilish heritage". For there are no watertight compartments of the divine and devilish natures ; it is one's works that determine one's character on every occasion and at each stage of life. In fact the Gita itself recognizes this when, towards the end of the discourse, man is asked to shun the three portals of hell.

Having said this, let me say that the disparaging remark of a Christian critic, that in this list of virtues it is only "the passive virtues that are most prominent", is wholly mistaken. To understand what these virtues mean to him who lives them, one has but to turn to Jnaneshvara's scores of *ovi* stanzas describing the implications of each of them.

Let it be noted that fearlessness which is at the head of the list is perhaps the most positive of the virtues. The *Upanishads* thus laid down the conditions of fearlessness: "When he realized that there was no other than he, his fear fled; for it is the 'otherness' from which proceeds fear" * (*Brh. Up.* 1. 4. 2); "He who has known the joy of *Brahman* never fears" § (*Tait. Up.* 2. 4); "When he is securely established in that invisible, inconcrete, fearless, he becomes fearless" † (*Tait. Up.* 2. 7). All other virtues naturally flow from this virtue. And Gandhiji has often said: "When we fear God, we shall fear no man, no matter how high-placed he may be. If you want to follow the vow of truth, fearlessness is the necessary consequence."

In the second verse follow non-violence and truth — *ahimsa* and *satya,* both of which may be called the obverse and reverse of the coin of fearlessness. If truth presupposes fearlessness, inoffensiveness or non-violence is, as Gandhiji has said, "the acme of fearlessness".]

द्वौ भूतसर्गौ लोकेऽस्मिन् दैव आसुर अेव च ।
दैवो विस्तरशः प्रोक्त आसुरं पार्थ मे श्रृणु ।।६।।

6. There are two orders of created beings in this world — the divine and the devilish; the divine order has been described in detail, hear from Me now of the devilish, O Partha.

प्रवृत्तिं च निवृत्तिं च जना न विदुरासुराः ।
न शौचं नापि चाचारो न सत्यं तेषु विद्यते ।।७।।

---

* सोऽबिभेत्तस्मादेकाकी बिभेति सहायमीक्षांचक्रे यन्मदन्यन्नास्ति कस्मान्नु बिभेमीति तत अेवास्य भयं वीयाय कस्माद्ध्यभेष्यद् द्वितीयाद्वै भयं भवति।

बृहदारण्यक. १. ४. २

§ आनन्दं ब्रह्मणो विद्वान् न बिभेति कदाचन।।

तैत्तिरीय. २. ४

† यदा ह्येवैष अेतस्मिन्नदृश्येऽनात्म्येऽनिरुक्तेऽनिलयनेऽभयं प्रतिष्ठां विन्दते। अथ सोऽभयं गतो भवति। तैत्तिरीय. २. ७

7. Men of the devil do not know what they may do and what they may not do; neither is there purity, nor right conduct, nor truth to be found in them.

असत्यमप्रतिष्ठं ते जगदाहुरनीश्वरम् ।
अपरस्परसंभूतं किमन्यत् कामहैतुकम् ॥८॥

8. 'Without truth, without basis, without God is the universe,' they say; 'born of the union of the sexes, prompted by naught but lust.'

अेतां दृष्टिमवष्टभ्य नष्टात्मानोऽल्पबुद्धयः ।
प्रभवन्त्युग्रकर्माणः क्षयाय जगतोऽहिताः ॥९॥

9. Holding this view, these depraved souls, of feeble understanding and of fierce deeds, come forth as enemies of the world to destroy it.

काममाश्रित्य दुष्पूरं दंभमानमदान्विताः ।
मोहाद् गृहीत्वाऽसद्ग्राहान् प्रवर्तन्तेऽशुचिव्रताः ॥१०॥

10. Given to insatiable lust, possessed by pretentiousness, arrogance and conceit, they seize wicked purposes in their delusion, and go about pledged to unclean deeds.

चिंतामपरिमेयां च प्रलयान्तामुपाश्रिताः ।
कामोपभोगपरमा अेतावदिति निश्चिताः ॥११॥

11. Given to boundless cares that end only with their death, making indulgence or lust their sole goal, convinced that that is all;

[These cares are "sorrows of the world" which work death, but not "godly sorrow which worketh repentance to salvation." (2. Cor. 7. 10)]

आशापाशशतैर्बद्धाः कामक्रोधपरायणाः ।
ओहन्ते कामभोगार्थम् अन्यायेनार्थसंचयान् ॥१२॥

12. Caught in a myriad snares of hope, slaves to lust and wrath, they seek unlawfully to amass wealth for the satisfaction of their appetites.

अिदमद्य मया लब्धम् अिमं प्राप्स्ये मनोरथम् ।
अिदमस्तीदमपि मे भविष्यति पुनर्धनम् ॥१३॥

13. 'This have I gained today; this aspiration shall I now attain; this wealth is mine; this likewise shall be mine hereafter;

असौ मया हतः शत्रुर् हनिष्ये चापरानपि ।
अीश्वरोऽहमहं भोगी सिद्धोऽहं बलवान् सुखी ॥१४॥

14. 'This enemy I have already slain, others also I shall slay; lord of all am I; enjoyment is mine, perfection is mine, strength is mine, happiness is mine;

आढयोऽभिजनवानस्मि कोऽन्योऽस्ति सदृशो मया ।
यक्ष्ये दास्यामि मोदिष्य अित्यज्ञानविमोहिताः ॥१५॥

15. 'Wealthy am I, and high-born. What other is like unto me? I shall perform a sacrifice! I shall give alms! I shall be merry!' Thus think they, by ignorance deluded;

अनेकचित्तविभ्रान्ता मोहजालसमावृताः ।
प्रसक्ताः कामभोगेषु पतन्ति नरकेऽशुचौ ॥१६॥

16. And tossed about by diverse fancies, caught in the net of delusion, stuck deep in the indulgence of appetites, into foul hell they fall.

आत्मसंभाविता स्तब्धा धनमानमदान्विताः ।
यजन्ते नामयज्ञैस्ते दंभेनाविधिपूर्वकम् ॥१७॥

17. Wise in their own conceit, stubborn, full of the intoxication of pelf and pride, they offer nominal sacrifices for show, contrary to the rule.

अहंकारं बलं दर्पं कामं क्रोधं च संश्रिताः ।
मामात्मपरदेहेषु प्रद्विषन्तोऽभ्यसूयकाः ॥१८॥

18. Given to pride, force, arrogance, lust and wrath they are deriders indeed, scorning Me in their own and others' bodies.

तानहं द्विषतः क्रूरान् संसारेषु नराधमान् ।
क्षिपाम्यजस्रमशुभान् आसुरीष्वेव योनिषु ॥१९॥

19. These cruel scorners, lowest of mankind and vile, I hurl down again and again, into devilish wombs.

[Cf. Koran : "Leave Me to deal with the deniers, lords of ease and comfort." (73. 11)]

आसुरीं योनिमापन्ना मूढा जन्मनि जन्मनि ।
मामप्राप्यैव कौन्तेय ततो यांत्यधमां गतिम् ॥२०॥

20. Doomed to devilish wombs, these deluded ones, far from ever coming to Me, sink lower and lower in birth after birth.

त्रिविधं नरकस्येदं द्वारं नाशनमात्मनः ।
कामः क्रोधस्तथा लोभस् तस्मादेतत् त्रयं त्यजेत् ॥२१॥

21. Three-fold is this gate of hell, leading man to perdition — Lust, Wrath and Greed; these three, therefore, should be shunned.

एतैर्विमुक्तः कौन्तेय तमोद्वारैस्त्रिभिर्नरः ।
आचरत्यात्मनः श्रेयस् ततो याति परां गतिम् ॥२२॥

22. The man who escapes these three gates of Darkness, O Kaunteya, works out his welfare and thence reaches the highest state.

यः शास्त्रविधिमुत्सृज्य वर्तते कामकारतः ।
न स सिद्धिमवाप्नोति न सुखं न परां गतिम् ॥२३॥

23. He who forsakes the rule of *shastra* and does but the bidding of his selfish desires, gains neither perfection, nor happiness, nor the highest state.

Shastra does not mean the rites and formulae laid down in the so-called *dharmashastra,* but the path of self-restraint laid down by the seers and the saints.

तस्माच्छास्त्रं प्रमाणं ते कार्याकार्यव्यवस्थितौ ।
ज्ञात्वा शास्त्रविधानोक्तम् कर्म कर्तुमिहार्हसि ॥२४॥

24. Therefore let *shastra* be thy authority for determining what ought to be done and what ought not to be done; ascertain thou the rule of the *shastra* and do thy task here (accordingly).

Shastra here too has the same meaning as in the preceding *shloka.* Let no one be a law unto himself, but take as his authority the law laid down by men who have known and lived religion.

[23-24. *Shastra.* Gandhiji has in his note rightly warned the readers against taking *shastra* in its commonly accepted sense. But it may not be quite necessary, as he has done, to define *shastra* differently. The *shastra* referred to here is none other than the *shastra* expounded by the Gita — the doctrine of detached or dedicated or selfless action. The very first part of *shl.* 23 makes it clear: the rule of the *shastra* as against working at the bidding of one's selfish desires. In the field of devotion, *shastra* is the *shastra* of which the exposition was concluded with

xv. 20 (q. v.). That doctrine is the doctrine of the worship of one God, Purushottama who pervades, penetrates and supports the universe, and not the worship of gods and spirits.

That *shastra* cannot here mean the so-called scriptures needs no argument. It would be absurd if, after expounding so thoroughly the doctrine of selfless work and of the worship of the One, the Gita should spring a surprise upon the readers by asking them to go to the scriptures for determining the course of their conduct.

In another connection Gandhiji said: "Nothing that is inconsistent with the main theme of the Gita is *shastra*, no matter where it is found printed." Also:

"Gita is the key to a knowledge of the *shastra.* It enunciates the principles on which all conduct must be based. It sums up the whole of the *shastras.*" (Gandhiji in *Harijan,* 22-12-'33)]

अिति श्रीमद्भगवद्गीतासु अुपनिषत्सु ब्रह्मविद्यायां योगशास्त्रे श्रीकृष्णार्जुनसंवादे
दैवासुरसंपद्विभागयोगो नाम षोडशोऽध्यायः ॥१६॥

Thus ends the sixteenth discourse, entitled '*Daivasurasampadvibhaga Yoga*' in the converse of Lord Krishna and Arjuna, on the science of *Yoga* as part of the knowledge of *Brahman* in the Upanishad called the Bhagawadgita.

DISCOURSE XVII

On being asked to consider Shastra (conduct of the worthy) as the authority, Arjuna is faced with a difficulty. What is the position of those who may not be able to accept the authority of Shastra but who may act in faith? An answer to the question is attempted in this discourse. Krishna rests content with pointing out the rocks and shoals on the path of one who forsakes the beaconlight of Shastra (conduct of the worthy). In doing so he deals with faith and sacrifice, austerity and charity, performed with faith, and their divisions according to the spirit in which they are performed. He also sings the greatness of the mystic syllables AUM TAT SAT — a formula of dedication of all work to God.

[17th Discourse: See my note on XVI. 23-24. As Lord Krishna has already told Arjuna that the doctrine of selfless work — the *shastra* expounded in the Gita — is the sole authority in conduct, there may appear to be no occasion for the question in the first *shloka* here. There is, however. For, in XVI. 23-24 the sphere of conduct was under consideration, here it is that of devotion that is in question. Arjuna has been told in IX. 23-25 that there are people who worship gods and manes and spirits. These too worship in faith — faith in a scripture of some kind or other, or some kind of religious faith, as we have seen in VII. 21. Arjuna therefore asks: 'How should one classify these worshippers, who worship in faith, but who neglect the rule of the *shastra* to worship one God?' The whole of the discourse is in reply to that question. Sacrifice, austerity, charity may be taken to be forms of worship, or devotional conduct which is coloured by a man's faith or belief in the scriptures as he understands them. He will not only sacrifice to a particular kind of gods, but do so in a particular kind of spirit.

I have taken this line of argument in "My Submission" (pp. 95-97) and analysed the seventeenth discourse accordingly. Here in the text I have not presumed to disturb Gandhiji's argument or translation.]

अर्जुन अुवाच ।
ये शास्त्रविधिमुत्सृज्य यजन्ते श्रद्धयाऽन्विताः ।
तेषां निष्ठा तु का कृष्ण सत्त्वमाहो रजस्तमः ॥१॥

Arjuna said :

1. What, then, O Krishna, is the position of those who forsake the rule of *Shastra* and yet worship with faith? Do they act from *sattva* or *rajas* or *tamas*?

श्रीभगवानुवाच ।
त्रिविधा भवति श्रद्धा देहिनां सा स्वभावजा ।
सात्त्विकी राजसी चैव तामसी चेति तां शृणु ॥२॥

The Lord said :

2. Threefold is the faith of men, an expression of their nature in each case; it is *sattvika, rajasa* or *tamasa*. Hear thou of it.

सत्त्वानुरूपा सर्वस्य श्रद्धा भवति भारत ।
श्रद्धामयोऽयं पुरुषः यो यच्छ्रद्धः स अेव सः ॥३॥

3. The faith of every man is in accord with his innate character; man is made up of faith; whatever his object of faith, even so is he.

[See my note on IX. 25.]

यजन्ते सात्त्विका देवान् यक्षरक्षांसि राजसाः ।
प्रेतान् भूतगणांश्चान्ये यजन्ते तामसा जनाः ॥४॥

4. *Sattvika* persons worship the gods; *rajasa* ones, the Yakshas and Rakshasas; and others — men of *tamas* — worship manes and spirits.

अशास्त्रविहितं घोरं तप्यन्ते ये तपो जनाः ।
दंभाहंकारसंयुक्ताः कामरागबलान्विताः ।।५।।

5. Those men who, wedded to pretentiousness and arrogance, possessed by the violence of lust and passion, practise fierce austerity not ordained by *shastra*;

कर्षयन्तः शरीरस्थम् भूतग्राममचेतसः ।
मां चैवान्तःशरीरस्थं तान् विद्ध्यासुरनिश्चयान् ।।६।।

6. They, whilst they torture the several elements that make up their bodies, torture Me too dwelling in them; know them to be of unholy resolves.

आहारस्त्वपि सर्वस्य त्रिविधो भवति प्रियः ।
यज्ञस्तपस्तथा दानम् तेषां भेदमिमं श्रृणु ।।७।।

7. Of three kinds again is the food that is dear to each; so also are sacrifice, austerity, and charity. Hear how they differ.

आयुःसत्त्वबलारोग्यसुखप्रीतिविवर्धनाः ।
रस्याः स्निग्धाः स्थिरा हृद्या आहाराः सात्त्विकप्रियाः ।।८।।

8. Victuals that add to one's years, vitality, strength, health, happiness and appetite; are savoury, rich, substantial and inviting, are dear to the *sattvika*.

कट्वम्ललवणात्युष्णतीक्ष्णरूक्षविदाहिनः ।
आहारा राजसस्येष्टा दुःखशोकामयप्रदाः ।।९।।

9. Victuals that are bitter, sour, salty, over-hot, spicy, dry, burning, and causing pain, bitterness and disease, are dear to the *rajasa.*

यातयामं गतरसं पूति पर्युषितं च यत् ।
अुच्छिष्टमपि चामेध्यं भोजनं तामसप्रियम् ॥१०॥

10. Food which has become cold, insipid, putrid, stale, discarded and unfit for sacrifice, is dear to the *tamasa.*

अफलाकांक्षिभिर्यज्ञो विधिदृष्टो य अिज्यते ।
यष्टव्यमेवेति मनः समाधाय स सात्त्विकः ॥११॥

11. That sacrifice is *sattvika* which is willingly offered as a duty without desire for fruit and according to the rule.

अभिसंधाय तु फलं दंभार्थमपि चैव यत् ।
अिज्यते भरतश्रेष्ठ तं यज्ञं विद्धि राजसम् ॥१२॥

12. But when sacrifice is offered with an eye to fruit and for vain glory, know, O Bharatashreshtha, that it is *rajasa.*

विधिहीनमसृष्टान्नं मंत्रहीनमदक्षिणम् ।
श्रद्धाविरहितं यज्ञं तामसं परिचक्षते ॥१३॥

13. Sacrifice which is contrary to the rule, which produces no food, which lacks the sacred text, which involves no giving up, and which is devoid of faith is said to be *tamasa.*

[*Asrishtannam,* (असृष्टान्नम्) ordinarily translated 'in which no food is distributed', is deliberately translated by Gandhiji thus: 'which produces no food'. In doing so, he seems to rely both on Manu and the Gita (See III. 14): Sacrifice produces rain which produces food. All sacrifice must be creative.

Gandhiji's interpretation of '*adakshinam*' (अदक्षिणम्) as 'which involves no (*dakshina*) giving up' is also different from the usual interpretation, 'devoid of prescribed fees to the priests'. Apart from the crude selfishness involved in the orthodox interpretation, the term '*dakshina*' (gift) has certainly been used in a highly spiritual sense in the *Upanishads,* as is apparent from *Chh. Up.* 3. 17. 4 where "austerity, charity, uprightness, non-violence and truthfulness" * are said to be the "gifts" to be offered at the sacrifice. The "giving up" in Gandhiji's translation means the giving up of something one holds dear. But the *Chh. Up.* would go even further and suggest the giving by the sacrificer of a promise to lead a life of the cardinal vows mentioned above. That is giving of oneself — a pure sacrifice.

Under my line of argument, however, even the orthodox interpretation would do, the sense being that the worst sacrifice would be that in which even the orthodox *shastric* rule of feeding the *Brahmanas* etc. is not satisfied.]

देवद्विजगुरुप्राज्ञपूजनं शौचमार्जवम् ।
ब्रह्मचर्यमहिंसा च शारीरं तप उच्यते ॥१४॥

14. Homage to the gods, to *Brahmanas*, to *gurus* and to wise men ; cleanliness, uprightness, *brahmacharya* and non-violence — these constitute austerity (*tapas*) of the body.

[Non-violence with which Gandhiji has familiarized us is what St. Augustine calls "inoffensiveness". As Gandhiji defines it — "Avoiding injury or offence to anything on earth in thought, word and deed."]

अनुद्वेगकरं वाक्यं सत्यं प्रियहितं च यत् ।
स्वाध्यायाभ्यसनं चैव वाङ्मयं तप उच्यते ॥१५॥

---

* अथ यत्तपो दानमार्जवमहिंसा सत्यवचनमिति ता अस्य दक्षिणाः ।
छान्दोग्य. ३. १७. ४

15. Words that cause no hurt, that are true, loving and helpful, and spiritual study constitute austerity of speech.

मनःप्रसादः सौम्यत्वं मौनमात्मविनिग्रहः ।
भावसंशुद्धिरित्येतत् तपो मानसमुच्यते ॥१६॥

16. Serenity, benignity, silence, self-restraint, and purity of the spirit—these constitute austerity of the mind.

[Regarding silence see note on XII. 19. Also Gandhiji: "Silence is essential for one whose life is an incessant search for truth. Silence also helps one to suppress one's anger as perhaps nothing else does. How is one to give vent to one's wrath if one is silent? Not by eyes. Surely not by physical violence, when one is pledged to non-violence. Not by writing, for the wrath would disappear in the very process of writing." Mechanically it is a kind of self-restraint. True self-restraint is the fruit of silence consciously pursued. "Purity of the spirit which is the only true fruit of the soul and without which all external activity is vain," says a Western mystic.]

श्रद्धया परया तप्तं तपस्तत् त्रिविधं नरैः ।
अफलाकांक्षिभिर्युक्तैः सात्त्विकं परिचक्षते ॥१७॥

17. This threefold austerity practised in perfect faith by men not desirous of fruit, and disciplined, is said to be *sattvika*.

सत्कारमानपूजार्थं तपो दंभेन चैव यत् ।
क्रियते तदिह प्रोक्तं राजसं चलमध्रुवम् ॥१८॥

18. Austerity which is practised with an eye to gain praise, honour and homage and for ostentation is said to be *rajasa*; it is fleeting and unstable.

मूढग्राहेणात्मनो यत् पीडया क्रियते तपः ।
परस्योत्सादनार्थं वा तत् तामसमुदाहृतम् ॥१९॥

19. Austerity which is practised from any foolish obsession, either to torture oneself or to procure another's ruin, is called *tamasa*.

दातव्यमिति यद् दानं दीयतेऽनुपकारिणे ।
देशे काले च पात्रे च तद् दानं सात्त्विकं स्मृतम् ॥२०॥

20. Charity, given as a matter of duty, without expectation of any return, at the right place and time, and to the right person is said to be *sattvika*.

यत् तु प्रत्युपकारार्थं फलमुद्दिश्य वा पुनः ।
दीयते च परिक्लिष्टं तद् दानं राजसं स्मृतम् ॥२१॥

21. Charity, which is given either in the hope of receiving in return, or with a view to winning merit, or grudgingly, is declared to be *rajasa*.

अदेशकाले यद् दानम् अपात्रेभ्यश्च दीयते ।
असत्कृतमवज्ञातं तत् तामसमुदाहृतम् ॥२२॥

22. Charity given at the wrong place and time, and to the undeserving recipient disrespectfully and with contempt is declared to be *tamasa*.

ॐ तत् सदिति निर्देशो ब्रह्मणस्त्रिविधः स्मृतः ।
ब्राह्मणास्तेन वेदाश्च यज्ञाश्च विहिताः पुरा ॥२३॥

23. *AUM TAT SAT* has been declared to be the threefold name of *Brahman* and by that name were created of old the *Brahmanas*, the Vedas and sacrifices.

तस्मादोमित्युदाहृत्य यज्ञदानतपःक्रियाः ।
प्रवर्तन्ते विधानोक्ताः सततं ब्रह्मवादिनाम् ।।२४।।

24. Therefore, with *AUM* ever on their lips, are all the rites of sacrifice, charity and austerity, performed always according to the rule, by *Brahmavadins*.

तदित्यनभिसंधाय फलं यज्ञतपःक्रियाः ।
दानक्रियाश्च विविधाः क्रियन्ते मोक्षकांक्षिभिः ।।२५।।

25. With the utterance of *TAT* and without the desire for fruit are the several rites of sacrifice, austerity and charity performed by those seeking Freedom.

सद्भावे साधुभावे च सदित्येतत् प्रयुज्यते ।
प्रशस्ते कर्मणि तथा सच्छब्दः पार्थ युज्यते ।।२६।।

26. *SAT* is employed in the sense of 'real' and 'good'; O Partha, *SAT* is also applied to beautiful deeds.

यज्ञे तपसि दाने च स्थितिः सदिति चोच्यते ।
कर्म चैव तदर्थीयं सदित्येवाभिधीयते ।।२७।।

27. Constancy in sacrifice, austerity and charity, is called *SAT*; and all work for these purposes is also *SAT*.

The substance of the last four *shlokas* is that every action should be done in a spirit of complete dedication to God. For *AUM* alone is the only Reality. That only which is dedicated to It counts.

[24-27 : For *AUM* see note on VIII. 11-13. The *Brahmavadin* in *shl*. 24 and 'those seeking Freedom' in *shl*. 25 are the same, and both terms are used for the worshipper who uses the triple designation of *Brahman* and dedicates all his worship, charity and austerity to the Supreme. *Shlokas* 25-27 declare the virtue of each of the designations, but the whole is one composite formula of dedication to God. *AUM* is an expression of the Being subsisting everywhere in all times ; *TAT* expresses the Supreme in its detachment ; and *SAT* expresses Truth and Goodness and Beauty. The worshipper, by doing everything to the glory of this Triple Name, pledges himself to constancy, detachment, truth, beauty, and goodness.]

अश्रद्धया हुतं दत्तं तपस्तप्तं कृतं च यत् ।
असदित्युच्यते पार्थ न च तत् प्रेत्य नो अिह ॥२८॥

28. Whatever is done, O Partha, by way of sacrifice, charity or austerity or any other work, is called *Asat* if done without faith. It counts for naught hereafter as here.

अिति श्रीमद्भगवद्गीतासु अुपनिषत्सु ब्रह्मविद्यायां योगशास्त्रे श्रीकृष्णार्जुनसंवादे
श्रद्धात्रयविभागयोगो नाम सप्तदशोऽध्यायः ॥१७॥

Thus ends the seventeenth discourse, entitled '*Shraddhatrayavibhaga Yoga*' in the converse of Lord Krishna and Arjuna, on the science of *Yoga*, as part of the knowledge of *Brahman* in the Upanishad called the Bhagawadgita.

DISCOURSE XVIII

This concluding discourse sums up the teaching of the Gita. It may be said to be summed up in the following: "Abandon all duties and come to Me, the only Refuge" (66). That is true renunciation. But abandonment of all duties does not mean abandonment of actions; it means the abandonment of the desire for fruit. Even the highest act of service must be dedicated to Him, without the desire. That is Tyaga (abandonment), that is Sannyasa (renunciation).

अर्जुन उवाच ।

संन्यासस्य महाबाहो तत्त्वमिच्छामि वेदितुम् ।
त्यागस्य च हृषीकेश पृथक् केशिनिषूदन ॥१॥

Arjuna said:

1. Mahabahu! I would fain learn severally the secret of *sannyasa* and of *tyaga*, O Hrishikesha, O Keshinishudana.

श्रीभगवानुवाच ।

काम्यानां कर्मणां न्यासं संन्यासं कवयो विदुः ।
सर्वकर्मफलत्यागं प्राहुस्त्यागं विचक्षणाः ॥२॥

The Lord said:

2. Renunciation of actions springing from selfish desire is known as *sannyasa* by the seers; abandonment of the fruit of all action is called *tyaga* by the wise.

[The reference here is to the doctrine which must have been prevalent at the time and which we find defined in

Manusmriti thus:* "No action is here seen to be done by one who is without desire; the spring of whatever action one does is desire." Hence the extreme position of the school of *sannyasa* that all action should be abandoned. As against this, the position taken by the Gita is that it is not desire that vitiates the act, but selfish desire, i.e. the desire for fruit, and all actions from which the desire for fruit is withdrawn cease to be binding. The abandonment of the desire for fruit is both *sannyasa* and *tyaga,* both having the etymological meaning 'giving up'. The *tyaga* or *sannyasa,* whatever one may call it, must of course be *sattvika,* as the author will presently tell us.]

त्याज्यं दोषवदित्येके कर्म प्राहुर्मनीषिणः ।
यज्ञदानतपःकर्म न त्याज्यमिति चापरे ।।३।।

3. Some thoughtful persons say: 'All action should be abandoned as an evil'; others say: 'Action for sacrifice, charity and austerity should not be relinquished'.

निश्चयं श्रृणु मे तत्र त्यागे भरतसत्तम ।
त्यागो हि पुरुषव्याघ्र त्रिविधः संप्रकीर्तितः ।।४।।

4. Hear my decision in this matter of *tyaga,* O Bharatasattama; for *tyaga,* too, O mightiest of men, has been described to be of three kinds.

[Three kinds: described in *shls.* 7-9.]

यज्ञदानतपःकर्म न त्याज्यं कार्यमेव तत् ।
यज्ञो दानं तपश्चैव पावनानि मनीषिणाम् ।।५।।

5. Action for sacrifice, charity and austerity may

---

* अकामस्य क्रिया काचित् दृश्यते नेह कर्हिचित् ।
यद् यद् हि कुरुते किंचित् तत् तत् कामस्य चेष्टितम् ।। २.४

not be abandoned; it must needs be performed. Sacrifice, charity and austerity are purifiers of the wise.

[Bhide Shastri who goes one better than Tilak in reading *Karmayoga* in every *shloka* of the Gita translates the second half of this *shloka* in a remarkable way: "Sacrifice, charity and austerity performed by the wise are purifying (for the world)" and adds in a note that the wise — the men of Self-realization — are already purified, they have no purification to achieve, theirs is the duty of purifying the world, and so even after obtaining *jnana*, they must perform sacrifice, charity, austerity for the guidance of the world (III. 20). The meaning is certainly possible. Let it be however noted that the whole thing ultimately turns on the meaning one gives to *manishinam* (मनीषिणाम्) translated here, 'of the wise'. Shankaracharya translates: 'Men who have no desire for fruit'. But the point is, even if one were to mean by *manishin* a *jnanin*, why should not sacrifice, charity etc. not purify him, and therefore necessarily every one else? Can any one maintain spiritual equipoise all the moments he breathes in the flesh? Only those who know can say!]

अेतान्यपि तु कर्माणि संगं त्यक्त्वा फलानि च ।
कर्तव्यानीति मे पार्थ निश्चितं मतमुत्तमम् ॥६॥

6. But even these actions should be performed abandoning all attachment and fruit; such, O Partha, is my best and considered opinion.

नियतस्य तु संन्यासः कर्मणो नोपपद्यते ।
मोहात् तस्य परित्यागस् तामसः परिकीर्तितः ॥७॥

7. It is not right to renounce one's allotted task; its abandonment, from delusion, is said to be *tamasa*.

दुःखमित्येव यत् कर्म कायक्लेशभयात् त्यजेत् ।
स कृत्वा राजसं त्यागं नैव त्यागफलं लभेत् ॥८॥

8. He who abandons action, deeming it painful and for fear of straining his limbs, he will never gain the fruit of abandonment, for his abandonment is *rajasa.*

कार्यमित्येव यत् कर्म नियतं क्रियतेऽर्जुन ।
संगं त्यक्त्वा फलं चैव स त्यागः सात्त्विको मतः ॥९॥

9. But when an allotted task is performed from a sense of duty and with abandonment of attachment and fruit, O Arjuna, that abandonment is deemed to be *sattvika.*

न द्वेष्टयकुशलं कर्म कुशले नानुषज्जते ।
त्यागी सत्त्वसमाविष्टो मेधावी छिन्नसंशयः ॥१०॥

10. Neither does he disdain unpleasant action, nor does he cling to pleasant action — this wise man full of *sattva,* who practises abandonment, and who has shaken off all doubts.

न हि देहभृता शक्यं त्यक्तुं कर्माण्यशेषतः ।
यस्तु कर्मफलत्यागी स त्यागीत्यभिधीयते ॥११॥

11. For the embodied one cannot completely abandon action ; but he who abandons the fruit of action is named a *tyagi.*

अनिष्टमिष्टं मिश्रं च त्रिविधं कर्मणः फलम् ।
भवत्यत्यागिनां प्रेत्य न तु संन्यासिनां क्वचित् ॥१२॥

12. To those who do not practise abandonment accrues, when they pass away, the fruit of action which is of three kinds : disagreeable, agreeable, mixed ; but never to the *sannyasins.*

[11-12 : *Tyagi* (abandoner) and *sannyasi* (renouncer) are really one, as the *sannyasi* and *yogi* were shown to be one in the fifth discourse.]

पंचैतानि महाबाहो कारणानि निबोध मे ।
सांख्ये कृतान्ते प्रोक्तानि सिद्धये सर्वकर्मणाम् ॥१३॥

13. Learn, from me, O Mahababu, the five factors mentioned in the *Sankhyan* doctrine for the accomplishment of all action :

['*Sankhyan* doctrine': Whether this means the doctrine of the system known as *Sankhya* (as many take it), or Vedanta doctrine (as Shankaracharya takes it), or both (as Jnaneshvara takes it), is difficult to say. The five factors as such are nowhere to be found in any known work of *Sankhya* philosophy. Keith mentions *Ahirbudhnya Samhita* where the *Sankhya* system is described as a *Tantra* with several divisions — which include all the *Sankhyan* principles and other conceptions among which we find *karta* (doer) and *daiva* (unseen or fate), mentioned in *shl.* 14. Hill goes to the length of making an attempt to make the fivefold list correspond to the usual twenty-fourfold *Sankhyan* division thus: (1) *adhishthana* (field) is the unmanifest *prakriti*; (2) *karta* (author) includes *buddhi* and *ahankara*; (3) *karanas* are the mind and the five organs of perception; (4) *cheshtas* are the five organs of action; (5) *daiva* meaning the realm of the five gross and five subtle elements presided over by their gods. This is certainly a bold and ingenious if far-fetched attempt. How far it is justified, only the author of the Gita can say! The word *Sankhya* to mean the *Sankhyan* system would, then, be taken to have been used for the first and the last time here in the Gita. The use of *Sankhya* in the sense of knowledge, however, is much more common, and perhaps the least dogmatic interpretation would be to take the phrase to mean 'any doctrine of knowledge' — whether Vedantic or *Sankhya*.]

अधिष्ठानं तथा कर्ता करणं च पृथग्विधम् ।
विविधाश्च पृथक्चेष्टा दैवं चैवात्र पंचमम् ॥१४॥

14. The field, the doer, the various means, the

several different operations, the fifth and the last, the Unseen.

शरीरवाङ्मनोभिर्यत् कर्म प्रारभते नरः ।
न्याय्यं वा विपरीतं वा पंचैते तस्य हेतवः ॥१५॥

15. Whatever action, right or wrong, a man undertakes to do with the body, speech or mind, these are the five factors thereof.

तत्रैवं सति कर्तारम् आत्मानं केवलं तु यः ।
पश्यत्यकृतबुद्धित्वान् न स पश्यति दुर्मतिः ॥१६॥

16. This being so, he who, by reason of unenlightened intellect, sees the unconditioned *Atman* as the agent — such a man is dense and unseeing.

यस्य नाहंकृतो भावो बुद्धिर्यस्य न लिप्यते ।
हत्वाऽपि स इमान् लोकान् न हन्ति न निबध्यते ॥१७॥

17. He who is free from all sense of 'I', whose motive is untainted, slays not nor is bound, even though he slay all these worlds.

This *shloka* though seemingly somewhat baffling is not really so. The Gita on many occasions presents the ideal to attain which the aspirant has to strive but which may not be possible completely to realize in the world. It is like definitions in geometry. A perfect straight line does not exist, but it is necessary to imagine it in order to prove the various propositions. Even so, it is necessary to hold up ideals of this nature as standards for imitation in matters of conduct. This then would seem to be the meaning of this *shloka*: He who has made ashes of 'self', whose motive is untainted, may slay the whole world, if he will. But in reality he who has annihilated 'self' has annihilated his flesh too, and he whose motive is untainted sees the past, present and future. Such a being can be one and only one — God. He acts and yet is no doer, slays and yet is no slayer. For mortal man the royal road — the conduct of the worthy — is ever before him, viz. *ahimsa* — holding all life sacred.

["If we believe Krishna to be God," said Gandhiji, in reply to a question asked him, with regard to this text, "we must impute to Him omniscience and omnipotence. Such an one can surely destroy. But we are puny mortals ever erring and ever revising our views and opinions. We may not, without coming to grief, ape Krishna, the inspirer of the Gita." (*Young India*, 30th April, 1925). Also, on another occasion he said: "Truth excludes the use of violence, because man is not capable of knowing the Absolute Truth and therefore not competent to punish." God alone is competent.]

ज्ञानं ज्ञेयं परिज्ञाता त्रिविधा कर्मचोदना ।
करणं कर्म कर्तेति त्रिविधः कर्मसंग्रहः ॥१८॥

18. Knowledge, the object of knowledge, and the knower compose the threefold urge to action; the means, the action and the doer compose the threefold sum of action.

ज्ञानं कर्म च कर्ता च त्रिधैव गुणभेदतः ।
प्रोच्यते गुणसंख्याने यथावच्छृणु तान्यपि ॥१९॥

19. Knowledge, action, and the doer are of three kinds according to their different *gunas*; hear thou these, just as they have been described in the science of the *gunas*.

सर्वभूतेषु येनैकं भावमव्ययमीक्षते ।
अविभक्तं विभक्तेषु तज्ज्ञानं विद्धि सात्त्विकम् ॥२०॥

20. Know that knowledge whereby one sees in all beings immutable entity — a unity in diversity — to be *sattvika.*

पृथक्त्वेन तु यज्ज्ञानं नानाभावान् पृथग्विधान् ।
वेत्ति सर्वेषु भूतेषु तज्ज्ञानं विद्धि राजसम् ॥२१॥

21. That knowledge which perceives separately in all beings several entities of diverse kinds, know thou to be *rajasa.*

यत् तु कृत्स्नवदेकस्मिन् कार्ये सक्तमहैतुकम् ।
अतत्त्वार्थवदल्पं च तत् तामसमुदाहृतम् ॥२२॥

22. And knowledge which, without reason, clings to one single thing, as though it were everything, which misses the true essence and is superficial is *tamasa.*

[20-22 : *Shl.* 20 repeats the thought of XIII. 30. The three *shlokas* deal with the three kinds of knowledge or apprehension that respectively harmonize, differentiate and exclude or confuse. Thus in philosophy, *sattvika* knowledge perceives the Unity of Self in diverse existences, the *rajasa* emphasizes the difference in them, and the *tamasa* refuses to see anything beyond the material existence of objects. The idea may be extended to all subjects. In religion, for instance, a man of *sattvika* vision will see one God and one spiritual truth in all religions and will have thus the same regard for all ; the man of *rajasa* vision will emphasize differences and claim superiority for his own form of religion ; and the man of *tamasa* vision will claim an exclusive revelation for his religion, regard all others as false, declare those not belonging to his fold as doomed to damnation, and will even wage a war to bring them to his fold. In brief, *sattva* will always find out points of contact or unity in seemingly different things, *rajas* will emphasize differences, *tamas* will cloud and warp the vision.

Herbert Spencer's division of knowledge is a close parallel. See 'My Submission' p. 33.]

नियतं संगरहितम् अरागद्वेषतः कृतम् ।
अफलप्रेप्सुना कर्म यत् तत् सात्त्विकमुच्यते ।।२३।।

23. That action is called *sattvika* which, being one's allotted task, is performed without attachment, without like or dislike, and without a desire for fruit.

यत् तु कामेप्सुना कर्म साहंकारेण वा पुनः ।
क्रियते बहुलायासं तद् राजसमुदाहृतम् ।।२४।।

24. That action which is prompted by the desire for fruit, or by the thought of 'I', and which involves much dissipation of energy is called *rajasa*.

अनुबंधं क्षयं हिंसाम् अनपेक्ष्य च पौरुषम् ।
मोहादारभ्यते कर्म यत् तत् तामसमुच्यते ।।२५।।

25. That action which is blindly undertaken without any regard to capacity and consequences, involving loss and hurt, is called *tamasa*.

मुक्तसंगोऽनहंवादी धृत्युत्साहसमन्वितः ।
सिद्ध्यसिद्ध्योर्निर्विकारः कर्ता सात्त्विक अुच्यते ।।२६।।

26. That doer is called *sattvika* who has shed all attachment, all thought of 'I', who is filled with firmness and zeal, and who recks neither success nor failure.

रागी कर्मफलप्रेप्सुर् लुब्धो हिंसात्मकोऽशुचिः ।
हर्षशोकान्वितः कर्ता राजसः परिकीर्तितः ।।२७।।

27. That doer is said to be *rajasa* who is passionate, desirous of the fruit of action, greedy, violent, unclean, and moved by joy and sorrow.

अयुक्तः प्राकृतः स्तब्धः शठो नैष्कृतिकोऽलसः ।
विषादी दीर्घसूत्री च कर्ता तामस उच्यते ॥२८॥

28. That doer is called *tamasa* who is undisciplined, vulgar, stubborn, knavish, spiteful, indolent, woebegone, and dilatory.

बुद्धेर्भेदं धृतेश्चैव गुणतस्त्रिविधं श्रृणु ।
प्रोच्यमानमशेषेण पृथक्त्वेन धनंजय ॥२९॥

29. Hear now, O Dhananjaya, detailed fully and severally, the threefold division of understanding and will, according to their *gunas*.

प्रवृत्तिं च निवृत्तिं च कार्याकार्ये भयाभये ।
बंधं मोक्षं च या वेत्ति बुद्धिः सा पार्थ सात्त्विकी ॥३०॥

30. That understanding, O Partha, is *sattvika* which knows action from inaction, what ought to be done from what ought not to be done, fear from fearlessness and bondage from release.

यया धर्ममधर्मं च कार्यं चाकार्यमेव च ।
अयथावत् प्रजानाति बुद्धिः सा पार्थ राजसी ॥३१॥

31. That understanding, O Partha, is *rajasa*, which decides erroneously between right and wrong, between what ought to be done and what ought not to be done.

अधर्मं धर्ममिति या मन्यते तमसाऽऽवृता ।
सर्वार्थान् विपरीतांश्च बुद्धिः सा पार्थ तामसी ॥३२॥

32. That understanding, O Partha, is *tamasa*, which, shrouded in darkness, thinks wrong to be right and mistakes everything for its reverse.

[Cf. Is 5. 20 : "Woe unto them that call evil good, and good evil, that put darkness for light, and light for darkness ; that put bitter for sweet and sweet for bitter."]

धृत्या यया धारयते मनःप्राणेन्द्रियक्रियाः ।
योगेनाव्यभिचारिण्या धृतिः सा पार्थ सात्त्विकी ॥३३॥

33. That will, O Partha, is *sattvika* which maintains an unbroken harmony between the activities of the mind, the vital energies and the senses.

[Cf. Durant on Plato's attitude to Justice (a term, by the way, very much akin to *yoga*): "And in individual justice is effective co-ordination, the harmonious functioning of the elements in a man, each in its fit place and each making its co-operative contribution to behaviour." The activities prompted by a *sattvika* will, will be all bent to the attainment of *moksha* — Freedom — as will be clear from the next *shloka*.]

यया तु धर्मकामार्थान् धृत्या धारयतेऽर्जुन ।
प्रसंगेन फलाकांक्षी धृतिः सा पार्थ राजसी ॥३४॥

34. That will, O Partha, is *rajasa* which clings, with attachment, to righteousness, desire and wealth, desirous of fruit in each case.

[The reference is to the four ends to be pursued by man. The *rajasa* will actuate man to the pursuit of *dharma* (righteousness or righteous works), *artha* (wealth), *kama* (desire for progeny etc.), to the exclusion of the fourth, viz.. *moksha* (Freedom) which ought to be made the prime end.]

यया स्वप्नं भयं शोकं विषादं मदमेव च ।
न विमुञ्चति दुर्मेधा धृतिः सा पार्थ तामसी ॥३५॥

35. That will, O Partha, is *tamasa*, whereby insensate man does not abandon sleep, fear, grief, despair and self-conceit.

सुखं त्विदानीं त्रिविधं शृणु मे भरतर्षभ ।
अभ्यासाद् रमते यत्र दुःखान्तं च निगच्छति ॥३६॥

36. Hear now from Me, O Bharatarshabha, the three kinds of pleasure.

Pleasure which is enjoyed only by repeated practice, and which puts an end to pain,

यत् तदग्रे विषमिव परिणामेऽमृतोपमम् ।
तत् सुखं सात्त्विकं प्रोक्तम् आत्मबुद्धिप्रसादजम् ॥३७॥

37. Which, in its inception, is as poison, but in the end as nectar, born of the serene realization of the true nature of *Atman* — that pleasure is said to be *sattvika.*

[36-37: The price of this pleasure is initial effort, striving, tribulation, and so apparent pain, in a word *tapasya.* Cf. Heb. 12. 11: "Now no chastening for the present seems to be joyous, but grievous; nevertheless afterward it yieldeth the peaceable fruit of righteousness unto them which are exercised thereby." Spinoza talks of the happiness of philosophy — *jnana* — in the same strain as *shl.* 36: "But the love towards a thing eternal and infinite alone feeds the mind with a pleasure secure from all pain.... The greatest good is the knowledge of the union which the mind has with the whole of Nature."]

विषयेन्द्रियसंयोगाद् यत् तदग्रेऽमृतोपमम् ।
परिणामे विषमिव तत् सुखं राजसं स्मृतम् ॥३८॥

38. That pleasure is called *rajasa* which, arising from the contact of the senses with their objects, is at first as nectar but in the end like poison.

[Cf. *Imitation of Christ*: "So all carnal joys enter pleasantly; but at the end bring remorse and death."]

यदग्रे चानुबन्धे च सुखं मोहनमात्मनः ।
निद्रालस्यप्रमादोत्थं तत् तामसमुदाहृतम् ॥३९॥

39. That pleasure is called *tamasa* which arising from sleep and sloth and heedlessness, stupefies the soul both at first and in the end.

न तदस्ति पृथिव्यां वा दिवि देवेषु वा पुनः ।
सत्त्वं प्रकृतिजैर्मुक्तं यदेभिः स्यात् त्रिभिर्गुणैः ।।४०।।

40. There is no being, either on earth or in heaven among the gods, that can be free from these three *gunas* born of *prakriti.*

ब्राह्मणक्षत्रियविशां शूद्राणां च परंतप ।
कर्माणि प्रविभक्तानि स्वभावप्रभवैर्गुणैः ।।४१।।

41. The duties of *Brahmanas, Kshatriyas, Vaishyas* and *Shudras,* are distributed according to their innate qualifications, O Parantapa.

शमो दमस्तपः शौचं क्षान्तिरार्जवमेव च ।
ज्ञानं विज्ञानमास्तिक्यं ब्रह्मकर्म स्वभावजम् ।।४२।।

42. Serenity, self-restraint, austerity, purity, forgiveness, uprightness, knowledge and discriminative knowledge, faith in God are the *Brahmana*'s natural duties.

शौर्यं तेजो धृतिर्दाक्ष्यं युद्धे चाप्यपलायनम् ।
दानमीश्वरभावश्च क्षात्रं कर्म स्वभावजम् ।।४३।।

43. Valour, spiritedness, constancy, resourcefulness, not fleeing from battle, generosity, and the capacity to rule are the natural duties of a *Kshatriya.*

कृषिगोरक्ष्यवाणिज्यं वैश्यकर्म स्वभावजम् ।
परिचर्यात्मकं कर्म शूद्रस्यापि स्वभावजम् ।।४४।।

44. Tilling the soil, protection of the cow and commerce are the natural functions of a *Vaishya*, while service is the natural duty of a *Shudra*.

[41-44 : See my note on '*Varna*' in 'My Submission', pp. 102-05. "A true *Brahmana* should be the very image of humility, and not be proud of his knowledge or wisdom. He will cease to be a *Brahmana* if he considers himself superior to others, as it is his duty to teach people to look upon a *Brahmana* and a *bhangi* (scavenger) with an equal eye. Again a *Brahmana* is hardly worth the name, if he does not have the courage of his own conviction." (*Harijan*, May 18, 1934)

Cf. with this Aristotle's *Kshatriya* and *Shudra* : "For he who can foresee with his mind is by nature intended to be lord and master ; and he who can work only with his body is by nature a slave." But not so thinks Gandhiji : "To say that *Brahmana* should not touch the plough is a parody of *Varnashrama dharma* and a prostitution of the meaning of the Bhagawadgita. Surely the qualities predominantly ascribed to the different divisions are not denied to the others. Is bravery to be the prerogative only of the *Kshatriya* and restraint only of the *Brahmana* ? Are *Brahmanas, Kshatriyas* and *Shudras* not to protect the cow ? Can any one remain a Hindu without readiness to die for a cow ?" (Gandhiji in *Young India*, 22-1-'25)]

स्वे स्वे कर्मण्यभिरतः संसिद्धिं लभते नरः ।
स्वकर्मनिरतः सिद्धिं यथा विन्दति तच्छृणु ।।४५।।

45. Each man, by complete absorption in the performance of his duty, wins perfection. Hear now how he wins such perfection by devotion to that duty.

यतः प्रवृत्तिर्भूतानां येन सर्वमिदं ततम् ।
स्वकर्मणा तमभ्यर्च्य सिद्धिं विन्दति मानवः ।।४६।।

46. By offering the worship of his duty to Him who is the moving spirit of all beings, and by whom all this is pervaded, man wins perfection.

[*Laborare est orare.* Cf. Carlyle, with whom "all true work is religion", and true work was contained in the commandment: "Know what thou canst work; and work at it, like a Hercules." Cf. also Spinoza with whom all virtue, i.e. action performed without expectation of reward, was "the serving of God".]

श्रेयान् स्वधर्मो विगुणः परधर्मात् स्वनुष्ठितात् ।
स्वभावनियतं कर्म कुर्वन्नाप्नोति किल्विषम् ॥४७॥

47. Better one's own duty, though uninviting, than another's which may be more easily performed; doing duty which accords with one's nature, one incurs no sin.

The central teaching of the Gita is detachment—abandonment of the fruit of action. And there would be no room for this abandonment if one were to prefer another's duty to one's own. Therefore one's own duty is said to be better than another's. It is the spirit in which duty is done that matters, and its unattached performance is its own reward.

[Cf. Marcus Aurelius: "Be not ashamed of any action which is in accordance with nature and never be misled by fear of censure or reproach."]

सहजं कर्म कौन्तेय सदोषमपि न त्यजेत् ।
सर्वारंभा हि दोषेण धूमेनाग्निरिवावृताः ॥४८॥

48. One should not abandon, O Kaunteya, that duty to which one is born, imperfect though it be; for all action, in its inception, is enveloped in imperfection, as fire in smoke.

[Man's birth and possession of this body here below are due to binding actions in the past, and so anything done by means of that body is imperfect in its inception.]

असक्तबुद्धिः सर्वत्र जितात्मा विगतस्पृहः ।
नैष्कर्म्यसिद्धिं परमां संन्यासेनाधिगच्छति ।।४९।।

49. He who has weaned himself from attachments of all kinds, who is master of himself, who is dead to desire, attains through renunciation the supreme perfection of freedom from action.

सिद्धिं प्राप्तो यथा ब्रह्म तथाऽऽप्नोति निबोध मे ।
समासेनैव कौन्तेय निष्ठा ज्ञानस्य या परा ।।५०।।

50. Learn now from Me, in brief, O Kaunteya, how he who has gained this perfection, attains to *Brahman*, the supreme consummation of knowledge.

बुद्धया विशुद्धया युक्तो धृत्याऽऽत्मानं नियम्य च ।
शब्दादीन् विषयांस्त्यक्त्वा रागद्वेषौ व्युदस्य च ।।५१।।

51. Equipped with purified understanding, restraining the self with firm will, abandoning sound and other objects of the senses, putting aside likes and dislikes,

विविक्तसेवी लघ्वाशी यतवाक्कायमानसः ।
ध्यानयोगपरो नित्यं वैराग्यं समुपाश्रितः ।।५२।।

52. Living in solitude, spare in diet, restrained in speech, body and mind, ever absorbed in *dhyanayoga*, anchored in dispassion,

अहंकारं बलं दर्पं कामं क्रोधं परिग्रहम् ।
विमुच्य निर्ममः शान्तो ब्रह्मभूयाय कल्पते ।।५३।।

53. Without pride, violence, arrogance, lust, wrath, possession, having shed all sense of 'mine' and at peace with himself, he is fit to become one with *Brahman*.

ब्रह्मभूतः प्रसन्नात्मा न शोचति न कांक्षति ।
समः सर्वेषु भूतेषु मद्भक्तिं लभते पराम् ॥५४॥

54. One with *Brahman* and at peace with himself, he grieves not, nor desires; holding all beings alike, he achieves supreme devotion to Me.

भक्त्या मामभिजानाति यावान् यश्चास्मि तत्त्वतः ।
ततो मां तत्त्वतो ज्ञात्वा विशते तदनंतरम् ॥५५॥

55. By devotion he realizes in truth how great I am, who I am; and having known Me in reality he enters into Me.

सर्वकर्माण्यपि सदा कुर्वाणो मद्व्यपाश्रयः ।
मत्प्रसादादवाप्नोति शाश्वतं पदमव्ययम् ॥५६॥

56. Even whilst always performing actions, he who makes Me his refuge wins, by My grace, the eternal and imperishable haven.

चेतसा सर्वकर्माणि मयि संन्यस्य मत्परः ।
बुद्धियोगमुपाश्रित्य मच्चित्तः सततं भव ॥५७॥

57. Casting, with thy mind, all actions on Me, make Me thy goal, and resorting to the *yoga* of even-mindedness fix thy thought ever on Me.

मच्चित्तः सर्वदुर्गाणि मत्प्रसादात् तरिष्यसि ।
अथ चेत् त्वमहंकारान् न श्रोष्यसि विनंक्ष्यसि ॥५८॥

58. Fixing thus thy thought on Me, thou shalt

surmount all obstacles by My grace; but if possessed by the sense of 'I' thou listen not, thou shalt perish.

यदहंकारमाश्रित्य न योत्स्य अिति मन्यसे ।
मिथ्यैष व्यवसायस्ते प्रकृतिस्त्वां नियोक्ष्यति ॥५९॥

59. If obsessed by the sense of 'I', thou thinkest, 'I will not fight', vain is thy obsession; (thy) nature will compel thee.

स्वभावजेन कौन्तेय निबद्धः स्वेन कर्मणा ।
कर्तुं नेच्छसि यन्मोहात् करिष्यस्यवशोऽपि तत् ॥६०॥

60. What thou wilt not do, O Kaunteya, because of thy delusion, thou shalt do, even against thy will, bound as thou art by the duty to which thou art born.

[Krishna knows Arjuna through and through, and so suggests that whilst it was certain that he was not going to escape the action to which his nature would drive him, and thus be subjected to bondage, it was open to him, and it would be better for him, to do the same thing at His bidding, without attachment and in a spirit of dedication, and thus incur no bondage.]

अीश्वरः सर्वभूतानां हृद्देशेऽर्जुन तिष्ठति ।
भ्रामयन् सर्वभूतानि यंत्रारूढानि मायया ॥६१॥

61. God, O Arjuna, dwells in the heart of every being and by His delusive mystery whirls them all, (as though) set on a machine.

[Plotinus brings out the same idea in a beautiful simile which sheds a flood of explanation on this important *shloka*: "We perpetually revolve round God the Principle of all things, but we do not always behold it. A band of singers moving about its leader may be diverted to the survey of something foreign to the choir, but when it turns itself to him, it sings well and truly subsists to him; thus also we perpetually revolve about the Principle of all things, even when we are loosened from it and we have no knowledge of it; but when we behold it we are no longer discordant, but form a divine dance about it." When we are "loosened" from Him, we dance to the tune of *prakriti*, when we behold Him we make *prakriti* dance to our tune, i.e. to His tune.]

तमेव शरणं गच्छ सर्वभावेन भारत ।
तत्प्रसादात् परां शांतिं स्थानं प्राप्स्यसि शाश्वतम् ॥६२॥

62. In Him alone seek thy refuge with all thy heart, O Bharata. By His grace shalt thou win to the eternal haven of supreme peace.

[Cf. the famous Biblical text: "Come unto Me and I will give you rest," which St. Augustine thus paraphrases: "Stand by Him, and ye shall stand fast. Rest in Him and ye shall be at rest."]

अिति ते ज्ञानमाख्यातं गुह्याद् गुह्यतरं मया ।
विमृश्यैतदशेषेण यथेच्छसि तथा कुरु ॥६३॥

63. Thus have I expounded to thee the most mysterious of all knowledge; ponder over it fully, then act as thou wilt.

सर्वगुह्यतमं भूयः शृणु मे परमं वचः ।
अिष्टोऽसि मे दृढमिति ततो वक्ष्यामि ते हितम् ॥६४॥

64. Hear again My supreme word, the most mysterious of all; dearly beloved thou art of Me, hence I desire to declare thy welfare.

मन्मना भव मद्भक्तो मद्याजी मां नमस्कुरु ।
मामेवैष्यसि सत्यं ते प्रतिजाने प्रियोऽसि मे ॥६५॥

65. On Me fix thy mind, to Me bring thy devotion, to Me offer thy sacrifice, to Me make thy obeisance; to Me

indeed shalt thou come — solemn is My promise to thee, thou art dear to Me.

सर्वधर्मान् परित्यज्य मामेकं शरणं व्रज ।
अहं त्वा सर्वपापेभ्यो मोक्षयिष्यामि मा शुचः ॥६६॥

66. Abandon all duties and come to Me the only refuge. I will release thee from all sins; grieve not!

[Cf. Koran: "But whosoever surrender his purpose to Allah while doing good his reward is with his Lord, and there shall no fear come upon them, neither shall they grieve." (2. 112; 10. 63). Also Is. 1. 25: "And I will turn my hand upon thee, and purely purge away thy dross and take away all thy sin." Also: "Call upon Me in the day of trouble; I will deliver thee."]

अिदं ते नातपस्काय नाभक्ताय कदाचन ।
न चाशुश्रूषवे वाच्यं न च मां योऽभ्यसूयति ॥६७॥

67. Utter this never to him who knows no austerity, has no devotion, nor any desire to listen, nor yet to him who scoffs at Me.

य अिदं परमं गुह्यं मद्भक्तेष्वभिधास्यति ।
भक्ति मयि परां कृत्वा मामेवैष्यत्यसंशयः ॥६८॥

68. He who will propound this supreme mystery to My devotees, shall, by that act of highest devotion to Me, surely come to Me.

न च तस्मान्मनुष्येषु कश्चिन् मे प्रियकृत्तमः ।
भविता न च मे तस्माद् अन्यः प्रियतरो भुवि ॥६९॥

69. Nor among men is there any who renders dearer service to Me than he; nor shall there be on earth any more beloved by Me than he.

It is only he who has himself gained the knowledge and lived it in his life that can declare it to others. These two *shlokas* cannot possibly have any reference to him, who no matter how he conducts himself, can give a flawless reading and interpretation of the Gita.

अध्येष्यते च य अिमं धर्म्यं संवादमावयोः ।
ज्ञानयज्ञेन तेनाहम् अिष्टः स्यामिति मे मतिः ॥७०॥

70. And whoso shall study this sacred discourse of ours shall worship Me with the sacrifice of knowledge. That is My belief.

श्रद्धावाननसूयश्च शृणुयादपि यो नरः ।
सोऽपि मुक्तः शुभांल्लोकान् प्राप्नुयात् पुण्यकर्मणाम् ॥७१॥

71. And the man of faith who, scorning not, will but listen to it, — even he shall be released and will go to the happy worlds of men of virtuous deeds.

[Released : Released from sin (Shankaracharya)]

[70-71. "I would like the Gita reciters to realize that mere recitation is not an end in itself. It should be an aid to the contemplation and assimilation of the meaning and the message of the Gita. By patience even a parrot can be taught to recite it by heart. But he would be no wiser for the recitation. The reciter of the Gita should be what the author expects him to be — a *yogi* in its broad sense. It demands from its votaries balance in every thought, word and deed and a perfect correspondence between the three." (Gandhiji in *Harijan*, 2-2-'34)]

कच्चिदेतच्छ्रुतं पार्थ त्वयैकाग्रेण चेतसा ।
कच्चिदज्ञानसंमोहः प्रणष्टस्ते धनंजय ॥७२॥

72. Hast thou heard this, O Partha, with a concentrated mind? Has thy delusion, born of ignorance, been destroyed, O Dhananjaya?

अर्जुन अुवाच ।

नष्टो मोहः स्मृतिर्लब्धा त्वत्प्रसादान्मयाऽच्युत ।
स्थितोऽस्मि गतसंदेहः करिष्ये वचनं तव ।।७३।।

Arjuna said :

73. Thanks to Thy grace, O Achyuta, my delusion is destroyed, my understanding has returned. I stand secure, my doubts all dispelled ; I will do Thy bidding.

संजय अुवाच ।

अित्यहं वासुदेवस्य पार्थस्य च महात्मनः ।
संवादमिममश्रौषम् अद्भुतं रोमहर्षणम् ।।७४।।

Sanjaya said :

74. Thus did I hear this marvellous and thrilling discourse between Vasudeva and the great-souled Partha.

व्यासप्रसादाच्छ्रुतवान् अेतद् गुह्यमहं परम् ।
योगं योगेश्वरात् कृष्णात् साक्षात् कथयतः स्वयम् ।।७५।।

75. It was by Vyasa's favour that I listened to this supreme and mysterious *Yoga* as expounded by the lips of the Master of *Yoga,* Krishna Himself.

राजन् संस्मृत्य संस्मृत्य संवादमिममद्भुतम् ।
केशवार्जुनयोः पुण्यं हृष्यामि च मुहुर्मुहुः ।।७६।।

76. O King, as often as I recall that marvellous and purifying discourse between Keshava and Arjuna, I am filled with recurring rapture.

तच्च संस्मृत्य संस्मृत्य रूपमत्यद्भुतं हरेः ।
विस्मयो मे महान् राजन् हृष्यामि च पुनः पुनः ।।७७।।

77. And as often as I recall that marvellous form of Hari, my wonder knows no bounds and I rejoice again and again.

[Cf. Dante

"Thenceforward, what I saw
Was not for words to speak......
. . . .
The Universal Form ; for that whene'er
I do but speak of it, my soul dilates
Beyond her proper self."

(Paradiso)]

यत्र योगेश्वरः कृष्णो यत्र पार्थो धनुर्धरः ।
तत्र श्रीर्विजयो भूतिर् ध्रुवा नीतिर्मतिर्मम ॥७८॥

78. Wheresoever Krishna, the Master of *Yoga,* is, and wheresoever is Partha the Bowman, there rest assured are Fortune, Victory, Prosperity, and Eternal Right.

[In one of his speeches of lofty eloquence during the Dandi March in 1930 Gandhiji identified Krishna with the righteousness of the end and Arjuna with the purity of means, and said : "I have faith in the righteousness of our cause and the purity of our weapons. Where the means are clean there God undoubtedly is present with His blessings and where the two combine there defeat is an impossibility."]

॥ हरिः ॐ तत् सत् ॥
अिति श्रीमद्भगवद्गीतासु अुपनिषत्सु ब्रह्मविद्यायां योगशास्त्रे श्रीकृष्णार्जुनसंवादे
संन्यासयोगो नाम अष्टादशोऽध्यायः ॥१८॥

Thus ends the eighteenth discourse, entitled '*Sannyasa Yoga*' in the converse of Lord Krishna and Arjuna, on the science of *Yoga*, as part of the knowledge of *Brahman* in the Upanishad called the Bhagawadgita.

INDEX

[Of proper names * — including books and authors quoted]

Abhimanyu, 138
Aditya, 291, 296
Agni, 301
" Ahirbudhnya Samhita ", 367
Airavata, 284-5
Akho, 86, 119
Albert Schweitzer, 6
Almora, 125
Amiel, 72
Anand, Swami, 125
Ananta, 285
Anantavijaya, 140
" Anasakti Yoga ", 3
Andal, 119
Andrews, C. F., 61
Angiras, 279
" Apology ", 240
" Arctic Home in the Vedas ", 263
Arctic Regions, 263
Arhat, 47
Aristotle, 32, 220, 376
Arnold, Edwin, 35, 60, 126
Arnold, Mathew, 46, 114, 229
Arseniew, 314
Aryaman, 285
Aryans, 263
" Ascent of Man ", 33, 328
Ashvaghosha, 182
Ashvattha Tree, 284, 338-9
Ashvatthaman, 138
Ashwins, 291, 296
Asquith, 119
Asuras, 296
" Atmabodha ", 267
Atri, 279
AUM, 245, 257-58, 271, 284, 360-62

Bacon, 32, 34, 187
Badarayana, 263
Bahikas, 139
Barnett, 250
Besant, Dr, 42
Bhagawata Dharma, 6, 14-5
" Bhagawata Purana ", 46, 50, 53, 71, 91, 103, 167, 289
Bhide Shastri, 279, 287, 311, 331, 365
Bhima, 111, 137, 138, 139, 140
Bhishma, 9, 57, 138, 139, 142, 149, 297, 299
Bible, 4, 19, 65, 198, 227, 318, 381,
of humanity — Gita, 13
Blavatsky, H. P., 152
Boehme, 321
Boswell, 175
" Brahma Sutra ", 257, 263
Brihadratha, 17
Brihaspati, 284
Broom, Dr, 260
Browning, 34, 66, 179, 247
Brutus, 13, 55
Buddha, 14, 36, 48, 244
" Buddhacharita ", 182
Buddhism, 6, 14
Bunyan, 119

Caird, Dr, 11
Caird, Principal, 112
Carlyle, 65, 104, 338, 377

* The names Gita, Arjuna, Krishna (including their epithets) which occur almost all over the book are not included. For various books of the Bible, see according to their names. All Upanishads are under one head, 'Upanishad' and in their alphabetical order.

Catherine of Siena, 86, 118, 227
Chaitanya, 119
Chedis, 137
Chekitana, 137
Chitraratha, 284
Chokhamela, 104
Christ, Jesus, 6, 9, 36, 51, 65, 85, 111, 120, 192, 255, 266, 309
Christianity, 65
1 Co. (Bible), 233, 275, 306
2 Co. (Bible), 249, 349
Col. (Bible), 9, 165, 224, 275
Coleridge, 93
Colophon of the Gita, 20, 147, 171, 193, 213, 227, 242, 252, 265, 277, 289, 306, 314, 327, 336, 345, 353, 362, 385
" Confessions ", 89, 165
" Constructive Survey of Upanishadic Philosophy ", 15, 18, 338
1 Cor. (Bible), 178, 186
2 Cor. (Bible), 95, 152, 198, 199
Curie, Madame, 119

Dadhichi, 111, 285
Damien, Fr., 119
Dandi March, 385
Dante, 385
Darwin, 22, 39
Davies, 168
Davis, 152
Delhi, 135
Deussen, Dr, 19
Devadatta, 140
Devaki, 9
Desai, Mahadev, 127 (See M. D. also)
" Dhammapada ", 190, 198, 230, 244
" Dharma Sutras ", 5
Dhrishtadyumna, 137, 141
Dhrishtaketu, 137
Dhritarashtra, 9, 10, 11, 55, 135-6, 141, 149, 164, 297
Draupadi 137, 138, 141
Drona, 57, 136, 137, 138, 142, 149, 297, 299
Drummond, Dr Henry, 22, 33, 36, 75, 89, 145, 328
Drupada, 137, 141
Durant, 373
Duryodhana, 57, 111, 136, 139, 140

" East & West in Religion", 5, 65
Eastern Church, Mystics of, 314
Eckhart, 45, 116, 118, 165, 170, 322
Edgar, 155 (See " King Lear ")
Eph. (Bible), 9, 95
Epictetus, 118, 163, 187, 188
" Epistle to the Romans ", 192, 309

Faust, 247
Fenelon, 119, 313
Fichte, 41, 42, 52
Flammarion, 40
Fox, 119
" From Yeravda Mandir ", 177, 179, 312

Gal. (Bible), 347
Gandharvas, 284, 296
Gandhiji, 3, 4, 5, 8, 9, 109, 122, 136, 160, 162, 166, 171, 173, 178, 183, 188, 196, 198, 210, 212, 220, 221, 222, 224, 230, 250, 254, 255, 264, 267, 270, 280, 304, 307, 311, 314, 324, 328, 333, 339, 348, 352, 353, 355, 357, 358, 359, 369, 376, 383, 385
Gandiva, 143
Garuda, 285-6
Gaudapada, 235
Gayatri, 287
George, Lloyd, 119
Ghora Angirasa, 9
" Gita Rahasya ", 6, 126
Goethe, 247
Gora, 104
Gordon, 119
Gospels (Bible), 19, 47

Hamlet, 13, 32
Hanuman, 141
" Harijan ", 178, 222, 255, 280, 353, 376, 383

Harishchandra, 118
Hastinapura, 135
Heb. (Bible), 67, 374
Hegel, 44
Hellen Keller, 112
Heraclitus, 40
Hercules, 105, 377
" Heroes ", 338
Hill, 5, 8, 168, 190, 210, 250, 270, 304, 311, 333, 343, 344, 367
Himalayas, 220, 284
Hinduism, its New Testament & Gospels, 19, 128-9
Hitler, 111, 119
Hopkins, 14
Howard, 119
Hume, 17, 19, 105, 107, 109
" Hyperion ", 151

" Idealist View of Life ", 21, 47, 79, 113
Igdrasil Tree, 338
Ikshvaku, 194
" Imitation of Christ ", 213, 231, 258, 271, 274, 318, 374. (See Kempis, Thomas A.)
" Indian Philosophy ", Vol. I, II, 5, 27, 250
Indra, 283
Inge, Dean, 120
Is. Bible, 67, 372, 382
Iss. (Bible), 152
Ishwarachandra's " Karika ", 24 (See " Sankhya Karika ")
Islam, 65, 250 (See Koran also)

James (Bible), 160
James, Prof., 43, 118
Jami, 289
Janaka, 62, 118, 131, 181-2
Jayadratha, 299
Jesuits, 109
Jesus, See Christ
Jnaneshvara, 119, 367
Job (Bible), 118
John (Bible), 84, 160, 276, 280
1 John (Bible), 209, 223
Johnson, Dr, 175
Julian, Sister, 118
" Julius Caesar ", 31

Kabir, 70, 86, 119, 217
Kalelkar, Kaka, 127
Kamadhenu, 285
Kapila, 22, 284
Karna, 111, 138, 297, 299
Kartikeya, 284
Kashiraja, 137, 141
Kauravas, 54, 135, 137, 156
Keats, 151
Keith, 26, 367
Kempis, Thomas A., 168
King Cimbeline's sons, 32
" King John ", 12, 55
" King Lear ", 155
Kirtikar, 40, 87
Koran, 4, 19, 47, 67, 89, 162, 176, 188, 198, 227, 230, 240, 245, 249, 268, 278, 281, 302, 317-18, 351, 382
— "The Glorious ", 67
Kosani, 125
Kratu, 279
Kripa, 138
Krishna Vasudev Cult, 3, 6-9, 14, 18
Kubera, 283
Kunti, 137, 138, 140
Kuntibhoja, 137
Kuru, 135, 136
Kurukshetra, 10, 54, 135
Kurús, 142, 164

Lady Blanch, 12, 55
Lao Tze, 229
Lessing, 119
" Light of Asia ", 35
Lincoln, 119
Locke, 34
Luke (Bible), 85, 266, 317

Macbeth, Lady, 12
Mackenzie, Prof., 19, 33, 104, 215
Madri, 141
Mahabharata, 8-10, 20, 21, 38, 42, 49, 50, 51, 54, 73, 104, 127-28, 136, 194
— Adi Parva, 127
— Drona Parva, 49

— Shanti Parva, 161, 179
— Udyoga Parva, 164
— War, 10
"Mahaparinibbana Sutra", 181
Manipushpaka, 140
Manu, 194, 357
"Manual of Ethics", 104
"Manusmriti", 118, 178, 207, 364
Marcus Aurelius, 118, 317, 377
Margashirsha, 287
Marichi, 279
Maruts, 291, 296
Mashruwala, Kishorlal, 127
Mat. (Bible), 183, 222, 238, 274
M. D., 307, 328
Meru, 283
Mirabai, 86, 119
Mithila, 63, 181-2
Mosaic Law, 198
"My Experiments with Truth", 125
Mystic, A Western (Quoted), 359
"Mysticism", 170, 227
"Mystics of Islam", See Nicholson

Nakula, 140-1
Narada, 17, 284
Narbuda, 139
Narsinha Mehta, 52, 86, 119, 203
"Nasadiya Sukta", 272
Nero, 63
Newman, Cardinal, 105, 114, 119
New Testament, 19
Nicholson, Prof., 39, 106, 169, 193, 275

Panchajanya, 140
Pandavas, 11, 54, 56, 135-7, 164, 288
Pandu, 10, 135-6, 140-41
"Paradiso", 385
Parashurama, 286
Partha, 11
Pascal, 109, 119, 324
Pasteur, 119
Patanjali, 226
Patmore, 49
Peter (Bible), 58
1 Peter (Bible), 58
2 Peter (Bible), 319
"Phaedo", 236
Phil. (Bible), 85
Pickthall, Marmaduke, 67
Planck, 79
Plato, 32, 236, 240, 370, 373
Plotinus, 73, 118, 166, 234, 380
Prahlad, 111, 285-6
Prajapati, 301
Prophet, Jewish, 67; The (of Islam), 47, 65, 89
Ps. (Bible), 83
Pulaha, 279
Pulastya, 279
Punjab, 139
Puranas, 49
Purujit, 137

Radhakrishnan, Dr, 5, 15, 21, 26, 38, 46, 65, 79, 108, 112, 236, 243, 250, 257
Raidas, 104
Rakshasas, 283, 300
Ramakrishna, Paramahamsa, 36, 86
Rama, 286
Ramadas, 119
Ramanujacharya, 249, 343
"Ramayana", 286
Ranade, Prof., 15, 17, 338
"Retractions", 65
Rev. (Bible), 39
Rig Veda, 175, 201, 263, 271, 272, 289
Rudras, 283, 291, 296
Rumi, Jalaluddin,, 118, 170, 274
Ruysbroeck, 100, 234

Sadhyas, 296
Sahadeva, 140-1
Sajana, 104
Sama Veda, 271, 283, 287
Sanatkumara, 17
Sand, George, 93
Sanjaya, 10, 56, 81, 101, 136, 147, 292, 384
"Sankhya Karika", 24, 235, 244

Satvalekar, Pandit, 203
Satyaki, 141
"Saul", 66
Savonarola, 119
Seal, Dr, 29
Sena, 104
Shabari, 84
Shaibya, 137-8
Shakespeare, 12-3, 31, 32, 55, 113
Shankaracharya, 91, 115-16, 118, 155, 161, 198, 200, 204, 216, 238, 243, 250, 251, 263, 265, 269, 270, 304, 324, 331, 333, 341, 365, 367, 383
Shankarananda, 289
Shashanka, 301
Shastra, 352-55
"Shatapatha Brahmana", 135, 249
Shibi, King, 111, Tribe, 138
Shikhandi, 141
Siddhas, 296, 300
Smritis, 21
Somadatta, 138, 139
"Song Celestial", 60, 126
Spencer, Herbert, 33, 371
Spinoza, 33, 44, 119, 163, 374, 377
St. Augustine, 64, 89, 118, 165, 180, 204, 224, 247, 268, 274, 358, 381
St. Catherine, See Catherine of Siena
St. Francis, 36, 71, 86, 118
St. Ignatius, 118
St. John, 108, 119, 166, 238
St. Matthew, 222
St. Paul, 8, 67, 81, 85, 118, 192, 309, 347
"Studies in Vedanta", 87
Subhadra, 138, 141
Sudhanva, 111
Sughosha, 140
Suso, 321
Swadeshi, 188-9

"Ta Te Ching", 200
"Tattvakaumudi", 38
Tauler, 235
Telang, 168
"Theologia Germanica", 170
Thomson, 78, 79
Thucydides, 12
Tilak, Lokamanya, 5, 115, 126, 161, 182, 198, 243, 250, 263, 279, 304, 331, 338, 365
Tolstoy, 161, 178, 179
Tukaram, 86, 87, 104, 119
Tulsidas, 119

Uchchaihshravas, 284-5
Underhill, Miss, 13, 48, 170, 227, 321
Upanishad, Brihad., 99, 244, 272, 321, 326, 348
— Chhandogya, 9, 16, 37, 180, 212, 217, 244, 262, 272, 292, 302, 358
— Isha, 16, 44, 216, 237, 321
— Katha, 18, 43, 77, 106, 153, 155, 191, 257, 340
— Kena, 21, 343
— Maitri, 16, 108, 257
— Mandukya, 258
— Muktik, 343
— Mundaka, 16, 18, 43, 68, 181, 210-1-2, 258, 264, 295, 321, 340, 344, 345
— Of the Mahabharata, 20
— Prashna, 16, 77, 212, 258, 264
— Shveta., 7, 219, 232, 237, 251, 301, 321, 340, 344-5
— Taittiriya, 258, 272, 321, 348
Upanishads, 4, 14-21, 49, 56, 93, 105-6, 109, 192, 212, 258, 262, 264, 320, 343, 358
Ushanas, 288
Uttamaujas, 138

Vaikhanas, 194
Vajasaneya Yaju. Samhita, 49
Vajra, 285
Valakhilya, 194
Varuna, 285, 301
Vasishtha, 279
Vasudeva, 8-9, 44, 75, 288 (See Krishna Vasudeva Cult)
Vasuki, 285

Vasus, 291, 296
Vayu, 301
Vedanta, 27, 343, 367
Vedas, 14, 17, 18, 49, 62, 80, 85, 129, 159-61, 210, 265, 271, 283, 304, 337, 343, 345, 360
Vedic Hymns, 9
Vedic Ritual, 59, 74, 115, 159-61, 211, 241
Vidyaranya, 118
Vikarna, 138
Vinoba, 127, 201, 311, 331, 332
Virata, 137, 141
" Vishnu Purana ", 38
Vivasvat, 194, 195
" Vivekachudamani ", 91
Vivekananda, Swami, 52
Voltaire, 175
Vrishnis, 288
Vyasa, 9, 10, 127, 288, 384

Wadia, Sophia, 200
Wesley, 119
" What I Believe ", 161
Williams, Monier, 37
Wordsworth, 60

Yajus (Veda), 271
Yakshas, 283, 296
Yama, 285, 301
Yaska, 38
Yeravda Central Prison, 6, 125
Yoga Bhashya, 235
" Yoga Sutras ", 53, 225, 239
" Young India ", 125, 162, 166, 168, 174, 184, 189, 197, 200, 221, 307, 328, 369, 376
Yudhamanyu, 138
Yudhishthira, 137, 138, 140